Food
and Beverage
Service

5th. edition

Dennis Lillicrap,

John Cousins and

Robert Smith

**Thames Valley University,
Ealing, London
and Slough, Berkshire**

**Birmingham College
of Food, Tourism and
Creative Studies**

Hodder & Stoughton

A MEMBER OF THE HODDER HEADLINE GROUP

Order queries: please contact Bookpoint Ltd, 39 Milton Park, Abingdon, Oxon OX14 4TD. Telephone: (44) 01235 400414, Fax: (44) 01235 400454. Lines are open from 9.00–6.00, Monday to Saturday, with a 24 hour message answering service. Email address: orders@bookpoint.co.uk

British Library Cataloguing in Publication Data
A catalogue record for this title is available from The British Library

ISBN 0 340 70531 0

First published 1998
Impression number   10 9 8 7 6 5
Year   2003 2002 2001 2000

Cover photograph by Owen Franken

Typeset by Wearset, Boldon, Tyne and Wear
Printed in Great Britain for Hodder & Stoughton Educational,
a division of Hodder Headline Plc, 338 Euston Road, London NW1 3BH
by J. W. Arrowsmith Ltd., Bristol.

CONTENTS

Acknowledgments   vi
Introduction and How to Use this Book   vii

Chapter 1

The food and beverage service industry   1
1.1   Introduction   2
1.2   Types of food and beverage operations   2
1.3   Sectors of the food and beverage service industry   4
1.4   Variables in food and beverage operations   7
1.5   The meal experience   9
1.6   Food and beverage service methods   11
1.7   Food and beverage service personnel   12
1.8   Attributes of food and beverage service personnel   20

Chapter 2

Food and beverage service areas and equipment   23
2.1   Introduction   24
2.2   Stillroom   25
2.3   Silver room or plate room   28
2.4   Wash-up   30
2.5   Hotplate   31
2.6   Spare linen store   34
2.7   Dispense bar   34
2.8   Automatic vending   39
2.9   Lighting and colour   43
2.10   Furniture   45
2.11   Linen   49
2.12   China   50
2.13   Tableware (flatware, cutlery and hollow-ware)   55
2.14   Glassware   58
2.15   Disposables   60

Chapter 3

The menu, menu knowledge and accompaniments   63
3.1   The menu   64
3.2   Food, accompaniments and covers   72

Chapter 4

Beverages – Non-alcoholic and alcoholic   95
4.1	Tea	96
4.2	Coffee	100
4.3	Other stillroom beverages	110
4.4	Non-alcoholic dispense bar beverages	110
4.5	Wine and drinks lists	114
4.6	Cocktails	118
4.7	Bitters	120
4.8	Wine	121
4.9	Tasting of wine	132
4.10	Matching food and drinks	135
4.11	Spirits	138
4.12	Liqueurs	141
4.13	Beer	142
4.14	Cider and perry	145
4.15	Storage	146

Chapter 5

The food and beverage service sequence   149
5.1	Basic technical skills	150
5.2	Interpersonal skills	157
5.3	Taking bookings	166
5.4	Preparation for service	168
5.5	The order of service (table service)	192
5.6	Taking customer food and beverage orders	195
5.7	Service of food	205
5.8	Service of alcoholic bar beverages and cigars	212
5.9	Service of non-alcoholic beverages	219
5.10	Clearing	224
5.11	Billing methods	232
5.12	Clearing following service	236

Chapter 6

The service of breakfast and afternoon tea   239
6.1	Breakfast service	240
6.2	Afternoon tea service	246

Chapter 7

Specialized forms of service   251
7.1	Introduction	252
7.2	Floor/room service	252
7.3	Lounge service	258
7.4	Hospital tray service	260
7.5	Home delivery	262
7.6	Airline tray service	263
7.7	Rail service	263

Chapter 8

Guéridon service   267

	8.1	Introduction	268
	8.2	Guéridon service	272
	8.3	Introduction to carving and jointing	275
	8.4	Dishes involving work on the guéridon	280

Chapter 9

Function catering   321

	9.1	Introduction	322
	9.2	Function administration	330
	9.3	Function organization	337
	9.4	Weddings	345
	9.5	Outdoor catering (off premises catering)	350

Chapter 10

Supervisory aspects of food and beverage service   353

	10.1	Legal considerations	354
	10.2	Food and beverage revenue control	370
	10.3	Beverage control	379
	10.4	Performance measures	386
	10.5	Customer relations	390
	10.6	Staff organization and training	393
	10.7	Sales promotion	403

Annex A

Foods in Season   407

Annex B

Glossary of cuisine terms   411

Annex C

Cocktail listing and recipes   419

Index   427

ACKNOWLEDGEMENTS

The revision of this book has drawn upon a variety of experience and literature. The authors would like to express their thanks to all the organizations and individuals who gave their assistance and support in the preparation of this text. In particular they would like to thank:

Academy of Food and Wine Service; Birmingham College of Food, Tourism and Creative Studies; Café Royal, London; The Carlton Hotel, Bournemouth; City and Guilds of London Institute; The Copthorne Hotel, Birmingham; Croners Catering, Croners Publications; Andrew Durkan, author and consultant formally of Ealing College (now part of Thames Valley University, London); Forte Posthouse, Aylesbury; The George Intercontinental Hotel, Edinburgh; Griersons Wine Merchants; The Holiday Inn Crowne Plaza, Leeds; Hospitality Training Foundation; Hotel and Catering, International Management Association; IFS Publications; The International Coffee Organisation; Restaurant Gilmore, Birmingham. The Restaurateurs' Association of Great Britain; Royal Doulton, (UK) Ltd; The Swallow Hotel, Birmingham; The Tea Council; Thames Valley University, London; Virgin Atlantic Airways, Plc.; Virgin Trains; Walley Catering Equipment Ltd; and The Wine and Spirit Education Trust.

The authors would also like to thank Lisa Hyde at Hodder and Stoughton, Editor; Gary Roberts for his photographs and Stuart Bennett, Cheryl Swain and Dawn Barnwell for their help during the photo shoot.

INTRODUCTION AND HOW TO USE THIS BOOK

The aim of this book is to cover the basic knowledge and skills necessary for those involved at a variety of levels in food and beverage service. The book also provides a framework on which to build further studies and on which to relate further acquired knowledge and experience.

In revising this fifth edition we have taken into account recent developments in examining and awarding body recommendations and syllabuses, as well as developments in teaching and the industry at large. In particular, the revision has taken into account the National Vocational Qualification (NVQ) and Scottish Vocational Qualification (SVQ) Standards for food and beverage service from levels 1 to 3.

The book has been prepared as being suitable to support studies for those wishing to be assessed at NVQ levels 1 to 3 in food and beverage service, and the City and Guilds (7066) Certificate, Diploma or Advanced Diploma in Food and Beverage Service. In addition, the book is intended to support the broader-based study requirements in food and beverage service for programmes leading to the award of the National Diploma, the General National Vocational Qualification, the Higher National Diploma, Degree Programmes and the Professional Certificate and Diploma Programmes of the Hotel and Catering International Management Association (HCIMA).

The basis for this text continues to be the recognition that food and beverage service is not an end in itself but part of the business of hotel and catering operations. Food and beverage operations in the hospitality industry is concerned with the provision of food and drink ready for immediate consumption (but excluding retailing and food manufacturing).

Food and beverage operations is therefore concerned with:

- The *markets* served by the various sectors of the industy and consumer needs

- The range of *policies* and business objectives of the various sectors and how these affect the methods adopted

- The *interpretation of demand* of the sectors for food and drink to be provided as well as other services

- The *planning and design of facilities* required for food and beverage operations and the plant and equipment required
- The development of appropriate *provisioning* methods to meet the needs of the production and service methods used within given operational settings
- Operational knowledge of technical methods and processes and ability in the *production and service processes and methods* available to the caterer, understanding the varying resources required for their operation, as well as decision making on the appropriateness of the various processes and methods to meet sectoral requirements
- *Controlling the costs* of materials as well as the costs associated with the operation of production and service and *controlling the revenue*
- The *monitoring of customer satisfaction*

The above may be seen as a sequence which may be referred to as the *catering cycle* (see Figure A). This definition serves our purposes in that it states succinctly what food and beverage operations are concerned with and illustrates that it is not merely production and service.

In order to provide a framework against which to revise this edition, a hierarchy of elements of operations was identified (Figure B).

These elements may be placed in the order given in Figure B, but may also be used to identify staff levels within food and beverage operations, as in Figure C, or levels of courses. The five levels indicated in Figure C roughly equate to the five levels identified by the NVQ/SVQ.

Figure A - Catering cycle

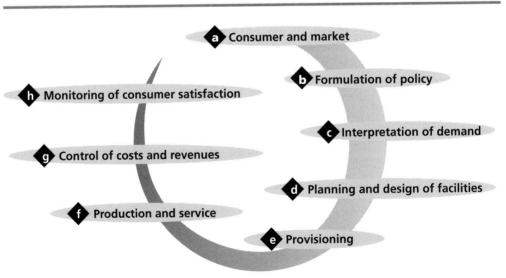

a Consumer and market

b Formulation of policy

h Monitoring of consumer satisfaction

c Interpretation of demand

g Control of costs and revenues

d Planning and design of facilities

f Production and service

e Provisioning

After Cracknell, H, Kaufman, R and Nobis, G *Practical Professional Catering*, Macmillan

*Figure B - **Operations hierarchy***

ELEMENT OF OPERATION	DESCRIPTION
SKILLS AND KNOWLEDGE	eg knowledge of food accompaniments, handling a spoon and fork
TASK	group of skills, eg glass washing
DUTY	group of tasks, eg preparing bar for service
METHOD	group of duties combined to achieve a particular service, eg silver service
OPERATION	combination of various methods, eg production, service, billing etc, thus creating a complete system for the provision of food and beverages within a specific type of outlet
SECTOR	business environment in which the operation exists

*Figure C - **Operations hierarchy and levels of staff***

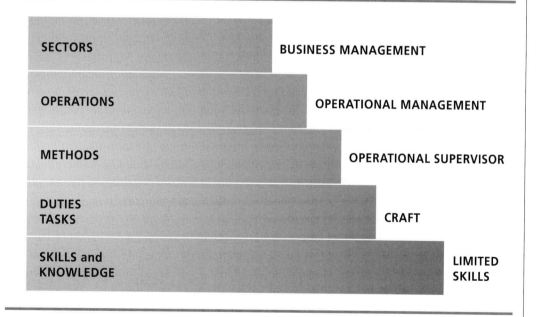

This approach has provided the thinking for the structure of this book.

Chapter 1 gives an overview of the food and beverage service industry, the sectors, types of premises, service methods and the reasons for eating out. This chapter also identifies service staff roles and the attributes needed by service personnel.

Chapters 2, 3 and 4 provides a base of underpinning knowledge about service areas and equipment **(Chapter 2)** the menu, its construction, example dishes and accompaniments **(Chapter 3)** and all types of beverages **(Chapter 4)**.

Chapter 5 details the basic skills, both interpersonal and technical, and indicates how these are applied to the service sequence (see page 11) for a variety of service settings.

The application of skills is then further developed for a variety of other service settings: breakfast and afternoon tea **(Chapter 6)**, specialised forms of service **(Chapter 7)**, guéridon service **(Chapter 8)** and function catering **(Chapter 9)**.

Finally, consideration is given to a number of supervisory aspects **(Chapter 10)** including legal requirements, control, performance measurement, customer relations, staffing and sales promotion. There are also three annexes which cover foods in season **(A)** a glossary of cuisine and service terms **(B)** and a cocktail listing with recipes **(C)**.

Throughout the book we have endeavoured to avoid sexist terms for job titles and job categories. These have been referred to as, for instance, manager, waiter, floor service staff, room attendants, servers and stewards. In all cases these terms, in line with general trends within the industry, refer to both male and female personnel.

The content of the book, whilst having its origins in classic cuisine and service (the context and the body of knowledge on which food and beverage operations are based) is also intended to reflect current practice within the industry. Therefore whilst the book gives information and describes various aspects of food and beverage service, it should not be seen as a prescriptive book. Clearly the actual operation of service will be substantially affected by the particular style of the operation.

Catering operations are continuing to enjoy tremendous improvement and development with considerable advances in quality. At the same time expansion of the industry, supported by greater demand from an increasingly knowledgeable and value conscious customer, is allowing increases in broader based forms of catering alongside some greater specialization of restaurants such as by type of cuisine, theme or particular country. However service both in level and standards of operation still varies greatly throughout the whole range of food and beverage operations.

Expansion of the industry has generally meant greater choice. This together with potential skill shortages and drives for efficiency is seeing a streamlining of operations with less emphasis on sophisticated service techniques in some sectors but more emphasis throughout the industry on product knowledge (food and beverages), technical skill, interpersonal skills, teamwork and generally better trained staff.

Increasing competition has also meant the quality of the service and the perceived value of the experience by customers, are the main differentiators between operations endeavouring to attract similar types of customer. It is against this background that the revisions for this fifth edition have taken place.

HOW TO USE THIS BOOK

The information in the book can be accessed in three main ways. Two of these are:

- using the contents list at the front of the book
- finding information through the use of the index which is at the back of the book

There are three annexes of supporting information which are also given at the back of the book.

In addition we have developed a new chart which takes account of the various examining and awarding body recommendations and assessment requirements, especially Vocational Qualifications. This chart is set out below and identifies the relevant chapter or section from this text. Because of the wide variety of hotel and catering operations the revised chart, now included in this edition, indicates only the broad range of knowledge and skills which will be relevant to a range of operations. The chart can therefore be used as a checklist to identify the relevance of a particular aspect to a particular operation, job or qualification requirement as well as a means of finding relevant information.

To use the chart, first select from the tasks and duties listing which aspect you are interested in. Then read off the chapter and/or section identified. Next go the detailed contents listing on pages iii–v to find the page number.

Although references given in this chart are to this book, there are two other texts in the suite for food and beverage service. The first is *The Beverage Book* (Andrew Durkan and John Cousins, published by Hodder and Stoughton) which will assist those who are looking for a more in-depth coverage of all aspects of beverage sales and service, both non-alcoholic and alcoholic, and the new *Learning About Food and Beverage* (John Cousins and Robert Smith, published by Hodder and Stoughton) which is specifically designed to advise and support those wishing to learn about, gain experience of and obtain qualifications in this noble profession.

Master reference chart

Task / Duties	Relevant Chapters /sections
Interpersonal Skills	
• **Balance the needs of the customer and the organisation**	1.1 to 1.6 and 10.4
• **Present a positive personal image to the customer**	1.7 and 1.8
• **Respond to feelings expressed by the customer**	5.2 and 10.5
• **Adapt methods of communication**	
Deal with:	
adults	
children	
those with mobility difficulties	5.2 and 5.6
those with communication difficulties	
customer complaints	
customer incidents	
Health, Safety and Security	
• **Maintain personal health and hygiene**	1.8
• **Maintain a safe environment**	
• **Maintain a secure environment**	
report suspicious items	10.1
report accidents	
• **Carry out procedures in the event of a fire**	
Underpinning Knowledge	
service areas and equipment	Chapter 2
menu, menu knowledge and accompaniments	Chapter 3 annexes A and B
non-alcoholic drinks	
wine	Chapter 4 and Annex C
other alcoholic beverages	
Service Sequence	
• **Establish and maintain working relationships**	1.7 and 1.8
• **Take bookings**	5.3
• **Prepare service areas**	5.4
• **Take orders for food and beverages and determine customer requirements**	5.2, 5.5 and 5.6
• **Serve food**	5.1 and 5.7

Task / Duties	Relevant Chapters /sections
● **Serve beverages**	
non-alcoholic beverages	
wine	5.8 and 5.9
other alcoholic beverages	
● **Clear during service**	5.10
● **Deal with payments**	5.11
● **Clear service areas after service**	5.12

Specialised service skills

● **Provide specialised forms of service**	
breakfast	6.1
afternoon teas	6.2
lounge service	7.2
room service	7.3
guéridon service	Chapter 8
prepare, cook and serve food	
in a food service area	

Function Catering

● **Prepare for and serve at functions**	Chapter 9
● **Contribute to function administration**	
● **Contribute to function organisation**	

Supervisory Responsibilities

● **Supervise operation within licensing (and other) laws**	10.1
● **Receive, store and return drinks**	10.3
● **Maintain cellars**	4.15
● **Maintain a practices and procedures for handling cash/cash equivalents**	5.11 and 10.2
● **Contribute to the control of food and beverage operations**	10.2, 10.3 and 10.4
● **Maintain cleaning programme in own area**	10.6
● **Maintain vending machine service**	2.8
● **Supervise the running of a function/event**	Chapter 9
● **Improve service reliability for customers**	10.5
● **Contribute to the development of teams and individuals**	10.6
● **Implement sales development activities**	10.7

CHAPTER 1

THE FOOD AND BEVERAGE SERVICE INDUSTRY

1.1	Introduction	2
1.2	Types of food and beverage operations	2
1.3	Sectors of the food and beverage service industry	4
1.4	Variables in food and beverage operations	7
1.5	The meal experience	9
1.6	Food and beverage service methods	11
1.7	Food and beverage service personnel	12
1.8	Attributes of food and beverage service personnel	20

1.1 Introduction

The Hotel and Catering or Hotel and Food Service Industry is now becoming widely known as the *Hospitality Industry*. The industry is usually defined by its *output of products* which satisfy demand for food, drink and accommodation (but it excludes food and drink manufacture and retailing).

Central to the industry is the need for operational personnel who are generally divided into *food and beverage staff* and *rooms division staff*. The industry in Britain currently employs 2.4 million people (source: Hospitality Training Foundation (HTF)) which represents 10% of the working population. The opportunities for advancement in food and beverage service are many: positions exist such as restaurant manager, banqueting manager, station head waiter, wine waiter, catering officer and so on, depending on the type of establishment in which one finally decides to work. Work is available in hotels and restaurants, catering organizations, hospital catering, welfare catering, clubs, industrial catering, residential catering, transport catering and outdoor catering. Once again, it all depends on the individual and on the type of catering in which one is most interested. Also there are many chances to see the world and travel around the countries of one's choice by land, sea or air, in such capacities as area or group manager, air steward, first class steward travelling on liners, public transport and so on. In this way a wealth of experience may be gathered by seeing the methods of food and beverage service in other countries.

Management has many responsibilities. These include the economics of menu costing, portion control, wastage of food, customer-staff relations, labour shortages and staff training. If good relations exist between management and staff, then problems should be few and the atmosphere should be pleasing to the customer. The food service staff play an important part in the achievement of such good relations. Since they are in contact with the customer and with management, their conduct influences the running of the establishment and the atmosphere created for the customer.

1.2 Types of food and beverage operations

The industry provides millions of meals per day in a variety of types of operations. These can be seen in the Standard Industrial Classification (SIC) (revised edition 1992).

The SIC attempts to describe the industry and it is widely used to classify official statistics. Figure 1.1 summarizes the activities listed in the 1992 SIC Class 'Hotel and Catering'.

However there are also a number of hospitality activities listed elsewhere. Division 9 of the 1992 SIC 'Other Services' for instance includes the following:

- Catering services ancillary to higher education institutions (activity 9310)
- Catering services ancillary to schools (activity 9320)

- Catering services ancillary to educational and vocational training not elsewhere specified (activity 9330)
- Soup kitchens (activity 9611)
- Social and residential homes (activity 9611)

Figure 1.1 Standard industrial Classification, Revised 1992 (summarized)

DIVISION 6			
CLASS	**GROUP**	**ACTIVITY**	
66			HOTELS AND CATERING
	661		RESTAURANTS, SNACK BARS, CAFES AND OTHER EATING PLACES
		6611	Eating places supplying food for consumption on the premises a Licensed places (hotels are classified to heading 6650 and night clubs etc to heading 6630) b Unlicensed places
		6612	Take-away food shops
	662	6620	PUBLIC HOUSES AND BARS
	663	6630	NIGHT CLUBS AND LICENSED CLUBS (sports and gaming clubs are classified to heading 9791)
	664	6640	CANTEENS AND MESSES a Catering contractors (canteens run by industrial establishments for their own employees are classified with the main establishment) b Other canteens and messes
	665	6650	HOTEL TRADE a Licensed premises b Unlicensed premises
	667	6670	OTHER TOURIST OR SHORT-STAY ACCOMMODATION a Camping and caravan sites b Holiday camps c Other tourist or short-stay accommodation not elsewhere specified (charitable rest homes are classified to heading 9611 and convalescent homes and rest homes with medical care to heading 9510)
(Source: CSO – Standard Industrial Classification, Revised 1992)			

1.3 Sectors of the food and beverage service industry

The Standard Industrial Classification (Figure 1.1) indicates that there are many types of food and beverage operations. It also indicates that some operations are primarily concerned with the provision of food and drink, for example restaurants and take-aways, whereas other operations are what can be called *secondary operations*, ie the provision of food and drink is part of another business, for example welfare catering and industrial catering.

The SIC classifies the industry by types of food and beverage premises. This does not necessarily indicate the type of demand being met or the conditions under which provision is being made. For example, cafeterias may be found in motorway service stations, in airline terminals, on rail stations, in retail catering, in industrial and in welfare catering. It should therefore be understood that similar types of food and beverage operations may be found in a variety of different sectors. For the purpose of this book, sectors are defined by the nature of demand being met, as shown in Figure 1.2. An historical summary of each sector is also given.

This identification of sectors also provides a framework for those studying the food and beverage service industry to which further studies and experience may be related.

In order to be seen in more detail each sector may be analysed by reference to a set of variables that exist in the different sectors (Figure 1.3). These variables represent elements

Figure 1.3 Variables in catering sectors

Historical background	Interpretation of demand/catering concept
Reasons for customer demand	Technological development
Influences	Primary/secondary activity
State of sector development	Types of outlets
Size of sector: in terms of outlets	Profit orientation/cost provision
in terms of turnover	Public/private ownership
Policies: Financial	
Marketing	
Catering	

which vary in particular sectors and thus provide a basis for examining the operation of outlets within specific sectors. They enable comprehensive pictures of industrial sectors to be compiled, and also provide for intercomparison of sectors.

Two further issues come out of the identification of sectors. Firstly, some sectors are providing food and drink for profit whereas others are working within the constraints of a given budget, often called *cost provision* (eg welfare and industrial). Secondly, some sectors are providing services to the general public whereas others provide them for restricted groups of people.

Figure 1.2 Sectors of the food and beverage service industry

SECTOR	PURPOSE OF SECTOR	HISTORICAL SUMMARY
HOTELS and other tourist accommodation	Provision of food and drink together with accommodation	Developed from inns. Supported by developments in transport and increases in business and leisure related tourism
RESTAURANTS including: conventional, specialist, 'Carveries', themed and ethnic	Provision of food and drink generally at medium to high price with medium to high levels of service	Grew out of hotel restaurants (Escoffier/Ritz influenced which were originally highly formal) through chefs wishing to start their own business
POPULAR CATERING including: cafés, pizza, 'Wimpy', grills, specialist coffee shops, 'Little Chefs', steak houses	Provision of food and drink generally at low to medium price with limited levels of service	Developed from ABC and Lyons concepts. Gone through various phases. Latterly American influenced
FAST FOOD eg: 'McDonalds', 'Burger King'	Provision of food and drink in highly specialized environment characterized by high investment, high labour costs and vast customer throughput	Grew from combination of popular catering and take-away, heavily influenced by American companies: sophisticated meal packaging and marketing
TAKE-AWAY including: ethnic, spuds, 'KFC', snacks, fish and chips, sandwich bars, kiosks	Provision of food and drinks quickly	Developed from original fish and chips concept. Influenced by America and trends in food tastes
RETAIL STORES	Provision of food and drink as adjunct to provision of retailing	Developed from prestigious stores wishing to provide food and drink as part of retailing concept
BANQUETING/ CONFERENCES/ EXHIBITIONS	Provision of food and drink on large scale, usually pre-booked	Originally associated with hotels but has now become major sector in its own right
LEISURE ATTRACTIONS eg: theme parks, galleries, theatres, airline terminals	Provision of food and drink for people engaged in another leisure pursuit	Increases in leisure have made profit from food and drink attractive to leisure and amenity providers

SECTOR	PURPOSE OF SECTOR	HISTORICAL SUMMARY
MOTORWAY SERVICE STATIONS	Provision of food together with retail and petrol services for motorway travellers, often in isolated locations	Born in 1960s with advent of motorway building. Influenced by America and became specialized because of government regulations on provision of catering, retail and petrol as well as location
WELFARE including: hospitals, schools, colleges, universities, forces, prisons, other welfare	Provision of food and drink to people through social need, primarily determined by an authority social conscience	Regulated and given substantial boost by Welfare State creation in 1948 and maintained now through
INDUSTRIAL CATERING either in-house operations or provided by catering contractor	Provision of food and drink to people at work	Born out of recognition that better fed workers work better. Given boosts in 1st and 2nd World Wars by legislation. Further developed by unions' wish to preserve conditions and emergence of professional contractors
LICENSED TRADE including: public houses, wine bars, licensed clubs, members clubs	Provision of food and drink in environment dominated by licensing requirements	Developed from inns; also origin of steak houses, eg 'Berni' in 1960s
TRANSPORT including: railways, airline, marine	Provision of food and drink to people on the move	Grew out of need to meet requirements of travelling public. Originally services were mainly of high levels reflecting the type of traveller. Eventually changed to meet need of wide range of travelling public
OUTDOOR CATERING (ODC) ('off premises' catering)	Provision of food and drink away from home base and suppliers	Developed through need to provide services at special events. The term ODC is misleading as little of this catering actually takes place outside

It is useful to define these different types of market as follows:

• **General market**	*Non-captive:*	Customers have a full choice
• **Restricted market**	*Captive:*	Customers have no choice, eg welfare
	Semi-captive:	Customers have a choice before entering, eg marine, airline, trains, some hotels and some leisure activities. The customers could have chosen alternatives to these but, once chosen, have little choice of food and drink other than that on offer

Defining the nature of the market in this way helps us to understand why different methods of organization may be in operation; eg in captive markets customers might be asked to clear their own tables, whereas in non-captive markets this is unlikely to be successful.

Taking the above points into account a general summary of sectors may be drawn up as seen in Figure 1.4.

Figure 1.4 Summary of sectors in the food and beverage service industry

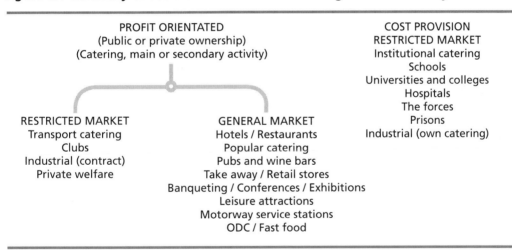

PROFIT ORIENTATED
(Public or private ownership)
(Catering, main or secondary activity)

COST PROVISION
RESTRICTED MARKET
Institutional catering
Schools
Universities and colleges
Hospitals
The forces
Prisons
Industrial (own catering)

RESTRICTED MARKET
Transport catering
Clubs
Industrial (contract)
Private welfare

GENERAL MARKET
Hotels / Restaurants
Popular catering
Pubs and wine bars
Take away / Retail stores
Banqueting / Conferences / Exhibitions
Leisure attractions
Motorway service stations
ODC / Fast food

1.4 Variables in food and beverage operations

The list of types of outlets in Figure 1.1 indicates by itself very little in terms of methods adopted and the management of them. In a similar way to the identifying variables for sectors (Figure 1.3), variables can also be identified for outlets/operations. These variables have been identified from a variety of published sources as well as from experience. They can be separated into three groups:

- Organizational
- Performance measures
- Customer experience

These groups provide for the systematic examination and inter-comparison of types of food and beverage operations through profiles of differing operations that can be drawn, based upon these variables (Figure 1.5).

Performance measures are further dealt with under Chapter 10 (Supervision). Customer experience variables are discussed in Section 1.5. The remainder of this book presents further information on a variety of organizational variables.

It should also be pointed out, for example, that a restaurant may be being operated

Figure 1.5 Variables in food and beverage service operations

ORGANIZATIONAL	
Service methods	Dining arrangements
Specialized service requirements	Nature of market
Legislative controls	Range of choice
Billing methods	Style of menu/drinks list
Checking methods	Staff working hours
Marketing/merchandising	Staff organization
Control method costs/revenue	Number of staff
Provisioning and storage methods	Opening times/service period
Production methods	Scale of operation
Clearing methods	Seating time
Dishwashing methods	Number of covers available
Type of equipment	Capacity

PERFORMANCE MEASURES	
Seat turnover/customer throughput	Sales/profit per sq m (or ft)/per seat
Customer spend/average check	Sales analysis
Revenue per member of staff	Departmental profit
Ratio of food and beverage sales to	Stock turnover
total sales	Stock holding
Productivity index	

CUSTOMER EXPERIENCE	
Food and drink available	Level of service and other services
Price range/value for money	Cleanliness and hygiene
Atmosphere (eg decor, lighting, air	
conditioning, acoustics, noise, size and	
shape of room, other clientele, attitude	
of staff)	

within the Restaurant Sector as a stand-alone operation. Alternatively a restaurant may be operated within say an hotel, in the Hotel Sector. Both sets of common variables will need to be examined to give a clear picture of the operation and business as a whole. In a small business the proprietor/manager would be concerned with the management of the whole business (ie factors indicated by applying both sets of variables). However, the food and beverage manager of an hotel would be principally concerned with the common operational variables.

1.5 The meal experience

The main aim of food and beverage operations is to achieve customer satisfaction. In other words, to meet the customer's needs. The needs that the customer might be seeking to satisfy include:

- *Physiological*: for example, the need to sate one's appetite or quench the thirst; the need for special foods (diabetic, vegetarian)
- *Economic*: for example, the need for good value; rapid, fast service; a convenient location
- *Social*: for example, when desiring enjoyable company; going out with friends or business colleagues; attending functions to meet others
- *Psychological*: for example, the need for enhancement of self-esteem; fulfilling life-style needs; the need for variety; as a result of advertising and promotion
- *Convenience*: for example, as a result of being unable to get home (shoppers, workers) or having to attend some other event (cinema, theatre); the desire for someone else to do the work; the physical impossibility of catering at home (weddings and other special functions)

Customers may be wanting to satisfy some or all of these needs.

It is important to recognize that the specific reasons behind a customer's choice determine the customer's satisfaction (or dissatisfaction) rather than the food and beverage service by itself. A good example is the social need to go out with friends: if one person fails to turn up or behaves in a disagreeable way, then the customer may be dissatisfied with the meal.

The customer who is not able to satisfy his/her needs will be a dissatisfied customer. The customer may, for instance, be dissatisfied with unhelpful staff, cramped conditions or the lack of choice available. These aspects are the responsibility of the food and beverage operation. However, sometimes the reasons for the customer being dissatisfied might be beyond the operation's control, eg location, the weather, other customers or transport problems.

In *non-captive markets* the customer has a choice of eating out opportunities both in terms of the food and drink to be consumed and the type of operation they may wish to patronize. Whilst it is true that certain types of catering operations might attract certain types of customer, this is by no means true all the time. The same customers may patronize a variety of different operations depending on the needs they have at the time, eg a romantic night out, a quick office lunch or a wedding function.

In *semi-captive markets* this is also important. The customers may choose, for example, a certain airline or boat or hotel based upon the identification of certain needs they may wish to satisfy. Also in *captive markets* where the customer does not have a choice of operation, there is still a need for satisfaction. For instance, it is generally recognized that better fed workers work better and that better fed patients recover quicker. 'Better fed' here, though, does not just refer to the food and drink provided but the whole experience of the meal.

From the food and beverage operator's point of view it is important to recognize that the customer's needs may vary and that food and beverage operators should be aware of factors which might affect the customer's meal experience. Much research has been carried out in recent years identifying these factors. They range from location to the acceptance of credit cards, and from attitudes of staff to the behaviour of other customers. These factors are summarized in Figure 1.6.

Figure 1.6 Meal experience factors

FACTORS	DESCRIPTION
FOOD AND DRINK	Range of food and drink on offer; type and variety; availability of special items; quality
LEVEL OF SERVICE	Method of service; speed of service; reliability; booking facility; acceptance of credit cards; availability of credit facilities etc
LEVEL OF CLEANLINESS AND HYGIENE	Cleanliness and hygiene of equipment, premises and staff
VALUE FOR MONEY/PRICE	Perceptions in the customer's mind of the value of the product (not just the food and drink) related to the price one is prepared to pay at the time
ATMOSPHERE	A fairly intangible concept but contributed to by aspects such as decor, lighting, heating, furnishing, acoustics, other customers and the attitude of staff

1.6 Food and beverage service methods

The service of food and beverages may be carried out in many ways depending on a number of factors:

- The type of *establishment*
- The type of *customer* to be served
- The *time* available for the meal
- The *turnover* of custom expected
- The type of *menu* presented
- The *cost* of the meal served
- The *site* of the establishment

Service staff are involved in a process or service sequence which essentially forms the link between the customer and the food production area, the stillroom, the cashiers and other departments. This process or service sequence can be summarized as a series of stages as in Figure 1.7.

Figure 1.7 Food and beverage service sequence

A	Preparation for service (which may include taking bookings)
B	Taking customer food and beverage orders
C	Service of food and beverages
D	Clearing
E	Billing (which may take place at the time of service, as in take away operations or later at the end of a meal as in a restaurant)
F	Dishwashing
G	Clearing following service

For each of these stages there are a variety of methods in which they may be carried out. The choice of method for the individual stage depends as much on the factors listed at the start of this section as it does on taking into account the process which the customer is to experience.

Essentially, the customer enters a food service area, orders or selects his/her choice and then is served (the customer may pay either at this point or later). Food and beverages are then consumed, following which the area is cleared.

Using this approach, five basic types of service can be identified. These are shown in Figure 1.8. In the first four the customer comes to where the food and beverages are provided, for example to the restaurant or take away. In the fifth the food and drink is

Figure 1.8 Simple categorization of the food and beverage customer process

SERVICE METHOD	FOOD AND BEVERAGE SERVICE AREA	ORDERING/ SELECTION	SERVICE	DINING/ CONSUMPTION	CLEARING
A TABLE SERVICE	Customer enters area and is seated	From menu	By staff to customer	At laid cover	By staff
B ASSISTED SERVICE	Customer enters area and is usually seated	From menu, buffet or passed trays	Combination of both staff and customer	Usually at laid cover	By staff
C SELF- SERVICE	Customer enters	Customer selects own tray	Customer carries	Dining area or take-away	Various
D SINGLE POINT SERVICE	Customer enters	Ordered at single point	Customer carries	Dining area or take-away	Various
E SPECIALIZED OR IN SITU SERVICE	In situ	From menu or predetermined	Brought to customer	Where served	By staff or customer clearing

taken to where the customer is, for example in guest rooms, lounges or to hospital patients.

The 15 service methods available to the food and beverage operator are identified in Figure 1.9 (pages 14 and 15) and grouped based upon the simple categorization of the food and beverage customer process (Figure 1.8).

A particular service method, eg *waiter*, requires a number of tasks and duties which are undertaken during the actual service of food and beverages. However, there are other tasks and duties which contribute to the service. These may be identified using the service sequence (see Figure 1.7). The level of complexity of food and beverage service in terms of staff skills, tasks and duties reduces from Group A (the most complex) to Group D. Group E contains specialized forms of service and these are further considered in Chapter 7.

1.7 Food and beverage service personnel

Typical organization charts for small and larger hotels are given in Figures 1.10 and 1.11. Among food and beverage operations that are not set within hotels, the organization might resemble the food and beverage section of the hotel organization charts. However, different terminology is used in differing types of establishment. In the section that follows, the variety of types of personnel in food and beverage operations is set out. Smaller operations may combine a number of these responsibilities.

Food and beverage manager

Depending on the size of the establishment, the food and beverage manager is either responsible for the implementation of agreed policies or for contributing to the setting of catering policies. The larger the organization the less likely the manager is to be involved in policy setting. In general, managers are responsible for:

- Ensuring that the required profit margins are achieved for each food and beverage service area in each financial period
- Updating and compiling new wine lists according to availability of stock, current trends and customer needs
- Compiling, in liaison with the kitchen, menus for the various food service areas and for special occasions
- The purchasing of all materials, both food and drink
- Ensuring that quality in relation to the price paid is maintained
- Determining portion size in relation to selling price
- Departmental training and promotions, plus the maintenance of the highest professional standards
- Employing and dismissing staff
- Holding regular meetings with section heads to ensure all areas are working effectively, efficiently and are well co-ordinated

Restaurant manager/supervisor

This person has overall responsibility for the organization and administration of particular food and beverage service areas. These may include the lounges, floors, grill rooms, restaurants and possibly some of the private banqueting suites. It is the restaurant manager who sets the standards for service and is responsible for any staff training that may have to be carried out on or off the job. He/she may make out duty rotas, holiday lists, and hours on and off duty so that all the service areas run efficiently and smoothly.

Reception head waiter

This staff member is responsible for accepting any bookings and for keeping the booking diary up to date. He/she will reserve tables and allocate these reservations to particular stations. The reception head waiter greets guests on arrival and takes them to the table and seats them.

Figure 1.9 Food and beverage service methods

TYPE OF SERVICE	DESCRIPTION
GROUP A: TABLE SERVICE	
Service to customers at a laid cover	
1 Waiter a Silver/English	Presentation and service of food to customer by waiting staff from food flat or dish
b Family	Main courses plated with vegetables placed in multi-portion dishes on tables for customers to help themselves; sauces offered
c Plate/American	Service of pre-plated foods to customers
d Butler/French	Presentation of food individually to customers by food service staff for customers to serve themselves
e Russian	Table laid with food for customers to help themselves (also sometimes confusingly used to indicate Guéridon or Butler service)
f Guéridon	Food served on to customer's plate at side table or trolley; also may include carving, cooking and flambage, preparation of salads and dressings, and fish filleting
2 Bar counter	Service to customers seated at bar counter (usually U-shaped) on stools
GROUP B: ASSISTED SERVICE	
Combination of table service and self-service	
3 Assisted	a Commonly applied to 'carvery' type operations. Some parts of the meal are served to seated customers; other parts are collected by the customers (also used for Breakfast service)
	b Buffets where customers select food and drink from displays or passed trays; consumption is either at tables, standing or in lounge area
GROUP C: SELF-SERVICE	
Self-service of customers	
4 Cafeteria a Counter	Customers queuing in line formation past a service counter choosing their menu requirements in stages and loading them on to a tray (may include a 'Carousel' – a revolving stacked counter saving space)
b Free-flow	Selection as in counter (above) but in food service area where customers move at will to random service points; customers usually exit via a till point
c Echelon	Series of counters at angles to customer flow within a free-flow area, thus saving space
d Supermarket	Island service points within a free-flow area

(Note: some 'call order' production may be included in cafeterias.)

TYPE OF SERVICE	DESCRIPTION

GROUP D: SINGLE POINT SERVICE

Service of customers at single point – consumed on premises or taken away

5 Take-away	a Customer orders and is served from single point, at counter, hatch or snackstand; customer consumes off the premises (some take-away establishments provide seating)
	b Drive-thru: form of take-away where customer drives vehicle past order, payment and collection points
	c Fast food: originally used to describe a service at a counter or hatch where customers receive a complete meal or dish in exchange for cash or ticket; commonly used nowadays to describe type of establishment offering limited range menu, fast service with take-away facility
6 Vending	Provision of food service and beverage service by means of automatic retailing
7 Kiosks	Outstation to provide service for peak demand or in specific location (may be open for customers to order or used for dispensing only)
8 Food court	Series of autonomous counters where customers may either order and eat (as in bar counter, above) or buy from a number of counters and eat in separate eating area, or take-away
9 Bar	Term used to describe selling point and consumption area in licensed premises

GROUP E: SPECIALIZED (OR IN SITU)

Service to customer's in areas not primarily designed for service

10 Tray	Method of service of whole or part of meal on tray to customer *in situ*, eg hospitals, aircraft; also used in ODC
11 Trolley	Service of food and beverages from trolley, away from dining areas, eg for office workers, in aircraft or on trains
12 Home delivery	Food delivered to customer's home or place of work, eg 'meals on wheels', pizza home delivery
13 Lounge	Service of variety of foods and beverages in lounge area
14 Room	Service of variety of foods and beverages in guest apartments or meeting rooms
15 Drive-in	Customers park motor vehicle and are served at the vehicles

(Note: banquet/function is a term used to describe catering for specific numbers of people at specific times in a variety of dining layouts. Service methods also vary. In these cases banquet/function 'catering' refers to the organization of service rather than a specific service method – refer to Chapter 9.)

Figure 1.10 Small hotel organization

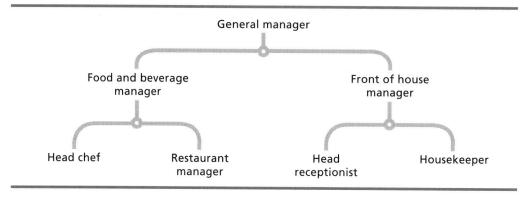

Figure 1.11 Larger hotel organization

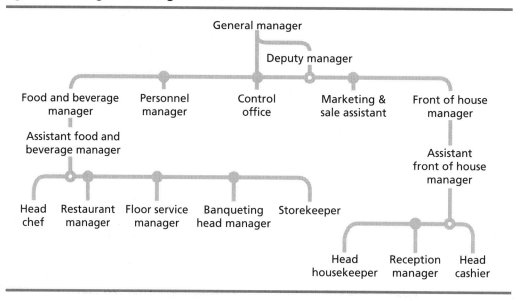

Head waiter/maître d'hôtel/supervisor

This person has overall charge of the staff team and is responsible for seeing that all the duties necessary for the pre-preparation for service are efficiently carried out and that nothing is forgotten. The head waiter will aid the reception head waiter during the service and will possibly take some orders if the station waiter is busy. The head waiter helps with the compilation of duty rotas and holiday lists, and may relieve the restaurant manager or reception head waiter on their days off.

Station head waiter/section supervisor

The station head waiter has the overall responsibility for a team of staff serving a set number of tables, which could be anything from four to eight in number, from one sideboard. The set of tables under the station head waiter's control is called a *station*.

The station head waiter must have a good knowledge of food and wine and its correct service, and be able to instruct other members of the staff. He/she will take the order (usually from the host) and carry out all the service at the table with the help of the chef de rang, who is the second in command of the station.

Station waiter/chef de rang

The chef de rang must be able to carry out the same work as the station head waiter and relieve him/her on days off. The chef de rang will normally have had less experience than the station head waiter. Both the chef de rang and the station head waiter must work together as a team to provide an efficient and speedy service.

Assistant station waiter/demi-chef de rang

The demi-chef de rang is a post usually found only on the Continent. As the term implies, this person is next in seniority to the chef de rang and assists where necessary.

Waiter/server/commis de rang

The commis de rang acts by instruction from the chef de rang. He/she mainly fetches and carries, may do a little service of either vegetables or sauces, and also offers rolls, places plates upon the table and so on, and helps to clear the tables after each course. During the pre-preparation period some of the cleaning and preparatory tasks will be carried out by the commis de rang.

Trainee commis/debarrasseur/apprentice

The debarrasseur is the 'learner', having just joined the food service staff, and possibly wishing to take up food service as a career. During the service this person will keep the sideboard well filled with equipment, and may help to fetch and carry items as required. The debarrasseur would carry out certain of the cleaning tasks during the pre-preparation periods. They may be given the responsibility of looking after and serving hors-d'oeuvre, cold sweets or assorted cheeses from the appropriate trolleys.

Carver/trancheur

The carver is responsible for the carving trolley and the carving of joints at the table as required. The carver will plate up each portion with the appropriate accompaniment.

Floor service staff/chef d'étage/floor waiter

The floor service staff are often responsible for a complete floor in an establishment or, depending on the size of the establishment, a number of rooms or suites. Floor service of all meals and beverages throughout the day is normally only offered by a first-class establishment. In smaller establishments floor service may be limited to early morning teas and breakfasts with the provision of in-room mini bars and tea and coffee facilities.

If a full floor service is in operation, the staff would consist of a head floor waiter with the appropriate number of floor waiters working for him/her. These staff are then responsible for the service of all meals and beverages (alcoholic and non-alcoholic) in rooms. A thorough knowledge of food and drink, and their correct service, is therefore essential. The importance of good liaison and co-operation with the housekeeping staff cannot be over-emphasized here. The floor service staff would normally work from a floor pantry or from a central kitchen with all food and drink reaching the appropriate floor and the required room by lift and in a heated trolley (refer to Section 7.2).

Lounge staff/chef de salle

Lounge staff may deal with lounge service as a specific duty only in a first-class establishment. In a smaller establishment it is usual for members of the food service staff to take over these duties on a rota basis. The lounge staff are responsible for the service of morning coffee, afternoon teas, aperitifs and liqueurs before and after both lunch and dinner, and any coffee required after meals. They would be responsible for setting up the lounge in the morning and maintaining its cleanliness and presentation throughout the day.

Wine butler/wine waiter/sommelier

The sommelier is responsible for the service of all alcoholic drinks during the service of meals. The wine butler must also be a sales person. This employee should have a thorough knowledge of all drink to be served, of the best wines to go with certain foods and of the licensing laws in respect of the particular establishment and area.

Cocktail bar staff

The person who works on the cocktail bar must be responsible, well versed in the skills of shaking and stirring cocktails and should have a thorough knowledge of all alcoholic and non-alcoholic drinks, the ingredients necessary for the making of cocktails and of the licensing laws.

Buffet assistant/buffet chef/chef de buffet

The chef de buffet is in charge of the buffet in the room, its presentation, the carving and portioning of food and its service. This staff member would normally be a member of the kitchen team.

Cashier

The cashier is responsible for the takings of the food and beverage operation. This may include making up bills from food and drink checks or, alternatively, in a cafeteria, for example, charging customers for their selection of items on a tray (refer to Section 10.2).

Counter assistants

These would be found in cafeterias where they would stock the counter and sometimes serve or portion food for customers. Duties may also include some cooking of call order items.

Table clearers

Again found in seating areas where the service is not waiter service. These people are responsible for clearing tables on to trolleys specially designed for good stacking of crockery, glassware, cutlery etc.

Function catering/banqueting staff

In establishments with function catering facilities there would normally be a certain number of permanent staff. These would include the banqueting manager, one or two assistant banqueting managers, one or two banqueting head waiters, a dispense person and a secretary to the banqueting manager. All other banqueting staff required are normally engaged on a casual basis. In small establishments where there are fewer functions the necessary administrative and organizational work would be undertaken by the manager, the assistant manager and the head waiter.

Staff requirements

The staff requirements in various establishments will differ for a number of reasons. The following is a guide to the food and beverage service staff whom you are likely to find in five main types of establishment.

Medium class hotel
Hotel Manager ⎱ responsible
Assistant manager ⎰ for booking
Head waiter   functions
Waiters
Wine waiter
Cashier

Department store
Catering manager
Assistant catering manager
Supervisor
Assistant supervisors
Cashier
Dispense staff
Wine waiting staff
Waiting staff

Cafeteria
Catering manager
Supervisors
Assistant supervisors
Counter service hands
Clearers
Cashier

Industrial concern
Catering manager
Assistant catering manager
Supervisors
Assistant supervisors
Waiter
Steward/butler
Counter service staff
Clearers
Cashiers

Popular price restaurant
Restaurant manager/supervisor
Waiting staff
Dispense bar assistant

1.8 Attributes of food and beverage service personnel

As has been said earlier (see Section 1.5) the product of food and beverage operation is not just the food and drink itself. Any member of staff coming into contact with the customer is also part of the product. No matter how good the quality of the food, beverage, decor and equipment, poorly-trained, scruffy or unhelpful staff can destroy the customer's potential satisfaction with the product. It is also true that well-trained, smart and helpful staff can sometimes make up for aspects which are lacking elsewhere in the operation.

Below are listed the principal attributes necessary in food and beverage service personnel.

A professional and hygienic appearance

How you look and the first impression you create are more often than not seen as a reflection of the hygiene standards of your establishment and the quality of service to come.

All staff should be aware of the factors listed below and it is their individual responsibility to ensure that they are put into practice:

- A shower or bath should be taken daily
- Always use deodorants
- Aftershave and perfumes should not be too strong
- Sufficient sleep, an adequate and healthy intake of food, and regular exercise will keep you in a healthy condition and allow you to cope with the pressures and stress of work
- Pay particular attention to your hands. They must always be clean, free of nicotine stain and with clean, well-trimmed nails
- No nail varnish should be worn
- Males should be clean shaven with any moustache neatly trimmed
- Females should only wear light make-up
- Ear-rings should not be worn with the possible exception of studs
- Your uniform should be clean, starched as appropriate and neatly pressed. All buttons must be present
- Hair must at all times be clean and well groomed. Should staff have long hair, then it must be tied 'up' or 'back'
- Shoes must be comfortable and clean, and of a plain, neat design. Fashion is not important here (ie high heels and trainers), but rather safety and foot comfort
- Your teeth should be brushed immediately before coming on duty
- Cuts and burns should be covered with the correct dressings
- Any colds or other possible infections should be reported immediately

- Your hands should be washed immediately after using the toilet, smoking or dealing with refuse. Use hot water and soap
- Try to avoid any 'mannerisms' that you may have, such as running your fingers through your hair, chewing gum, or scratching your face
- Excessive jewellery must not be worn. Follow your establishment policy

Knowledge of food and drink

The staff must have sufficient knowledge of all the items on the menu and wine list in order to advise and offer suggestions to customers. Furthermore they must know how to serve correctly each dish on the menu, what its accompaniments are, the correct cover, the make-up of the dish and its appropriate garnish, and also how to serve various types of drink, in the correct glass and at the right temperature.

Punctuality

Punctuality is all important. If the staff are continually late on duty it shows lack of interest in work and a lack of respect for management and customers.

Local knowledge

In the interest of customers the staff should have a certain knowledge of the area in which they work so they may be able to advise the guests on the various forms of entertainment offered, the best means of transport to places of interest and so on.

Personality

The staff must be tactful, courteous, good humoured and of an even temper. They must converse with the customer in a pleasing and well spoken manner and the ability to smile at the right time pays dividends. With these attributes the staff will help the management by becoming good sales people.

Attitude to customers

The correct approach to the customer is of the utmost importance. The staff must not be servile, but anticipate the customer's needs and wishes. A careful watch should be kept on customers at all times during the service without staring. Care should always be taken when dealing with difficult customers. (There is really no such thing as a 'difficult' customer – they are normally people whom one is uncertain how to handle.) Customers should never be argued with as this will only aggravate the situation, but all complaints should be referred to someone in authority in the food service area.

Memory

This is an essential asset to food and beverage service staff. It may help them in various ways in their work if they know the likes and dislikes of customers, where they like to sit in the food service area, what are their favourite drinks and so on.

Honesty

This is all important to the staff in dealings with both the customer and the management. If there is trust and respect in the triangle of staff, customer and management relationships, then there will be an atmosphere of work which encourages efficiency and a good team spirit amongst the food and beverage service operators.

Loyalty

The staff's obligations and loyalty are firstly to the establishment in which they are employed and its management.

Conduct

The staff's conduct should be impeccable at all times, especially in front of customers. The rules and regulations of an establishment must be followed, and respect shown to all senior members of staff.

Sales ability

Staff reflect the image of the establishment. They are salespeople and must therefore have a complete knowledge of all forms of food and drink and their correct service.

Sense of urgency

So that the establishment has the maximum amount of business over the service period with as high a net profit as possible, the staff must develop a sense of urgency.

Customer satisfaction

The food and beverage service staff must see that the guests have all they require and are completely satisfied. It is of great importance to anticipate a customer's needs. If he/she is comfortable in the surroundings then this is because of the warm and friendly atmosphere in the food service area, and the team spirit amongst the waiting staff.

Complaints

The staff should have a pleasant manner, showing courtesy and tact, an even temper and good humour, and never displeasure even though at times things may be difficult. They should never argue with a customer and, if they cannot deal with the situation, it should be referred immediately to a senior member of the team who, because of his/her greater experience, will be able to calm the guest and put right any fault. Remember loss of time in dealing with complaints only makes the situation worse.

CHAPTER 2

FOOD AND BEVERAGE SERVICE AREAS AND EQUIPMENT

2.1	**Introduction**	24
2.2	**Stillroom**	25
2.3	**Silver room or plate room**	28
2.4	**Wash-up**	30
2.5	**Hotplate**	31
2.6	**Spare linen store**	34
2.7	**Dispense bar**	34
2.8	**Automatic vending**	39
2.9	**Lighting and colour**	43
2.10	**Furniture**	45
2.11	**Linen**	49
2.12	**China**	50
2.13	**Tableware (Flatware, cutlery and hollow-ware)**	55
2.14	**Glassware**	58
2.15	**Disposables**	60

2.1 Introduction

In any establishment a customer's first impressions on entering the service area are of great importance. A customer may be gained or lost on these impressions alone. The creation of atmosphere by the right choice of furnishings and equipment is therefore a contributing factor to the success of the food and beverage service area. A careful selection of items in terms of shape, design and colour enhances the overall décor or theme and contributes towards a feeling of total harmony. The choice of furniture and its placing, linen, tableware, small equipment and glassware will be determined by considering:

- The type of *clientele* expected
- The *site* or location
- The *layout* of the food and beverage service area
- The type of *service* offered
- The *funds* available

The general points that must be considered when purchasing equipment for a food and beverage service area are:

- Flexibility of use
- Type of service being offered
- Type of customer
- Design
- Colour
- Durability
- Ease of maintenance
- Stackability
- Cost and funds available
- Availability in the future – replacements
- Storage
- Rate of breakage, ie china
- Shape
- Psychological effect on guests
- Delivery time

There are many *service areas* behind the scenes, or what may be termed 'back-of-house', which are required to be well organized, efficiently run and supervised, and stocked with appropriate equipment, depending on the style of operation. It is necessary for all these factors to come together like a well-oiled machine to determine overall a successful back-up to the food and beverage operation.

The service areas are usually between the kitchen and food service areas. They are important units in the make-up of a catering establishment, acting as the link between kitchen or food preparation unit and the restaurant or food service units. They are meeting points for staff of various departments as they carry out their duties, and therefore there must be close liaison between these various members of staff and the departments under whose jurisdiction they come.

The service areas themselves are some of the busiest units of a catering establishment, especially over the service periods. Because of this, it is most important that department heads ensure that all staff know exactly what their duties are and how to carry them out efficiently and quickly. A pride in the job and in doing it well means that the staff will co-operate with one another to give a complete and efficient service to the customer.

In general, especially in large operations, five main service areas can be distinguished:

- Stillroom
- Silver or plate room
- Wash-up
- Hotplate
- Spare linen store

A well-structured layout of these areas is most important to ensure an even flow of work by the various members of staff. However, the layout itself may vary with different catering establishments according to their needs.

We shall deal firstly with those service areas at the 'back-of-house' and then look at the equipment necessary.

2.2 Stillroom

The main function of the stillroom is to provide items of food and beverages required for the service of a meal and not catered for by the other major departments in a hotel, such as the kitchen, larder and pastry.

The duties performed in this service area will vary according to the type of meals offered and the size of establishment concerned.

Staff

In a large first-class establishment a stillroom supervisor is in charge of the stillroom. Depending on its size and the duties to be performed, he/she may have a number of staff under his/her control. The person in charge is responsible for the compilation of work rotas for all the stillroom staff so that all duties are covered and so that it is fully staffed from first thing in the morning until last thing at night. A further responsibility of the stillroom supervisor is the ordering of supplies from the main dry goods store and the effective control of these items when issued to various departments.

When ordering goods from the main dry goods store, all requirements should be written out on a requisition sheet in duplicate. The top copy goes to the store to be retained by the storekeeper after issuing the goods and the duplicate remains in the requisition book as a means of checking the receipt of goods from the store by a member of the still-room staff. No goods should be issued by the storekeeper unless the requisition has been signed by the stillroom supervisor.

Because of the number of hours that the stillroom has to remain open and running efficiently, the staff normally work on a straight shift basis, doing an early shift one week and a late shift the next. They are responsible for washing up all their own equipment.

Equipment

Since the requirements of most stillrooms are basically the same, it follows that the equipment in all stillrooms is of a similar nature. A wide range of food items is offered and, therefore, to ensure their correct storage, preparation and presentation, a considerable amount of equipment is used. The following are examples of items needed:

- *Refrigerator*: for storage of milk, cream, butter, fruit juices and so on
- *Beverage making facilities*
- *Large double sink and draining board*: for washing-up purposes and a washing-up machine of a size suitable for a particular stillroom and large enough to ensure efficient turnover of equipment
- *Salamander or toasters*: for the preparation of breakfast or melba toast
- *Bread slicing machine*
- *Working top table* and *cutting board*
- The necessary *storage space* for all the *small equipment* such as china, glassware and silverware that is in everyday use
- *Storage cupboard*: for all dry goods held in stock, and for such miscellaneous items as doilies, kitchen papers, paper napkins, etc
- *Coffee grinding machine*: to ensure the correct 'grind' of coffee for the brewing method to be used

Provisions

As a basic guide, the following food items would normally be dispensed from the still-room:

- *All beverages* such as coffee, tea, chocolate, tisanes, Bovril, Horlicks, Ovaltine and other food drinks
- *Assorted fruit juices*: orange, tomato, pineapple and grapefruit
- *Milk and cream*
- *Sugars*: loaf, pre-wrapped portions, brown coffee crystals, demerara, etc
- *Preserves*: marmalade, cherry, plum, raspberry, strawberry, apricot and honey. For the purpose of control and saving with regard to wastage, many

establishments now offer pre-portioned jars or pots of preserve at breakfast and for afternoon tea, rather than a preserve dish.

- *Butter*: either passed through a butter pat machine, curled or pre-wrapped portions.

- *Sliced and buttered brown, white and malt bread*

- *Rolls, brioche and croissant*

- *Melba toast*: very thin toasted bread slices.

- *Breakfast toast*: thick sliced bread, toasted both sides, with crusts removed, cut into two triangles and placed in a toast-rack

- *Gristicks and starch-reduced rolls*

- *Dry cracker, digestive and water biscuits*: for service with the cheeseboard; sweet biscuits for service with early morning and afternoon teas

- *Assorted breakfast cereals*: Cornflakes, Weetabix, Shredded Wheat, Rice Crispies, muesli and so on. In many establishments cereals of all types are offered in a pre-wrapped, portion controlled packets.

- *Toasted scones and teacakes*

- *Pastries, gâteaux and sandwiches*: In a large establishment the pastries and gâteaux will come from the Pastry department, and the assorted savoury sandwiches from the Larder. In a smaller establishment the pastries and gâteaux may be bought from an outside firm but issued from the stillroom, and sandwiches would be made and issued from the stillroom.

  If the stillroom prepares the sandwiches, it is useful to know that an ordinary loaf contains 25 slices and that a 'quarten' contains 50. This then makes 12 and 25 rounds of sandwiches respectively. Once prepared, the sandwiches should be kept covered with a moist cloth and the crusts removed only immediately before serving

- *Porridge and boiled eggs*: often provided by the stillroom in small establishments

Control

There are two main ways of checking for goods to be issued, namely:

- By issuing items in bulk on receipt of a requisition received from a food service area. The requisition must be signed by someone in authority. This would include such food items as butter, preserves, sugar, and so on.

- By issuing tea, coffee or any other beverage required in the necessary portions on receipt of a waiters check.
  Morning coffee and afternoon tea are controlled in this way, the pastries, gâteaux, toasted teacakes, sandwiches, bread and butter and preserves being issued on receipt of a waiter's check, either in portions with the beverage, or in bulk by the sale or return method.

2.3 Silver room or plate room

In the larger more luxurious establishments, the silver room, or plate room as it is sometimes known, is a separate service area. In the small establishments it is more often than not combined with the pantry wash-up.

Equipment

The silver room should hold the complete stock of silver required for the service of all meals, together with a slight surplus stock in case of emergency. Silver for banqueting service may be a different design and kept specifically for that purpose.

The large silver such as flats, salvers, soup tureens, and cloches, will be stored on shelves, with all the flats of one size together, and so on. All shelves should be labelled showing where each different item goes. This makes it easier for control purposes and for stacking. When stacking silver the heavier items should go on the shelves lower down and the smaller and lighter items on the shelves higher up. This helps to prevent accidents. All cutlery and flatware, together with the smaller items of silver such as ashtrays, cruets, butter dishes, special equipment, tables numbers and menu holders, are best stored in drawers lined with green baize. This helps to prevent noise and stops the various items sliding about the drawer when it is opened and closed and so becoming scratched and marked.

Staff

All the service silver should be cleaned and burnished on a rota basis. It is the duty of the head plate person to ensure that this is carried out and that all silver is cleaned regularly. Obviously those items in constant use will require more attention. He/she will also put on one side any articles of silver broken or that require buffing up or replating, so that they may be sent to the manufacturers for any faults to be corrected.

The head plate person may have a number of staff under him/her depending on the size of the establishment. In the smaller medium class establishment, however, where the plate room is possibly combined with the pantry wash-up, it would be the duty of either the washing-up staff or the waiting staff to ensure that all the service silver is kept clean.

Silver cleaning methods

There are various methods of silver cleaning, and the method used generally depends on the size and class of establishment. The larger establishments use a burnishing machine which would be in constant use all through the day, whereas the smaller establishments which possibly could not afford a burnishing machine, would use a manual method.

The main methods used are as follows:

Burnishing machine

This is a revolving drum with a safety shield. It may be plumbed into the mains or remain portable with the water being poured in by means of a hose from a tap. Depending on the size of burnishing machine in use, it may be divided into compartments to hold specific sizes of silver. It may also be possible to insert a rod through the centre of the drum from one end to the other. This rod is removable and is passed through the handles of teapots, coffee pots, milk jugs, sugar basins, etc, to hold them in position while the drum is revolving.

In order for the burnishing machine to run effectively and efficiently it is approximately half-full of ball-bearings. To these a certain amount of soap powder is added according to the maker's instructions. The silver is placed inside and then the lid clamped down tightly. The main water supply is then turned on to ensure a constant flow of water. If the machine is not plumbed in, then water should be poured into the drum until the ball-bearings are covered, before the lid is clamped down. The machine is then switched on. As the drum revolves the mixture of water and soap powder acts as a lubricant between the silver and the ball-bearings. Thus any tarnish is removed but the silver is not scratched. On being removed from the burnishing machine the silver should be rinsed in hot water and dried with a clean tea cloth.

This method of silver cleaning keeps the silver in good condition with minimum effort and gives a lasting polish. The ball-bearings must always be kept covered with water otherwise they rust very easily.

Polivit

A polivit is an aluminium metal sheet containing holes which is best used in an enamel or galvanized iron bowl. The polivit is placed in the bowl together with some soda. The silver to be cleaned is then put into the bowl, ensuring that at least one piece of silver has contact with the polivit. Sufficient boiling water is poured into the bowl to cover the silver being cleaned. A chemical reaction takes place between the polivit, soda, boiling water and silver, which causes the tarnish to be lifted. After three to four minutes the silver should be removed from the bowl and placed into a second bowl of boiling water and rinsed. On removal from the second bowl the silver is allowed to drain and then polished with a clean, dry tea cloth.

Plate powder

This is a pink powder which needs mixing with a little methylated spirit to obtain a smooth paste. The reason for using methylated spirit to mix the powder is that when the paste is rubbed on the article the spirit evaporates much more quickly than would water and the silver is therefore ready for polishing much more quickly. If, however, methylated spirit is not available, then water may be used, but the cleaning process takes a little longer.

The smooth paste, once prepared, is rubbed onto the article being cleaned with a clean piece of cloth. The paste must be rubbed well in to remove all tarnish. The article is then left until the paste has dried and the paste is then rubbed off with a clean cloth. It is advisable to rinse the article well in very hot water and to give a final polish with a clean dry tea cloth. When silver is cleaned that has a design or engraving on, a small toothbrush may be used to brush the paste into the design and a clean one used to remove it. This method is both time-consuming and messy, but produces very good results.

Silver dip

This is a pink coloured liquid which must be used in a plastic bowl. The silver to be cleaned is placed into a wire basket and dipped into the plastic bowl containing the silver dip. All the silver articles being cleaned should be covered by the liquid. The silver should be left in the bowl only a very short while and then lifted out and drained. After draining it is placed in warm water, rinsed and then polished with a clean dry tea cloth. This method is very quick and produces good results, but it is harder on the silver than the other methods because of the chemical reaction between the liquid and the silver. However, it is a popular method in the medium-sized establishment because it is quicker than other methods.

2.4 Wash-up

Organization

The wash-up is a most important service area and must be sited correctly so that staff can work speedily and efficiently when passing from the food service areas to the kitchens. Servers should stack trays of dirties correctly at the sideboard, with all the correct sized plates together, and tableware stacked on one of the plates with the blades of the knives running under the arches of the forks. All glassware should be stacked on a separate tray and taken to a separate wash-up point.

The wash-up service area should be the first section the waiter enters from the food service area. Here he/she deposits all the dirty plates, stacking them correctly and placing all the tableware in a special wire basket or container in readiness for washing. The server must place any debris into the bin or bowl provided. All used paper serviettes, doilies or kitchen paper should be placed in a separate bin. The china itself may be washed by one of two main methods.

Dishwashing methods

Manual (tank) method

The dirty china is placed into a tank of hot water containing a soap detergent. After washing, the plates are placed into wire racks and dipped into a second sterilizing tank containing clean hot water at a temperature of approximately 75°C (179°F). The racks are left for two minutes and then lifted out and the china left to drain. If sterilized in water at this temperature the china will dry by itself without the use of drying-up cloths. This is therefore more hygienic. After drying, the china is stacked into piles of the correct size and placed on shelves until required for further use.

Semi automatic

Many of the larger establishments have dishwashing machines. These are necessary because of the high usage of china. The instructions for use of a washing-up machine are generally supplied by the manufacturer together with details of detergent to be used, and in what quantity. These directions should be strictly adhered to. The china itself has any debris removed and is then placed into wire racks. The racks are then passed through the machine, the china being washed, rinsed, and then sterilized in turn. Having passed through the machine the china is left to drain for two to three minutes and is then stacked and placed on shelves until required for further use. As with the tank method the plates do not require drying with tea cloths. Development of this method includes the automatic conveyor and the flight conveyor. See Figure 2.1.

Figure 2.1 Summary of dishwashing methods (Courtesy of Croner's Catering)

METHOD	DESCRIPTION
MANUAL	Soiled ware washed by hand or brush machine
SEMI-AUTOMATIC	Soiled ware loaded manually into dishwashing machine by operators
AUTOMATIC CONVEYOR	Soiled ware loaded in baskets, mounted on a conveyor, by operators for automatic transportation through a dishwashing machine
FLIGHT CONVEYOR	Soiled ware loaded within pegs mounted on a conveyor, by operators for automatic transportation through a dishwashing machine
DEFERRED WASH	Soiled ware collected together, stripped, sorted and stacked by operators for transportation through a dishwashing machine at a later stage

2.5 Hotplate

Organization

The hotplate or pass may be regarded as the meeting point between the food service staff and the food preparation staff. Active co-operation and a good relationship between the staff of these two service areas helps a great deal to ensure that the customer receives an efficient and quick service of the meal, from a polite courteous waiter who has not been 'roused' because of bad service at the hotplate. This co-operation will also ensure that all the dishes served are well and attractively presented. At the same time all orders written by the waiter must be legible to the aboyeur so that there is no delay in 'calling-up' a particular dish.

Aboyeur

The *aboyeur* (or barker) is in charge, and controls the hotplate over the service period. As an aid to the food service staff the aboyeur would control the 'off board' which tells the waiter immediately any dish is 'off'. It should be sited in a prominent position for all to see. The hotplate itself should be stocked up with all the china necessary for the service of a meal. This would include some or all of the following items: soup plates, fish plates, joint plates, sweet plates, consommé cups, platters, soup cups and demi-tasse.

The silver required for service is often placed on the top of the hotplate and used as required. The hotplate is usually gas or electrically operated and should be lit well in advance of the service to ensure all the necessary china and silver is sufficiently heated.

The aboyeur who controls the hotplate over the service period will initially receive the food check from the waiter. He/she checks that it is legible and that none of the dishes ordered are 'off' the menu. Then the order from the various corners of the kitchen is called up as each particular dish is required. It is important that, if a dish required has to be prepared and cooked to order, then the aboyeur orders this to be done before the waiter comes to the hotplate to collect it. Then there will be no major delay for the waiter who is going to serve the dish, or for the customer who is waiting for the next course to be served. When a food check is finished with it is placed into a control box. This 'box' is kept locked and can only be opened by a member of staff from the 'control department' who, for control purposes, marries the copy of the food check from the kitchen with the copy the cashier has and the duplicate copy of the bill.

Hotplate language and terminology

To ensure there is no delay in any food dish reaching the hotplate, the aboyeur should call it up allowing time for preparation, cooking and presentation. To this end, special kitchen terms are used to warn the food preparation staff working in various corners to get ready certain dishes.

These terms are as follows:

- *Le service va commencer*; general warning to kitchen that the service is about to commence

- *Ça marche trois couverts*: indication to the kitchen of the number of covers

- *Poissonnier, faites marcher trois soles Véronique*: 'partie' concerned informed of the order required

- *Poissonnier, envoyez les trois soles Véronique*: when the order is required at the hotplate by the waiter, the aboyeur calls it up from the appropriate 'partie'

- *Oui*: the reply given by the 'chef de partie' to the order called out by the aboyeur

- *Bien soigné*: the term called out by the aboyeur before the actual order when an extra special order is required

- *Dépêchez-vous*: the words used to hurry up an order

- *Arrêtez*: the term used to cancel an order

- Foods requiring special degrees of cooking are given the following terms:
  (1) Omelette *baveuse*: soft inside

(2) Steak grillé: (a) *bleu*: (rare) surfaces well-browned, inside raw

(b) *saignant*: underdone

(c) *à point*: medium

(d) *bien cuit*: cooked right through, well done

All food service staff should be familiar with these terms in order to appreciate exactly what is going on at the hotplate and how the particular 'kitchen French' terms help to ensure quick and efficient service. Many establishments however now use English for these instructions. Again though staff do need to know the system for their establishment.

Carvery-type operations

As the carvery menu is restricted and guests are able to help themselves to expensive joints and other dishes, the most important factor in the success of a carvery is the accuracy of estimates related to the:

- *Average weight* of each portion
- *Type of meat* people will choose
- *Number of people* coming on any particular day

As a guide the average main course portion with vegetables is in the region of 525 g (1 lb 5 oz), but in estimating costs the average main course is assumed to be 600 g (1 lb 8 oz) – the additional 75 g (3 oz) being wastage. There is weight loss after cooking as well as wastage in carving.

After cooking, the joints are normally put into a hot closet where they can be held at a temperature somewhere between 78 and 82°C (170–180°F). If the temperature were higher than this, the joints would start cooking again. Even when holding joints at this temperature prior to carving, it is almost inevitable that joints of lamb commence cooking again. Thus lamb joints should never be fully roasted in the oven. If the temperature of the hot closet is too low there can be bacteriological problems.

On the carvery itself the meat and other dishes are maintained at a temperature of around 74–82°C (160–180°F) by the use of overhead infra-red heat lamps. These lamps are generally mounted on telescopic stands so various sized joints may be accommodated and carving may be carried out safely.

The demand for a particular type of meat in this style of operation may vary due to social and agricultural influence.

The anticipated turnover can be calculated through a number of factors:

- Figures from the previous week
- Figures for the same week the year before
- Adjustment of figures according to any local conditions, eg the situation of the establishment, the number of people resident, local attractions such as exhibitions and theatres

2.6 Spare linen store

Another back-of-house service area that is generally found within establishments is the spare linen cupboard or store. This is normally the responsibility of a senior member of the food service staff and is kept locked for control purposes. This spare linen stock is held near the food service area in case of emergency. The linen is changed when necessary on a basis of 'one clean for one dirty'.

2.7 Dispense bar

The term *dispense bar* is recognized to mean any bar situated within a food and beverage service area that dispenses only wine or other alcoholic drinks to be served to a guest consuming a meal. However, in many establishments because of the planning and layout, wine and other alcoholic drinks for consumption with a meal are sometimes dispensed from bars situated outside the food and beverage service area itself – in other words, from one of the public bars. All drinks dispensed must be checked for and controlled in some way (this will be dealt with in Sections 5.6 and 10.3). All alcoholic drinks are served by that member of the restaurant team known as the *sommelier* or wine butler, unless it is the custom for the food service waiter to serve his/her own guests with the drink they require.

Equipment

In order to carry out efficiently the service of all forms of drink requested, the bar should have available all the necessary equipment for making cocktails, decanting wine, serving wine correctly, making fruit cups and so on. The equipment should include the following items.

Main items

- *Cocktail shaker*: the ideal utensil for mixing ingredients that will not normally blend together well by stirring. A three-part utensil
- *Boston shaker*: consists of two cones, one of which overlaps the other to seal in the 'mix'. Made of stainless steel, glass or plated silver. The mix is strained using a Hawthorn strainer
- *Mixing glass*: like a glass jug without a handle, but has a lip. Used for mixing clear drinks which do not contain juices or cream
- *Strainer*: there are many types, the most popular being the Hawthorn. This is a flat spoon-shaped utensil with a spring coiled round its edge. It is used in conjunction with the cocktail shaker and mixing glass to hold back the ice after the drink is prepared. A special design is available for use with liquidizers and blenders

- *Bar spoon*: for use with the mixing glass when stirring cocktails. The flat 'muddler' end is used for crushing sugar and mint in certain drinks

- *Bar liquidizer or blender*: used for making drinks that require puréed fruit

- *Drink mixer*: used for drinks that do not need liquidizing, especially those containing cream or ice-cream. If ice is required, use only crushed ice

Figure 2.2 Examples of cocktail bar equipment

1 Boston shaker
2 Silver cocktail shaker
3 Stainless steel cocktail shaker

1 Bar tidy
2 Mixing glass with bar spoon
3 Juicer
4 Appetiser tray
5 Hawthorn strainer
6 Mini whisk

Other items

- Assorted glasses
- Measures
- Ice buckets and stands
- Small ice buckets and tongs
- Wine baskets
- Soda syphons
- Water jugs
- Coloured sugars
- Assorted bitters: peach, orange, angostura

- Cutting board and knife
- Optics/spirit measures
- Coasters
- Cooling trays
- Refrigerator
- Small sink unit or bar glass washing machine
- Bottle opener
- Cork extractor
- Ice crushing machine
- Ice pick
- Muslin and funnel

- Ice making machine
- Lemon squeezing machine
- Drinking straws
- Swizzle sticks
- Cocktail sticks
- Strainer and funnel
- Carafes
- Service salvers
- Wine and cocktail lists
- Wine knife and cigar cutter
- Plentiful supply of glass cloths, serviettes and service cloths

Food items

- Olives
- Maraschino cherries
- Worcester sauce
- Tabasco sauce
- Salt and pepper
- Cinnamon
- Nutmeg
- Cloves
- Angostura bitters
- Cube sugar

- Caster sugar
- Demerara
- Eggs
- Cream
- Mint
- Cucumber
- Orange
- Lemon
- Coconut cream

Glassware

The choice of the right glass is a vital element if the cocktail is to be invitingly presented. Well-designed glassware combines elegance, strength and stability, and should be fine rimmed and of clear glass. All glassware should be clean and well polished (see Section 2.14).

Figure 2.3 Examples of bar equipment

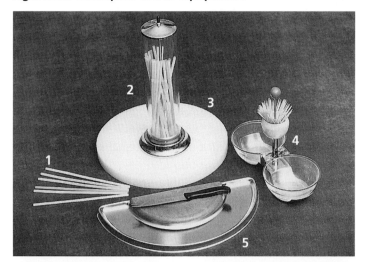

1 Straws
2 Straw dispenser
3 Cutting board
4 Appetiser tray
5 Slicing board

1 Drip tray
2 Thimble measures
3 & 4 Bottle pourers
5 Optic
6 Spare optic cork

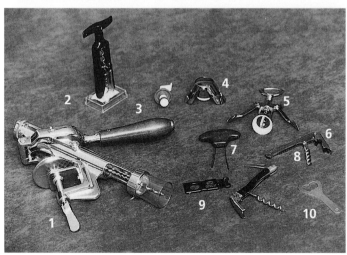

1 Bar cork remover
2 Wine bottle opener
3 Bottle stopper
4 Champagne bottle stopper
5, 6, 7 & 8 Wine bottle openers
9 Cigar cutter
10 Crown cork opener

Planning of the bar

There are certain essentials necessary in the planning of every bar and it is as well to bear these in mind now. They are factors which should be given prime consideration when one has to plan a bar or set up a bar for a particular function. They are as follows:

Area

The barstaff must be given sufficient area or space in which to work and move about. There should be a minimum of 1 m (3 ft) from the back of the bar counter to the storage shelves and display cabinets at the rear of the bar.

Layout

Very careful consideration must be given, in the initial planning, to the layout. Adequate storage must be provided, in the form of shelves, cupboards and racks, for all the stock required and equipment listed. Everything should be easily to hand so that the barstaff do not have to move about more than necessary to give a quick and efficient service.

Plumbing and power

It is essential to have hot and cold running water for glass washing. Power is necessary to provide the effective working of cooling trays, refrigerators and ice-making machines.

Safety and hygiene

Great care must be observed so that the materials used in the make-up of the bar are hygienic and safe. Flooring must be non-slip. The bar top should be of a material suited to the general decor that is hard wearing, easily wiped down and has no sharp edges. The bar top should be of average working height – approximately 1 m ($3\frac{1}{4}$ ft) and a width of 0.6 m (20 in).

Site of the bar

A major factor is the siting of the bar. The position should be chosen so that the bar achieves the greatest possible number of sales.

2.8 Automatic vending

In the broadest sense, *automatic vending* may be defined as 'selling by automation'. It is a form of automatic retailing using one of the following:

- Coin
- Token
- Banknote
- Moneycard

The types of service available may be broken into two areas, namely, *service and facilities* and *consumables*, eg:

Service and facilities	Consumables
• TV time	• Hot and cold beverages
• Gas	• Meals
• Water	• Confectionery
• Electricity	• Tobacco
• Shoe cleaning	• Alcoholic drinks
• Car parking	
• Toilets	
• Baggage store	

Within the catering framework 'automatic vending' refers to the supply of a wide variety of food and beverages, both hot and cold, through coin/token operated machines.

Two sectors of the catering industry benefit most at the present time from automatic vending, namely industrial and transport catering. Vending machines are found sited in canteens, factories, offices, industrial concerns, railway stations, garages (including motorways) schools, hospitals, leisure centres and hotels.

Advantages

The machines themselves may be used in conjunction with the conventional kitchen approach to catering. At the same time they relieve some of the pressure of work on the counter hands and cashier by taking some of the customers away from the counter and to the machines. This is especially true where only hot or cold beverages are required together with a limited range of snacks for a certain percentage of those being catered for.

This is one of the many advantages of automatic vending. Other advantages are:

- *24-hour service*: automatic vending machines provide a round the clock 24-hour service

- *Low cost*: automatic vending machines are cheaper to operate than conventional methods of service

- *Increase in productivity*: it is generally recognized that good staff facilities mean an increase in productivity. To this end, the correct siting of the automatic vending machines can give a boost to the employees' moral by providing for their needs 24 hours a day. This should ensure that staff do not have to move any great distance from their place of work or waste time in queuing.

- *Food cost control*: this is a great advantage because automatic vending allows for strict portion control

- *Economy of labour*: which results in a reduction in the wages bill

- *Natural tea-break*: with the advent of these machines the fixed tea-break has given way to the natural tea-break, with the result that less working time is lost due to workers slowing down in anticipation of the break and being back a few minutes late from their break. This also means that productivity is increased

- *Fresh beverages*: whilst a main meal may be served, if beverages are available by machine then they are fresh, piping hot and taken as and when required. This means the beverage does not then go cold whilst the main meal is being consumed

- *Variety*: automatic vending machines offer at the present time a wide variety of hot and cold snacks and beverages, all contained within a space considerably smaller than is necessary for the conventional forms of large equipment. This must be another important consideration and saving, as 'space' is so costly

- *Hot meals*: automatic vending machines are also being used in conjunction with the microwave oven. Here all snacks and meals are kept in refrigerated compartments. The customer chooses his/her meal, takes it from the machine, and then places it in the microwave oven to reheat

- *Reduced wastage*: as long as the customer demand has been correctly gauged, wastage may be reduced to the minimum. This is also provisional on the 'right machines' providing the 'right items' at the 'right price' having been sited in the 'right place'

- *Ease of maintenance*: a member of the permanent staff can be trained to do the replenishing daily

Disadvantages

There are disadvantages to automatic vending and these have to be considered in relation to the total operation before making a final decision on usage. These may be summarized as follows:

- *Speed of service*: for a beverage this is approximately 10 seconds; a cafeteria operator would be faster. It is also important to bear in mind that conventional systems are more suitable for large-scale operations
- *Quality*: although quality has improved in both the product and its packaging, customer resistance still exists
- *Human presence*: there may be very little, if any, 'human presence'. Manufacturers have researched this problem and attempted to overcome it with attractively designed and colourful machines
- *Electricity*: the machines are subject to power failure and power surges
- *Maintenance*: automatic vending machines require regular daily servicing and cleaning. Depending upon the style of operation, the machines may require servicing and cleaning twice a day
- *Vandalism*: most modern machines are robust, but loss of revenue and lack of service result in frustration to all concerned.
- *Breakdown*: can take vital hours to repair.

Types of machine

These include:

- *Merchandiser*: sells its product as seen visually by the customer, eg confectionery machines
- *Beverage vendor*: mixes the ingredients to produce the product
- *In-cup system*: ingredients are already in individual cups to which water is added
- *Micro-vend system*: provides a range of hot or cold foods from which the customer may make a selection and heat in an accompanying microwave oven.

Catering services

The catering services provided may come in the form of:

- *Hot beverages*: by use of powdered ingredients

- *Cold beverages*: by use of post-mix syrup and water (carbonated or non-carbonated)

- *Hot meals*: by internal heating or with the use of microwaves and time cards/tokens

- *Meals and snacks*: by means of refrigeration

The numbers and types of machines required will depend on their location, the type and numbers of people they are providing a service for, the cost factor and the variety of food and beverage items required.

The machines required may be installed either individually or in small groups, to supplement the conventional catering establishment or to cover a small sales demand that does not warrant the expense of employing the extra labour and plant. The opposite to this would be the installation of a complete vending service where demand is highly volatile, space is limited and the use of staffed operations would be uneconomical.

A further advancement in the development of microwave oven techniques in conjunction with vending is the micro-vend buffet. This is a complete refreshment unit for both hot and cold meals and hot and cold drinks. Here complete meals are prepared to standard recipes and retained in refrigerated conditions. With each meal the customer receives a small token which enables him/her to operate a microwave oven incorporated in the automatic vending unit. *General factors* which should be considered prior to purchasing and in relation to vending equipment may be summarized as follows:

- *Cup sales*: may be one to two drinks per person per day when charged but could double if offered free

- *Ingredient capacity*: related to required periods of restocking

- *Number of selectors (items) available*: this will often relate to the demand (anticipated number of customers)

- *Hygiene*: ease of cleaning

- *Extraction efficiency*: for heat/steam systems

- *Restocking*: ease of filling

- *Maintenance*: regular servicing contract

- *Physical dimension/acceptability*: whether the machine will fit into the environment and blend in with the decor

- *Siting*: as close as is feasible to those using the machine, that is, either on the work floor or in a food service area so as to maximize use

- *Weight (floor loading)*: ease of moving for cleaning and siting purposes

- *Availability*: of power and plumbing

- *Capital available*: whether the machine should be leased, purchased or taken on a contract basis

- *Training*: whether staff can be trained easily to replenish, clean and maintain machines
- *Policy*: there must be clear guidelines linked to failure of a machine and insurance cover

Cleaning of vending machines

'Automatic', vending machines are neither self-cleaning nor self-maintained and human help is needed here. Therefore, regular *service contract* maintenance is required and should be guaranteed if all is to run smoothly and without the problems of mechanical breakdown. The regularity of the service contract would be determined by the type of vending machine and the demand put upon it.

Regular daily cleaning and replenishment is nearly always required although demand may necessitate two or even three daily visits for cleaning and replenishment.

Staff should be trained in the techniques of cleaning and replenishing vending machines. The following check-list stresses the key factors to be considered:

1. Clean at times when demand is at its lowest to avoid unnecessary loss of sales
2. To avoid electrical accidents, use the minimum amount of water while cleaning or disconnect from the mains where possible.
3. Read the supplier's recommendations carefully and use only nominated cleaning agents
4. Ensure the temperature controls stated are functioning correctly
5. Always wipe down the complete outside of the vending machine to protect an image of good hygiene
6. Ensure all 'sales items' are clearly visible and operating instructions are easy to follow
7. When replenishing the machine, check the sell-by dates and put older items to the front
8. Ensure all packaging and labelling is correct
9. Check slow moving 'sales items' very carefully for the correct 'use by' dates and any deterioration in the commodity
10. Refill appropriate containers with the relevant powders for the products being sold
11. Ensure as appropriate that cups, plates and napkins are available in the machines

Note: at all times extreme care must be taken concerning the various aspects of hygiene and safety when foods and beverages are being served in this way.

2.9 Lighting and colour

Modern designs tend towards a versatile system of lighting by which a food and beverage service area may have bright lighting at lunchtime and a more diffused form of lighting in the evening. It is also an advantage to be able to change the colour of the lights for special functions, cabarets, etc. The caterer must find a colour and lighting scheme that will attract and please as many people as possible. Basically restaurants may select from two main kinds of interior illumination: incandescent and fluorescent lighting.

Incandescent lighting is warmer in colour but less efficient to operate than fluorescent bulbs of the same wattage. It can be easily directed to specific spots such as a particular table or pointing. However, its warmth appeal can cause a colour problem. It may make surroundings cheerful and inviting, but the yellowish hue of its bulbs, especially when dimmed, makes meats and lettuce appear muddy in colour. Warmer bulbs such as pink light make red meats look natural but salads unappetizing.

The main virtue of *fluorescent lighting* is its lower operating cost, but it is often criticized for giving a dull and lifeless illumination. Food may be made to look appealing by using blue-white light from fluorescent fixtures, but the blue-white glow may also detract from a warm romantic atmosphere.

A balance is usually needed for both warmth and good food appearance. Many experts recommend a lighting system made up of 70% cool or blue-white fluorescent bulbs and 30% incandescent. This will give mood and a pleasant and natural appearance for food.

The food service area needs more than proper décor lighting. Functional lighting is a must, giving proper illumination for cooks to prepare food, staff to serve it and guests to order and eat it. Functional lighting may amount to as much as 75% of a restaurant's total lighting system. In the dining room two basic areas require functional lighting: the table and the room as a whole. The aim therefore is to mix the right blend of décor and functional lighting at the lowest possible cost.

Table lighting is most flattering to guests when it shines down from the ceiling. Incandescent ceiling lights serve the purpose well here. Care must be taken, however, to ensure that the bulbs used do not give off too bright a light creating too much contrast between dark and light spots. Clean and well-polished silver, glassware and china on a dining table or a well-polished reflective tabletop in the lounge will bounce light gently upwards acting as a softener to overhead lights.

Functional lighting in the dining room must serve a number of purposes. Namely:

- Fixtures directing light on to ceilings and walls should indicate to guests the dimensions of the room, together with any special attractions, such as pictures and old oak beams. Low wattage incandescent bulbs are best suited for this purpose

- The lighting should project a subdued atmosphere with contrasts between bright and dark areas and tabletops capturing much of the light whilst ceilings and upper walls remain dark

- It may be necessary to feature special areas of a dining room, such as a buffet or self-service salad bar

The average food and beverage service area needs to have the correct mix of décor and functional lighting. It is only the fast food areas that may successfully eliminate décor or mood lighting altogether. It appears that brighter lights subconsciously tell the guests to eat more quickly and leave. It is the recommended way to illuminate for quick turnover and high volume throughput.

There is a definite association between colour and food which must be considered. The following colours are regarded as most acceptable: *pink, peach, pale yellow, clear green, beige, blue* and *turquoise*. These colours reflect the natural colours found in good and well-presented food-stuffs. The colour scheme should assist in reflecting the character of the restaurant. A well-designed colour scheme can easily be spoilt by a badly planned lighting system and therefore the two aspects should be considered together at the design stage.

The restaurant surroundings can contribute a great deal towards the price-quality relationship in the minds of potential guests. It is realized that what may be suitable for a fast food operation would be entirely unsuitable for a restaurant operation catering for an executive market. Bright illumination may be found in bars with light colours on the walls, but food service areas are better with dimmer illumination and warmly coloured walls, giving a more relaxed and welcoming atmosphere. Colour should also contribute to a feeling of cleanliness.

Just as colour and light play an important role, so will table accessories need careful choice: slip cloths, serviettes and place mats will help to make the environment more attractive.

2.10 Furniture

Furniture must be chosen according to the needs of the establishment. The type of operation being run determines one's specific needs as far as the dining arrangements are concerned. What these *dining arrangements* may be is indicated in Figure 2.4.

Very often by using different materials, designs and finishes and by careful arrangement one can change the atmosphere and appearance of the food service area to suit different occasions.

There are various types of wood and wood grain finishes, each suitable to blend with a particular décor. Wood is strong and rigid and resists wear and stains. It is found as the principal material in chairs and tables in use in all food and beverage service areas with the exception of canteens, some staff dining-rooms and cafeterias.

Although wood predominates, more metals, mainly aluminium and aluminium-plated steel or brass, are gradually being introduced into dining-room furniture. Aluminium is lightweight, hardwearing, has a variety of finishes, is easily cleaned and the costs are reasonable. Nowadays one often finds a wooden-topped table with a metal base, or a chair with a lightweight metal frame and a plastic finish for the seat and back.

Formica or plastic-coated table tops may be found in many cafeterias or staff dining-rooms. These are easily cleaned, hardwearing and eliminate the use of linen. The table tops come in a variety of colours and designs suitable for all situations. If desired, place-mats may take the place of linen.

Figure 2.4 Dining arrangements (Based on a chart from Croner's Catering)

TYPE	DESCRIPTION OF FURNITURE
LOOSE RANDOM	Freestanding furniture positioned in no discernable pattern within a given area
LOOSE MODULE	Freestanding furniture positioned within a given area to a pre-determined pattern with or without the use of dividers to create smaller areas within a whole
BOOTH	Fixed seating, usually high backed, used to create secluded seating
HIGH DENSITY	Furniture, with minimum dimensions and usually fixed, is positioned within a given area to create maximum seating capacity
MODULE	Seating incorporates tables and chairs constructed as one and may be fixed
IN SITU	Customers served in areas not designed for service, eg aircraft and hospital beds
BAR AND LOUNGE AREAS	Customers served in areas not conventionally designed

Plastics and fibreglass are now being used extensively to produce dining-room chairs. These materials are easily moulded into a single-piece seat and back to fit the body contours, the legs usually being made of metal. The advantages are that these are durable, easily cleaned, lightweight, may be stacked, are available in a large range of colours and designs and are relatively inexpensive. They are more frequently found in bars, lounges and staff dining-rooms at the moment rather than in the first-class hotel or restaurant.

Chairs

Chairs come in an enormous range of designs, materials and colours to suit all situations and occasions. Because of the wide range of styles, the chairs vary in height and width, but as a guide, a chair seat is 46 cm (18 in) from the ground, the height from the ground to the top of the back is 1 m (39 in) and the depth from the front edge of the seat to the back of the chair is 46 cm (18 in).

Points to note in purchasing are as in Section 2.1, although some of the first considerations here should be size, height, shape and even the variety of seating required – banquette, armchairs, straight-backed padded chairs, giving the guest a choice. A leather or wool fabric is much easier to sit on than PVC which tends to become uncomfortable around the back and seat.

Certain principles should be borne in mind when planning food and beverage service areas to maximize the seating area. An example in relation to a cafeteria style operation follows:

Care should be taken when planning a cafeteria that the customers waiting for a meal from the various service points do not interrupt the flow of customers around the tables, or those going out through the main entrance. If this is not carefully watched then the flow and speed of service will be slowed quite considerably.

The seating arrangements will depend on:

- The size and shape of the food service area
- The design of tables and chairs used
- The allowance made for gangways and clearing trolleys
- The type of establishment

As a guide, an allowance of $2\frac{1}{2}$–4 sq m (10–12 sq ft) per person is sufficient; this takes into account seating, table space, gangways and access to counters. The type of furniture used here must be pleasant to look at, hardwearing, durable and easy to clean. The chairs used are usually of the stacking variety as this takes up less storage space when the food service area is being used for other types of functions and for cleaning. The tables themselves should be a variety of shapes, thus breaking the monotony of the layout of the room. The tops are usually of formica which facilitates cleaning. The edges and corners of the tables must be reinforced to avoid chipping and cracks when knocked by trolley, trays, etc. The formica top may come in a variety of colours and should tone in with the décor.

Tables

Tables come in three main shapes: round, square and rectangular. An establishment may have a mixture of shapes to give variety, or tables of all one shape according to the shape of the room and the style of service being offered. These tables will seat two or four people and two tables may be pushed together to seat larger parties, or extensions may be provided in order to cope with special parties, luncheons, dinners, weddings, etc. By using these extensions correctly a variety of shapes may be obtained allowing full use of the room, and getting the maximum number of covers in the minimum space. In many instances the table top may be found to have a plasticized foam back or green baize covering which is heat resistant and non-slip so the tablecloth will not slide about as it would on a polished wooden top table. This type of covering also deadens the sound of china and cutlery being laid. As a guide tables may be said to be approximately the following sizes:

Square
76 cm (2 ft 6 in) square to seat two people
1 m (3 ft) square to seat four people

Round

1 m (3 ft) in diameter to seat four people
1.52 m (5 ft) in diameter to seat eight people

Rectangular

137 cm × 76 cm (4 ft 6 in × 2 ft 6 in) to seat four people, extensions being added for larger parties

Sideboards

The style and design of a sideboard varies from establishment to establishment. It is dependent upon:

- The style of service and the menu offered
- The number of waiters or waitresses working from one sideboard
- The number of tables to be served from one sideboard
- The amount of equipment it is expected to hold

It is essential that the sideboard is of minimum size and portable so that it may be moved easily if necessary. If the sideboard is too large for its purpose it is then taking up space which could be used to seat more customers. Some establishments use smaller fixed sideboards and use 'tray jacks' (movable folding tray stands) when serving and clearing. The top of a sideboard should be of a heat resistant material which can be easily washed down. After service the sideboard is either completely emptied out or restocked for the next service. In some establishments the waiters are responsible for their own equipment on their station. After service they restock their sideboard and it is then locked. Where this

Figure 2.5 Examples of sideboards

system is carried out the sideboard also carries its own stock of linen, ie everything necessary to equip a particular waiter's station or set of tables. The material used in the make-up of the sideboard should blend with the rest of the décor.

The actual lay-up of a sideboard depends firstly on its construction – the number of shelves and drawers for tableware, etc – and, secondly, on the type of menu and service offered. Therefore the lay-up in every establishment could vary slightly, each being suited to its own needs and style of service and presentation. It is suggested, however, that in each particular establishment the sideboards be laid up in the same fashion. If this is done the staff get used to looking for a certain item in a certain place and this facilitates speedy service which is essential. The items to be found in a sideboard are given on page 171. These would be required if the service was a full silver service from a large table d'hôte menu running in conjunction with a limited à la carte menu. The items required would be adjusted according to the style of service.

2.11 Linen

This is perhaps one of the more costly items within overheads, and therefore its control is of the utmost importance. The generally recognized routine in the majority of establishments is an exchange of 'one for one'. In other words, one clean item is issued for each dirty item handed in.

The original stock of clean linen is issued upon receipt of a requisition form written in duplicate and signed by a responsible person from the food service department. The top copy of the requisition form goes to the housekeeping department or linen room and the duplicate copy remains in the requisition book held in the food and beverage service area. A surplus linen stock is usually held in the food service area in case of emergency.

At the end of each service the dirty linen should be noted and sent to the housekeeping department to be exchanged for clean. Because of the high cost of laundering such linen, where a tablecloth is perhaps only a little grubby, a slip cloth would be placed over it for the succeeding service. This is not as expensive to have re-laundered as would be a tablecloth. Dirty serviettes when being exchanged for clean ones should be tied in bundles of ten.

It is as well to mention here the wide range of disposable serviettes, place-mats and tablecloths available in varying colours and qualities. There are also now reversible tablecloths with a thin polythene sheet running through the centre, preventing any spillages from penetrating from one side to the other. Although the expense may seem high, there are many advantages and comparable laundry charges may well be higher. For information on disposables, refer to Section 2.15.

Linen should be stored on paper-lined shelves, the correct sizes together, and with the inverted fold facing outward, which facilitates counting and control. If the linen is not stored in a cupboard it should be covered to avoid dust settling on it. There are many qualities of linen in present day use, from the finest Irish linen and cotton to the synthetic materials such as nylon and viscose. The type of linen used would depend on the class of establishment, type of clientele and cost involved, and the style of menu and service to be offered. The main items of linen normally to be found are:

Tablecloths
137 cm × 137 cm (54 in × 54 in) to fit a table 76 cm (2 ft 6 in) square or a round table 1 m (3 ft) in diameter
183 cm × 183 cm (72 in × 72 in) to fit a table 1 m (3 ft) square
183 cm × 244 cm (72 in × 96 in) to fit rectangular shaped tables
183 cm × 137 cm (72 in × 54 in) to fit rectangular shaped tables

Slipcloths
1 m × 1 m (3 ft × 3 ft) used to cover a 'grubby' tablecloth

Serviette
46–50 cm (18–20 in) square if linen
36–42 cm (14–17 in) square if paper

Buffet cloths
2 m × 4 m (6 ft × 12 ft) – this is the minimum size; where there are longer tables there may be longer cloths

Waiter's cloths or service cloths
These are used by every waiter as protection against heat and to keep uniforms clean

Tea and glass cloths
The best are made of linen or cotton

Correct usage of linen

Linen should be used only for its intended purpose in the restaurant and not for cleaning purposes as this often results in permanent soiling which will render the item unusable in the future.

2.12 China

The china must blend in with the rest of the items on the table and also with the general décor of the establishment.

More and more people are eating out and they like to see china which is cheerful and colourful in design and pattern similar to that used in their own homes. An establishment generally uses one design and pattern of china, but when an establishment has a number of different food service areas it is easier from the control point of view to have a different design in each service area. This may not at first seem practical, but nowadays forward thinking manufacturers are producing a range of perhaps ten patterns, and will guarantee a supply for a period of ten years to replace breakages, etc.

Very few caterers can afford to buy high-quality china for normal day-to-day use because of the high initial capital outlay and replacement costs. The caterer therefore has to turn to what is termed 'earthenware'. This has been vastly improved over the last few years both in appearance and durability. Badged china at the present time is not so popular and patterned china is the more acceptable.

When purchasing china the points previously mentioned should be borne in mind. Other factors to consider here are:

- Every item of earthenware should have a complete cover of glaze to ensure a reasonable length of life
- China should have a rolled edge which will give added reinforcement at the edge. One word of caution here is that hygiene is most important – chipped china can harbour germs
- The pattern should be under rather than on top of the glaze. However this demands additional glaze and firing. Patterns on top of the glaze will wear and discolour very quickly. Therefore china with the pattern under the glaze is more expensive but its life will be longer
- China must be dishwasher-proof

Some manufacturers stamp the date, month and year on the base of the item. From this, the life of the china can be determined with some accuracy.

Very often earthenware produced for catering purposes is given a trade name by the manufacturer to indicate its strength. Some examples of these are:

- Vitreous
- Vitrock
- Vitrex
- Vitresso
- Ironstone
- Vitrified

Of these, *vitrified* ware is recognized to be the strongest, but this does not always mean that every caterer buys vitrified hotelware as other factors apart from strength and economy have to be taken into account.

Two newer forms of crockery are known as 'Steelite' and 'Micratex'. *Steelite* is advertised as vitreous china and has a high chip resistance. Other features are said to be its heat-retaining quality, its low absorption level which minimizes the risk of bacterial contamination, and the ability of the glaze to withstand high temperatures and pressures. It comes in a variety of shapes and patterns to suit most needs. *Micratex* is a form of crockery where the body strength of the china has been reinforced by a technique employed in grinding the clay. This is to make the article stronger without adding to the weight.

Catering china

There are various classifications of catering china. Very briefly these are as follows:

Bone china

This is very fine, hard china that is very expensive. The decorations are to be found under the glaze only. It can be made to thicker specifications, if requested, for hotel use. The price of bone china puts it out of reach of the majority of everyday caterers, and only a few of the top-class hotels and restaurants would use it. Obviously the price of a meal in these establishments is high in order to cover this aspect of the overheads. The range of design, pattern and colour is very wide, and there is something to suit all occasions and situations.

Hotel earthenware

This is produced in the United Kingdom in vast quantities and is the cheapest and least durable hotelware. Its main uses are in institutional catering where price rather than durability is the main consideration.

It is the normal earthenware which can be made stronger than that designed for domestic use. It is not, however, guaranteed to the British Standard 4034 as is vitrified hotelware. The specification for BS 4034 demands that vitrified tableware be non-porous which is also a guarantee of its strength. This form of tableware is cheaper than bone china. There is a standard range of designs and patterns in varying colours. As it is the only type of hotel earthenware to come up to BS 4034 specifications, it is dearer than the other classifications of hotel earthenware, but the price/durability ratio is far better than that of normal hotel earthenware.

Vitrified earthenware is particularly economical where it is in continuous use 24 hours a day, has heavy handling with a high turnover, and where hygiene is particularly important, eg in motorway cafeterias and hospitals.

A domestic weight earthenware is also available, but this is lighter and thinner than the hotel earthenware or vitrified hotelware previously mentioned. Because of its short life, lack of strength and possible high breakage rate it is not regarded as suitable for the average caterer, except perhaps for the seaside boarding house or similar operation.

Stoneware

This is a natural ceramic material traditionally made in the United Kingdom and fired at a very high temperature, about 120°C (284°F). It is shaped by traditional hand-crafting techniques so there is a wide variety of shapes and finishes available, from matt to a high-gloss glaze. It is non-porous and extremely durable with high thermal and shock resistance. The price is slightly higher than earthenware due to a long-life guarantee.

Porcelain

This is of a completely different composition with a semi-translucent body, normally blue/grey, and has a high resistance to chipping.

Storage

China should be stored on shelves in piles of approximately two dozen. Any higher may result in their toppling down. They should be stored at a convenient height for placing on and removing from the shelves without any fear of accidents occurring. If possible china should be kept covered to prevent dust and germs settling on it.

Sizes

There is a wide range of items available (see Figure 2.6), and their exact sizes vary according to the manufacturer and the design produced. As a guide, the sizes are as follows:

- Sideplate: 15 cm (6 in) diameter
- Sweet plate: 18 cm (7 in) diameter
- Fish plate: 20 cm (8 in) diameter
- Soup plate: 20 cm (8 in) diameter
- Joint plate: 25 cm (10 in) diameter
- Cereal/sweet plate: 13 cm (5 in) diameter
- Breakfast cup and saucer: 23–28 cl (8–10 fl oz)
- Tea cup and saucer: 18.93 cl ($6\frac{2}{3}$ fl oz)
- Coffee cup and saucer (demi-tasse):   9.47 cl ($3\frac{1}{2}$ fl oz)
- Teapot: 28.4 cl ($\frac{1}{2}$ pt)

  56.8 cl (1 pt)

  85.2 cl ($1\frac{1}{2}$ pt)

  113.6 cl (2 pt)

Other items of china required include:

- Salad crescent
- Hot water jugs
- Milk jugs
- Cream jugs
- Coffee pots
- Hot milk jugs
- Consommé cup and saucer

- Sugar basin
- Butter dishes
- Ashtrays
- Egg cups
- Soup bowl/cup
- Platter (oval plate)

Figure 2.6 Selection of china (Royal Doulton (UK) Ltd)

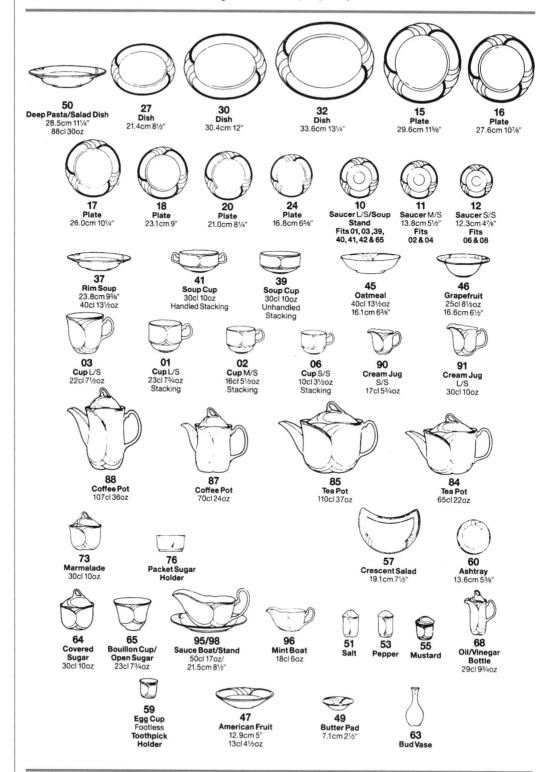

50
Deep Pasta/Salad Dish
28.5cm 11¼"
88cl 30oz

27
Dish
21.4cm 8½"

30
Dish
30.4cm 12"

32
Dish
33.6cm 13¼"

15
Plate
29.6cm 11⅝"

16
Plate
27.6cm 10⅞"

17
Plate
26.0cm 10¼"

18
Plate
23.1cm 9"

20
Plate
21.0cm 8¼"

24
Plate
16.8cm 6⅝"

10
Saucer L/S/Soup
Stand
Fits 01, 03, 39,
40, 41, 42 & 65

11
Saucer M/S
13.8cm 5½"
Fits
02 & 04

12
Saucer S/S
12.3cm 4⅞"
Fits
06 & 08

37
Rim Soup
23.8cm 9⅜"
40cl 13½oz

41
Soup Cup
30cl 10oz
Handled Stacking

39
Soup Cup
30cl 10oz
Unhandled
Stacking

45
Oatmeal
40cl 13½oz
16.1cm 6⅜"

46
Grapefruit
25cl 8½oz
16.6cm 6½"

03
Cup L/S
22cl 7½oz

01
Cup L/S
23cl 7¾oz
Stacking

02
Cup M/S
16cl 5½oz
Stacking

06
Cup S/S
10cl 3½oz
Stacking

90
Cream Jug
S/S
17cl 5¾oz

91
Cream Jug
L/S
30cl 10oz

88
Coffee Pot
107cl 36oz

87
Coffee Pot
70cl 24oz

85
Tea Pot
110cl 37oz

84
Tea Pot
65cl 22oz

73
Marmalade
30cl 10oz

76
Packet Sugar
Holder

57
Crescent Salad
19.1cm 7½"

60
Ashtray
13.6cm 5⅜"

64
Covered
Sugar
30cl 10oz

65
Bouillon Cup/
Open Sugar
23cl 7¾oz

95/98
Sauce Boat/Stand
50cl 17oz/
21.5cm 8½"

96
Mint Boat
18cl 6oz

51
Salt

53
Pepper

55
Mustard

68
Oil/Vinegar
Bottle
29cl 9¾oz

59
Egg Cup
Footless
Toothpick
Holder

47
American Fruit
12.9cm 5"
13cl 4½oz

49
Butter Pad
7.1cm 2½"

63
Bud Vase

2.13 Tableware (flatware, cutlery and hollow-ware)

Types of tableware

Tableware is a term recognized as embracing all items of flatware, cutlery and hollow-ware. It may be classified as follows:

- *Flatware* in the catering trade denotes all forms of spoon and fork

- *Cutlery* refers to knives and other cutting implements

- *Hollow-ware* consists of any item made from silver, apart from flatware and cutlery, eg teapots, milk jugs, sugar basins, oval flats

Manufacturers are producing varied patterns of flatware, hollow-ware and cutlery in a range of prices to suit all demands. One new pattern of flatware and cutlery is scaled down to three-quarters the normal size specifically for tray service. This demonstrates the manufacturer's desire to keep in touch with the caterer's needs.

The majority of food service areas use either plated silverware or stainless steel. Once again, the points mentioned previously concerning purchasing should be borne in mind. In addition, when purchasing flatware and cutlery it is important to consider:

- The type of menu and service offered

- The maximum and average seating capacity

- The rush hour turn-over

- The washing-up facilities and its turn-over

Silver

Manufacturers will often quote 20, 25 or 30 year plate. This denotes the length of life a manufacturer may claim for their plate subject to fair or normal usage. The length of life of silver also depends upon the weight of silver deposited. The term A1 often heard in connection with silver plate has no significance whatsoever. There is no standard laid down and the quality of A1 plate differs with every manufacturer. There are three standard grades of silver plate – full standard plate, triple plate and quadruple plate.

Caterers in doubt about the quality of silver plated tableware and stainless steel will be able to refer to British Standard 5577. The aim of the standard was to end the use of such terms as *A1* and *20 year plate*, and to ensure that details of component materials were provided. This standard was introduced in 1978.

In silverplated tableware two grades have been specified:

- *Standard* for general use

- *Restaurant* thicker grade for restaurant use and marked with an 'R'

The minimum thickness of silver plating quoted should give a life of at least 20 years, depending on usage.

The hallmark on silver tells two things. The two symbols represent the standard of silver used and the Assay office responsible. The two letters are the maker's mark and the date letter.

Plain cutlery and flatware is more popular than patterned for the simple reason that it is cheaper and easier to keep clean. The best investment is knives with handles of hard soldered silver plate, nickel or good stainless steel. (Handles are an important factor in cutlery.) Plastic materials, however, are much cheaper and usually satisfactory. The 'Sanewood' handled stainless steel is very good. This is a material which is impervious to boiling water and will not crack or chip.

Stainless steel

Stainless steel flatware and cutlery is available in a variety of grades. The higher priced designs usually have incorporated in them alloys of chromium (which makes the metal stainless) and nickel (which gives a fine grain and lustre). Good British flatware and cutlery is made of 18/8 stainless steel. This is 18% chromium and 8% nickel.

Stainless steel is finished by different degrees of polishing:

- High polish finish
- Dull polish-finish
- A light grey matt, non reflective finish

It is worth noting that stainless steel resists scratching far more than other metals and may therefore be said to be more hygienic. At the same time it neither tarnishes nor stains.

Storage

Careful storage of cutlery and flatware is most important. Ideally, there should be boxes or drawers for each specific item, each box or drawer being lined with baize to prevent the items concerned sliding about and becoming scratched and marked. Other items of hollow-ware should be stored on shelves which are labelled showing where the different items go. They must be stored at a convenient height for placing on and removing from the shelves.

Theoretically all flatware, cutlery and hollow-ware should be stored in a room or cupboard which can be locked since they constitute a large part of the capital of the restaurant. Cutlery and flatware may be stored in cutlery trolleys or trays of which there are a number now on the market to suit all purposes.

There is an almost unlimited range of flatware, cutlery and hollow-ware in use in the catering industry today. These items are those necessary to give efficient service of any form of meal at any time of the day. Everyone is familiar with the knife, fork, spoon, flats, vegetable dishes and lids, entrée dishes and lids, soup tureens, teapot, hot water jugs, sugar basins and so on that we see in every day use. Over and above these, however, there are a number of specialist items of equipment provided for use with specific dishes. Some of these more common items of specialist equipment are listed in Figure 2.8, together with a brief note of the dishes which they may be used for.

Figure 2.7 Examples of cutlery and flatware
Left to right: *1 soup spoon 2 fish knife 3 fish fork 4 joint knife 5 joint fork 6 side knife 7 sweet spoon 8 sweet fork 9 tablespoon 10 teaspoon 11 coffee spoon*

Figure 2.8 Items of specialist equipment and their use

EQUIPMENT	USE
1 Asparagus holder	1 Used to hold asparagus spears when eating
2 Pastry slice	2 Sweet trolley – serving portions of gâteau
3 Oyster fork	3 Shellfish cocktail/oysters
4 Pastry fork	4 Afternoon tea
5 Corn-on-the-cob holders	5 One to pierce each end of the cob
6 Lobster pick	6 To extract the flesh from the claw
7 Butter knife	7 To serve butter portion
8 Sauce ladle	8 Service from sauce boat
9 Fruit knife and fork	9 Dessert – cover
10 Nutcrackers	10 Dessert – fruit basket
11 Grape scissors	11 To cut and hold a portion of grapes
12 Grapefruit spoon	12 Grapefruit halves
13 Ice-cream spoon	13 For all ice-cream dishes served in coupes
14 Sundae spoon	14 Ice-cream sweet in a tall glass
15 Snail tongs	15 Used to hold the snail shell
16 Snail dish	16 Dish is round with two ears, having six indentations to hold a portion (6) of snails
17 Snail fork	17 Used to extract the snail from its shell
18 Cheese knife	18 Cheese board
19 Stilton scoop	19 Service of Stilton cheese
20 Gourmet spoon	20 Sauce spoon for cover
21 Preserve spoon	21 Used with jam dish
22 Sugar tongs	22 Required for cube sugar

Figure 2.9 Specialised equipment as listed in Figure 2.8

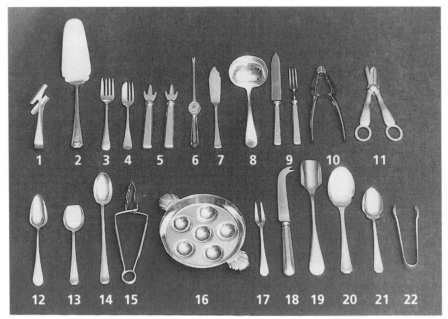

2.14 Glassware

Types and sizes of glassware

Glass also contributes to the appearance of the table and the overall attraction of the room. There are many standard patterns available to the caterer. Most manufacturers now supply hotel glassware in standard sizes for convenience of ordering, availability and quick delivery.

Except in certain speciality restaurants or high-class establishments, where either coloured glassware or cut glassware may be used, hotel glassware is usually plain. The one

Figure 2.10 Range of glasses that may be found in the dispense bar
Left to right: 'dock' glass port/sherry, cocktail, elgin sherry, Highball, slim Jim, cocktail, 12 oz short stem 'Worthington', lager (Pilsner), 1 pt draught beer 'straight', 1 pt dimple beer

Figure 2.11 Types of glasses
Left to right: *copita sherry, club goblet, Paris goblet, white wine goblet, German/Alsace wine glass, red wine goblet, tulip/flute sparkling/rosé wine glass, brandy balloon, elgin liqueur*

Figure 2.12 Sizes of glassware

GLASS	SIZE
WINE GOBLETS	14.20, 18.93, 22.72 cl (5, 6$\frac{2}{3}$, 8 fl oz)
GERMAN/ALSACE	18, 23 cl (6, 8 fl oz)
FLUTE	18, 23 cl (6, 8 fl oz)
SAUCER CHAMPAGNE	18, 23 cl (6, 8 fl oz)
COCKTAIL GLASSES	4, 7 cl (2, 3 fl oz)
SHERRY, PORT	5 cl (1.75 fl oz)
HIGHBALL	23, 28 cl (9, 10 fl oz)
WORTHINGTON	28, 34 cl (10, 12 fl oz)
LAGER GLASS	28, 34 cl (10, 12 fl oz)
BRANDY BALLOON	23, 28 cl (8, 10 fl oz)
LIQUEUR GLASS	2.5 cl (0.88 fl oz)
TUMBLER	28.40 cl ($\frac{1}{2}$ pint)
BEER	25, 50 cl ($\frac{1}{2}$, 1 pint)

exception sometimes found is Hock glasses with brown stems – the same colour as the Hock bottle – and Moselle glasses with green stems – the same colour as the Moselle bottle. However, many establishments now use a clear stemmed glass for both Hock and Moselle wines. In this way there is a saving in the quantity to be purchased since the same glass may be used for the service of both wines, and therefore a saving in both storage space and cost. The tulip-shaped glass for champagne is more usual now than the traditional 'saucer' shape, because it retains longer the sparkle and effervesence.

A good wine glass should be plain and clear so that the colour and brilliance of a wine can be clearly seen; it should have a stem for holding the wine glass so that the heat of one's hand does not affect the wine on tasting; there should be a slight incurving lip to help hold the aroma and it should be large enough to hold the particular wine being tasted.

Storage

Glasses are normally stored in a glass pantry and should be placed in single rows on paper-lined shelves, upside down to prevent dust settling in them. An alternative to this is to have plastic coated wire racks made specifically for the purpose of stacking and storing the glasses. Such racks are also a convenient method of transporting glassware from one point to another which cuts down on breakages.

Tumblers should not be stacked inside one another as this may result in heavy breakages and cause accidents to staff.

2.15 Disposables

The growth in the use of 'disposables' over the past 20 years has been considerable. Over a third of those sold are expected to be multi-ply rather than single-ply. This seems to suggest that it is the better quality grades that are set to expand in this 'throw away' market. Part of the expansion is due to the emergence of public-house catering as a competitor to the fast-food and take-away establishments.

Customer critique is very evident and the various materials and methods employed by manufacturers to produce them show in turn differences in 'feel' and 'performance'. In other words, a material which drapes well may not fold well and it is therefore better as a tablecover than as a napkin. Degrees of softness vary and, in the case of napkins, the way they feel against the mouth is important and can be critical to their acceptance.

It is the trend in many establishments today to use disposables to help cut costs. At the same time, the disposables must be both attractive, presentable and acceptable to the client and also help to attract customers. The choice of which disposables to use may be determined by:

1 *Necessity* because of situations such as:

- Outdoor catering
- Automatic vending
- Fast food

2 *Cost* considerations such as:

- Cost of laundry
- Savings on wash-up

The growth in the market of disposables, or 'throw-aways' as they are sometimes called, is due to a number of factors, namely:

- The need to reduce costs
- The difficulty of obtaining labour for washing up
- The cutting of the high cost of laundering
- Improved standards of hygiene

- Breakage cost minimization
- Reduction in storage space required
- Changes in cooking and storage technology, eg cook/chill and cook/freeze
- The needs of 'transport' caterers on trains, boats and planes
- Fast-food developments – related to increased customer acceptability

Types of disposables

The main varieties of disposables available are used broadly speaking in the following areas:

- *Storage* and *cooking* purposes
- *Service* of food and beverages, eg plates, knives, forks, cups
- *Décor* – napkins, tablecloths, slip cloths, banquet roll, place mats
- *Hygiene* – wipes
- *Clothing*, eg aprons, chef hats, gloves
- *Packaging* – for marketing and presentation purposes

The types of disposables that may be used to replace the normal restaurant linen would be serviettes, place mats, traycloths, tablecloths, coasters, etc. When considering hygiene, it is in the use of the conventional glass cloth for drying up that cross infection is more likely to occur. This risk is eliminated when disposables are used. The caterer must always bear in mind that his/hers is an industry where eye-appeal and the creation of the right atmosphere are particularly important, and therefore disposables must be made to fit into all levels of catering establishments.

Most forms of disposables can today be of various colours, patterned or have the house-style motto or crest reproduced on them. A disposable serviette is not so inclined to slip off the knee as a linen serviette. There again, with the vast range of colours available one can ring the changes in a food and beverage service area with different colours for each meal, provided that they blend in with the surroundings. Throw-away packs of knives, forks and spoons are more convenient and hygienic where the turnover of custom is very high over very short periods of time. This might apply in industrial canteens and transport catering. It will eliminate delays at service points where the speed of washing-up is inadequate.

In hospitals, where any form of cross infection should be avoided, a great variety of disposables are used. This gives a substantial saving in staff times and costs.

A considerable advance in the range of disposables available has been the introduction of disposables whose approximation to china tableware is very close. For instance they may have a high quality, overall finish and a smooth, hard, white surface. The plates themselves are strong and rigid with no tendency to bend or buckle, and a plasticising ingredient ensures that they are grease- and moisture-proof, even against hot fat and gravy. Oval luncheon plates, snack trays and compartments plates are all available to the caterer.

Advantages of disposables

- *Equipment and labour*: disposables reduce the need for washing-up equipment, staff and materials
- *Hygiene*: usage improves the standard of hygiene in an establishment
- *Time*: disposables may speed up service, eg for fast food
- *Properties*: they have good heat retention and insulation properties
- *Marketing*: disposables can be used as a promotional aid
- *Capital*: usage reduces the amount of capital investment
- *Carriage*: they are easily transported
- *Cost*: disposables are cheaper than hiring conventional equipment

Disadvantages of disposables

- *Acceptability*: customer acceptability may be poor
- *Cost*: disposables can be more expensive than some conventional equipment
- *Storage*: back-up quantities are required
- *Supply*: there is heavy reliance on supply and delivery time

CHAPTER 3

THE MENU, MENU KNOWLEDGE AND ACCOMPANIMENTS

3.1   **The menu**   64

3.2   **Food, accompaniments and covers**   72

63

3.1 The Menu

Origin of the menu

The menu is primarily a selling aid. Originally the bill of fare (English) or menu (French) was not presented at the table. Banquets generally consisted of two courses each made up of a variety of dishes, anything from 10 to 40 in number. The first set of dishes were placed on the table before the diners entered – hence the work entrée – and, when consumed, these dishes were removed or relieved by another set of dishes – hence the words reléves or removes.

It is said that in the year 1541 Duke Henry of Brunswick was seen to refer to a long slip of paper. On being asked what he was looking at he said it was a form of programme of the dishes, and by reference to it he could see what was coming and reserve his appetite accordingly. Thus we may presume that the provision of a menu developed from some such event.

The bill of fare was originally very large and was placed at the end of the table for everyone to read. As time progressed the menu became smaller in size and a number of copies made which allowed individuals to read their own copy.

Classic Menu Sequence

Over the years the sequence of the menu has taken on a classical format or order of dishes. This format is used to lay out menus as well as to indicate the order of the various courses. Although the actual number of courses on a menu, and dishes within each course, will depend on the size and class of the establishment, most follow the classic sequence. This sequence is as follows:

1 Hors-d'oeuvres

Traditionally this consisted of a variety of salads but now includes items such as pâtés, mousses, fruit, charcuterie and smoked fish.

2 Soups (*potages*)

This includes all soups, both hot and cold.

3 Egg dishes (*oeufs*)

There are a wide variety of egg dishes beyond the usual omelettes but these have not retained their popularity on modern menus.

4 Pasta and rice (*farineux*)

This includes all pasta and rice dishes. Can be referred to as farinaceous dishes.

5 Fish (*poisson*)

This course consists of fish dishes, both hot and cold. Fish dishes such as smoked salmon or prawn salad are mainly considered to be hors-d'oeuvres.

6 Entrée

Entrées are generally small, well garnished dishes which come from the kitchen ready for service. They are usually accompanied by a rich sauce or gravy. Potatoes and vegetables are not usually served with this course if it is to be followed by a main course. If this is the main meat course then it is usual for potatoes and vegetable to also be offered. Examples of this type of dish are tournedos, noisettes, sweetbreads, garnished cutlets or filled vol-au-vent cases.

7 Sorbet

Traditionally sorbets (sometimes called granites) were served to give a pause within a meal, allowing the palate to be refreshed. They are lightly frozen water ices, often based on un-sweetened fruit juice and may be served with a spirit, liqueur or even Champagne poured over. Russian cigarettes also used to be offered at this stage of a meal.

8 Relevé

This refers to main roasts or other larger joints of meat.

9 Roast (*rôti*)

This traditionally refers to game or poultry dishes.

10 Vegetables (*légumes*)

Certain vegetables (for example asparagus and artichokes) may be served as a separate course instead of with the main course. These types of dishes are now more commonly served as starters.

11 Salad (*salade*)

This refers to a small plate of salad that is taken after main course (or courses), and is quite often literally a green salad and dressing.

12 Cold Buffet (*buffet froid*)

This includes a variety of cold meats and fish items together with a range of salads.

13 Sweets (*entremets*)

Includes both hot and cold puddings.

14 Cheese (*fromage*)

15 Savoury (*savoureaux*)

Sometimes simple savouries, such as Welsh rarebit and other items on toast or in pastry or savoury soufflés, are served at this stage.

16 Fruit (*dessert*)

Fresh fruit, nuts and perhaps candied fruits.

17 Beverages

Traditionally this referred to coffee but nowadays a much wider range of beverages is generally available including tea, tisanes, chocolate and proprietary beverages. Although listed here to show the sequence, beverages are not counted as a course as such and therefore should not be included when the number of courses of a meal is stated. Thus if a meal is quoted as having four courses, this must mean that there are four food courses and that the beverages are in addition to these.

The sequence outlined above is used throughout the Hotel and Catering Industry when menus are compiled. However a number of courses are often grouped together. At its most simple this might comprise:

- starters – courses 1 to 4
- main courses – courses 5,6 and 8 to 12
- afters – courses 13 to 16
- beverages

This sequence is also used as a guide for the compilation and the determination of the order of the courses of function and special party menus.

Although this sequence shows sweets before the cheese course it is now more common in Britain for cheese to be offered before the sweet. This allows for the drier main course wines to be consumed with the cheese course, thereby preventing its taste from being destroyed by the change to a sweet dish. Furthermore, changing from savoury to sweet and then back to savoury does not follow a logical pattern of taste sensation and this may affect the enjoyment of the meal. Despite this either sequence may be found.

Note: The classic menu sequence outlined above is derived from traditional European (mainly French) cuisine influences. The menu structure changes in the various continents as do some of the terms, for instance in the USA a main course is commonly called an entrée and sweets commonly called dessert. The term dessert is also becoming more commonly used to denote sweets generally.

Classes of menu

Menus may be divided into two classes, traditionally called à la carte (from the card) and table d'hôte (table of the host). The key difference between these two is that the à la carte menu has dishes separately priced, whereas the table d'hôte menu has an inclusive price either for the whole meal or for a specified number of courses, for example any two or any four courses. There are however usually choices within each course.

Other menu terms used are 'carte du jour' (literally card of the day) – which is usually a fixed meal with one or more courses for a set price. A 'prix fixe' (fixed price) menu is similar. Sometimes the price of the meal also includes wine or other drinks.

The table d'hôte menu

The key characteristics are:

- the menu has a fixed number of courses
- there is a limited choice within each course
- the selling price is fixed
- the food is usually available at a set time

The à la carte menu

The key features are:

- the choice is generally more extensive
- each dish is priced separately
- there may be longer waiting times as some dishes are cooked or finished to order

Figure 3.1 Example of a table d'hôte menu, Courtesy of the Swallow Hotel Birmingham

D I N N E R

Tuesday 29th July, 1997

Cream of mushroom soup

Warm poached egg on mushroom glazed with hollandaise sauce

Pressed fish terrine with a saffron and garlic mayonnaise

Scottish smoked salmon carved at the table
(£7.50 supplement per person)

Char - grilled salmon on a potato cake

Roasted brill with girolle mushrooms

Pan - fried lemon sole with a avocado and tomato salsa

Loin of lamb with smoked bacon and aubergine caviar

Roasted chicken in a mushroom and herb boullion

Roasted halloumi cheese on a warm potato
salad

Each main course is complemented with its own vegetable

Chocolate torte with a vanilla sauce

Fresh strawberries with a mixed summer fruit sorbet

Croustillant of raspberries with it's own coulis

Filter or decaffeinated coffee served
with petits fours

£27.00 for three courses
£32.00 for four courses

Figure 3.2 Example of part of an à la carte menu, Courtesy of the Swallow Hotel Birmingham

Ravioli of goats cheese and spinach with asparagus
£18.50

Fillet of pork wrapped in parma ham with
roasted peppers, sun-dried tomatoes and
a parmesan macaroni
£ 21.50

Calves liver on a confit of red onions and
marsala sauce
£21.50

Rib of beef topped with a sweet shallot and
Rosemary butter
£22.00

Rack of lamb with a herb crust and a
bouquetiere of vegetables
£22.50

Loin of venison with broad beans, girolles
and foie gras
£23.00

Crown of Barbary duck with a blueberry sauce
£42.00 for 2

All main courses are complemented
with their own vegetables

*Those who smoke are kindly requested to show
consideration towards other diners.*

Chef de Cuisine   Restaurant Manager
Jonathan Harrison   Vito Scaduto

All prices are inclusive of VAT

5/97

Figure 3.3 Example of a Brasserie style menu, Courtesy of the Copthorne Hotel Birmingham

APPETISERS

PAN-FRIED BLACK PUDDING,
with roasted apple & mustard jus, topped
with a poached egg £4.95

FRESHLY MADE SOUP OF THE DAY £2.95

SALMON GRAVADLAX
accompanied by a lemon & dill fromage frais £6.50

DUCK PARFAIT AND KUMQUAT COMPOTE
laid on rocket leaves with toasted brioche
£4.95

A MEDITERRANEAN KEBAB OF SCAMPI,
CAPSICUMS & PINEAPPLE
set on a bed of wild rice with a red wine
& thyme sauce £7.50

SEASONAL MELON & BLACK CHERRIES
with a coconut & mint syrup (v) £4.95

DEEP FRIED GOATS CHEESE
laid on a bed of French leaves with a honey
vinaigrette (v) £5.95

'LES ESCARGOTS'
traditionally served snails in garlic & parsley butter
£5.95

A WARM TOMATO, BASIL & ONION TARTLET
served on marinated & roasted peppers (v)
£3.95

THAI BEEF SALAD
on a bed of noodles flavoured with a
lemon grass marinade £6.95

MAIN COURSES

FRESH RED SNAPPER FILLET,
pan-fried & set on bean sprouts & ginger with a
mild yellow bean sauce £9.95

CHAR-GRILLED RUMP OF LAMB,
raised on haricot vert beans & fondant potatoes in a
cream of wild mushrooms & rosemary sauce
£12.95

SALMON & PRAWN FISHCAKES,
served on a tomato & cucumber salsa £8.50

VIETNAMESE CHICKEN CURRY
with braised wild rice & fresh lime £9.95

BRAISED KNUCKLE OF PORK
placed on garlic roasted vegetables & an orange
Cognac sauce £9.95

HALF A ROAST DUCK
with turned vegetables in a black cherry &
Kirsh sauce £14.95

ROAST CRIPSY COD
set on a bed of creamed leeks with a port wine sauce
£9.95

TART OF HOLOUMI CHEESE & AUBERGINE
set on a pesto & olive oil dressing (v) £9.50

8oz SIRLOIN STEAK : £14.95
10OZ RIB EYE STEAK : £14.25

Chargrilled to your liking with tomato, mushrooms and
a choice of fries or jacket potato.
For an extra £1.00 why not try a Diane
or Pepper Sauce

DESSERTS

APRICOT CRUMBLE
with homemade custard £3.50

BANANA BREAD & BUTTER PUDDING
£4.50

PROFITEROLES FILLED WITH PASTRY CREAM
with a warm chocolate sauce £4.50

EXOTIC FRESH FRUIT SALAD
& a scoop of vanilla ice cream £3.95

A SELECTION OF ENGLISH & CONTINENTAL CHEESES
with savoury biscuits £4.90

BLACKCURRANT MOUSSE
on a vanilla sponge base with a mango sauce
£3.95

WINE LIST

WHITE WINES	Glass	50cl	75cl
1 FRANCE: CUVEE MARACHAL	1.95	6.75	9.25
2 GERMANY - NIERSTEINER GUTES DOMTAL	2.20	7.50	11.25
3 ITALY - CHARDONNAY DELLE TRE VENEZIE			12.25
4 FRANCE - MUSCADET DE NEUVILLE	2.50	8.75	12.95
5 AUSTRALIA PROSPECT HILL SEMILLON / CHARDONNAY	2.65	9.25	13.75
7 FRANCE - BOURGOGNE ALIGOTE			21.25

Brasserie, coffee shop and popular catering menus

These may be regarded as limited forms of à la carte menus with all the dishes listed and priced separately. It allows, for instance, guests to have a snack with a beverage, a full meal or just a beverage.

Influences on the menu

Modern day menus are the result of the mix of a number of factors. Menu content, traditionally based on classic cuisine, is continually being influenced by food trends, fads and fashions. Additionally customer demand is being affected by a greater understanding of:

- the relationship between health and eating
- special diets
- cultural and religious influences
- vegetarianism.

Because of these influences there is now a greater emphasis in offering alternatives such as low fat milks, eg skimmed or semi-skimmed, non dairy creamers for beverages, alternatives to sugar as sweeteners, sorbets alongside ice creams and polyunsaturated fat and non animal fats as alternatives to butter. There has also been a great influence on cooking ingredients and methods, the development of lower fat dishes, lighter cuisine and attractive and decent alternatives for non-meat eaters with greater use of animal protein substitutes such as Quorn and tofu.

Health and eating

The key issue in the relationship between health and eating is the balance of the diet, not that individual foods are somehow unhealthy. Customers are increasingly looking for the availability of choices which will enable them to achieve a balanced diet. Also customers are requiring more specific information on methods of cooking, eg low fat, low salt. General consensus suggests that the regular diet should be made up of at least one third based on a range of bread, cereals and potatoes, one third based on a variety of fruit and vegetables and the balance based on dairy foods, including low fat milk, low fat meats and fish and small amounts of fatty and sugary food. In addition there are a variety of medical conditions, including allergies, which are more common than was generally understood. Customers do need to know about ingredients as in some circumstances eating certain things may make them very ill and at worse could be fatal.

Special diets

Customers may be required to undertake special diets for medical reasons (including the prevention of allergic reactions). Customer with these needs will usually know what they can and can't eat but is important that when asked, a server is able to accurately describe the dishes so that the customer can make the correct choice. *Never, never guess.*

Special diets may include:

Allergies

Food items where allergies are known include the gluten in wheat, rye and barley (known as coeliac), peanuts and their derivatives, sesame seeds and other nuts such as cashew, pecan, brazil and walnuts as well as milk, fish, shellfish and eggs.

Diabetic

This is the inability of the body to control the level of glucose within the blood. Diets may include foods as in the low cholesterol list below and the avoidance of high sugar dishes.

Low cholesterol

Diets will include polyunsaturated fats and may include limited quantities of animal fats. Other items eaten may include lean poached or grilled meats and fish, fruit and vegetables and low fat milk, cheese and yoghurt.

Low sodium/salt

This requires a reduction of sodium or salt consumed. Diets will include low sodium/salt foods and cooking with very limited or no use of salt.

Cultural and religious dietary influences

Various faiths have differing requirements with regard to the dishes/ingredients which may be consumed and these often also cover preparation methods, cooking procedures and the equipment used. A summary of these needs is given below:

Hindus

All do not eat beef and rarely pork. In addition some will not eat any other meats, fish or eggs. Diets may include cheese, milk and vegetarian dishes.

Jews

Allows for the consumption of 'clean' (kosher) animals and therefore all do not eat pork or pork products, shellfish or animal fats and gelatine from beasts considered to be unclean or not slaughtered according to the prescribed manner. There are restrictions placed on methods of preparation and cookery and also the preparation and eating of meat and dairy products at the same meal is not allowed.

Muslims

Will not eat meat, offal or animal fat unless it is halal (lawful, as required under Islamic Dietary Law) meat.

Sikhs

Do not eat beef or pork. Some will keep to a vegetarian diet. Others may eat fish, mutton, cheese and eggs. Sikhs will not eat halal meat.

Roman Catholics

Restrictions on diet are very limited. Usually will not eat meats on Ash Wednesday or Good Friday. Some keep with the past requirement for no meat to be eaten on Fridays. Fish and dairy products may be taken instead.

Vegetarianism

Vegetarianism may derive from cultural, religious, moral or physiological considerations. It is therefore important that food descriptions are accurate. The various forms of vegetarianism may be summarized as:

Vegetarians: semi

These will not eat red meats, or all meats other than poultry, or all meats. Diets will include fish and may include dairy produce and other animal products.

Vegetarians: lacto-ovo

These will not eat all meat, fish, poultry but may eat milk, milk products and eggs.

Vegetarians: lacto

These will not eat all meat, fish, poultry and eggs but may eat milk and milk products.

Vegans

These will not eat any foods of animal origin. Diets will mainly consist of vegetables, vegetable oils, cereals, nuts, fruits and seeds.

Frutarians

This is a more restricted form of vegetarianism. Excluded are all foods of animal origin together with pulses and cereals. Diets may include mainly raw and dried fruit, nuts, honey and olive oil.

3.2. Food, accompaniments and covers

Introduction

Knowledge about the product is at the core of successful food and beverage service. This knowledge enables the server to advise the customer of the content, the methods used in making the dishes and also to ensure that the customer is provided with an appropiate service lay-up and the correct accompaniments. This section provides information on a variety of individual food items used in food service and this is followed by information on the lay-ups and accompaniments for a selection of menu items by course. Additional information is contained in the list of Foods in Season (Annex A page 407) and the Glossary of Classic Cuisine and Service Terms (Annex B page 411).

There are a number of dishes where traditional accompaniments are normally served. Additionally there are also traditions indicating the appropiate lay-up or cover for certain dishes. This section contains a guide to these lay-ups and accompaniments. However, this guide is not intended to be a prescription as changes are constantly taking place and new accompaniments being tried. Also the desire for healthier eating has led to changes: alternatives to butter, such as Flora are often provided and frequently bread is not buttered in advance thereby allowing the customer to choose his or her requirements. In addition the availability of lower fat milks, non-dairy creamers and non-sugar sweeteners is now standard.

Accompaniments offered with certain dishes are mainly to assist in improving the flavour or to counteract richness. For the lay-up the most important consideration is to aid eating. The use of fish knives and forks, for instance, is becoming less fashionable (the original reason for this cutlery revolved around simply being concerned to keep them separate from other cutlery) and small (demi-tasse) coffee cups are now seen less often in restaurants.

The use of underplates also varies. Underplates are used for four main purposes. These are:

- to improve presentation on the table
- to make carrying of soup plates, bowls and other bowl shaped dishes easier
- to isolate the hand from hot dishes
- to allow cutlery to be carried along with the item

The use of doilies, dish papers or napkins on underplates can also improve presentation, reduce noise and help to prevent the dish being carried slipping on the underplate. As a general guide it is worth considering the use of underplates wherever a food item is being served in a cup or bowl shaped dishes. This also applies to vegetable dishes.

Food items used in food service

Depending on the nature, style and extent of the menu on offer, there will be a variety of food items available which support the service of a range of dishes. Some of these items have specific use for particular dishes and others are used generally across a number of dishes. Examples of a variety of these items and their use is given in Figure 3.4 below.

A note on sauces

Although there appear to be a wide variety of sauces, they are almost always variations on the same base sauces. These are:

fond brun	basic brown meat sauce
velouté	white sauce using fish, meat or vegetable stock
allemande	a velouté thickened with cream and egg yolks
béchamel	savoury white sauce made with milk
tomato sauce	made with fresh, tinned or puréed tomatoes
mayonnaise	cold sauce made from egg yolks, oil, vinegar, salt pepper and mustard
Hollandaise	hot sauce made from melted butter, egg yolks, shallots and vinegar
vinaigrette	cold sauce made form mixing oil, vinegar and a selection of seasonings

These sauces provide the fundamental elements for other sauces. By adding a variety of different ingredients, for example adding cheese to a béchamel sauce to create a mornay sauce, a wide range of sauces are created.

Figure 3.4 Examples of food items used in food service

ITEM	DESCRIPTION	USE
Ailloli	Garlic mayonnaise	Cold fish dishes and as a salad dip
Balsamic vinegar	Aromatic vinegar, acid product made from sweet grape wine, aged in oak	Dressings
Cayenne	Hot, red pepper (actually a powdered species of capsicum)	Oysters, smoked salmon
Chilli sauce	Hot sauce, mostly Chinese made	With Chinese style foods
Chilli vinegar	Vinegar flavoured with chillies	Oysters
Chutney	Generic name for Indian sauces. Common varietes are sweet mango or hot mango also Piccalilli and others such as Branston	Indian chutneys for Tandoori and other Indian dishes. Other chutneys for cold meats and ploughman's lunch
Cider vinegar	Acid product made from cider	Can be used in salad dressings. Seen by some as a product for the health conscious
Cocktail gherkins	Small gherkins	Appetisers or garnish for charcuterie
Cocktail onions	Small pearl onions	Appetisers or garnish for charcuterie
Cranberry sauce	Sauce, made from cranberries, usually available as a proprietary sauce. Can be served hot or cold	Roast turkey
Croûtons	Small cube of fried or toasted bread	Garnish for soups and used in some salad dishes
Cumberland sauce	Sweet-and-sour sauce including, orange and lemon juice and zest, redcurrent jelly and port. Can be kitchen made or proprietary bottled	Game dishes and for charcuterie
Dill pickle	Pickled gherkins or cucumbers flavoured with dill	Meats, salads dishes, charcuterie and cheese

ITEM	DESCRIPTION	USE
French dressing	Dressing made from oil and usually wine vinegar, or lemon juice, with seasoning. Mustard and herbs may be added	Salads
Ginger	Spicy root used in many forms, ground ginger is most common in restaurants	Melon
Gros sel	Literally 'fat salt', not finely ground. Also called rock salt	Boiled beef but also widely used in table grinders
Horseradish sauce	Hot sauce made from horseradish root, usually available as proprietary sauce, often needs creaming down	Roast Beef and Chicken Maryland and also for cold smoked fish dishes when creamed down
HP sauce	Brown proprietary, spicy vinegar-based sauce	Cold meats and other dishes
Indian pickles	Un-sweetened, hot pickles, featuring limes, mango , brinjals, etc	Accompaniment for Indian (and other) savoury dishes
Kasundi	Hot Indian pickle featuring chopped mango	Accompaniment for Indian (and other) savoury dishes
Ketchup, mushroom	Old-style English proprietary sauce now seldom seen. Chinese mushroom sauce is substituted	Flavouring in lamp cookery and for other dishes
Ketchup, tomato	Sauce of tomato pulp, vinegar and sweetening. Usually available as a poprietary sauce	Grills, fish, burgers
Lemon	Citrus fruit (slices, segments or halves	Infinite variety of uses, especially smoked fish, fried fish and a range of drinks including tea
Lime	Citrus fruit (slices, segments or halves)	Similar to lemon above,

ITEM	DESCRIPTION	USE
Mayonnaise	Made from liaison of oil and egg yolks, flavoured with vinegar, herbs and seasoning	Dressing for eg poached fish, and sauce for salads
Malt vinegar	Acid product of brewed malted barley	Dressings and traditionally for chips
Mint sauce	Vinegar-based sauce with chopped mint and sweetening. Poprietary versions usually used	Roast lamb
Mint jelly	Sweetish jelly made with mint. Proprietary versions usually used	Roast lamb, as alternative to mint sauce
Mixed pickles	Assortment of vegetables pickled in vinegar	Cold meats, charcuterie
Mustard, English	Generally the hottest available as powder for making up or as proprietary bottled, sometimes with other ingredients such as whole seeds	Roast beef, boiled beef, grills, cold meats, pâtés and as ingredient in dressings eg vinaigrette
Mustard, other	Wide variety including French au poivre, vert, Bordeaux, Meaux, Dijon, Douce, German (senf)	Cold meats, grills, dressings
Mustard sauce	Warm sauce, generally kitchen made but also available as proprietary sauce	Traditionally grilled herring but is used for other meat and fish dishes
Oil, general	Many varieties, usually low in unsaturated fats	Dressings and increasingly for cooking
Oriental vinegars	Several varieties	Give character to dressings and food dishes
Paprika	Powdered, mild, red capsicum	Garnish on wide variety of dishes. Sometimes deep fried with fish
Parmesan	Italian hard cheese (grated or shredded)	Soups (eg minestrone), pasta
Pepper	Ground white pepper	Traditional form of pepper

ITEM	DESCRIPTION	USE
Peppercorns	Green are usually pickled in brine and soft	In food dishes
	White and black	Black used for the table in peppermills but sometimes mixed
Piccalilli	Mixed pickle in thickened, spiced sauce (predominately tumeric and sugar)	Cold meats, ploughman's lunch, buffet, snacks
Piri-piri	Hot chilli sauce of Portuguese/ African origin	Prawns, crayfish, chicken
Redcurrant jelly	Proprietary sauce	Traditionally offered with hare. Also traditionally offered with roast mutton but now commonly offered with roast lamb
Sea salt	Salt derived from evaporated sea water	Seasoning, especially with boiled beef and used in grinders
Salt, refined	Ground table salt	Traditionally used as salt in table cellar or shakers
Soy sauce	Clear, dark brown sauce usually Chinese, made from Soy beans	Chinese and sometimes other dishes
Tabasco	Hot spicy pepper proprietary sauce	Oysters, clams, other seafood and in other dishes
Vinaigrette	Liason of oil and vinegar or lemon juice with seasoning. May also include mustards and herbs	Dressings
Wine vinegar	Acid product of wine, red or white	Dressings
Worcestershire sauce	Maceration of blend of spices and fruit in vinegar. Often known by the brand name 'Lea and Perrins'	Tomato juice, Irish stew, seafood cocktails and in dressings. Also used in a variety of other dishes

Hors-d'oeuvre and other appetizers

Hors-d'oeuvre

Traditionally hors-d'oeuvres are a selection of salads, fish and meats. The selection was served onto a cold fish plate and the cover was a fish knife and fork. The cover nowadays is more likely to be dictated by the type of food being served and its presentation. Oil and vinegar were also traditionally offered but this has become less common because the foods are usually already well dressed. Brown bread and butter is also less often offered, thereby allowing the customer a choice or either butter or alternatives.

Service can be a pre-plated selection or offered as a selection, in individual ravier dishes, from a tray, guéridon or from the traditional hors-d'oeuvre trolley as illustrated in Figure 3.5.

Common hors-d'oeuvre items include:

Salads

Plain or compound. Examples of plain salads include fish and meat salads, cucumber salad, tomato salad, potato salad, beetroot salad, red cabbage and cauliflower. Compound salads include for example Russian (mixed vegetables in mayonnaise) Andalouse (celery, onions, peppers, tomatoes, rice and vinaigrette), Italienne (vegetable salad, cubes of salami, anchovy fillets and mayonnaise) and Parisienne (slices of crayfish, truffles, Russian salad and bound with mayonnaise and aspic).

Fish

May include items such as anchovies, herring (fresh or marinated) lobster, mackerel (marinated, smoked or fresh), smoked eel (filleted or sliced) and prawns (plain, in cocktail sauce or in a mousse).

Meats

Includes items such as foie gras, ham (raw, boiled or smoked) and salami of all sorts.

Figure 3.5 Hors-d'oeuvre trolley

Canapés

These are slices of bread with the crusts removed, cut into a variety of shapes, then toasted or fried in oil or butter and garnished. Garnishes can include smoked salmon, foie gras, prawns, cheese, asparagus tips, tomato, egg, capers, gherkins, salami and other various meats.

Eggs

These can be poached, in aspic, hard boiled, cut in two, garnished and stuffed with various fillings which include the yolk.

Other Appetizers

Asparagus (*Asperges*)

Fresh asparagus can be eaten hot with for example melted butter or Hollandaise sauce or cold with vinaigrette or mayonnaise. It is useful to place an upturned fork under the right hand side of the plate to tip the plate so that the sauce will form in a well at the bottom of the plate towards the left hand side. Eating can with be with a side knife and fork, with an asparagus holder or with the fingers. If with the fingers, then a finger bowl and a spare napkin should be offered.

Avocado

Generally served in halves with a salad garnish on a fish plate. Can be served with vinaigrette (now more likely to be made with a wine vinegar) which is served separately or with prawns in a cocktail sauce. There are also special dishes to hold half an avocado. Brown bread and butter is less common now. Alternative methods of presentation are also found, for example where the avocado is sliced and fanned out. A side knife and sweet fork are then laid.

Caesar Salad

Salad of cos (or Romaine) lettuce, dressed with vinaigrette or other similar dressing (originally containing near-raw egg), garlic, croûtons and grated (or shaved) parmesan cheese. There are a number of variations to these ingredients. Side knife and sweet fork are laid. Sometimes this salad is served in a bowl.

Caviar

Served with a caviar knife (broad blade knife) or side knife, on the right hand side of the cover. Served onto a cold fish plate and accompaniments include blinis (buckwheat pancakes) or hot breakfast toast, butter, segments of lemon, chopped shallots and chopped egg yolk and egg white. Portion size is usually about 30g (1oz).

Charcuterie

This can include a selection of a range of meat (mainly pork) items including Bayonne ham, salamis, smoked ham, Parma ham and also pâtés and terrines. Cover is a side knife and sweet fork, or a joint knife and fork if taken as a main course. Accompaniments are peppermill and cayenne pepper, gherkins and sometimes onions. Occasionally a small portion of potato salad is offered. Bread is usually offered but brown bread and butter is now less common.

Corn on the cob

These are usually served with special holders which are like small swords or forks. Three wooden cocktail sticks in each end will also do the job, but avoid trying to use two sweet forks as it is possible to painfully catch teeth on the prongs. There are special dishes available, but a soup plate will do to provide a reservoir for the melted butter or Hollandaise sauce. A finger bowl and spare napkin might be advisable. A peppermill is offered.

Fresh fruit

Either served on a plate or in a bowl. Eaten with side knife and sweet fork if served on a plate and sweet spoon and fork if served in a bowl. Usually no accompaniment is offered although some people might like caster sugar. Both caster sugar and ground ginger are offered with melon if it is served by itself. (For guéridon preparation of fruit see page 316)

Fruit cocktails

Usually served in a glass or some form of bowl. These are eaten with a teaspoon and caster sugar is offered where there is grapefruit included in the cocktail.

Fruit juices

Usually served in a glass. Sometimes caster sugar is offered in which case a teaspoon should be given to stir in the sugar. For tomato juice, salt and Worcestershire sauce are offered and again a teaspoon should also be given to aid mixing in these accompaniments.

Globe artichokes

This vegetable is usually served whole as a starter. The edible portion of the leaves is 'sucked off' between the teeth after dipping them in a dressing (for example vinaigrette if served cold or melted butter or Hollandaise sauce if served hot). The leaves are held with the fingers. The heart is finally eaten with a side knife and sweet fork. A finger bowl and spare napkin are essential. There are special dishes for this vegetable, but a fish plate with a small bowl for the dressing will also do the job. In this case there would have to be a spare plate for the discarded leaves. Alternatively a joint plate may be used.

Mousses and pâtés

Normally these are eaten using a side knife and sweet fork. Hot, unbuttered breakfast toast or another bread is offered. Butter may be offered and other accompaniments would be appropiate to the dish itself, eg lemon segments with fish mousses, although lemon is often offered with meat based pâtés .

Niçoise Salad

There are a number of versions of this salad. Generally it includes boiled potatoes, whole French beans, tomatoes, hard-boiled eggs (quartered or sliced) stoned black olives, flakes of tuna fish and anchovy fillets. This salad is usually made up and plated. Vinaigrette is often offered.

Other smoked fish

As well as the accompaniments offered with smoked salmon, creamed horseradish has become a standard offering with all other smoked fish including trout, mackerel, cod, halibut and tuna.

Other salads

Salads can be made up and served plated or constituted at the guéridon. Dressings are various. Cover is usually related to the main ingredient ie fish knife and fork for fish based salads but a side knife and fork can be used for all. For guéridon service of salads see Chapter 8 page 295.

Oysters (*hûitres*)

Cold oysters are usually served in one half of the shell on a bed of crushed ice in a soup plate. An oyster fork is usually offered but a small sweet fork can also be used. Because oysters are usually eaten by holding the shell in one hand and the fork in the other, a finger bowl and an extra napkin could be offered. Accompaniments include half a lemon and the oyster cruet (cayenne pepper, pepper mill, chilli vinegar and Tabasco sauce). Traditionally brown bread and butter was also offered.

Potted shrimps

A fish knife and fork or a side knife and sweet fork should be laid. Accompaniments include hot, unbuttered, breakfast toast (there is plenty of butter already in this dish), cayenne pepper, a peppermill and segments of lemon.

Seafood cocktails

These are usually made up and served in glasses or bowls. A teaspoon and small fork are often laid for eating. Sometimes the tableware is placed on the underplate and placed on the table with the dish. Accompaniments are lemon segment, peppermill, sometimes cayenne pepper and traditionally brown bread and butter, although this is less common now.

Smoked salmon (*saumon fumé*)

Usually eaten with a fish knife and fork or a side knife and sweet fork. Traditional accompaniments are half a lemon (which may be wrapped in muslin to prevent the juice squirting onto the customer when the lemon is squeezed), Cayenne pepper, peppermill and brown bread and butter. Often nowadays a variety of unbuttered bread is offered with butter and alternatives served separately. Oil is sometimes offered and also chopped onions, and capers.

Snails (*escargots*)

Snail tongs are place on the left and a snail fork on the right. The snails are served in an escargot dish which has six or twelve indentations. French bread is offered for mopping up the sauce. Half a lemon may be given and a finger bowl and an extra napkin could be offered.

Soups

Soups are divided into a number of categories. These include, consommés, veloutés crèmes, purées, potages, bisques (shell fish soups) broths and various national soups.

Consommé

Clarified soup made from poultry, beef , game or vegetable bouillon. Usually served in consommé cups with a sweet spoon. These soups were once drunk from the cup using the handles and the spoon was provided to help in eating the garnish. The tradition continues of the use of the cup but this is now presented at the table. The handles on some styles of cups have become merely representative ears. Although consommé is usually served hot is can also be served cold or jellied (en gelée).

Veloutés, crèmes and purées

These soups are usually eaten from a soup plate with a soup spoon. It is however common now to see soup bowls of varying designs. Traditionally croûtons were only offered with purées and Cream of Tomato soups but they are now commonly offered with a range of soups.

Potages, broths and bisques

These are also served generally in soup plates and eaten with a soup spoon but again bowls of varying designs are also used.

National soups

These soups usually have special treatments. Examples are:

Batwinia (Russian) Purée of spinach, sorrel, beetroot and white wine, with small ice cubes served separately. Served very cold.

Bortsch (Polish) Duck flavoured consommé garnished with duck, diced beef and turned vegetables: the accompaniments are sour cream, beetroot juice and bouchées filled with duck pâté. A soup plate is often used here as there are a large amount of accompaniments.

Bouillabaisse (French) This is really a form of fish stew. Although a soup plate and soup spoon are used it is common for a knife and fork to also be given. Thin slices of French bread, dipped in oil and grilled are also offered (sippets).

Cherry (German) Bouillon consisting of cherry purée, cherry juice and red wine, served with stoned cherries and sponge finger biscuits.

Cock-a-leekie (Scottish) Veal and chicken consommé garnished with shredded leeks and chicken. Served with prunes: these may have been put into the soup plate at the service point.

Kroupnich (Russian) Barley and sections of poultry offal garnished with small vol-au-vents stuffed with poultry meat.

Mille fanti (Italian) Consommé with a covering of bread crumbs, Parmesan cheese and beaten eggs.

Minestrone (Italian) Vegetable paysanne soup with pasta. Traditional accompaniments are grated Parmesan cheese and grilled flutes.

Petit Marmite (French) Beef and chicken flavoured soup garnished with turned root vegetables and dice of beef and chicken. Served in a special marmite pot which resembles a small casserole. A sweet spoon is used to eat this soup as it is easier to get this spoon into the pot. Accompaniments are grilled flutes, poached bone marrow and Parmesan cheese. Sometimes the bread and cheese are done as a croût on top of the soup before serving at the table.

Potage Germiny (French) Consommé thickened before service with egg yolks and cream. Cheese straws are offered.

Shchy (Russian) Bortsch consommé, garnished with sauerkraut. Beetroot juice and sour cream are offered separately.

Soupe à l'oignon (French) French onion soup, often served in a consommé cup or soup bowl. Can be served with grilled flutes and parmesan cheese but is often topped with a slice of French bread gratinated with cheese.

Turtle, clear (English) Beef, poultry and turtle consommé, with strong aromatic herb flavouring, garnished with diced turtle meat. This soup was traditionally served in a consommé cup and accompaniments were cheese straws, lemon segments and brown bread and butter. Warmed Madeira or sometimes sherry was put into the soup just before serving. This soup is not seen now but there are substitutes used.

Eggs

Eggs dishes as separate courses have a chequered history. Omelettes have retained their popularity but dishes such as eggs en cocotte occasionally feature on menus.

The following egg dishes have specific service requirements:

Oeuf sur la plat
The egg is cooked in the oven in the oeuf sur la plat dish and is then served to the customer in this dish on an underplate. A sweet spoon and fork are used but a side knife may be given depending on the garnishes. A sur la plat dish is a small round white earthenware or metal dish with two ears.

Oeuf en cocotte
The egg is cooked in the cocotte dish, with various garnishes and served in this dish to the customer. The dish is placed on an underplate and a teaspoon is used to eat the dish. A cocotte dish is a small round earthenware dish with straight sides about the size of a small teacup.

Omelettes
As an egg course an omelette is eaten with a joint fork and is served onto a hot fish plate. The joint fork is placed on the right hand side of the cover. Omelettes are often plated but may be served from a flat using two forks or two fish knives. The ends may also be trimmed as part of this service.

Pasta and rice dishes

These dishes which are also referred to as farinaceous dishes, include all pastas such as spaghetti, macaroni, nouilles, ravioli and also rice dishes such as pilaff or risotto. It also includes dishes such as Gnocchi Piedamontaise (potato), Parisienne (choux paste) and Romaine (semolina).

For spaghetti, a joint fork should be laid in the right hand side of the cover and a sweet spoon on the left. For all other dishes a sweet spoon and fork are used. Grated Parmesan cheese is normally offered with all these dishes. Sometimes the Parmesan cheese is now shaved from the piece rather than being grated.

Fish dishes

Traditionally fish dishes were eaten with a fish knife and fork but this practice is declining. For a fish course the usual lay-up is a fish plate and side knife and fork. For fish as a main course it is a joint plate with fish knife and fork or a joint knife and fork. General accompaniments for fish dishes are:

Hot fish dishes with a sauce
There are not usually any accompaniments.

Hot fish dishes without sauces
These often have Hollandaise offered or another hot butter-based sauce. Lemon segments may also be offered.

Fried fish which has been breadcrumbed (*à l'Angalise*)
These dished often have tartare sauce, or another mayonnaise based sauce, offered together with segments of lemon.

Fried or grilled fish dishes not breadcrumbed
These dishes are usually offered with lemon. Sometimes sauces such as Hollandaise or tartare are offered.

Deep fried fish which has been dipped in batter (*à l'Orly*)
A (kitchen made) tomato sauce is sometimes offered together with segments of lemon. Proprietary sauces can also be offered as can vinegar if chips are being served.

Cold poached fish dishes
Usually mayonnaise or another mayonnaise-based sauce such as Sauce Vert are offered together with segments of lemon.

Fish dishes with special service requirements include:

Grilled Herring (*hareng grillé*)
Usually served with a mustard sauce.

Whitebait (*blanchailles*)
Served on a hot fish plate and traditionally eaten with a fish knife and fork. Accompaniments are Cayenne pepper, peppermill, segments of lemon and brown bread and butter.

Mussels (*moules marinière*)

Usually served in a soup plate or bowl on an underplate with brown bread and butter, or more commonly now various breads, and Cayenne pepper being offered. A fish knife and fork and sweet spoon are often laid for eating. A plate for the debris is often placed on the table together with a finger bowl and a spare napkin..

Cold Lobster (*homard froid*)

Cover is a fish knife and fork and a lobster pick together with a spare debris plate and a finger bowl with a spare napkin. Lemon and sauce mayonnaise are the usual accompaniments.

Meats, poultry and game

Roast meats

In all cases roast gravy is offered. For dishes where the roast is plain (ie not roasted with herbs for instance) then the following are usually offered:

Roast beef (*boeuf rôti*)

Horseradish sauce, mustards and Yorkshire pudding.

Roast lamb (*agneau rôti*)

Mint sauce and also now more commonly, redcurrant jelly.

Roast mutton (*mouton rôti*)

Traditionally this was redcurrant jelly and sometimes onion sauce.

Roast pork (*porc rôti*)

Apple sauce and sage and onion stuffing.

Boiled meats

Boiled mutton (*mouton bouilli*)

Caper sauce is usually served.

Salt beef (*silverside*)

Turned root vegetables, dumplings and the natural cooking liquor.

Boiled fresh beef (*beouf bouilli*)

Turned root vegetables, natural cooking liquor, rock salt and gherkins.

Boiled ham (*jambon bouilli*)

Parsley sauce or white onion sauce.

Other meat dishes

Irish Stew

This stew is often served in a soup plate and a sweet spoon offered together with the joint knife and fork. Accompaniments are Worcestershire sauce and pickled red cabbage.

Curry (*kari*)

General accompaniments are poppadums (crisp, highly seasoned pancakes) Bombay

Duck (dried fillet of fish from the Indian Ocean) and mango chutney. Also offered is a Curry Tray which will have items such as diced apple, sultanas, sliced bananas, yoghurt and desiccated coconut.

Mixed grill and other grills

These dishes may be garnished with cress, tomato and fried potatoes. Various mustards and sometimes proprietary sauces act as accompaniments.

Steaks

As for mixed grill and also sauce Béarnaise is offered with Châteaubriand (double fillet) and sometimes with other steaks.

Poultry

Roast chicken (*poulet rôti*)

The accompaniments are bread sauce, roast gravy and parsley and thyme stuffing. Sage and onion stuffing is also used.

Roast duck (*caneton rôti*)

Sage and onion stuffing, apple sauce and roast gravy are served.

Wild duck (*caneton sauvage*)

Roast gravy and traditionally an orange salad with an acidulated cream dressing is offered as a side dish.

Roast goose (*oie rôti*)

Sage and onion stuffing, apple sauce and roast gravy.

Roast turkey (*dinde rôti*)

Cranberry sauce, chestnut stuffing, chipolata sausages, game chips, watercress and roast gravy are the usual accompaniments.

Furred game

Jugged Hare

Heart shaped croûtons, forcemeat balls and redcurrant jelly.

Venison (*venaison*)

Cumberland sauce and redcurrant jelly.

Feathered game

When roasted the accompaniments for all feathered game, including for instance partridge (*perdreau*), grouse (*lagopède*) and pheasant (*faisan*), are fried breadcrumbs, hot liver pâté spread on a croûte on which the meat sits, bread sauce, game chips, watercress and roast gravy may all be served.

Baked potato

A baked potato (*pomme au four*) is often served separately on a hot side plate, with a sweet fork on the plate to aid eating. Accompaniments are Cayenne pepper, peppermill and butter (or substitutes). Butter is not often now automatically put on the top of the potato.

Sweets

Most sweets are generally served onto sweet plates or are pre-plated. Puddings and various hot dishes can be pre-plated onto or served into various bowls. The lay-up is usually the sweet spoon and fork. Often a sugar sifter may be required by the customer. Various items may require different cutlery for instance a sundae spoon, ice cream spoon or teaspoon. The main consideration is always to aid eating.

The serving of sauces, eg custard, and whipped cream can be out of sauce boats (ladled not poured) or there may be individual portion jugs. Alternatively the sauce boats may be left (on an underplate) on the table for the customers to help themselves. If sauces are served then it is usual not to serve these over the item but around it – unless the customer specifically requests it.

Cheese

Cheeses are distinguished by flavour and categorized according to their texture. They differ from each other for a number of reasons, mainly arising through variations in the making process. Differences occur in the rind and how it is formed, in the paste and in the cooking process, relating here to both time and temperature. Also cheeses vary because the milk used comes from such different animals as cows, sheep and goats.

Cheese should be stored in a cool, dark place with good air circulation or in a refrigerator. If it is not covered in its original wrapping, it should be wrapped in either cling film or aluminium foil to prevent any drying out taking place. It should also be stored away from food items that absorb flavours/odours, such as dairy produce.

Dependent upon use, cheeses may be purchased either whole or pre-portioned. Depending upon the type of establishment, the latter is more often the case as there is less wastage and no loss in quality, flavour or aroma.

The texture of a cheese depends largely on the period of maturation. The recognized categories are:

- Fresh
- Soft
- Semi-hard
- Hard
- Blue

Examples of cheeses commonly available are:

Fresh cheese

Cottage
Unripened low-fat, skimmed milk cheese with a granular curd. Originated in the USA and now has many variations

Cream

Similar to *cottage cheese* but is made with full milk. There are a number of different varieties available, some made from non-cow milks

Mozzarella

Italian cheese made now from cow's milk but originally from buffalo milk

Ricotta

Italian cheese made from the whey of cow's milk. A number of other Italian varieties are available made from sheep's milk

Soft cheese

Bel Paese

This light and creamy Italian cheese has a name which means 'beautiful country' and was first produced in 1929

Brie

Famous French cheese made since the eighth century. Other countries now make this style of cheese, distinguishing it by the country's name, eg *German brie*

Camembert

Famous French cheese which is stronger and can be more pungent than *Brie*

Carré de l'est

A soft cheese produced in France that is made from pasteurized cow's milk, and packed in square boxes. Like *Camembert*, it softens on ripening and is darker in colour than *Brie*. When ripe it has a mild flavour

Feta

Greek cheese made from both goat's and sheep's milk

Liptauer

Hungarian cheese spread made from sheep's and cow's milk. Often found with various additions, eg onions, mustard or spices

Munster

French Vosges cheese similar to *Camembert* in shape but with an orange red rind. American, German and Swiss versions are also available

Semi-hard cheese

Appenzeller

Typical example of Swiss cheese textures. The name is from the Latin for 'abbot's cell'

Caerphilly

Buttermilk-flavoured cheese with a soft paste. Some people will find it almost soapy. Originally a Welsh cheese but now manufactured all over Britain

Cheddar

Classic British cheese now made all over the world and referred to as, for example, *Scottish cheddar, Canadian cheddar*

Cheshire

Crumbly, slightly salty cheese, available as either white or red. It was originally made during the twelfth century in Cheshire but is now made all over Britain

Chèvre

The name means 'goat', which denotes the origin of the milk from which this cheese, and the wide variety of variations, is made

Derby

English Derbyshire cheese now more often known by the sage-flavoured variety, *Sage Derby*

Edam

Similar to, but harder than, *Gouda*, this Dutch cheese has a fairly bland, buttery taste and a yellow or red wax coated rind. It is sometimes flavoured with cumin

Emmenthal

The name of this Swiss cheese refers to the Emme Valley. It is similar to *Gruyère*, although it is softer and slightly less tasty

Esrom

Similar to the French *Port Salut*, this Danish cheese has a red rather than yellow rind

Gloucester/Double Gloucester

Full-cream, classic English cheeses originally made only from the milk of Gloucestershire cows

Gouda

Buttery textured, soft and mild flavoured well-known Dutch cheese with a yellow or red rind

Gruyère

Mainly known as a Swiss cheese but both the French and Swiss varieties can legally be called by this name. It has small pea-size holes and a smooth relatively hard texture. The French varieties may have larger holes

Jarlsberg

Similar to *Emmenthal*, this Norwegian cheese was first produced in the late 1950s. It has a yellow wax coating

Lancashire

Another classic English cheese similar to *Cheshire*; (white *Cheshire* is sometimes sold as *Lancashire*)

Leicester

Mild flavoured and orange coloured English cheese

Limberger

Often quite pungent, this originally Belgian cheese is now also available from Germany

Monterey

Creamy, soft American cheese with many holes. A harder version known as *Monterey Jack* is suitable for grating

Pont l'Evêque

Similar to *Camembert*, but square in shape, this French cheese originates from Normandy

Port Salut

Mild flavoured cheese with a name meaning 'Port of Salvation', referring to the abbey where exiled Trappist monks returned after the French Revolution

Reblochon

Creamy, mild flavoured cheese from the Haute-Savoie region of France. The name comes from the illegal 'second milking' from which the cheese was originally made

Tilsit

Strong flavoured cheese from the East German town of the same name where it was first produced by Dutch living there. Now available from other parts of Germany

Wensleydale

Yorkshire cheese originally made from sheep's or goat's milk but now from cow's milk. This cheese is the traditional accompaniment to apple pie.

Hard cheese

Caciocavallo

Originating from ancient Roman times, the name means 'cheese on horseback' because its shape is said to resemble saddlebags

Kefalotyri

Literally Greek for 'hard cheese', this is a tasty, grating-type cheese from Greece

Parmesan

Classic Italian hard cheese, more correctly called *Parmigiano Reggiano*, and predominantly known as the grated cheese used in and for sprinkling over Italian dishes

Blue cheese

Blue de Bresse

Fairly soft and mild flavoured French cheese from the area between Soane-et-Loire and the Jura

Blue Cheshire

One of the finest of the blue cheeses which only becomes blue accidentally, although the makers endeavour to assist this process by pricking the cheese and maturing it in a favourable atmosphere

Danish Blue

One of the most well-known of the blue cheeses. Softish and mild flavoured, it was one of the first European blue cheeses to gain popularity in Britain

Dolcelatte

Factory made version of *Gorgonzola*. The name is Italian for 'sweet milk' and the cheese is fairly soft with a creamy texture and greenish veining

Dorset Blue

A strong, hard pressed cheese, being close textured and made from skimmed milk. It is straw coloured with deep blue veins, rather crumbly and has a rough rind

Gorgonzola

Softish, sharp flavoured, classic Italian cheese with greenish veining, which is developed with the addition of mould culture

Roquefort

Classic, sheep's milk cheese from the southern Massif Central in France. The maturing takes place in caves which provide a unique humid environment which contributes to the development of the veining

Stilton

Famous and classic English cheese made from cow's milk; so called because it was noted as being sold in the Bell Inn at Stilton by travellers stopping there. According to legend it was first made by a Mrs Paulet of Melton Mowbray. Traditionally served by the spoonful but nowadays usually (and perhaps preferably) portioned. The pouring of port on to the top of a whole Stilton, once the top rind had been removed, was also popular but this practice is also on the decline. The *White Stilton* has also become popular and is slightly less flavoursome than the blue variety

Cover, accompaniments and service

The cover for cheese is:

- Side plate
- Side knife
- Sometimes a small fork (sweet)

Accompaniments set on the table may include:

- Cruet (salt, pepper, and mustard)
- Butter or alternative
- Celery served in celery glass part filled with crushed ice, on an underplate
- Radishes, when in season, placed in glass bowl on underplate with teaspoon
- Castor sugar for cream cheeses
- Assorted cheese biscuits (cream crackers, Ryvita, sweet digestive, water biscuits, etc) or breads

If not plated the cheeseboard or trolley will be presented to the customer containing a varied selection of cheeses in ripe condition together with sufficient cheese knives for cutting and portioning the different cheeses. If cheese is wrapped in foil this must be removed by the waiter before serving. If the cheese rind is not palatable it is also removed by the waiter. This is not necessary in the case of Camembert and Brie as the rind of these two French cheeses is palatable.

Savouries

On the lunch and dinner menu a savoury may generally be served as an alternative to sweet. In a banquet it may be a separate course served in addition to either a sweet or cheese course.

Savouries may be:

On toast
Usually shaped pieces of toast with various toppings such as anchovies, sardines, mushrooms, smoked haddock, and the classic Welsh rarebit (toasted seasoned cheese, egg and béchamel sauce mixture), or Buck rarebit (Welsh rarebit with a poached egg on the top)

Canapés or croûtes
Shaped pieces of bread about 6 mm (¼ inch) thick, brushed with melted butter and grilled, or may be shaped shallow fried bread. Examples include:
Scotch woodcock (scrambled egg, topped with a trellis of anchovies and studded with capers
Croûte Diane (chicken livers wrapped in streaky bacon)
Croûte Derby (ham puree garnished with a pickled walnut)
Devils on horseback (prunes wrapped in bacon)
Angels on horseback (poached oysters wrapped in bacon)
Canapé Charlemagne (shrimps in a curry sauce)
Canapé Quo Vadis (grilled roes garnished with small mushrooms)

Tartlettes
Round pastry cases with various fillings such as mushrooms, cheese soufflé mixtures with various garnishes or prawns or other fish in various sauces

Barquettes
Filled boat-shaped pastry cases, similar to tartlettes

Bouchées
Filled small puff pastry (vol-au-vent) cases

Omelettes
Two and three egg omelettes with various flavours/fillings such as parsley, anchovy, cheese or fines herbes (fine herbs)

Soufflés
Made in a soufflé dish with various flavours such as mushroom spinach, sardine, anchovy, smoked haddock or cheese

Flans

Either single or portioned savoury flans such as Quiche Lorraine

Cover, accompaniments and service

The main cover for a savoury is usually a side knife and a sweet fork.

Accompaniments are:

- salt and pepper
- Cayenne pepper
- Pepper mill
- Worcestershire sauce (usually only with meat savouries)

Savouries are usually pre-portioned by the kitchen and served onto a hot fish plate. The savoury is served plated to the guest after the cover and accompaniments have been laid on the table. Where a savoury is being served as an alternative to sweets or cheese, with other guests in the party taking these, then the convention of serving all cold dishes before hot dishes (irrespective of the host) usually applies.

Dessert (fresh fruit and nuts)

Dessert may include all types of fresh fruits and nuts according to season, although the majority of the more popular items are now available all the year round. Some of the more popular items are: dessert apples, pears, bananas, oranges, mandarins, tangerines, black and white grapes, pineapple and assorted nuts such as brazils. Sometimes a box of dates may appear on the fruit basket.

The dessert is usually dressed up in a fruit basket by the larder section and may be used as a central piece on a cold buffet until required.

Cover, accompaniments and service

The cover to be laid for dessert is:

- Fruit plate
- Fruit knife and fork: traditionally interlocked on the fruit plate
- Spare napkin
- One finger bowl: on a sideplate and containing lukewarm water and a slice of lemon. It will be placed at the top right-hand corner of the cover and may be used by the customer for rinsing his/her fingers
- One finger bowl: on a sideplate and containing cold water for rinsing the grapes. It will be placed on the top left-hand corner of the cover
- Nut crackers and grape scissors: to be placed on the fruit basket
- Spare sideplate for shells and peel

The following accompaniments should be set on the table:

- Castor sugar holder on a sideplate
- Salt for nuts

The fruit basket is presented to the guest who makes his/her choice of a portion of fresh fruit or nuts.

If the guest chooses nuts as part of his/her portion, then the nut-crackers would be removed from the fruit basket, placed on a sideplate and left on the table at the head of the cover. If grapes are chosen then the waiter rests the fruit basket on the table supporting it with one hand and cuts off the selected portion of grapes with the aid of the grape scissors. These are so made that they will grip the stem once the portion has been cut and removed from the main bunch, and thus by holding the portion with the grape scissors they may be rinsed in the finger bowl at the top left-hand corner of the cover and placed on the fruit plate. If guéridon service is being used, the procedure will be the same but takes place from the guéridon or trolley. Guéridon preparation of fruit is described in Chapter 8, page 316.

Beverages

Traditionally the term beverages on a menu referred to coffee but it has become more common now for it to encompass tea, tisanes, milk drinks (hot or cold) and proprietary drinks such as Bovril or Horlicks.

Fairly rigid guidelines used to exist for the service of tea and coffee:

- Morning coffee was traditionally served in tea cups, with hot milk and white sugar only.
- In the evening the demi-tasse (half cups) were used for coffee and cream might have been offered. Brown sugar was usually the only one available.
- Similarly with tea breakfast cups were used in the morning and the standard tea cup in the afternoon and in the evening – if you were lucky enough to be offered tea!
- Lemon was offered only with China tea and milk with other teas.

Fortunately there is now more choice available. Both tea, coffee (in both standard and de-caffeinated versions) and a range of other beverages are commonly available throughout the day with a choice of milks, creams (including non-dairy creamers) and sugars (including non-sugar sweeteners). The use of the small coffee cup (demi-tasse) is on the decline.

CHAPTER 4

BEVERAGES – NON-ALCOHOLIC AND ALCOHOLIC

4.1	**Tea**	96
4.2	**Coffee**	100
4.3	**Other stillroom beverages**	110
4.4	**Non-alcoholic dispense bar beverages**	110
4.5	**Wine and drinks list**	114
4.6	**Cocktails**	118
4.7	**Bitters**	120
4.8	**Wine**	121
4.9	**Tasting of wine**	132
4.10	**Matching food and drinks**	135
4.11	**Spirits**	138
4.12	**Liqueurs**	141
4.13	**Beers**	142
4.14	**Cider and Perry**	145
4.15	**Storage**	146

4.1 Tea

History

Tea was discovered by accident over 5000 years ago when leaves from a tea bush accidentally dropped into some boiling water and delicately flavoured the liquid. Tea was originally drunk for its medicinal benefits and it was not until the 1700s that it began to be consumed as the delicious beverage that we know today.

What is tea?

Tea is prepared from the leaf bud and top leaves of a tropical evergreen bush called *Camellia sinensis*. It produces what is regarded as a healthy beverage containing approximately only half the caffeine of coffee and at the same time it aids muscle relaxation and stimulates the central nervous system. It is regarded as a profitable beverage with caterers serving over 10 billion cups of tea a year.

Producing countries

Tea is grown in more than 25 countries around the world. The crop benefits from acidic soil, and warm climate and where there is at least 130cm of rain a year. It is an annual crop and its flavour, quality and character is affected by the location, altitude, type of soil and the climate.

The main tea producing countries are:

China This is the oldest tea growing country and is known for speciality blends such as Keemun, Lapsang Souchong, Oolongs and green tea.

East Africa (Kenya, Malawi, Tanzania and Zimbabwe) This area produces good quality teas which are bright and colourful and used extensively for blending purposes. Kenya produces bright and colourful teas which are easily discernible and have a reddish or coppery tint, and a brisk flavour.

India The largest producer of tea representing about 30% of the world's tea. Best known are teas from Assam, strong and full bodied, Darjeeling, delicate and mellow tea and also Nilgiri which is second only to Assam and produces teas similar to those of Sri Lanka.

Indonesia Teas produced here are light and fragrant with bright colouring when made and are used mainly for blending purposes.

Sri Lanka (formerly Ceylon) Teas here are inclined to have a delicate, light lemon flavour. They are generally regarded as excellent afternoon teas and also lend themselves to being iced.

Purchasing tea

Tea may be purchased in a variety of forms, a caterer's exact requirements being determined by a number of factors such as type of establishment and clientele, the occasion, method of service, storage facilities available and cost.

The different means of purchasing are:

1 *Bulk* (leaf) allowing the traditional method of serving
2 *Tea bags* which are heated sealed and contain either standard or speciality teas. These tea bags come in one cup, two cup, pot for one or bulk brew form. The bulk brew may be 2–4–8 pint
3 *String and tag*: this comes as a one cup bag with string attached and a tag that remains outside the cup or teapot for easy and quick identification of the tea by the customer
4 *Envelopes*: this is again a string and tag but in an envelope for hygienic handling. It is regarded as ideal for trays in a room service operation
5 *Instant*: instant tea granules

The leaf particle size is referred to as grades. These are Pekoe (pecko) – delicate top leaves, Orange Pekoe – rolled leaf with a slim appearance and Pekoe Dust – smallest particle of leaf size. In between these grades there are a set of grades known as fannings. In tea terminology, 'flush' refers to a picking which can take place at different times of the year.

The blend

The word *blend* indicates that a named tea on the market for sale to the public may be composed of a variety of different teas to produce one marketable tea acceptable to the average consumer palate.

For instance, what is sometimes termed a *standard* tea may contain somewhere in the region of 15 different teas, some of which would almost certainly be Indian tea for strength, African tea for colour and China tea for flavour and delicacy.

Most teas used are blended teas sold under proprietary brands or names. All teas are fermented (oxidized) during the process of manufacture which gives them their black colour. The one exception is China tea which is classed as a green tea.

Storage

Tea should be kept:

- in a dry, clean and covered container
- in a well ventilated area
- away from excess moisture
- must not be kept near any strong smelling foods as tea very quickly absorbs strong odours

Making of tea

The type of tea used will of course depend on the customer's choice and cost, but most establishments carry a varied stock of Indian, Ceylon, China and speciality tea together with a variety of tisanes available upon request.

The quantities of dry tea used per pot or per gallon may vary slightly with the type of tea used, but as an approximate guide the following may be used:

- 42.5–56.7 grams (1½–2 oz) dry tea per 4.546 litres (1 gallon)
- ½ litre (1 pt) of milk will be sufficient for 20–24 cups
- ½ kilogram (1 lb) sugar for approximately 80 cups

When brewing smaller amounts in the stillroom, such as a pot for one or two, it is often advisable to install a measure. This then ensures standardization of brew and control on the commodity in use. Other means of pre-portioning tea may be used, such as tea bags. When making tea in bulk and calculating quantities of tea required for a party, allow approximately ⅙ litre (⅓ pint) per cup or 24 cups per 4.546 litres (1 gallon). If breakfast cups are used, capacity approximately ¼ litre (½ pint), then allow only 16 cups to 4.546 litres (1 gallon).

Because tea is an infusion and therefore the maximum flavour is required from the brew, a few simple rules carefully observed will obtain satisfactory results. These are:

- Heat the pot before putting in the dry tea so that the maximum heat can be obtained from the boiling water
- Measure the dry tea and freshly drawn cold water exactly
- Use freshly boiled water
- Make sure the water is boiling on entering the pot
- Allow it to brew 3–4 minutes to obtain maximum strength from the brew
- Remove the tea leaves at the end of this period if making in multi-pot insulated urns
- Ensure all the equipment used is scrupulously clean

Indian or Ceylon Blend

Indian or Ceylon Blend tea may be made in either china or metal teapots. Usually both are offered with milk. Sugar would be offered separately.

China

This is made from a special blend of tea which is more delicate in flavour and perfume than any other tea, but lacks body. Less dry tea is required than for making Indian or Ceylon tea.

It is made in the normal way and is best made in a china pot. China tea is normally drunk on its own, but may be improved, according to taste, by the addition of a slice of lemon. Slices of lemon would be offered on a sideplate with a sweet fork. China tea is rarely served with milk. Sugar may be offered.

Russian or lemon tea

This may be brewed from a special blend similar to China tea, but more often than not is made from either Indian or Ceylon tea. It is made in the normal way and is usually served with a slice of lemon. The tea is served in quarter litre (half pint) glasses, which stand in a silver holder with a handle, and on a sideplate with a teaspoon. A slice of lemon may be placed in the glass and a few slices of lemon served separately on a doily on a sideplate with a sweet fork. Sugar would be served separately.

Iced tea

Make strong tea and chill well. This iced tea may then be strained and stored chilled until required. It should be served in a tumbler, on a doily, on a sideplate, and with a teaspoon. A slice of lemon may be placed in the glass and some lemon should be served separately as for Russian tea.

Multi-pot

There are many occasions when tea has to be produced in bulk. Such occasions might be a reception tea, tea-breaks in an industrial catering concern, or functions catering for large numbers. In these instances tea may be made in multi-pots/urns which may be described as teapots or urns, varying in capacity from 4.546 to 23 litres (1 to 5 gallons). These containers have infusers which hold the required quantity of tea-leaves for the size of pot/urn being used. The infuser would be placed in the pot/urn and freshly boiled water added. The mix would then be allowed to brew for a number of minutes – a maximum of 10 minutes for a 5 gallon urn – and the infuser removed to ensure a good quality product would be served. The quantity of tea made should always relate to the number to be served – this will ensure minimum delay in the service and minimum wastage.

Speciality teas

There are a variety of special tea blends, some examples of which are listed below:

Assam a rich full and malty flavoured tea, suitable for service at breakfast, usually with milk.

Darjeeling a delicate tea with a light grape flavour and known as the 'Champagne of Teas'. Usually served as an afternoon or evening tea with either lemon or a little milk if preferred.

Earl Grey a blend of Darjeeling and China tea, flavoured with oil of Bergamot. Usually served with lemon or milk.

Jasmine a green (unoxidized) tea which is dried with Jasmine Blossom and produces a tea with a fragrant and scented flavour.

Kenya a consistent and refreshing tea usually served with milk.

Lapsang Souchong a smoky, pungent and perfumed tea, delicate to the palate which may be said to be an acquired taste. Usually served with lemon.

Sri Lanka makes a pale golden tea with a good flavour. Ceylon Blend is still used as a trade name. Served with lemon or milk.

Tisanes

These are fruit flavoured teas and herbal infusions which are often used for medicinal purposes and are gaining in popularity with trends towards more healthy eating and drinking. Often these do not contain caffeine. Examples are:

Herbal Teas	*Fruit Teas*
● Camomile	● Cherry
● Peppermint	● Lemon
● Rosehip	● Blackcurrant
● Mint	● Mandarin Orange

These teas are usually made in china pots, or can be made by the cup or glass, and served sometimes with sugar.

4.2 Coffee

History

There is evidence to suggest that coffee trees were cultivated about 1000 years ago in the Yemen. The first commercial cultivation of coffee is thought to have been in the Yemen district of Arabia in the fifteenth century. By the middle of the sixteenth century coffee drinking had spread to Aden, Egypt, Syria and Turkey. The first coffee house in England was opened in Oxford in 1650. Coffee spread from Britain to America, but it was not until 1773 and the resultant Boston Tea Party that the American palate changed from drinking tea as a beverage to coffee.

What is coffee?

Coffee is a natural product grown in many countries of the tropical and sub-tropical belt in South and Central America, Africa and Asia. It is grown at different altitudes in different basic climates and in different soils and is looked upon as an international drink consumed throughout the world. Brazil is the world's largest grower of coffee, Columbia is second, the Ivory Coast third and Indonesia fourth.

The trees which produce coffee are the genus *Coffea* which belongs to the *Rubiaceae* family. There are somewhere in the region of 50 different species, although only two of these are commercially significant. These are known as *Coffea arabica* and *Coffea camephora* which is usually referred to as *robusta*. Arabica accounts for some 75% of world production.

The coffee tree is an evergreen shrub which reaches a height of two to three metres when cultivated. The fruit of the coffee tree is known as the 'cherry' and these are about 1.5 cm in length and have an oblong shape. The cherry usually contains two coffee seeds. The coffee tree will not begin to produce fruit until it is 3–5 years old and it will then usually yield good crops for up to 15 years.

The blend

Companies who sell coffee have their own blending experts whose task it is to ensure that the quality and taste of their particular coffee brand is consistent, despite the fact that the imported beans will vary from shipment to shipment.

Samples of green coffee beans are taken from bags in the producing countries and the port of arrival and sent to prospective buyers whose experts roast, brew and taste samples to test their quality before deciding on the type of blend for which the particular coffee is suitable.

Most brands of coffee sold in shops are, in fact, a blend of two or more batches of beans. Because they have no smell or taste, green beans have to be roasted in order to release the coffee aroma and flavour. The correct roasting should give a uniform colour. The output of different roastings are used to form different blends.

The common degrees of roasting are:

Light or pale roastings suitable for mild beans to preserve their delicate aroma

Medium roastings give a stronger flavour and are often favoured for coffees with well defined character

Full roastings: popular in many Latin countries and have a bitterish flavour

High roasted coffee accentuates the strong bitter aspects of coffee, although much of the original flavour is lost

Commercial coffee roasters can either convert the beans into instant (soluble) coffee or prepare them for sale as roasted or ground beans. The higher the roast, the less acidity and the more bitterness there is in the coffee.

The grind

Roasted coffee must be ground before it can be used to make the brew. Coffee is ground to different grades of fineness which suit the many different methods of brewing. The most suitable grinds for some common methods of brewing coffee are:

Method	Grinding grade
Filter/Drip	Fine to medium
Jug	Coarse
Turkish	Pulverized
Cafetière	Medium
Vacuum infusion	Medium fine to fine
Espresso	Very fine
Percolator	Medium

Storage

When storing coffee:

- Store in a well ventilated storeroom

- Use an air-tight container for ground coffee to ensure that the oils do not evaporate, causing loss of flavour and strength

- Keep it away from excess moisture

- It must not be stored near any strong smelling foods, as coffee will absorb their odour.

Making coffee

Methods of brewing can vary, ranging from instant coffee brewed by the cup, through $1\frac{1}{2}$–3 litre (3–6 pints) units and up to machines that may cope with large functions. Coffee beans may be purchased and then ground according to requirements. The beans should not be ground until immediately before they are required as this will ensure the maximum flavour and strength from the oils within the coffee bean. If ground coffee is purchased it normally comes in vacuum packed packets in order to maintain it until use. These packets contain set quantities to make 4.5 litres (1 gallon) and 9 litres (2 gallons) and so on.

When making coffee in bulk 283.5–340 g (10–12 oz) of ground coffee is sufficient to make 4.5 litres (1 gallon) of black coffee. Assuming that cups with a capacity of $\frac{1}{3}$ pint will be used then 283.5–340 g (10–12 oz) of ground coffee is sufficient to provide 24 cups of black coffee or 48 cups if serving half coffee and half milk. When breakfast cups are used then 16 cups of black coffee or 32 cups of half coffee and half milk will be available. Capacity, at a dinner where demi-tasse, $\frac{1}{13}$ litre ($\frac{1}{6}$ pint), are used, is 48 cups of black coffee or 96 cups half black coffee and half milk.

The rules to be observed when making coffee are as follows:

- Use freshly roasted and ground coffee

- Buy the correct grind for the type of machine in use

- Ensure all equipment is clean before use

- Use a set measure of coffee to water: 283.5–340 g per 4.5 litres (10–12 oz per gallon)

- Add boiling water to the coffee and allow to infuse
- The infusion time must be controlled according to the type of coffee being used and the method of making
- Control the temperature since to boil coffee is to spoil coffee: the coffee develops a bitter taste
- Strain and serve
- Add milk or cream separately
- The best serving temperatures are 82°C (180°F) for coffee and 68°C (155°F) for milk

Characteristics of good coffee

- Good flavour
- Good aroma
- Good colour with milk or cream – not grey
- Good body

Reasons why bad coffee is produced:

Weak Coffee

- Water has not reached boiling point
- Insufficient coffee
- Infusion time too short
- Stale or old coffee used
- Incorrect grind of coffee used for equipment in operation

Flat Coffee

- All points for weak coffee
- Coffee left in urn too long before use, or kept at wrong temperature
- Dirty urn or equipment
- Water not fresh, or boiled too long
- Coffee reheated

Bitter Coffee

- Too much coffee used
- Infusion time too long
- Coffee not roasted correctly
- Sediment remaining in storage or serving compartment
- Infusion at too high a temperature
- Coffee may have been left in urn too long before use

Figure 4.1 Brewing methods

Jug

Vacuum or glass balloon coffee maker

Plunger pot/Cafetière

Automatic filter

Filter (drip) method

Turkish/Greek/Arabic coffee

Espresso and cappuccino

Coffee may be made in many ways and the service depends on the method used. Figure 4.1 shows ways in which coffee may be made and served.

Instant

This may be made in individual coffee or teacups or in large quantities. It involves the mixing of soluble coffee solids with boiling water. When making instant coffee in bulk, approximately 71 g (2½ oz) to each gallon of water should be allowed. This form of coffee may be made very quickly, immediately before it is required, by pouring freshly boiled water onto a measured quantity of coffee powder. Stir well. Hot or cold milk, cream and sugar may be added to taste.

Saucepan or jug method

This is an American method of making coffee more often used in the home than in a catering establishment. A set measure of ground coffee is placed in a saucepan or jug and the required quantity of freshly boiled water is poured onto the coffee grounds. This should then be allowed to stand for a few minutes to extract the full flavour and strength from the ground coffee. It is then strained and served. Hot or cold milk, cream and sugar may be added as desired.

Cafetière (coffee or tea maker)

La cafetière makes coffee simply and quickly by the infusion method and to order. This in turn ensures that the flavour and aroma of the coffee are preserved. *La cafetière* comes in the form of a glass container with a lip held in a gold or chrome finished holder and sealed with a lid which also holds the plunger unit in position.

The method of making is completed simply by adding boiling water to the ground coffee, stirring and then placing the plunger unit and lid in position. It has a visual attraction and involves the client in completing the process by ensuring the plunger unit is pushed to the base of the glass container before serving.

A guideline to the quantity of coffee to be used might be:

2 level dessertspoonfuls for the 3 cup size
6 level dessertspoonfuls for the 8 cup size
9 level dessertspoonfuls for the 12 cup size

Infusion time is from 3 to 5 minutes.

Percolator method

This method is again used more in the home than commercially. A set quantity of coffee grounds are placed in the percolator, which is then filled with freshly drawn water. The water, upon reaching boiling point, rises up through a tube and percolates the coffee grounds, extracting the full flavour, colour and strength. Hot or cold milk, cream and sugar may be added to taste.

The length of infusion time is determined by the strength of coffee required, which in turn is controlled by thermostat. When this infusion time has been completed the coffee liquid no longer continues to infuse with the coffee grounds but is held in the main body of the percolator at the correct serving temperature of 82°C (180°F).

Vacuum infusion ('cona')

This method of making coffee has considerable visual appeal in the restaurant, and has the advantage that the coffee served is always fresh as only limited quantities are made at one time. It also avoids making too much coffee and therefore prevents wasting or serving old, flat, bitter coffee during another food service period.

Banks of these machines may be used for varying requirements, housing two, three, four or five containers at one time. They are compact and portable and very easy to keep clean. The method of making the coffee is fairly simple in itself but is best supervised to ensure the best results and a constant standard.

The filters in this vacuum-type equipment are sometimes glass, but more often than not are made of plastic or metal. The bowls are either glass or metal.

The method of making coffee is similar to the percolator method. The lower bowl is filled with cold water or, to speed up the operation, freshly heated but not boiled water, up to the water level. The filter is placed in the upper bowl, ensuring it is securely fixed, and the required quantity of ground coffee is added according to the amount of water being used. The upper bowl is then set in the lower bowl, making sure it is securely in place, and the water is heated.

As the water reaches boiling point, it rises up the tube into the upper bowl, mixing with the ground coffee. As it rises in the upper bowl, it is often best to stir the mixture gently to ensure that all coffee grounds infuse with the liquid, as sometimes the grounds are inclined to form a cap on top of the liquid and therefore do not fully infuse. At the same time, care must be taken that the filter is not knocked as this may cause grains to pass into the lower bowl.

On reducing the heat, the coffee liquid passes back into the lower bowl leaving the grounds in the upper bowl. The upper bowl and filter are then removed and washed ready for re-use. The coffee in the lower bowl is ready for use and should be served at a temperature of approximately 82°C (180°F). The coffee may be served with hot or cold milk or cream, with sugar to taste.

Filter (café filtre)

This is a method originating from and traditionally used in France. The filter method produces excellent coffee. Fresh boiled water is poured into a container with a very finely meshed bottom which stands on a cup/pot. Within the container is the required amount of ground coffee. The infusion takes place and the coffee liquid falls into the cup/pot. Filter papers may be used to avoid the grounds passing into the lower cup, but this will depend on how fine or coarse is the ground coffee being used.

By this method, coffee may be made individually by the cup or in bulk for a party of up to six guests. Before starting to make coffee by this method, ensure that all equipment is hot. Otherwise the resulting coffee cools very rapidly.

'Pour through' filter method

This is an excellent method of making *filter* coffee which has increased in popularity in Britain over the past few years. Many of these 'pour through' filter machines are available for purchase, or on loan from a number of the main coffee suppliers.

It is seen as a very good method of coffee making for the *bar top/back bar* in a public house, where coffee may be served in conjunction with hot or cold snacks or where it may be offered at the end of a meal. When coffee is made by this method, ensure that:

- The machine is plugged in and switched on at the mains
- The 'brew' indicator light is on. This tells the operator that the water already held in the machine is at the correct temperature for use
- The correct quantity of fresh ground coffee, which will usually come in the form of a vacuum sealed pack, is used. A fresh pack should be used for each new brew of filter coffee being made
- A new clean filter paper is used for each fresh brew

The logic behind this method is that the measured quantity of freshly drawn water poured into the top of the 'pour through' filter machine displaces the hot water already in the machine. This hot water infuses with the ground coffee and runs into the serving container as a coffee liquid ready for immediate use. It takes approximately 3–4 minutes to make one brew.

An alternative to the 'pour through' which serves a similar purpose when one is unsure of the quantity required is the automatic 'Melitta'. It makes 2–8 cups of coffee in about 5 minutes and may be set up on either the bar top or any small space available. This is a fully automatic coffee machine.

Individual filter

This is an alternative in the making of filter coffee. It is a plastic, disposable, individual filter, bought with the required amount of coffee already sealed in the base of the filter. Each individual filter is sufficient for one cup and after use the whole filter is thrown away. The advantage of this method is that every cup may be made to order. It also appeals to the customers as they see that they are receiving entirely fresh coffee as well as it having a certain novelty value.

When making a cup of coffee by this method, freshly boiled water should be poured into the filter cup to the required level. The liquid then falls into the cup. A lid should be placed over the water in the filter to help retain the temperature. Time of making is approximately 3–4 minutes.

Espresso

This method, Italian in origin, came to Britain in the 1950s. The machines used in making this form of coffee can provide cups of coffee individually in a matter of seconds, some machines being capable of making 300–400 cups of coffee per hour. With this type of machine, the coffee used must be finely ground.

The method involves passing steam through the finely ground coffee and infusing under pressure. The advantage is that each cup is made freshly for the customer. Served black, the coffee is known as *Espresso* and is served in a small glass cup. If milk is required, it is heated for each cup by a high pressure steam injector and transforms a cup of black coffee into *Cappuccino*. As an approximate guide, from $\frac{1}{2}$ kg (1 lb) of coffee used, 80 cups of good strength coffee may be produced. The general rules for making coffee apply here but, with this special and delicate type of equipment, extra care should be taken in following any instructions.

Still-set

This method normally consists of a small central container into which the correct sized filter paper is placed. A second, fine-meshed metal filter with a handle is then placed on the filter paper and the ground coffee placed on top of this. There is an urn on either side of varying capacities according to requirements. The urns may be $4\frac{1}{2}$, 9, 13 or 18 litres (1, 2, 3, 4 gallons) in size.

These still-sets are easy to operate, but must be kept very clean at all times and regularly serviced. The urns should be rinsed before and after each brew until the water runs clear. This removes the thin layer of cold coffee which clings to the side of the urn that, if left, will spoil the flavour and aroma of the next brew.

Boiling water is passed through the grounds and the coffee passes into the urns at the side. Infusion should be complete in 6–8 minutes for $4\frac{1}{2}$ litres (1 gallon) of coffee, using medium ground coffee. The *milk* is heated in a steam jacket container. It should be held at a constant temperature of 68°C because if held at too high a temperature or boiled or heated too soon, on coming into contact with the coffee it will destroy its flavour and taste. At the same time, the milk itself becomes discoloured. The coffee and milk should be held separately, at their correct temperatures ready for serving.

Decaffeinated

Coffee contains caffeine which is a stimulant. Decaffeinated coffee is made from beans after the caffeine has been extracted. The coffee is made in the normal way.

Iced

Strong black coffee should be made in the normal way. It is then strained and chilled well until required. It may be served mixed with an equal quantity of cold milk for a smooth beverage, or with cream. It is served in a tall glass, with ice cubes added and with straws. The glass should stand on a doily on a sideplate with a teaspoon and, where necessary, some cream served separately.

Turkish or Egyptian

This is made from darkly roasted Mocha beans which are ground to a fine powder. The coffee is made in special copper pots which are placed on top of a stove or lamp and the water is then allowed to boil. The sugar should be put in at this stage to sweeten the coffee as it is never stirred once poured out. The finely ground coffee may be stirred in or the boiling water poured onto the grounds. The amount of coffee used is approximately one heaped teaspoonful per person. Once the coffee has been stirred in, the copper pot is taken off the direct heat and the cooling causes the grounds to settle. It is brought to the boil and allowed to settle twice more and is then sprinkled with a little cold water to settle any remaining grains. The coffee is served in small cups. While making the coffee, it may be further flavoured with vanilla pods but this is optional.

Irish and speciality coffees

An 18.93 cl (6⅔ fl oz) Paris goblet should be heated and sugar added as required by the guest. (A certain amount of sugar is always required when serving this form of coffee as it is an aid to floating the double cream on the surface of the hot coffee; the waiter must ensure the guest realizes this.) A teaspoon is then placed in the goblet to conduct the heat and avoid cracking the goblet as the piping hot, strong black coffee is poured in. The coffee should be stirred well to dissolve the sugar and then one measure of Irish whiskey added. At this stage, it is important to ensure that everything is thoroughly blended. The liquid should now be within 2½ cm (1 in) of the top of the goblet. Double cream should then be poured slowly over the back of a teaspoon onto the surface of the coffee until it is approximately 1.9 cm (¾ in) thick. The coffee must not be stirred: the best flavour is obtained by drinking the whiskey-flavoured coffee through the cream.

This method of making coffee may be carried out at the table and has visual appeal. As the fat content of cream is much higher than that of milk, less may be used and it should not be heated.

When the Irish coffee has been prepared, the goblet should be put on a doily on a sideplate and placed in front of the guest. If brandy is used instead of whiskey, the coffee is known as *Café Royale*.

Figure 4.2 Tray laid for service of Irish coffee

Irish coffee is normally served by the waiter at the table. The following equipment is required:

- Silver salver
- Serviette
- 18.93 cl (6⅔ fl oz) Paris goblet on an underplate
- Teaspoon
- Jug of double cream
- 6 out measure
- Coffee pot
- Sugar basin of coffee sugar with a teaspoon
- Bottle of Irish whiskey

Order of ingredients in the glass

1 Sugar
2 Black coffee

3 Spirit or liqueur
4 Double cream

Other forms of speciality connoisseur coffees

Monk's Coffee:	Benedictine	*Calypso Coffee:*	Tia-Maria
Russian Coffee:	Vodka	*Highland Coffee:*	Scotch Whisky
Jamaican Coffee:	Rum	*Seville Coffee:*	Cointreau

Different catering outlets may put a different name to a speciality coffee containing the same liqueur or spirit. For example:

Café Royale:	Brandy	*Caribbean:*	Rum
Café Parisienne:	Brandy	*Jamaican:*	Rum

4.3 Other stillroom beverages

Other beverages may also be offered from the stillroom such as cocoa, drinking chocolate, 'Horlicks', 'Ovaltine' and 'Bovril', and these should be readily available. They should be prepared and served according to the maker's instructions.

If milk shakes are requested, then the following basic ingredients are required:

● Chilled milk

● Syrups (flavouring)

● Ice-cream

These would normally be served with a straw in a tall glass after making in a mixer or blender.

4.4 Non-alcoholic dispense bar beverages

Non-alcoholic dispense bar beverages may be classified into five main groups:

1 Aerated waters
2 Natural spring waters or mineral waters

3 Squashes
4 Juices
5 Syrups

Aerated waters

These beverages are charged or aerated with carbonic gas. Artificial aerated waters are by far the most common. The flavourings found in different aerated waters are imparted from various essences.

Some examples of these aerated waters are as follows:

- *Soda water*: colourless and tasteless
- *Tonic water*: colourless and quinine flavoured
- *Dry ginger*: golden straw coloured with a ginger flavour
- *Bitter lemon*: pale cloudy coloured with a sharp lemon flavour

Other flavoured waters which come under this heading are:

- 'Fizzy' lemonades
- Orange
- Ginger beer
- Coca-cola, etc.

Natural spring waters/mineral waters

The EU has divided bottled water into two main types: mineral water and spring water. *Mineral water* has a mineral content (which is strictly controlled), while *spring water* has fewer regulations, apart from those concerning hygiene. Water can be still, naturally sparkling or carbonated during bottling.

Bottle sizes for mineral and spring waters vary considerably from 1.5 litres to 200 millilitres. Some brand names sell in both plastic and glass bottles, whilst other brands prefer either plastic or glass bottles depending on market and the size of container preferred by that market.

Figure 4.3 Different varieties of mineral water

NAME	TYPE	COUNTRY
APPOLLINARIS	Naturally sparkling	Germany
CONTREX	Still	France
PERRIER	Naturally sparkling or in fruit flavours	France
ROYAL FARRIS	Naturally sparkling	Norway
SAN PELLEGRINO	Carbonated	Italy
SPA	Still, naturally sparkling or in fruit flavours	Belgium
SPA MONOPOLE	Still or sparkling	Belgium
VICHY CELESTINES	Naturally sparkling	France
VITTEL	Naturally sparkling	France
VOLVIC	Still	France

Figure 4.4 Different varieties of spring water

NAME	TYPE	COUNTRY
ASHBOURE	Still or sparkling	England
BADOIT	Slightly sparkling	France
BUXTON	Still or carbonated	England
EVIAN	Still	France
HIGHLAND SPRING	Still or carbonated	Scotland
MALVERN	Still or carbonated	England

Natural spring waters are obtained from natural springs in the ground, the waters themselves being impregnated with the natural minerals found in the soil and sometimes naturally charged with an aerating gas. The value of these *mineral waters*, as they are sometimes termed, has long been recognized by the medical profession.

Where natural spring waters are found, there is usually what is termed a *Spa*, where the waters may be drunk or bathed in according to the cures they are supposed to effect. Many of the best known mineral waters are bottled at the springs.

The mineral waters are usually classified according to their chemical properties which are as follows.

Alkaline waters

These are the most numerous of all the mineral waters. It is said they help treatment of gout and rheumatism. Some examples are:

Perrier   Saint-Galmier
Malvern   Aix-les-bains
Vichy   Aix-la-chapelle
Evian   Selters

Aperient waters

So named because of their saline constituents, these being in the main sulphate of magnesia or sulphate of soda. Some examples are:

Cheltenham
Montmirail
Leamington-Spa
Seidlitz

Chalybeate waters

These mineral waters are of two kinds, being either carbonated or sulphated. It is recognized that they act as a stimulant and a tonic. Some examples are:

Forges
Passy
Saint Nectaire
Vittel

Lithiated waters

These are rich in Lithia salts. Some examples are:

Baden-Baden
Carlsbad
Saint Marco
Salvator

Sulphurous waters

These waters are impregnated with hydrogen. Some examples are:

St. Boes
Harrogate
Challes

Table waters

These waters are recognized to be much less highly mineralized than other natural spring waters, and are mainly alkaline. They may be taken between meals or at meal time, either alone or mixed with light wine or spirits.

Squashes

Squashes may be served on their own, mixed with spirits or cocktails, or used as the base for such drinks as fruit cups. They are indispensable in the bar and an adequate stock should always be held. Examples are:

- orange
- lemon
- grapefruit } squash
- lime juice

Juices

The main types of juices held in stock in the dispense bar are:

Bottled or canned

- orange juice
- pineapple juice
- grapefruit juice
- tomato juice

These are normally purchased in small bottles termed 'babies' which contain 11.36 centilitres (4 fl oz). They may also be obtained canned.

Fresh

- orange juice
- grapefruit juice
- lemon juice

It is often necessary to keep a small stock of these juices, made from fresh fruits. They would be used for cocktails and for mixing with spirits.

Syrups

The main use of these concentrated, sweet, fruit flavourings is as a base for cocktails, fruit cups or mixed with soda water as a long drink. The main ones used are:

- *grenadine* (pomegranate)
- *cassis* (blackcurrant)
- *citronelle* (lemon)
- *gomme* (white sugar syrup)
- *framboise* (raspberry)
- *cerise* (cherry)
- *orgeat* (almond)

Syrups are also available as 'flavouring agents' for cold milk drinks such as milk shakes.

Information concerning the service of non-alcoholic bar beverages may be found in Section 5.9, page 222.

4.5 Wine and drinks lists

Function of the wine list

The function of the wine list is similar to that of the menu and is a selling aid. Careful thought is needed in its planning, design, layout, colour and overall appearance to ensure it complements the establishment's style and profitability.

The *sommelier* should have a good knowledge of all the wines available and of their main characteristics. He/she should also have an extensive knowledge of which wines are most suitable to offer with certain foods (see Section 4.10).

The contents are commonly listed in the order in which they may be consumed, namely:

- Apéritifs – which alongside sparkling and still wines (p. 125 and p. 126) can include a range of aromatized wines (p. 127), fortified wines (p. 127) and natural spring and mineral waters (p. 111).
- Cocktails (p . 118)

- Spirits (p. 138) and associated mixers (aerated waters p. 111)

- Wines – sparkling and still

- Beers (p. 142), cider (p. 145) minerals (p. 111) and squashes (p. 113)

- Digestifs – which as well as liqueurs (p. 141) can included brandies (p. 138), malt whiskies (p. 141), ports, other fortified wines, sweet table wines, and vin doux naturels (page 127).

- Speciality coffees and cigars can also be included in lists.

Nowadays many lists also include low calorie and low alcohol beverages.

Wines are usually listed area by area, with the white wines of one region first, followed by the red wines of that region. A more modern trend is to list all the white wines available area by area, followed by the red wines arranged in a similar way. This type of layout is often more useful to the customer. In all wine lists, sparkling wines, and therefore the champagnes, are normally listed before all other wines available.

Traditional approach for listing wines

- Champagne
- Sparkling
- White Bordeaux
- Red Bordeaux
- White Burgundy
- Red Burgundy
- Loire valley
- Rhône valley
- Alsace
- Other French regions
- Rhine wines
- Mosel wines
- Italian wines
- Spanish wines
- Portuguese wines
- English wines
- Other European wines
- Californian wines
- Australian wines
- South African wines
- House wines

Less Traditional approach for listing wines

- Red wines
- White wines
- Rosé wines
- Sparkling wines

General information required:

Wines
- Bin number
- Name of wine
- Quality indication, eg AOC, QMP etc

- Shipper
- Château/Estate bottled
- Descriptive comments as appropriate
- Vintage if applicable
- Price per ½ bottle/bottle/magnum/carafe (+volume)

Other drinks
- Brand name
- Style (eg sweet, dry, etc)
- Description, eg cocktails

Legal requirements
See Chapter 10, page 360.

Types of wine and drinks lists
Bar and cocktail lists

These may range from a basic standard list offering the common everyday apéritifs such as sherries, vermouths, bitters, and a selection of spirits with mixers, beers and soft drinks together with a limited range of cocktails to a very comprehensive list offering a good choice in all areas. The actual format and content would be determined by the style of operation and clientele you wish to attract.

Dependent on this, the emphasis may be in certain areas such as:

- Cocktails: traditional or fashionable
- Malt whiskies
- Beers
- New World wines
- Non-alcoholic drinks

Cocktail lists may be found in Annex C on page 419.

Restaurant wine lists

These may take the following format:

1 A full and very comprehensive list of wines from all countries, with emphasis on the classic areas such as Bordeaux/Burgundy plus a fine wine/prestige selection
2 A middle of the road, traditional selection, eg some French, German, Italian, together with some New World wines
3 A small selection of well-known or branded wines – a prestige list
4 Predominantly wines of one specific country

After meal drinks lists (digestifs)

1 These are often combined with the wine list – although occasionally presented as a separate liqueur list
2 The list should offer a full range of liqueurs, together with possibly a specialist range of brandies and/or a specialist range of malt whiskies. Vintage and LBV port may also be offered here
3 A range of speciality liqueur/spirit coffees might also be included (see Section 4.2)

Banqueting wine lists

1 The length will generally depend on the size and style of operation
2 In most instances there is a selection of popular wine names/styles on offer
3 There would be a range of prices from house wines to some fine wines to suit all customer preferences
4 In some instances the banqueting wine list is the same as the restaurant wine list

For further information see Chapter 9.

Room service drinks lists

1 There may be a mini-bar or choice from a standard bar list
2 A limited range of wines is often offered
3 The price range varies according to establishment
4 Special orders are required for champagne, etc

Alcoholic strength
Three scales of measurement

The main scale of measurement of alcoholic strength may be summarized as:

- OIML Scale (European): range 0% to 100%
- Sikes Scale (United Kingdom old scale): range 0° to 175°. 'Proof' was the point 100°, 70° is equal to 40% alcohol by volume
- American Scale (USA): range 0° to 200°. Similar to Sikes but has scale of 200° rather than 175°

The OIML Scale

Previously called Gay Lussac Scale, the *Organisation Internationale Métrologie Légale (OIML) Scale* is directly equal to the percentage of alcohol by volume in the drink at 20°C. It is the universally accepted scale for the measurement of alcohol.

The by volume measurement indicates the amount of pure alcohol in a liquid. Thus a liquid measured as 40% alcohol by volume will have 40% of the contents as pure alcohol. The alcoholic content of drinks, by volume, is now almost always shown on the label.

Approximate alcoholic strengths of drinks are:

not more that 0.05%	alcohol free
not more than 0.5%	de-alcoholized
up to 1.2%	low alcohol
3 – 6%	beer, cider and 'alcopops'* with any of these being up to 10%
8 – 15%	wines, usually around 10 – 13%
14 – 22%	fortified wines (liqueur wines) such as sherry and port, aromatized wines such as vermouth, vin doux naturels such as Muscat de Beaumes-de-Venise and Sake**
37.5 – 45%	spirits, usually at 40%
17 – 55%	liqueurs, very wide range

* 'alcopops' is a term used to describe manufactured flavoured drinks (generally sweet and fruity) which have had alcohol, such as gin, added to them. They are also known as alcoholic soft drinks or alcoholic lemonade. Usually 3.5 to 5% but can be up to 10%.

** Sake is a strong (18%), slightly sweet, form of beer made from rice .

4.6 Cocktails

History

The origin of the cocktail is claimed by England, Mexico, America and France. There are many stories but no one knows the authenticity of any. However, it was in the United States that cocktails first gained major popularity.

At this stage, the cocktail was as much a pre-mixed stimulant mixture for taking on sporting occasions as it was a bar drink. Universal interest in cocktails came in the 1920s when prohibition in the USA changed everyone's drinking habits. The term cocktail is now recognized to mean all mixed drinks. A cocktail is normally a short drink of $3\frac{1}{2}$–4 fluid ounces – anything larger being called a 'mixed drink' or 'long drink'.

Types of cocktails

Included under the heading 'cocktails' come those drinks known as:

Blended drinks: Using a liquidizer

Champagne Cocktails: Such as 'Bucks Fizz' which has the addition of orange juice

Cobblers: Wine and spirit based, served with straws and decorated with fruit

Collins: Hot weather drinks, spirit based, served with plenty of ice

Coolers: Almost identical to the Collins but usually containing the peel of the fruit cut into a spiral; spirit or wine based

Crustas: May be made with any spirit, the most popular being brandy; edge of glass decorated with powdered sugar; crushed ice placed in glass

Cups: Hot weather, wine based drinks

Daisies: Made with any spirit; usually served in tankards or wine glasses filled with crushed ice

Egg Noggs: Traditional Christmas drink; rum or brandy and milk based; served in tumblers

Fixes: Short drink made by pouring any spirit over crushed ice; decorated with fruit and served with short straws

Fizzes: Similar to a Collins; always shaken and then topped with soda; must be drunk immediately

Flips: Similar to Egg Noggs, containing egg yolk but never milk; spirit, wine or sherry based

Frappés: Served on crushed ice

Highball: 'American', simple drink that is quickly prepared; spirit with 'mixer'

Juleps: 'American', containing mint with claret, madeira or bourbon whisky base

Pick-Me-Ups: To aid digestion

Pousse-Café: Specific densities; layered

Smashes: Smaller version of a Julep

Sours: Always made with fresh juices to sharpen the flavour of the drink

Swizzles: Take their name from the stick used to stir the drink; 'Swizzling' creates a frost on outside of glass

Toddies: Refreshers that may be served hot or cold; contain lemon, cinnamon, nutmeg

Making cocktails

A true cocktail is made by one of two methods: *shaking* or *stirring*. Such a beverage ordered by a customer has two or more ingredients in its make up. The art of making a good cocktail is to blend all the ingredients together by shaking or stirring so that upon tasting no one ingredient is predominant.

A rule of thumb to determine whether a cocktail should be shaken or stirred is that if it contains a fruit juice as one of the ingredients then it should be shaken, whilst if the ingredients are wine based and clear then it should be stirred.

The key equipment required when making a cocktail depends on the method being used:

Shaken
Cocktail shaker or Boston shaker with Hawthorn strainer
Blender (for mixes)

Stirred
Bar mixing glass
Bar spoon with muddler
Hawthorn strainer

Points to note

- Ice should always be clear and clean
- Do not overfill the cocktail shaker
- Effervescent type drinks should never be shaken
- To avoid spillage, do not fill glasses to brim
- When egg white or yolk is an ingredient, first break the egg into separate containers
- Serve cocktails in chilled glasses
- To shake, use short and snappy actions
- Always place ice in the shaker or mixing glass first, followed by non-alcoholic and then alcoholic beverages
- To stir, stir briskly until blend is cold
- As a general rule the mixing glass is used for those cocktails based on liqueurs or wines (clear liquids)
- The shakers are used for cocktails which might include fruit juices, cream, sugar and similar ingredients
- When egg white or yolk is an ingredient then the Boston shaker should always be used
- Always add the garnish after the cocktail has been made; add it to the glass
- Always measure out ingredients; inaccurate amounts spoil the balance of the blend and taste
- Never use the same ice twice

A comprehensive listing of cocktails is given in Annex C, page 419.

4.7 Bitters

Bitters are used either as apéritifs or for flavouring mixed drink and cocktails. The most popular varieties are:

Amer Picon:

A very black and bitter French apéritif. Grenadine or Cassis is often added to make the flavour more acceptable. Traditionalists add water in a proportion 2:1.

Angostura bitters:

Takes its name from a town in Bolivia. However, it is no longer produced there but in Trinidad. Brownish red in colour, it is used in the preparation of pink gin and the occasional cocktail and may be regarded as mainly a flavouring agent.

Byrrh:

(Pronounced beer.) This is a style of bitters made in France near the Spanish border. It has a base of red wine and is flavoured with quinine and herbs and fortified with brandy.

Campari:

A pink, bitter-sweet Italian aperitif that has a slight flavour of orange peel and quinine. Serve in an 18.93 cl (6⅔ fl oz) Paris goblet or Highball glass. Use one 6 *out* measure on ice and garnish with a slice of lemon. Top up according to the guest's requirements with soda or water (iced).

Fernet Branca:

The Italian version of Amer Picon. Best served diluted with water or soda. Good for hangovers!

Underberg:

A German bitter which looks like and almost tastes like iodine. It may be taken as a pick-me-up with soda.

Other bitters:

Orange and peach bitters are used principally as cocktail ingredients. Other well known bitters are Amora Montenegro, Radis, Unicum, Abbots, Peychaud, Boonekamp and Welling. Many are used to cure that 'morning after the night before' feeling. Cassis or Grenadine are sometimes added to make the drink more palatable.

4.8 Wine

Introduction

Wine is the alcoholic beverage obtained from the fermentation of the juice of freshly gathered grapes. The fermentation takes place in the district of origin, according to local tradition and practice.

Only a relatively small area of the world is 'wine producing'. This is because the grape will only provide juice of the quality necessary for conversion into a drinkable wine where two climatic conditions prevail:

- There must be enough sun to ripen the grape
- The winter must be moderate, yet sufficiently cool to give the vine a chance to rest and restore its strength for the growing and fruiting season

These climatic conditions prevail in two main wine producing zones which lie between latitudes 50° and 30° north and south of the equator.

Three quarters of the world's wine is produced in Europe and just under half in the EU. France and Italy produce the most wine, with Italy being the largest producer. Next in order comes the former Soviet republics, Argentina, Spain, USA and Germany.

Factors that influence the quality of wine

1 Climate and microclimate
2 Nature of the soil and subsoil
3 Vine family and grape species
4 Method of cultivation – viticulture
5 Chemical composition of the grape
6 Yeast and fermentation
7 Methods of wine making – vinification
8 Luck of the year
9 Ageing and maturing process
10 Method of shipping or transportation
11 Storage temperature

Pests and diseases

The vine is subject to pests and diseases in the form of birds, insects, fungi, viruses and weeds. Examples are:

Phylloxera vastatrix

A louse-like, almost invisible aphid which attacks the roots of the vine. *Phylloxera* arrived in Europe in the mid 1800s almost by accident, transported on American vines imported into various European countries from the eastern states of North America. It ravaged many of the vineyards of Europe at this time. The cure was to graft the European vine onto resistant American root stocks. This practice has become standard throughout the world wherever *Vitis vinifera* is grown.

Grey rot or *Pourriture gris (Botrytis cinerea)*

In warm damp weather, this fungus attacks the leaves and fruit of the vine. It is recognized by a grey mould. As a result of this fungus, an unpleasant flavour is imparted to the wine.

Noble rot or *Pourriture noble*

This is the same fungus in its beneficent form, which may occur when humid conditions are followed by hot weather. The fungus punctures the grape skin, the water content evaporates and the grape shrivels, thus concentrating the sugar inside. This process gives the luscious flavours characteristic of Sauternes, German Trockenbeerenauslese and Hungarian Tokay Aszu.

Vinification

The process central to vinification is fermentation – the conversion of sugar to alcohol. This process is necessary to the making of all alcoholic beverages – not only to still, sparkling and fortified wines, but also to spirits, liqueurs and beers (although some variations and further processes will be applied for individual beverages).

The grape

The grape itself may be broken into a number of elements:

- skin – tannins and colour
- stalk – tannins
- pips – bitter oils
- pulp – sugar, fruit acids, water, pectins

The colour in wine comes from the skin of the grape, being extracted during the fermentation process. Red wine can only be made from red grapes, but white wine can be made from white or red grapes, provided that, in the latter case, the grape skins are removed before fermentation begins.

The yeast required for the fermentation process is found on the outside of the grape skin in the form of a whitish bloom.

Vine species

The vine species grown that produces grapes suitable for wine production and that stocks the vineyards of the world is named *Vitis vinifera*. All varieties now planted in Europe have evolved from this species through cross-breeding, to suit local soils and climates.

The same vine variety, grown in different regions and processed in different ways, will produce wines of differing characteristics. A few examples are:

Black

Carbernet Sauvignon of Bordeaux, the Loire, California, Australia, Chile, Bulgaria and Spain

Pinot Noir of Northern Burgundy, Champagne, California, South America and Germany

Gamay from the Beaujolais wine producing region

Sangoivese of Chianti of Italy

Grenache of Châteauneuf-du-Pape in the Rhône, California and Spain

Note: the same vine variety in different regions can be, and often is, given a different name, eg *Grenache* of the Rhône as *Garnacha* producing fine Spanish wines.

White

Sémillon produces the fine sweet Sauternes

Sauvignon blanc of Pouilly sur Loire and Bordeaux, Chile, California and Australia

Chardonnay producing Champagne and fine white Burgundies, Californian, New Zealand and Australian wines

Riesling and Sylvaner of Germany and Alsace

Palomino used in the production of sherry

Faults in wine

Faults occasionally develop in wine as it matures in bottles. Nowadays, through improved techniques and attention to detail regarding bottling and storage, faulty wine is a rarity. Here are the more common causes.

Corked wines

These are wines affected by a diseased cork caused through bacterial action or excessive bottle age. The wine tastes and smells foul. This is not to be confused with cork residue in wine which is harmless.

Maderization or oxidation

This is caused by bad storage – too much exposure to air, often because the cork has dried out in these conditions. The colour of the wine browns or darkens and the taste very slightly resembles Madeira, hence the name. The wine tastes 'spoilt'.

Acetification

This is caused when the wine is overexposed to air. The vinegar microbe develops a film on the surface of the wine and acetic acid is produced making the wine taste sour, resembling wine vinegar (*vin vinaigre*).

Tartare flake

This is the crystallization of potassium bitartrate. These crystal-like flakes, sometimes seen in white wine, may cause anxiety to some customers as they spoil the appearance of the wine which is otherwise perfect to drink. If the wine is stabilized before bottling, this condition should not occur.

Excess sulphur dioxide (SO$_2$)

Sulphur dioxide is added to wine to preserve it and keep it healthy. Once the bottle is opened, the stink will disappear and, after a few minutes, the wine is perfectly drinkable.

Secondary fermentation

This happens when traces of sugar and yeast are left in the wine in bottle. It leaves the wine with an unpleasant, prickly taste that should not be confused with the petillant, spritzig characteristics associated with other styles of healthy and refreshing wines.

Foreign contamination

Examples include splintered or powdered glass caused by faulty bottling machinery or re-used bottles which previously held some kind of disinfectant.

Hydrogen sulphide (H$_2$S)

The wine smells and tastes of rotten eggs. Throw it away.

Sediment, lees, crust or dregs

This is organic matter discarded by the wine as it matures in cask or bottle. It can be removed by racking, fining or, in the case of bottled wine, by decanting.

Cloudiness

This is caused by suspended matter in the wine, disguising its true colour. It may be due to extremes in storage temperatures.

Classification of wine types

Still wine

This is the largest category. The alcoholic strength may be between 9% and 15%, by volume. The wines may be:

- *Red*: being fermented in contact with grape skins from which the wine gets its colour. Normally dry wines.

- *White*: usually produced from white grapes, but the grape juice (must) is usually fermented away from the skins. Normally dry to very sweet.

- *Rosé*: made in three ways – from black grapes fermented on the skins for up to 48 hours; by mixing red and white wines together; or by pressing grapes so that some colour is extracted. It may be dry or semi-sweet. These are called blush wines in the USA when made wholly from red grapes.

Sparkling wines

- The most famous is Champagne. This is made by the *méthode champenoise* (secondary fermentation in the bottle) in an area of north-eastern France.

- Effervescent wines made outside this area are called *vins mousseux* or sparkling wines and are made by either the *méthode champenoise* (now called *méthode traditionelle*), the *Charmat* method (tank fermented and sometimes termed the *méthode cuve close*), the transfer method, or the carbonation method.

- Sparkling wines are available from France, Spain, Italy and many other countries.

Figure 4.5 Key differences in methods of production of sparkling wines

METHOD	FERMENTATION AND MATURATION	REMOVAL OF SEDIMENT
Méthode traditionelle	In bottle	By the processes of remuage and dégorgement
Charmat or *méthode cuve close*	In tank	By filtration process
Transfer method	In bottle	By transfer to vat under pressure and then filtering
Carbonation	Sometimes termed 'impregnation' where carbon dioxide is injected into a vat of still wine which has been chilled and which is then bottled under pressure. Least expensive method	

- They may vary from *brut* (very dry), *sec* (medium dry), *demi-sec* (medium sweet), to *doux* (sweet).
- Semi-sparkling wines are known by the term *pétillant*.

Sweetness in sparkling wine

The sugar content is indicated by the label:

extra brut	very dry	up to 6 g
brut	very dry	less than 15 g
extra-sec	dry	12 to 20 g
sec	slightly sweet	17 to 35 g
demi-sec	sweetish	35 to 50 g

Other sparkling wine terms

French
Vin mousseux: sparkling wine other than Champagne
Méthode traditionelle: sparkling, made by the traditional method
Pétillant/perlant: slightly sparkling
Cremant: less sparkling than mousseux

German
Spritzig: slightly sparkling
Flaschengarung nach dem traditionellen Verfahren: sparkling made by the traditional method
Sekt: sparkling (also used to mean the wine itself)
Schaumwein: sparkling of lesser quality than Sekt
Perlwein: slightly sparkling

Italian
Spumante: sparkling
Frizzante: semi-sparkling

Portuguese
Espumante: sparkling
Vinho verde: meaning 'green wine', slightly sparkling

Spanish
Espumosos: sparkling
Metodo tradicional: sparkling, made by the traditional method
Cava: sparkling, made by the traditional method

Organic wines

These wines, also known as 'green' or 'environmentally friendly' wines, are made from grapes grown without the aid of artificial insecticides, pesticides or fertilizers. The wine itself will not be adulterated in any way, save for minimal amounts of the traditional preservative, sulphur dioxide, which is controlled at source.

Alcohol-free, de-alcoholized and low alcohol wines

Alcohol free: maximum 0.05% alcohol
De-alcoholized: maximum 0.50% alcohol
Low alcohol: maximum 1.25% alcohol

These wines are made in the normal way and the alcohol is removed either by hot treatment – distillation – which unfortunately removes most of the flavour as well, or, more satisfactorily, by a cold filtration process, also known as reverse osmosis. This removes the alcohol by mechanically separating or filtering out the molecules of alcohol through membranes made of cellulose or acetate. To this, at a later stage, water and a little *must* are added, thus attempting to preserve much of the flavour of the original wine.

Vins doux naturels

These are sweet wines that have had their fermentation muted by the addition of alcohol in order to retain their natural sweetness. Muting takes place when the alcohol level reaches between 5% and 8% by volume. They have a final alcohol strength of about 17% by volume.

Fortified wines

Fortified wines such as Sherry, Port and Madeira have been strengthened by the addition of alcohol, usually a grape spirit.

These are now known within the EU as liqueur wines or *vins de liqueur*. Their alcoholic strength may be between 15% and 22%, by volume.

- *Sherry* (from Spain) 15–18% – fino (dry), amontillado (medium), oloroso (sweet)
- *Port* (from Portugal) 18–22% – ruby, tawny, vintage character, late bottled vintage, vintage
- *Madeira* 18% (made on the Portuguese island of Madeira) – Sercial (dry), Verdelho (medium), Bual (sweet), Malmsey (very sweet)
- *Marsala* 18% – a dark sweet wine from Marsala in Sicily

Another example is muscat and muscatel, made from the Muscat grape. Most are sweet and raisin-like with a strong bouquet. One of the best known is Muscat de Beaumes-de-Venise, named after a village in the Côtes du Rhône where it is made. The wine is fortified with spirit before fermentation is complete so that some of the natural sugar remains in the wine. It is drunk young.

Aromatized wines

These are flavoured and fortified wines.

Vermouth

The four main types of vermouth are:

Dry vermouth: often called French vermouth or simply French. It is made from dry white wine that is flavoured and fortified.

Sweet vermouth/bianco: made from dry white wine, flavoured, fortified and sweetened with sugar or mistelle.

Rosé vermouth: made in a similar way to Bianco but it is less sweet and is coloured with caramel.

Red vermouth: often called Italian vermouth, Italian or more often It (as in Gin and It). It is made from white wine and is flavoured, sweetened and coloured with a generous addition of caramel.

POPULAR BRANDS

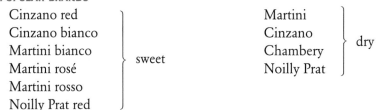

Cinzano red		Martini	
Cinzano bianco		Cinzano	
Martini bianco		Chambery	dry
Martini rosé	sweet	Noilly Prat	
Martini rosso			
Noilly Prat red			

Chamberyzette

Made in the Savoy Alps of France. It is flavoured with the juice of wild strawberries.

Punt-e-mes

From Carpano of Turin; this is heavily flavoured with quinine and has wild contrasts of bitterness and sweetness.

Dubonnet

Dubonnet is available in two varieties: *blonde* (white) and *rouge* (red) and is flavoured with quinine and herbs.

St Raphael

Red or white, bitter-sweet drink from France flavoured with herbs and quinine.

Lillet

Popular French apéritif made from white Bordeaux wine and flavoured with herbs, fruit peel and fortified with Armagnac brandy. It is aged in oak casks.

Pineau de Charente

Although not strictly an aromatized or fortified wine, Pineau de Charente has gained popularity as an alternative aperitif or digestif. It is available in white, rosé or red and is made with grape must from the Cognac region and fortified with young Cognac to about 17% alcohol by volume.

Reading a wine label

The label on a bottle of wine can give a lot of useful information about the wine. The language used will normally be that of the country of origin. The information always includes:

- The country where the wine was made
- Alcoholic strength in percentage by volume (% vol)
- Contents in litres, cl or ml
- Name and address or trademark of supplier

It may also include:

- The year the grapes were harvested, called the vintage
- The region where the wine was made
- The quality category of the wine
- Details of bottler

The European Community has strict regulations that govern what is printed on the bottle label. These regulations also apply to wine entering the EU.

Still wines of the standard size bottled after 1988 when EU regulations on content came into force must contain 75 cl, though bottles from previous years, containing 70 cl for example, will still be on sale for some years to come.

An example of the kind of information given on a label may be seen below.

Figure 4.6 Examples of information provided on a wine label

Quality control

Most of the world's wine-makers must ensure that their products conform to strict quality regulations covering such aspects as where the vineyards are, what variety of grape is used, how the wine is made and how long it is matured.

European Community directives lay down general rules for quality wines produced in specified regions (QWPSR) or, in French, *vin de qualité produit en regions determinés (VQPRD)*. Wines which meet these requirements include VDQS and AC wines of France, QbA and QmP wines of Germany, DOC and DOCG wines of Italy, DO wines of Spain and regiao demarcado wines of Portugal.

France

Vin de table: this is ordinary table wine in the cheapest price range. It is not recognized under quality control standards.

Vin de pays: the lowest official category recognized. Wines of medium quality and price, made from certain grapes grown within a defined area. The area must be printed on the label. A minimum alcohol content is specified.

Vin delimité de qualité supérieure (VDQS): A quality wine just below appellation controlled standard. Area of production, grape varieties, minimum alcohol content, cultivation and vinification methods are specified.

Appellation d'origine contrôlée (AC or AOC): Quality wine from approved areas. Grape varieties and proportions, pruning and cultivation method, maximum yield per hectare, vinification and minimum alcohol content are specified.

Germany

Tafelwein: table wine made from a blend of wines from Germany and other EC countries. It must be stated that this is so in the language of the country of sale.

Deutscher Tafelwein: cheaper wine made from one of the four wine regions designated for table wine (Rhein and Mosel, Main, Neckar and Overrhein). It is often blended. A minimum alcohol content is specified.

Landwein: quality wine from one of 17 designated districts. it can be *trocken* (dry) or *halbtrocken* (medium dry). A minimum alcohol content is specified.

Qualitätswein bestimmter Anbaugebiete (QbA): quality wine in medium price range (includes Liebfraumilch) from one of the 13 designated regions (*Anbaugetieten*). It must carry an *Amtliche Prüfungsnummer* (control number).

Qualitätswein mit Prädikat (QmP): quality wines of distinction and special characteristics. They have no added sugar. The Prädikat describes how ripe the grape was when it was harvested – generally the riper the grape, the richer the wine. There are six categories:

- *Kabinett:* made from grapes harvested at the normal time, usually October, but in a perfect state of ripeness
- *Spätlese:* made from grapes harvested late

- *Auslese:* made from selected bunches of ripe grapes
- *Beerenauslese:* made from selected ripe grapes affected by noble rot
- *Eiswein:* made from ripe grapes left on the vine to be picked and pressed when frozen
- *Trockenbeeranauslese:* made from selected single grapes heavily affected by noble rot.

Italy

Vino da tavola: ordinary table wine, unclassified.

Vino tipico/Vino da tavola con indicazione geografica: wine from a defined area.

Denominazione de origine contrallata (DOC): quality wine from an approved area. Grape varieties, cultivation and vinification methods and maximum yields are specified.

Denominazione di origine controllata e garantia (DOCG): guaranteed quality wines from approved areas. Grape variety and proportions, maximum yield, vinification methods, pruning and cultivation and minimum alcohol content are specified.

Spain

Vine de meas: ordinary table wine.

Denominaction de origen (DO): quality wines from specified regions.

Reserva: red wines which have aged for at least one year in oak casks and two years in the bottle; white and rosé wines aged for at least two years including six months in oak casks.

Gran reserva: red wines which have aged for at least two years in oak casks and three years in the bottle; white and rosé wines aged for at least four years including at least six months in oak casks.

Portugal

Vinho de meas: ordinary table wine from no particular region and may be a blend from several regions.

Vinho de meas regional: table wine from a specified region.

Vinho regional: quality wine from a particular place within a named region.

Regiao demarcado: quality wines from specified regions.

Selo de garantia: the quality and authenticity of the wine is guaranteed.

Estate bottled

The following indicate that the wine was bottled on the estate:

Mise en bouteille au domaine or *Mise du domaine* (France)

Erzeugerabfullung or *Aus eigenem Lesegut* (Germany)

Imbottligliato all'origine or *Imbottigliato al'origine nelle cantine della fatoria dei* – bottled at source in the cellars of the estate of (Italy)

Embottelado or *Engarrafado de origen* (Spain)

Engarrafado na origem (Portugal)

Other terms used in France

Mise en bouteille au château: means the wine was bottled at the château (literally means castle) printed on the label. It is seen mostly on wines from Bordeaux.

Mise en bouteille dans nos caves: means the wine was bottled in the cellars of the person (*négociant*) whose name usually appears on the label.

Mise en bouteille par: means the wine was bottled by the company or individual whose name appears after these words.

4.9 Tasting of wine

The *sommelier*, as well as having an extensive knowledge of the wine list, should have a good knowledge of the characteristics of the different wines offered. To ensure this, he/she must know the correct approach to tasting wine.

Tasting may be said to be an analysis of wine by the senses. It is the appreciation by our senses of the qualities of a wine.

- *Sight*: indicating the clarity and colour of the wine
- *Smell*: determines the bouquet of a wine by means of a vigorous swirling in the glass.
- *Taste*: allows detection of the aroma in the mouth.

The taste-character of wine is detected in different parts of the mouth but especially by the tongue: sweetness at the tip, acidity on the upper edges, saltiness at the sides, bitterness at the back. Dryness and sweetness are immediately obvious, as is acidity, which generally provides liveliness and crispness. Astringency or tannin content, associated with some red wines, will give a dry coating effect especially on the teeth and gums.

The combination of smell and taste gives what is often termed 'flavour'. This might be, for example, the amount of tannin content in the wine, its degree of dryness or sweetness, whether it is a light or heavy bodied wine, etc.

To appreciate the tasting of wine to the full you must work in the correct environment. That is:

- No noise to distract the taster
- Good ventilation to eliminate odours

- Sufficient light, not artificial, but daylight if possible
- Temperature of the room at about 20°C (68°F)

The tasting of wines includes looking at, smelling and tasting the wine (see Figure 4.8).

The tool of the taster is the glass, which must be the correct shape. A wine glass with a stem and of sufficient capacity should be chosen (see Figure 4.7). The glass should be fairly wide but narrowing at the top. This allows the 'elements' making up the bouquet to become concentrated and thus better assessed. The wine glass should never be filled to more than one-third capacity. This allows the taster to swirl the wine round the glass more easily. It goes without saying that the tasting glass should be spotlessly clean.

Figure 4.7 Wine taster's glass

Figure 4.8 Observations on wines

SENSE	CHARACTERISTIC		DESCRIPTION
Sight	Clarity		Bright/clear/hazy/cloudy
	Colour	Red	Purple/ruby/red/red-brown/ mahogany/brown-amber
		Rosé	Orange-pink/onion skin/pink/rose/blue-pink
		White	Pale yellow/pale green/straw/ yellow/gold/yellow-brown/maderised
Smell	Bouquet	Depth	Full/deep/light/nondescript
		Character	Clean/unclean/acetic/fruity/ fragrant/sweet/musty/woody/baked
Taste	Dryness		Bone dry/dry/medium/sweet/ very sweet
	Body		Full-bodied/medium/light
	Flavour		Acid/bitter/spicy/grapy
	Tannin		Hard/silky/soft
	Acid		Tart/green/piquant/cloying
Summing up			Austere/severe/coarse/tough/ vigorous/robust/well-balanced/ delicate/rich/fat/luscious/flabby

The Wine Taste Guide

Developed by the Wine Promotion Board and accepted as standard within the industry, this is a quick and easy method of telling at a glance whether a white wine is bone dry or lusciously sweet. Very dry wines like Chablis are graded as 1; Moscatel is at the other extreme and is graded 9. The Wine Taste Guide also clarifies the degrees of sweetness in between.

The Red Wine Taste Guide works in the same way but is based not on sweetness or dryness, but on fullness. The biggest, richest reds rate at E and, at the other end of the scale, light, summery reds are classified as A.

Figure 4.9 Red and white wine guide (chart courtesy of Griersons Wine Merchants)

The Red Wine Guide

The five categories marked A to E identify styles of red wines in terms of light styles to big, full-bodied heavy wines.

 Bardolino
Beaujolais
Valdepeñas

 Côtes du Roussillon
Merlot
Navarra
Pinot Noir from all countries
Red Burgundy
Valencia
Valpolicella

 Bordeaux Rouge/Claret
Côtes du Rhône
Rioja

 Cabernet Sauvignon from Australia
Bulgaria, California, Chile, New Zealand,
Romania and South Africa
Châteauneuf du Pape
Chianti
Dão
Hungarian Red

 Barolo
Crozes Hermitage
Cyprus Red
Greek Red
Shiraz from Australia and South Africa

Dry to Sweet White Wine Guide

Number 1 signifies very dry white wines. Number 9 indicates maximum sweetness. The numbers in between span the remaining dryness-to-sweetness spectrum.

 Muscadet
Champagne
Chablis
Dry White
Bordeaux
Manzanilla Sherry
Tavel Rosé

 Soave
White Burgundy
Fino Sherry
Sercial Madeira
Rioja
Penedes

 Brut Sparkling Wine
Gewürztraminer d'Alsace
Dry Amontillado Sherry
Medium Dry Montilla
Dry White Vermouth
Anjou Rosé
Medium Dry English

 Vinho Verde
Mosel Kabinett
Rhein Kabinett
Laski and
Hungarian Olasz
Riesling,
Medium Dry
Portuguese Rosé

 Vouvray
Demi-Sec
Liebfraumilch
Medium
British Sherry
Verdelho
Madeira

 Demi-Sec
Champagne
Spanish
Medium
Sherry
All Golden
Sherry types

 Asti Spumante
Rhein Auslesen
Premières Côtes
de Bordeaux
Tokay Aszu
Pale Cream
Sherry
Montilla Cream
Bual Madeira
Rosso, Rosé and
Bianco
Vermouths

 Austrian
Beerenauslesen
Spanish Sweet
Wine
Sauternes
Barsac
Cream and
Rich Cream
Sherry types

 Malmsey
Maderia
Muscat de
Beaumes
de Venise
Marsala

4.10 Matching food and drinks

A few general pointers are set out below that may be followed when advising the customer on which beverage to choose to accompany a meal. However, it must be stressed that customers should at all times be given complete freedom in their selection of wines, etc.

1 Apéritifs are alcoholic beverages that are drunk before the meal. If wine will be consumed with the meal, then the apéritif selected should be a 'grape' (wine-based) rather than a 'grain' (spirit-based) apéritif, since the latter can spoil or dull the palate.

   The apéritif is usually a wine-based beverage. It is meant to stimulate the appetite and therefore should not be sweet. Dry and medium dry sherries, dry vermouths and Sercial or Verdelho Madeira are all good examples of apéritifs.

2 The starter courses are best accompanied by a dry white or dry rosé wine.

3 National dishes should be complemented by the national wines of that country. Thus, for instance, Italian red wine should be served with pasta.

4 Fish and shellfish dishes are most suited to well-chilled dry white wines.

5 Red meats such as beef and lamb blend and harmonize well with red wine.

6 White meats such as veal and pork are acceptable with medium white wines.

7 Game dishes require the heavier and more robust red wines to complement the full flavour of these dishes.

8 Sweets and desserts are served at the end of the meal and here it is acceptable to offer well-chilled sweet white wines that may come from either the Loire, Sauternes, Barsac or Hungary. These wines harmonize best with dishes containing fruit.

9 The majority of cheeses blend well with port and other dry robust red wines. Port is the traditional wine harmonizing best with Stilton cheese.

10 The grain- and fruit-based brandies and liqueurs all harmonize well with coffee.

A few general guidelines will ensure that the most appropriate wines are selected to accompany a meal:

- Champagne or sparkling complement most foods
- Consume red wine with red meat and white wine with white meat
- If unsure, often a rosé will suffice
- Consume white wine before red wine
- Consume dry wine before sweet wine
- Consume a 'good' wine before a 'great 'wine
- Commence with a grape apéritif rather than a grain apéritif prior to the meal
- Make sure your wine is at the correct temperature

Hors-d'oeuvre

- Fino or Manzanilla sherry
- Sancerre or Gewürztraminer

Soups

- These do not really require an accompaniment, but sherry or dry port or Madeira could be tried
- Consommés, turtle soup and lobster or crab bisque can be uplifted by adding a glass of heated sherry or Madeira before serving

Foie gras

- Beaujolais or a light, young, red wine
- Some people like sweet wines such as Sauternes

Omelettes and quiches

- Ideally, no wine should be served
- An Alsatian Riesling or Sylvaner is probably the most suitable if wine is required

Farinaceous dishes

- Italian red wines such as Valpolicella, Chianti, Barolo, Santa Maddalena, Lago di Caldaro

Fish

- *Oysters and shellfish*: dry white wines, Champagne, Chablis, Muscadet, Soave or Frascati
- *Smoked fish*: white Rioja, Hock, white Graves, Verdicchio
- *Fish dishes with sauces*: these require fuller white wines such as Vouvray, Montrachet or Yugoslav Riesling
- *Shallow fried, poached or grilled fish*: Vinho Verde, Moselle, Californian Chardonnay, Australian Sémillon or Chardonnay

White meats

The type of wine to serve is dependent on whether the white meat (chicken, turkey, rabbit, veal or pork) is served hot or cold:

- *Served hot with a sauce or savoury stuffing*: either a rosé such as Anjou or light reds like Beaujolais, New Zealand Pinot Noir, Californian Zinfandel, Saint Julien, Bourg and Blaye, Passe-tout-grains and Corbières

- *Served cold*: fuller white wine such as Hocks, Gran Viña Sol, Sancerre and the rosés of Provence and Tavel

Other meats

- *Duck and goose*: big red wines that will cut through the fat, eg Châteauneuf-du-Pape, Hermitage, Barolo and the Australian Cabernet Shiraz
- *Roast and grilled lamb*: Medoc, Saint Emilion, Pomerol and any of the Cabernet Sauvignons
- *Roast beef and grilled steaks*: big red Burgundies, Rioja, Barolo, Dão and wines made from the Pinot Noir grape
- *Meat stews*: lighter reds, eg Zinfandel, Côtes du Rhône, Clos du Bois, Bull's Blood
- *Hare, venison and game*: reds with distinctive flavour, eg Côte Rotie, Bourgeuil, Rioja, Chianti, Australian Shiraz, Californian Cabernet, Chilian Cabernet Sauvignon and fine red Burgundies
- *Oriental foods, Peking duck, mild curry, tandor chicken, shish kebab*: Gewürz-traminer, Lutomer Riesling, Vinho Verde, Mateus Rosé or Anjou Rosé

Cheese

The wine from the main course is often followed through to the cheese course but, if not, almost any wine will do as cheese and wine go together well.

- The light, cream cheeses go well with full bodied whites, rosés and light reds
- The strong, pungent (even smelly) and blue veined varieties cry out for big reds like Bordeaux and Burgundy, or tawny, vintage or vintage-style ports and even luscious sweet whites

Sweets and puddings

Most sweets and puddings are only barely comfortable with wines, perhaps because two sweet tastes in the mouth are almost too much of a good thing. However, certain wines can be recommended:

- Champagne works well with sweets and puddings
- The luscious Muscats (de Beaumes-de-Venise, de Sétubal, de Frontignan, Samos), Sainte-Croix-de-Mont, Sauternes, Banyuls, Monbazillac, Tokay and wines made from late gathered individual grapes in Germany all make a brave effort to satisfy. Despite this, it is perhaps preferable to save the wine until after the sweet course when it can be appreciated to the full

Dessert (fresh fruit and nuts)

- Sweet fortified wines, sherry, port, Madeira, Malaga, Marsala, Commande-ria, Yalumba Galway Pipe and Seppelt's Para

Coffee

- Cognac and other brandies such as Armagnac, Asbach, Marc, Metaxa, Grappa, Oude Meester, Fundador, Peristiani VO31
- Good aged malt whiskies
- Calvados, sundry liqueurs and ports

4.11 Spirits

Production

All spirits are produced by the distillation of alcoholic beverages. The history of distillation goes back over 400 years when it is said that stills were used in China to make perfumes and by the Arabs to make spirit based drinks.

The principle of distillation is that ethyl alcohol vaporizes (boils) at a lower temperature (78°C) than water (100°C). Thus where a liquid containing alcohol is heated in an enclosed environment the alcohol will form steam first and can be taken off, leaving water and other ingredients behind. This process raises the alcoholic strength of the resulting liquid. There are two main methods of producing spirits, either by the pot still method which is used for full, heavy flavoured spirits such as brandy, or the patent still (Coffey) method with produces the lighter spirits such as vodka.

Bases for spirits

The bases used in the most common spirits are listed in Figure 4.10. In each case the base is a fermented liquid.

Figure 4.10 Bases for spirits

SPIRIT	BASE
Whisky, gin and vodka	Barley, maize or rye (ie beer)
Brandy	Wine
Calvados	Cider
Rum	Molasses
Tequila	Pulque

Types of spirit

Aquavit

Made in Scandinavia from potatoes or grain and flavoured with herbs, mainly caraway seeds. To be appreciated fully, Aquavit must be served chilled.

Arrack

Made from the sap of palm trees. The main countries of production are Java, India, Ceylon and Jamaica.

Brandy

Brandy may be defined as a spirit distilled from wine. The word brandy is more usually linked with the names Cognac and Armagnac, but brandy is also made in almost all wine producing areas.

Eau de vie

Eau de vie is the fermented and distilled juice of fruit. Much of the best comes from the Alsace area of France, Germany, Switzerland and Yugoslavia. Examples are:

Himbergeist from wild raspberries (Germany)
Kirschwasser (Kirsch) from cherries (Germany)
Mirabelle from plums (France)
Quetsch from plums (Alsace and Germany)
Poire William from pears (Switzerland and Alsace)
Slivovitz from plums (Yugoslavia)
Fraise from strawberries (France, especially Alsace)
Framboise from raspberries (France, especially Alsace)
Eau de vie, especially the *alcohol blanc* variety, should be water-clear in appearance.

Gin

The term 'gin' is taken from the first part of the word *Genièvre* which is the French term for juniper. Juniper is the principal botanica (flavouring agent) used in the production of gin. The word Geneva is the Dutch translation of the botanical, juniper. Maize is the cereal used in gin production in the United Kingdom. However, rye is the main cereal generally used in the production of Geneva gin and other Dutch gins.

Malted barley is an accepted alternative to the above cereals. The two key ingredients (botanicals) recognized for flavouring purposes are juniper berries and coriander seeds.

Types of gin are:

Fruit gins As the term implies, these are fruit flavoured gins that may be produced from any fruit. The most popular are sloe, orange and lemon.

Geneva gin This is made in Holland by the pot still method alone and is generally known as 'Hollands' gin.

London Dry Gin This is the most well-known and popular of all the gins. It is unsweetened.

Old Tom This is a sweet gin made in Scotland. The sweetening agent is sugar syrup. As the name implies, it was traditionally used in a Tom Collins cocktail.

Plymouth Gin This has a stronger flavour than London Dry and is manufactured by Coates in Devon. It is most well known for its use in the cocktail Pink Gin, together with the addition of Angostura Bitters.

Grappa

An Italian style brandy produced from the pressings of grapes after the required must – unfermented grape juice – has been removed for wine production. It is similar in style to the French marc brandy.

Marc

Local French brandy made where wine is grown. Usually takes the name of the region, eg Marc de Borgogne.

Mirabelle

A colourless spirit made from plums. The main country of origin is France.

Pastis

Pastis is the name given to spirits flavoured with anis and/or liquorice, such as Pernod. The spirit is made in many Mediterranean countries and is popular almost everywhere. It has taken over from the infamous *absinthe*, once known as the 'Green Goddess'. The latter has since been banned in France.

Quetsch

A colourless spirit with plums being the main ingredient. The key countries of production are the Balkans, France and Germany. It has a brandy base.

Rum

This is a spirit made from the fermented by-products of sugar cane. It is produced in countries where sugar cane grows naturally and is available in dark and light varieties. Some examples of these are Jamaica, Cuba, Trinidad, Barbados, Guyana and the Bahamas.

Schnapps

A spirit distilled from a fermented potato base and flavoured with caraway seed. The main countries of production are Germany and Holland.

Tequila

A Mexican spirit distilled from the fermented juice of the agave plant. It is traditionally drunk after a lick of salt and a squeeze of lime or lemon.

Vodka

A highly rectified (very pure) patent still spirit. It is purified by being passed through activated charcoal which removes virtually all aroma and flavour. It is described as a colourless and flavourless spirit.

Whisk(e)y

Whisky or whiskey is a spirit made from cereals: Scotch whisky from malted barley, Irish whiskey usually from barley, North American whiskey and Bourbon from maize and rye. The spelling whisky usually refers to the Scotch or Canadian drink and whiskey to the Irish or American.

Scotch whisky is primarily made from barley, malted (hence the term malt whisky) then heated over a peat fire. Grain whiskies are made from other grains and are usually blended with malt whisky.

Irish whiskey differs from Scotch in that hot air rather than peat fire is used during malting, thus Irish does not gain the smoky quality of Scotch. It is also distilled three times (rather than two as in the making of Scotch) and is matured longer.

Canadian whisky is usually a blend of flavoured and neutral whiskies made from grains such as rye, wheat and barley.

American whiskey is made from various mixtures of barley, maize and rye. Bourbon is made from maize.

Japanese whisky is made by the Scotch process and is blended.

4.12 Liqueurs

Liqueurs are defined as sweetened and flavoured spirits. They should not be confused with liqueur spirits which may be whiskies or brandies of great age and quality. For instance, a brandy liqueur is a liqueur with brandy as a basic ingredient, whilst a liqueur brandy may be defined as a brandy of great age and excellence.

Production

Liqueurs are made by two basic methods:

- *Heat or infusion method*: best when herbs, peels, roots, etc are being used as heat can extract the oils, flavours and aromas

- *Cold or maceration method*: best when soft fruits are used to provide the flavours and aromas

The heat method uses a pot still for distillation purposes whilst the cold method allows the soft fruit to soak in brandy in oak casks over a long period of time.

For all liqueurs a spirit base is necessary and this may be brandy, rum or neutral spirit. Many flavouring ingredients are used and the following list gives some indication of these:

aniseed	rind of citrus fruit	blackcurrants
caraway seeds	wormwood	apricots
kernels of almonds	rose petals	coriander
cherries	cinnamon	nutmeg

Types of liqueurs

Figure 4.11 shows some of the more popular liqueurs that may be found on the liqueur trolley. The service of liqueurs is discussed on page 217.

4.13 Beer

Introduction

Beer in one form or another is an alcoholic beverage found in all bars and areas dispensing alcoholic beverages . They are fermented drinks, deriving their alcoholic content from the conversion of malt sugars into alcohol by brewers yeast.

The alcoholic content of beer varies according to type, usually between 3.5–10% alcohol by volume.

Beer types

Draught beer in cans These draft-flow beers have an internal patented system which produces a pub-style, smooth creamy head when poured from the can. A range of beers are available in this format.

Bitter Pale, amber-coloured beer served on draft. May be sold as light bitter, ordinary bitter or best bitter.

Mild Can be light or dark depending of the colour of the malt used in the brewing. Generally sold on draft and has a sweeter and more complex flavour than bitter.

Burton Strong, dark, draft beer. This beer is also popular in winter when it is mulled or spiced and offered as a winter warmer.

Old ales Brown, sweet and strong. Can also be mulled or spiced.

Strong ales Colour varies between pale and brown and taste between dry and sweet. Alcoholic content also varies.

Barley wine Traditionally an all-malt ale. This beer is sweet and strong and sold in small bottles or nips (originally 1/3 of a pint now 190ml).

Stout Made from scorched , very dark malt and generously flavoured with hops. Has a smooth malty flavour and creamy consistency. Sold on-draft or in bottles and traditionally not chilled.

Porter Brewed from charred malt, highly flavoured and aromatic. Gets its name from it popularity with market porters working in Dublin and London.

Lager The name comes from the German 'lagern' (to store). The yeast ferment at the bottom of the vessel and the beer is stored at low temperatures for up to six months, some for longer. Sold on-draft or in a bottle.

Figure 4.11 Popular liqueurs

LIQUEUR	COLOUR	FLAVOUR/ SPIRIT BASE	COUNTRY
Abricotine	Red	Apricot/brandy	France
Avocaat	Yellow	Egg, sugar/brandy	Holland
Anisette	Clear	Aniseed/neutral spirit	France, Spain, Italy, Holland
Arrack	Clear	Herbs, sap of palm trees	Java, India, Sri Lanka, Jamaica
Bailey's Irish Cream	Coffee	Honey, chocolate, cream whiskey	Ireland
Benedictine Dom	Yellow/green 'Deo Optimo Maiximo'	Herbs/brandy	France
Calvados	Amber	Apple/brandy	France
Chartreuse	Green (45% abv)	Herbs, plants/brandy	France
Chartreuse	Yellow (55% abv)	Herbs, plants/brandy	France
Cherry Brandy	Deep red	Cherry/brandy	Denmark
Cointreau	Clear	Orange/brandy	France
Crème de cacao	Dark brown	Chocolate, vanilla/rum	France
Drambuie	Golden	Heather, honey, herbs/whisky	Scotland
Grand Marnier	Amber	Orange/brandy	France
Glayva	Golden	Herbs, spice/whisky	Scotland
Kirsch	Clear	Cherry/neutral spirit	Alsace
Kahlua	Pale chocolate	Coffee/rum	Mexico
Kummel	Clear	Carraway seed/neutral spirit	East European countries
Maraschino	Clear	Maraschino cherry	Italy
Parfait amour	Violet	Violets, lemon peel, spices	France/Holland
Sambuca	Clear	Liquorice/neutral spirit	Italy
Slivovitz	Clear	Plum/brandy	East Europe
Southern Comfort	Golden	Peaches/oranges/whiskey	United States
Strega (The witch)	Yellow	Herbs/bark/fruit	Italy
Tia Maria	Brown	Coffee/rum	Jamaica
Van der hum	Amber	Tangerine/brandy	South Africa

Bottle-conditioned beers Also known as sediment beers, they tend to throw a sediment in the bottle whilst fermenting and conditioning takes place. These beers need careful storage, handling and pouring. Available in bottles only.

Reduced alcohol beer There are two categories of beer with reduced alcohol levels:

- Non-alcoholic beers (NABs) which, by definition, must contain less than 0.5% alcohol by volume
- Low alcohol beers (LABs) which, by definition, must contain less than 1.2% alcohol by volume

The beer is firstly made in the traditional way and then the alcohol is removed.

Beer measures

Nips	22.72 cl (7-8 fl oz)
Half pint	28.40 cl (10 fl oz)
Pint	56.80 cl (20 fl oz)

Draft beer containers

pin	20.457 l ($4\frac{1}{2}$ gallons)
firkin	40.914 l (9 gallons)
kilderkin	81.828 l (18 gallons)
barrel	163.656 l (36 gallons)
hogshead	245.484 l (54 gallons)
2 1/2 barrel tanks	205 l (45 gallons)
5 barrel tanks	410 l (90 gallons)

Mixed beer drinks

A selection of beverages based on beer is given below:

Mild and bitter
Stout and mild
Brown and mild
Light and mild
Shandy: draught bitter and lemonade or ginger beer
Black velvet: Guinness and champagne
Black and tan: half stout and half bitter
Lager and lime
Lager and blackcurrant

4.14 Cider and perry

Cider is an alcoholic beverage obtained through the fermentation of apple juice, or a mixture of apple juice and up to 25% pear juice. *Perry* is similarly obtained from pear juice and up to 25% apple juice.

Countries of production

Cider and perry are produced primarily in England and Normandy, but may also be made in Italy, Spain, Germany, Switzerland, Canada, the USA, Australia and New Zealand. The English areas of production are the counties of Devon, Somerset, Gloucester, Hereford, Kent and Norfolk where the best cider orchards are found.

Cider apples require:

- The sweetness of dessert apples
- The acid of culinary apples
- The bitterness of tannin to balance the flavour and help preserve the apple

Main types of cider

Draught

This is unfiltered. Its appearance, while not cloudy, is also not 'star-bright'. It may have sugar and yeast added to give it condition. Draught cider may be completely dry – known as scrumpy – or sweetened with sugar. It is marketed in oak casks or plastic containers.

Keg/bottled

This cider is pasteurized or sterile filtered to render it star-bright. At this stage one or more of the following treatments may be carried out:

- The cider may be blended
- It may undergo a second fermentation, usually in a tank, to make sparkling cider
- It may be sweetened
- Its strength may be adjusted
- It is usually carbonated by the injection of carbon dioxide gas.

Characteristics of keg and bottled ciders

Medium sweet (carbonated): 4% vol alcohol
Medium dry (carbonated): 6% vol alcohol
Special (some carbonated): 8.3% vol alcohol

Note

- some special ciders undergo a second fermentation to make them sparkling
- fermented apple juice over 8.5% vol alcohol becomes designated as apple wine for tax purposes.

Perry

Perry is more often made sparkling and comes into the special range. It may be carbonated or the sparkle may come from a second fermentation in sealed tanks. In the production of perry the processes of filtering, blending and sweetening are all carried out under pressure.

Perries are usually drunk on their own, chilled and in tulip/saucer-shaped sparkling wine glasses.

4.15 Storage

Beer

Faults

Although thunder has been known to cause a secondary fermentation in beer, thereby affecting its clarity, faults can usually be attributed to poor cellar management.

Cloudy beer

This may be due to too low a temperature in the cellar or, more often, may result from the beer pipes not having been cleaned properly.

Flat beer

Flat beer may result when a wrong spile has been used – a hard spile builds up pressure, a soft spile releases pressure. When the cellar temperature is too low, beer often becomes dull and lifeless. Dirty glasses, and those that have been refilled for a customer who has been eating food, will also cause beer to go flat.

Sour beer

This may be due to a lack of business resulting in the beer being left on ullage for too long. Sourness may also be caused by adding stale beer to a new cask, or by beer coming in contact with old deposits of yeast which have become lodged in the pipeline from the cellar.

Foreign bodies

Foreign bodies or extraneous matter may be the result of productional or operational slip-ups.

Beer storage and equipment

Beer engines

These are pumps pulled by hand using a handle in the bar. They must be cleaned weekly when the pipe-lines are cleaned and must be stripped down and inspected on a monthly basis. New washers may be needed, etc. Some engines work by carbon dioxide top pressure, which applies force downwards on to the beer in the cask and drives a measured amount up into the bar when a button is pressed.

Dip-sticks

These are used to determine how much beer is left in the cask. The dip-stick is placed into the cask through the shive.

Electrical impelled pumps

Electrical impelled pumps, situated in the cellar, dispense an accurate amount of beer into the glass in the bar when the bartender presses the button.

Filters

Filters must only be used in the cellar to return sound beer to the cask – for instance, beer which has been drawn out of the pipes before pipe-cleaning started. Filters must be kept clean and used with clean filter papers.

To filter beer is not in itself illegal, but to return to cask any over-spill or 'slops' is an offence. To mix or dilute beer in the cask, or to adulterate any produce for sale, is also an offence.

Pipe cleaning bottles

These are used to clean pressurized container pipe-lines. With the gas turned off, the assembly head should be taken from the keg and locked onto the two-gallon cleaning bottle containing cleaning fluid. The CO_2 should be turned on and the pipes filled with the fluid. After about one hour the process should be repeated using clean water. Automatic beer-line cleaning equipment is also now popular.

Scotches

Triangular blocks of wood which are used to prevent a beer cask from rolling from side to side.

Shives and spiles

Shives are round pieces of hard wood which are placed in the bung-hole of the beer cask just before it is sent out from the brewery after racking (filling). The shive has a small hole in the centre which does not go completely through the wood. When the cask is vented, the hole is completed by punching out the thin centre section with a wooden mallet. The hole will permit gas to escape from the cask. Spiles are used in the hole to allow or prevent the CO_2 gas from escaping. They are small pegs made of two different types of wood. The hardwood spile, when placed in the shive, does not allow any gas to escape. Instead, pressure builds up in the cask and the beer regains its condition (frothy head). The softer spile is made from bamboo and when placed in the shive, it allows the gas to escape and so prevents the beer from being too gassy and difficult to serve.

Stillions

Casks in use (on ullage) will be supported on stillions (or thrawls). A stillion is the wooden rack or brick platform upon which the casks are placed for service. Keg pressurized beer containers are usually situated together in one area of the cellar along with the necessary CO_2 gas cylinders strapped or bracketed to the wall.

Factors, determining good cellar management

- Good ventilation
- Cleanliness
- Even temperatures of 13–15°C (55–58°F)

- Strong draughts and wide ranges of temperatures should be avoided
- On delivery, all casks should be placed immediately upon the stillions
- Casks remaining on the floor should be bung uppermost to better withstand the pressure
- Spiling should take place to reduce any excess pressure in the cask
- Tappings should be carried out 24 hours before a cask is required
- Pipes and engines should be cleaned at regular intervals
- All beer lines should be cleaned weekly with a diluted pipe-cleaning fluid and the cellar floor washed down weekly with a weak solution of chloride and lime (mild bleach)
- Beer left in pipes after closing time should be drawn off
- Returned beer should be filtered back into the cask from which it came
- Care should be taken that the cellar is not overstocked
- All spiles removed during the service should be replaced after closing time
- All cellar equipment should be kept scrupulously clean
- Any ullage should be returned to the brewery as soon as possible.
- Re-ordering should be carried out on one set day every week after checking the bottle stocks of beers, wines, minerals, etc. Strict rotation of stock must be exercised, with new crates placed at the rear and old stock pulled to the front for first issue

Wine

Ideally, wine should be stored in a subterranean cellar which has a northerly aspect and is free from vibrations, excessive dampness, draughts and unwanted odours. The cellar should be absolutely clean, well ventilated, with only subdued lighting and a constant cool temperature of 12.5°C (55°F) to help the wine develop gradually.

Table wines should be stored on their sides in bins so that the wine remains in contact with the cork. This keeps the cork expanded and prevents air from entering the wine – a disaster which quickly turns wine to vinegar. White, sparkling and rosé wines are kept in the coolest part of the cellar and in bins nearest the ground (because warm air rises). Red wines are best stored in the upper bins. Commercial establishments usually have special refrigerators or cooling cabinets for keeping their sparkling, white and rosé wines at serving temperature.

Other drinks

Spirits, liqueurs, squashes, juices and mineral waters are stored upright in their containers, as are fortified wines. The exceptions are port-style wines which are destined for laying down.

See also section 10.3 (page 379) 'Beverage control'.

CHAPTER 5

THE FOOD AND BEVERAGE SERVICE SEQUENCE

5.1	**Basic technical skills**	150
5.2	**Interpersonal skills**	157
5.3	**Taking bookings**	166
5.4	**Preparation for service**	168
5.5	**The order of service (table service)**	192
5.6	**Taking customer food and beverage orders**	195
5.7	**Service of food**	205
5.8	**Service of alcoholic bar beverages and cigars**	212
5.9	**Service of non-alcoholic beverages**	219
5.10	**Clearing**	224
5.11	**Billing methods**	232
5.12	**Clearing following service**	236

5.1 Basic technical skills

There are six basic technical waiting skills. These are:

- Holding a service spoon and fork
- Carrying plates
- Using a service salver
- Using a service plate
- Carrying glasses
- Carrying trays

These basic technical skills have relevance specifically to *table service* and *assisted service*. However, some of these skills also have relevance in other forms of service, eg carrying trays for room service.

Holding a service spoon and fork

Expertise in this technique can only be achieved with a great deal of practice. The purpose of the service spoon and fork is to enable the waiter to serve food from a flat or dish on to the guest's plate quickly and present it well.

1 The ends of the service spoon and fork should be positioned in the centre of the palms of the serving hand as illustrated in Figure 5.1(a). This allows more control when serving various food items
2 The service fork should be positioned above, or on top of, the service spoon
3 The service spoon is held firmly in position by the fingers of the serving hand other than the forefinger (see Figure 5.1(b))
4 The forefinger or index finger is used together with the thumb to hold the handle of the service fork
5 Note that the spoon and fork should be held close to the tips of the fingers to allow the best possible manoeuvrability.
6 Using this method you are able to pick up food items from the serving dish in between the service spoon and service fork, and at the same time manipulate (turn) the service fork to mould with the shape of the items being served (see Figure 5.1(c))
7 There are, of course, occasions where two service forks may be used, or a slice, as this makes the service of the food item concerned more efficient

Carrying plates

This skill is necessary in carrying plates of pre-plated foods as well as for clearing. To be able to clear correctly ensures speed and efficiency around the table, avoids the possibility of accidents and creates minimum inconvenience to guests. In turn it also allows the stacking of dirties neatly and correctly on the sideboard with the minimum delay. The correct clearing techniques enables more to be cleared, in less time and in fewer journeys between

Figure 5.1 Hand positions for holding service spoon and fork

(a) Stage 1

(b) Stage 2

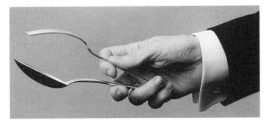

(c) Stage 3

Figure 5.2 Hand positions when clearing plates

(a) First plate cleared

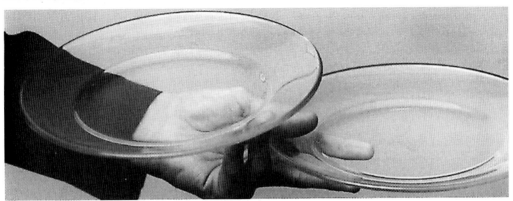

(b) Second plate cleared

sideboard and table. In the long term this speeds up the eating process and allows for greater seat turnover.

1 Figure 5.2(a) illustrates the initial hand position for the first plate. Care must be taken to ensure that the first plate is held firmly as succeeding dirty plates are built up from here. The second plate will rest firmly on the forearm and the third and fourth fingers

2 Figure 5.2(b) shows the second plate positioned on the left hand.

Using a service salver

A service salver is a round, silver or stainless steel, tray with a napkin on it. It may be used in a number of ways

- For carrying clean glasses and removing dirty glasses from a table
- For removing clean cutlery and flatware from the table
- For placing clean cutlery and flatware on the table
- For placing coffee services on the table
- As an underflat when silver serving vegetables

Carrying glasses

When carrying clean glasses on the service salver they should be placed the right way up to reduce the risk of them toppling over. When being placed on the table, the waiter should hold the stem and place the glass at the top right-hand corner of the cover and the correct way up. This ensures that the bowl of the wine glass is not touched.

Carrying clean cutlery and flatware

When removing from or placing clean cutlery and flatware on a table they should be carried on a service salver. The blades of the knives should be placed under the arch in the middle of the forks, and if carrying sweet spoons and forks the prongs of the fork should go under the arch in the middle of the spoon. The reason for this is to help to hold the items steady on the service salver, bearing in mind that the handles of the cutlery and flatware are generally the heaviest parts and this method prevents them sliding about too much.

Carrying coffee services

When taking coffee services (where a demi-tasse is used) to a table, the sideplates may be stacked in one pile on the service salver, the coffee saucers in another, all the demi-tasse together and all the coffee spoons laid flat on the service salver. When the waiter is at the table the coffee service is placed down from the right-hand side, having first set a coffee saucer on a sideplate, a demi-tasse on the saucer with a coffee spoon on the coffee saucer and to the right of the demi-tasse. He/she goes to the right-hand side of each guest, and completes this simple operation.

It is a speedier and safer method (especially when slightly larger numbers are involved) than putting the coffee services up at the sideboard and then carrying as many as possible to the table. The reason for putting the coffee service down from the right and placing it on the right-hand side of the cover is that the coffee will be served from the right. This avoids stretching across the front of the guest when laying the coffee service or serving the coffee – a small technical point which helps towards giving a first class service.

Tea and coffee cups can be carried using the salver, again by stacking the saucers, cups and teaspoons separately.

Silver serving vegetables

When silver serving vegetables and potatoes at the table an underflat should be used to hold either one large vegetable dish or a number of smaller ones depending on the guests' order (see page 207). The purpose of the underflat is:

- To add to the presentation of the food being served
- To give the waiter more control when using the service spoon and fork to serve the vegetables from the vegetable dish to the guest's plate
- To provide greater protection in case of spillage, therefore not detracting from the presentation of the food on the plate or the overall table presentation
- To give the waiter added protection against heat and possible spillage on the uniform

Using a service plate

A service plate is a joint plate with a napkin upon it. It has a number of uses during the meal service:

- For removing clean cutlery and flatware from the table
- For placing clean cutlery and flatware on the table
- For crumbing down after the main course, or any other stage of the meal if necessary
- For clearing sideplates and side knives
- For clearing accompaniments from the table as and when necessary

Crumbing down

'Crumbing down' is a procedure generally carried out by the waiter after the main course has been consumed and all the dirty items of equipment cleared from the table. The waiter then brushes any crumbs and other debris lying on the tablecloth on to the service plate with the aid of either the folded service cloth or a small brush used for this particular purpose. This procedure results in a freshness that will help to promote subsequent courses.

Figure 5.3 Crumbing down. Note the neatly folded service cloth

Clearing sideplates and knives

When clearing dirty sideplates and side knives after the main course has been consumed, by taking a service plate to the table the waiter has a larger area on which to stack the side knives and any debris. Using the correct 'clearing' hand position, the sideplates may be stacked above the service plate with all the debris in a separate pile and the side knives laid flat upon the service plate. This is a much safer and speedier method especially when large numbers are involved (see page 230).

Clearing accompaniments

The service plate is also used to clear such items as the cruet, cayenne pepper, pepper mill or other accompaniments which may not already be set on an underplate.

Carrying glasses

There are two basic methods of carrying glasses in the food and beverage service areas. These are either by hand or on a service salver.

Carrying by hand

The wine goblets should be positioned between alternate fingers as far as is possible. The wine goblets should only be carried in one hand, allowing the other hand to remain free to steady oneself in case of emergencies.

Figure 5.4 shows a close up of the wine goblets held in one hand showing how the base of each glass overlaps the next, allowing the maximum number of glasses to be held in one hand. This method allows wine goblets that are already polished to be handled. They can be carried about the room and set in their correct position on the table without the bowl of the glass being touched.

Figure 5.4 Carrying wine glasses

Carrying glasses on a service salver

The method of carrying clean wine goblets about the restaurant using the service salver is illustrated in Figure 5.5.

- Note the use of the service cloth on the palm of the hand, with the service salver placed upon it

Figure 5.5 Carrying clean wine glasses on a service salver

Figure 5.6 Carrying dirty glasses on a service salver

- The purpose of this is to allow the service salver to be rotated more easily in order to remove each wine goblet in turn by the base and to set it on the table

Figure 5.6 indicates the use of the service salver for clearing dirty wine goblets from the table.

- The first dirty wine goblet cleared should be placed on the service salver nearest the holding hand. The use of the thumb over the base of the first glass cleared to hold it steady whilst clearing further glasses is acceptable
- As the dirties are cleared, they should be placed on the service salver firstly nearest the holding hand, working out to fill the service salver as more glasses are added. This ensures a better and more even distribution of weight and lessens the likelihood of accidents occurring

For the purposes of carrying glasses about to set up for functions, use is often made of glass racks which enable the transportation of glasses in bulk once they have been washed and polished at a central point.

Carrying trays

Trays are used for:

- Carrying food from the kitchen to the restaurant sideboard
- Service in rooms and lounges
- Clearing from sideboards
- Clearing from tables (when customer is not seated at the table)
- Carrying equipment

The correct method of holding and carrying a tray is to position the tray lengthways onto the forearm and to support it by holding the tray with the other hand.

Figure 5.7 shows how to carry an oblong tray. Note the tray is organized so that the heaviest items are nearest the carrier. This helps the balancing of the tray. Also note that one hand is placed underneath the tray and the other at the side.

5.2 Interpersonal skills

Interpersonal skills in food and beverage service centre on the interactions between the customer and the food and beverage service staff. All other interactions are secondary to, and the result of, the prime interaction of customers and staff. This has implications for the way customers are treated. Conversations between customers and staff override conversations between staff and staff. When in conversation with customers, staff should not:

- Talk to other members of staff without first excusing themselves from the customer

Figure 5.7 Carrying a loaded oblong tray

- Interrupt interactions between customers and staff, but should wait until there is a suitable moment to catch the attention of the other member of staff so that they may excuse themselves from the customer first

- Serve customers whilst carrying on a conversation between themselves

- Talk across rooms either to each other or to customers

The customers should be made to feel that they are being cared for and not that they are an intrusion into the operation.

Interpersonal skills also relate to specific points of the service for example:

- Showing customers to their table – always walk with them at their pace

- Seating customers – ladies first descending in age unless the host is a lady

- Handling coats/wraps – handle with obvious care (see Section 10.1, page 365)

- Handing menus/wine lists to customers – offer the list and wait for the customer to take it

- Opening and placing a napkin – open carefully, do not shake it like a duster, place it on the customer's lap after saying excuse me to the customer

- When offering water, rolls say, for example: '*Excuse me Sir/Madam, would you like a bread roll?*'

- Offering accompaniments – only offer them if you have them at the table. Offering them when they are not at the table usually means 'I will get them if you really want them!'

- Serving and clearing – always say '*Excuse me*' before serving or clearing and '*Thank you*' after you have finished with each customer

- Explaining food and beverage items – use terms the customer understands (ie not technical terms such as *turned vegetable* or *pané*); use terms which make the item sound attractive, eg *casserole* not *stew*, *creamed* or *purée* potatoes not *mashed*; do not use abbreviations, eg *veg*

- Talking to customers – only when standing next to them – and looking at them.

Other procedures which contribute to good interpersonal skills are highlighted throughout the rest of this chapter. Also see Section 10.5, page 390.

Addressing customers

'*Sir*' or '*Madam*' should be used when the name is known, eg Mr Smith, Miss Jones. First names should only be used in less formal operations where the customer explicitly indicated that this is acceptable. If the customer has a title, then appropriate use should be made of the correct forms of address (see Section 9.3, page 342).

Greetings such as '*Good morning*' and '*Good evening*' should be used upon receiving customers, or when the member of staff first comes into contact with the customer (that is, when lounge service staff attend people already seated in the lounge and so on).

During service

When an unforeseen incident arises it must be coped with promptly and efficiently without causing any more disturbance than is necessary to any of the other guests. Quick action will very often soothe the irate customer and ensure a return visit to your establishment. It is worth remembering at this stage that in case of complaints, whatever their nature, they should be referred immediately to the supervisor. Delay can only cause confusion and very often the wrong interpretation may be put on a situation if left to be dealt with later. In the case of accidents, a report of the incident must be kept and signed by those involved.

Listed below are a few of those incidents which might occur and the suggested steps that should be taken in order to put right any fault.

Spillages

It is possible that during the service of a course a few drops of sauce or roast gravy may have fallen on the tablecloth. The following steps should be taken:

1 Check immediately that none has fallen on the guest being served. Apologize to the guest

2 If some has fallen on the guest's clothing, allow the guest to rub over the dirtied area with a clean damp cloth. This will remove the worst of the spillage

3 If it is necessary for the guest to retire to the cloakroom to remove the spillage then his/her meal should be placed on the hotplate until he/she returns

4 Depending on the nature of the spillage the establishment may offer to have the garment concerned cleaned

5 If the spillage has gone on the tablecloth, the waiter should first of all remove any items of equipment that may be dirtied or in his/her way

6 He/she should then mop or scrape up the spillage with either a clean damp cloth or a knife

7 An old menu card should then be placed on top of the table but under the tablecloth over the damaged area

8 A second menu should be placed on the tablecloth over the damaged area

9 A clean rolled serviette should then be brought to the table and rolled completely over the damaged area. The menu will prevent any damp from soaking into the clean serviette

10 Any items of equipment removed should be returned to their correct position on the table top

11 Any meals taken to the hotplate should be returned and fresh covers put down where necessary

12 Again apologies should be made to guests for any inconvenience caused

---

A glass of water is knocked over accidentally by a guest. The following steps should be taken:

---

1 Ensure none has gone on the guest

2 If some of the water has fallen on the guest's clothing then follow A2 and 3, above

3 Where possible, as this form of accident usually involves changing the tablecloth, the party of guests should be seated at another table and allowed to continue their meal without delay

4 If they cannot be moved to another table then they should be seated slightly back from the table so that the waiter can carry out the necessary procedures to rectify the fault speedily and efficiently

5 The guests' meals should be placed on the hotplate to keep warm

6 All dirty items should be removed on a tray to the waiter's sideboard ready to go to the wash-up area

7 All clean items should be removed and kept on the waiter's sideboard for relaying

8 The tablecloth should be mopped with a clean absorbent cloth to remove as much of the liquid as possible

9 A number of old menus should be placed on the table top but underneath the tablecloth

10 A clean tablecloth of the correct size should be brought to the table. It should be opened out and held in the correct manner as if one were laying a tablecloth during the pre-service preparation period. The table should then be clothed up in the usual manner except that when the clean cloth is being drawn across the table towards the waiter he/she is at the same time taking off the soiled tablecloth. The soiled tablecloth should be removed at the same time that the clean tablecloth is being laid so that none of the table top can be seen by the guests at any time. The old menus will prevent any dampness penetrating to the clean tablecloth

11 When the table has its clean tablecloth on it should be relaid as quickly as possible

12 The guests should then be re-seated at the table and the meals returned to them from the hotplate

Returned food

A guest suggests that the fish dish served is 'off '. The following steps should be taken:

1 Apologize to the guest
2 The dish should be removed to sideboard to be returned to aboyeur at hotplate
3 The guest should be offered the menu and asked if he/she would like another portion of the same dish or prefer to choose something else as an alternative
4 A special check for the new order should be written out:

Figure 5.8 Example of a returned food check

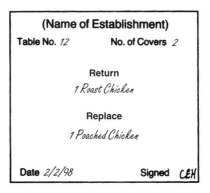

> (Name of Establishment)
>
> Table No. *12*   No. of Covers *2*
>
> **Return**
> *1 Roast Chicken*
>
> **Replace**
> *1 Poached Chicken*
>
> Date *2/2/98*   Signed *CEH*

This shows the dish being returned and what the guest is having in its place

5 A fresh cover should be laid
6 The new dish should be collected as soon as possible from the hotplate
7 It should be served to the guest
8 Apologies should be made for any inconvenience caused
9 The waiter must ensure that the aboyeur receives the dish being returned and checks it immediately, because it may mean that the particular dish concerned has to be taken off the menu to prevent the chance of food poisoning
10 The policy of the establishment would dictate whether or not the guest is to be charged for the alternative dish

Lost property

A waiter finds a wallet under a chair, recently vacated by one of the clients. The following steps should be taken:

1 A check should be made immediately as to whether or not the guest has left the service area. If he/she is still in the area, the wallet may be returned to him/her

2 If the guest has left the service area, the waiter should hand the wallet to the head waiter or supervisor in charge

3 The supervisor or head waiter should check with reception and the hall-porter to see if the guest has left the building

4 If the guest concerned is a resident, then reception may ring his/her room, stating the wallet has been found and can be collected at a convenient time

5 If the guest is a regular customer, it is possible that the head waiter or head porter may know where to contact him/her to call for the wallet

6 If the guest is a regular customer but cannot be contacted, the wallet should be kept in the lost property office until the customer's next visit

7 If the owner has not been found or contacted immediately, the head waiter or supervisor should list the items contained in the wallet with the waiter who found the wallet. The list should be signed by both the head waiter or supervisor and the finder (the waiter). The list must be dated and also indicate where the article was found and at what time

8 A copy of this list should go with the wallet to the lost property office where the contents of the wallet must be checked against the list before it is accepted. The details of the find are then entered in a lost property register

9 Another copy of the list should go to the hall porter in case any enquiries are received concerning a wallet. Anyone claiming lost property should be passed on to the lost property office

10 Before the lost property office hands over any lost property, a description of the article concerned and its contents should be asked for to ensure as far as possible that it is being returned to the genuine owner. The office should also see proof of identity of the person claiming ownership

11 In the case of all lost property, the above mentioned steps should be carried out as quickly as possible as this is in the best interests of the establishment and causes the guest minimum inconvenience. On receipt of lost property, the guest should be asked to sign for the article concerned, also giving his/her address

12 Any lost property unclaimed after three months may become the property of the finder who should claim it through the head waiter or supervisor

Illness

A guest falls ill in your establishment. The following steps should be taken:

1 As soon as it is noticed that a guest is feeling unwell while in the dining room or restaurant a person in authority should be immediately called to the spot
2 The person in authority must enquire if the guest needs assistance. At the same time he/she must try to judge whether the illness is of a serious nature or not
3 It is often advisable in cases such as this to take the guest to another room to see if they are able to recover in a few minutes
4 It this happens their meal should be placed on the hotplate until their return
5 If the illness appears to be of a serious nature, a doctor, nurse or someone qualified in first-aid should be called for immediately
6 The guest should not be moved until after a doctor has examined him/her
7 If necessary the area should be screened off
8 Although this is a difficult situation to deal with in front of the general public the minimum fuss should be made, and service to the rest of the guests carried on normally
9 It is best, if at all possible, to have the guest who has fallen ill immediately moved to another room where he/she may rest out of the heat of the dining area. This causes minimum fuss in the restaurant or dining room itself
10 The doctor should advise whether an ambulance should be called
11 If the guest falling ill is a woman then a female member of staff should attend her
12 The guest may have had a sudden stomach upset and wish to leave without finishing the meal. A taxi should be called to take the guest home
13 It should be left to the good judgement of the staff concerned whether the guest should be accompanied or not
14 Payment for that part of the meal consumed, and the taxi fare would be according to the policy of the establishment
15 It is most important that for all accidents, minor or serious, *all* details are recorded in an accident book. This is in case of a claim against the establishment at a later date
16 If after a short period of time the guest returns and continues with the meal, a fresh cover should be laid and the meal returned from the hotplate

Alcohol over-consumption

If a guest is suspected of having too much to drink the following steps should be taken:

1 If a prospective client asks for a table and the staff believe the client is possibly under the influence of drink they may refuse a table, even though there may be one available
2 It is not always possible, however, to recognize a guest who may prove objectionable later on
3 If difficulty is found in handling this type of person then assistance in removing the person from the eating area may come from the members of staff or the hall porter

4 If a guest is suspected of being drunk this must first of all be ascertained by the head waiter or supervisor

5 The guest should then be asked to leave rather than be allowed to become objectionable to other guests later on

6 If the guest has already consumed part of the meal but is not being objectionable then the remainder of the meal should be served in the normal fashion, but the head waiter or supervisor must ensure no more alcoholic beverage is offered

7 On finishing, the guest should be watched until he/she has left the premises

8 It is always advisable to make out a report of all such incidents, and they should be brought to the immediate attention of the restaurant manager in case of any claim at a later date concerning a particular incident

Unsatisfactory appearance

A customer's appearance is not satisfactory. The following steps should be taken:

1 If a guest's appearance is likely to give offence to others then they should be asked to correct their dress to the approved fashion

2 If the guest will not comply with the request, he/she should be asked to leave

3 If he/she has partly consumed a meal then whether he/she will be charged or not depends on the policy of the house and the discretion of the head waiter or supervisor

4 A report of this incident must be made and signed by the staff concerned

Records

It is advisable that when any incident occurs a report is made out immediately. The basic information that should be found in the report is as follows:

1 Place
2 Date
3 Time
4 Nature of incident
5 Individual reports from those concerned and signed
6 Action taken
7 Name, address and phone number of the guest involved, and also of the staff involved

All reports should be kept in case similar incidents occur at a later date, and for future reference should the need arise.

Lost children

Should a child be reported lost, the following steps should be taken:

1 Take a complete description of the child lost:

    (a) male/female

    (b) age

    (c) where last seen

    (d) clothing worn

    (e) any predominant features

    (f) colour of hair

    (g) any accessories, ie handbag/doll, etc

2 Immediately inform the supervisor/security

3 Constant watch on all entrances/exits

4 Check all cloakroom/rest areas and immediate vicinity where the child has been reported missing

5 Should nothing result from taking the above actions, immediately inform the local police

Dealing with children

Should children be amongst the customers arriving in your food service area then the lead concerning their welfare should be taken from the parents or accompanying adults.

    Where applicable, the following factors should be determined:

1 Are high chairs/seat cushions required?

2 Restrictions on the service of alcohol to minors (see page 360)

3 Are 'children's meal' menus required?

4 The portion size if ordered from the normal menu

5 The provision of children's 'give aways', ie crayons, colouring books, etc

6 For the safety of both children and others, the staff should be aware of children's movements

7 Should the children be of a more mature child's age, then they must be addressed as either '*Sir*' or '*Madam*'

Customer mobility

Extra awareness is needed to meet the requirements of customers who may have special needs, such as mobility problems. The following considerations should be given on these occasions:

1 Place wheelchair users at tables where there is adequate space for manoeuvrability

2 Position him/her out of the main thoroughfare of customer/staff movement

3 Position him/her with easy access to cloakrooms, exits and fire exits

4 Always ensure that menus, wine lists and the like are immediately available to any wheelchair user

5 Never move the wheelchair without the customer being asked first

6 Crutches/walking sticks should be placed in an accessible and readily available position

Blind and partially sighted customers

Awareness is also required to meet the needs of those customers who may be blind or partially sighted. Here the following considerations should be given:

1 Talk to and treat the customer with special needs as you would any other customer
2 Remember it is 'by touch' that blind people see and are made aware that they are involved in what is happening around them
3 Immediately prior to 'ordering', a gentle touch on the hand or arm attracts his/her attention to you
4 Offer to fillet/bone fish and meat items
5 Offer to cut up potato and vegetable items should it be necessary
6 Never overfill cups, glasses or soup bowls
7 Should you feel it appropriate, use 'bowls' instead of 'plates' for specific food items, but always ask the guest first

Ask if you should describe where the food items are on the plate. Use the clock method to explain the location of food on a plate eg, 6 o'clock for meat, 10 to 10 for vegetables, 10 past 2 for potatoes.

Customers with communication difficulties

You should also be aware of 'communication' problems that may arise when, for example, customers are deaf or hard of hearing or have little understanding of the English language. In these cases the following steps should be taken:

1 Speak directly at the customer
2 Stand in such a position that the customer is able to see your face clearly
3 Speak normally but more distinctly
4 Describe food/drink items in simple, precise and plain language
5 Seat customers away from possible excessive noise as this is most uncomfortable for customers wearing hearing aids
6 In these instances always read back the food or drink order received to confirm all requests
7 Listen attentively to what is being said to you to ensure you understand the customer's requirements

5.3 Taking bookings

Procedure

1 When the telephone rings, lift the receiver and say: '*Good morning* (state the name of the establishment), *may I help you?*'

2 If the customer is making the booking in person then say '*Good morning Sir/Madam, how may I help you?*'

3 When taking a booking the essential information required is as follows:
   - Day
   - Date
   - Name
   - Number of covers
   - Time
   - Any special requests

4 When you have received this information from the prospective customer it is advisable to repeat it all as confirmation to the customer

5 If a cancellation is being received then again confirm the cancellation with the customer by repeating his/her request over the telephone and then ask if you can take a booking for any other occasion in place of the cancellation

6 At the end of a telephone call for a booking one should say: '*Thank you for your booking, we shall look forward to seeing you.*'

The booking sheet

An example booking sheet is given in Figure 5.9. This form gives the maximum number of covers to be booked for that service period and provides for a running total of pre-booked covers to be kept. The form also has space for the customer's telephone number. For parties of six or more it may be the policy of the establishment to request written confirmation or to take a credit card number. Other information that might be sought is smoking or non-smoking if the operation has separate designated smoking areas.

Figure 5.9 Example of booking sheet

Restaurant.................	Day..................		Date..................		Maximum covers	
Name	**Tel No.**	**Covers**	**Arrival time**	**Running total**	**Special requirements**	**Signature**

If party bookings require special menus, the booking should be referred to the supervisor. Procedures similar to function catering booking will then be adopted (see Section 9.2, page 330).

5.4 Preparation for service

The duties to be carried out before the service commences are many and varied according to the particular food and beverage service area concerned. A list of the possible tasks and duties is shown below, but it should be noted that not all of them are applicable to every situation and there may be some jobs not listed which are peculiar to a particular establishment. The term *mise-en-place* ('preparation for service') is the traditional term used for all the duties that have to be carried out in order to have the room ready for service. A duty rota showing the tasks and duties to be completed before service, and which member of staff is responsible, is drawn up (see Section 10.6, page 393).

Daily duties

The daily duties might be stated as follows:

Supervisor

1 Check the booking diary for reservations
2 Make out the seating plan for the day and allocate customers accordingly
3 Make out a plan of the various stations and show where the staff will be working
4 Go over the menu with staff immediately before service is due to commence
5 Check that all duties on the duty rota are covered and that a full team of staff is present.

Housekeeping duties

Housekeeping duties include the reception area and may involve the following:

1 Every day, vacuum the carpet and brush surrounds
2 Clean and polish doors and glass
3 Empty wastebins and ash trays
4 Perform one of the following tasks, as appropriate:
    * *Monday*: brush and dust tables and chairs
    * *Tuesday*: polish all sideboards, window ledges and cash desk
    * *Wednesday*: polish all brasses
    * *Thursday*: clean and polish the reception area
    * Commence again as Monday
5 Each day, on completion of all duties, line up tables and chairs for laying up

Linen/paper

This applies not only to table, buffet and slip cloths, and glass and waiter cloths, but also to paper slip cloths and napkins plus dish papers and doilies.
    Duties might include:

1 Collecting the clean linen from the housekeeping department, checking items against list, distributing them to the various service points, laying tablecloths and folding serviettes. Spare linen should be folded neatly into the linen basket
2 Ensuring that stocks are sufficient to meet needs

3 Ensuring that glass cloths and waiters' cloths are available
4 Providing dish papers and doilies as required
5 The preparation of the linen basket for return to the linen room

Hotplate

1 Switch on the hotplate
2 Ensure all doors are closed
3 Items to be placed in the hotplate would be according to the menu offered, for example:
   - Soup plates
   - Consommé cups
   - Fish plates
   - Joint plates
   - Sweet plates
   - Coffee cups
4 Set out the required kitchen silver on top of the hotplate, including cloches
5 Stock up after each service with clean and polished china in readiness for the next meal service

Silver

Duties might include:

1 Collection of cutlery, flatware and hollow-ware from the silver room
2 Polishing and sorting on to trays the following items in quantities agreed with the supervisor:
   - Service spoons
   - Joint/service forks
   - Sweet spoons
   - Sweet forks
   - Soup spoons
   - Tea/coffee spoons
   - Fish knives
   - Fish forks
   - Joint knives
   - Side knives
   - Specialist silver as required for menu
   - Stocking of sideboards
3 Daily cleaning:
   - Spirit and electric heaters
   - Flare lamps, spirit and gas
   - Ashtrays
   - Carving trolley
4 Additional cleaning of cutlery, flatware and hollow-ware as per the daily rota, for example:
   - *Monday*: all round flats, all knives, large coffee pots and milk jugs
   - *Tuesday*: 41 cm, 46 cm, 56 cm (16, 18, 22 in) oval flats, all forks, small coffee pots and milk jugs

- *Wednesday*: round vegetable dishes and lids, all spoons, large coffee pots and milk jugs
- *Thursday*: oval vegetable dishes and lids, small items of special equipment, individual soup tureens
- *Friday*: any other items that it may be necessary to clean on a regular rota basis in order to ensure that everything is cleaned at regular intervals and nothing missed. At the same time by using this method anything broken or that may be in need of replacing can be noted and put on one side for repair

Crockery

Duties include:

1. The checking and polishing of sideplates ready for lay-up
2. The checking and polishing of crockery for hotplate according to menu and service requirements
3. Preparation of service plates/flats for sideboards
4. Preparation of stocks of crockery for sideboards:
   - Fishplates
   - Sideplates
   - Coffee saucers

Cruets, ashtrays, table numbers and butter dishes

Duties include:

1. The collection of cruets, ashtrays, table numbers and butter dishes from the silver room
2. Checking, filling and polishing the cruets
3. The laying on tables of cruets, ashtrays, table numbers and butter dishes with knives, according to the head waiter's instructions
4. Restoring following service

Stillroom

Duties include:

1. The ordering of stores requirements (check with the bar and accompaniments)
2. The preparation of
   - Coffee services and other beverage service items
   - Butter scrolls/butter pats
   - Melba toast
   - Other toast, bread and butter for special dishes
3. The clearing of the stillroom area following service
4. Polishing and refilling oil and vinegar stands, sugar basins and dredgers, peppermills and cayenne pepper pots
5. Preparing all accompaniments: tomato ketchup, French and English mustard, ground ginger, horseradish sauce, mint sauce, Worcester sauce, Parmesan cheese
6. Distributing the cruets to the tables and the accompaniments to the sideboards. For the

number of accompaniments and sets of cruets to prepare, check with the head waiter the number of sideboards and tables that will be in use

Sideboards

Items to be placed on the sideboard after ensuring it is polished:

- Assorted tableware from right to left: service spoon and forks, dessert spoons and forks, soup, tea and coffee spoons, fish knives and forks, joint knives, side knives
- Assorted china: joint plates, fish plates, side plates, sweet plates, coffee saucers, consommé saucers, etc, according to the menu
- Service plate and service salver
- Soup and sauce ladles
- Under-flats for vegetable and entrée dishes and for sauce boats
- Spirit or electric heater after it has been cleaned
- Roll basket
- Check pads, service cloths, menus
- Guéridons may have to be laid up in conjunction with the sideboards according to the type of service offered

Figure 5.10 Example of a sideboard lay-up

Key
1   Service spoons and forks
2   Sweet spoons and forks
3   Soup spoons, teaspoons, coffee spoons
4   Fish knives and forks
5   Joint knives
6   Side knives
7   Fish plates
8   Sweet plates
9   Sideplates
10   Coffee saucers
11   Underflats
12   Service salver
13   Dirty linen
14   Check pad on service plate
15   Assorted condiments
16   Ashtrays
17   Water jugs
18   Bread basket and butter
19   Hotplate
20   Trays

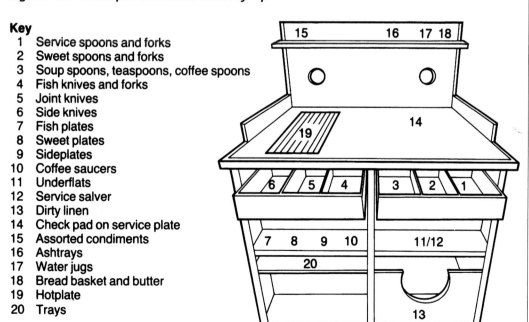

Figure 5.11 Laid sideboard

Dispense bar

Mise-en-place may involve the following duties:

1 Open the bar: remove the liqueur trolley from the bar area
2 Bar silver requiring cleaning to be taken to the silverman
3 Clear any debris left from the previous day
4 Wipe down bar tops
5 Clean shelves and swab out the bar floor
6 Check optics
7 Prepare ice-buckets, wine coolers, service trays and water jugs
8 Check pads and wine lists; line up, clean and polish aperitif glasses
9 Check the liqueur trolley for glasses, stock and bottle presentation
10 Prepare the bar service top according to the standards of the establishment which may include:

- Cutting board
- Fruit knife
- Fruit: Lemons
  Orange
  Apples
- Cucumber
- 1 egg (fresh)
- Mixing glass, spoons

- Hawthorn strainer
- Cocktail shaker
- Wine funnel
- Glass jar with olives
- Coloured sugar
- Angostura bitters
- Peach bitters
- Worcester sauce

- Cocktail sticks
- Cherries in glass
- Straws in sherry glass
- Tea strainer
- Wine coasters
- Spirit measures
- Soda syphon
- Ice bucket and tongs

Miscellaneous

1 Prepare and lay up the carving trolley, sweet trolley and hors-d'oeuvre trolley
2 Polish the sideplates and fish plates required for laying up
3 As the necessary preparatory work is completed the staff should report back to the head waiter who must check that the work has been carried out in a satisfactory manner and then reallocate the member of staff to work involving the laying-up of the room

So that the duties may be carried out efficiently, they should proceed in a certain order. It goes without saying that the dusting should not be done after the tables are laid, or the tables and chairs put in place before the vacuuming is completed. Therefore a suggested order of work might be as follows:

1 Dusting
2 Stacking chairs on the tables
3 Vacuuming
4 Polishing
5 Arrange tables and chairs according to the table plan
6 Linen
7 Accompaniments
8 Hotplate
9 Stillroom
10 Sideboards
11 Silver cleaning
12 Miscellaneous: trolleys

Some of these jobs will be carried out at the same time and the head waiter must ensure they are completed efficiently.

Display buffet

Duties include:

1 The preparation of the buffet table to the supervisor's instructions
2 The display of:
- Butter dishes and knives
- Accompaniments
- Food items
- Special cutlery and tableware as required (eg grapefruit spoons)
- Underplates for large butter dishes
- Service spoons and forks
- Sideplates with doilies if necessary
- Water jugs and joint knives for pâtés or mousses
- Cold fish plates
- Carving knife

Trolleys

Duties can include:

Carving trolley

1 Check the trolley for cleanliness
2 Check and refill methylated spirit burners
3 Fill the water reservoir with boiling water from the still
4 Lay up the bottom shelf only
5 Ensure the sauce and gravy reservoirs are in place under cover. They should be sited beside the plate platform
6 Lay up for the top shelf: folded linen napkin *only*
7 Lay up for the bottom shelf: service plate with
   - 1 joint knife
   - 6 service spoons and forks
   - 2 sauce ladles (set into a folded (pouch) napkin)
   - Service plate with carving knife, fork and steel (the steel placed between plates)

See Section 8.3, page 279 for a photograph of a carving trolley.

Sweet trolley

1 Check trolleys for cleanliness and polish
2 Place doilies or cloths on top tiers
3 Place on the bottom shelf on a folded slip cloth:
   - Sweet plates/bowls
   - Gâteau slice, pastry tongs (in the drawer or on a service plate)
   - Service spoons and forks
   - Joint knives
   - Sauce ladles (in a folded napkin)
   - Joint plate for dirty service gear

Cheese trolley

1 Check the trolley for cleanliness
2 The top and bottom shelves could be laid up as follows:

Top shelf:
   - Salt and pepper
   - Castor sugar
   - Flat or dish with assorted biscuits
   - Various cheeses on a cheeseboard
   - Knives and forks for cheese service
   - Celery glass on underplate

Bottom shelf:
   - Sideplates
   - Side knives

For reference, see page 209 for an example of a sweet/cheese trolley.

Clothing-up
Laying the tablecloth

Before laying the tablecloth the table and chairs should be in their correct position. The table top should be clean and the table level, with care being taken to ensure that it does not wobble. If the table wobbles slightly, a disc sliced from a cork will correct the problem.

Next, the correct size of tablecloth should be collected. Most tablecloths are folded in what is known as a *screen fold*.

The waiter should stand between the legs of the table to ensure the corners of the cloth cover the legs.

The screen fold should be opened out across the table in front of the waiter with the inverted and two single folds facing them ensuring that the inverted fold is on top. The cloth should then be laid in the following manner:

- place the thumb on top of the inverted fold with the index and third fingers either side of the middle fold
- spread out your arms as close to the width of the table as is possible and lift the cloth so that the bottom leaf falls free
- this should be positioned over the opposite edge of the table to where you are standing
- now let go of the middle fold and open the cloth out towards you until the table is covered with the cloth
- check that the cloth is even on all sides
- any adjustments should be made from the edge of the cloth

The points which should be noted if the tablecloth is laid correctly are as follows:

- The corners of the tablecloth should cover the legs of the table
- The overlap should be even all round the table: 30–45 cm (12–18 in)
- The creases of the tablecloth should all run the same way in the room
- If two tablecloths are necessary to cover a table for a larger party then the overlap of the two tablecloths should face away from the entrance to the room. This is for presentation purposes of both the room and the table

Nothing is more attractive in the room than tables clothed-up with clean, crisp and well-starched linen tablecloths. The tablecloth should be handled as little as possible and this will be ensured by laying the tablecloth in the correct manner.

Serviette folds

There are many forms of serviette fold to be found in use in the food and beverage service area. Some are intricate in their detail while others are more simple. The simpler folds are used in everyday service and some of the more complex and difficult folds may be used on special occasions, such as luncheons, dinners and weddings.

There are three main reasons why the more simple folds are better than the more complex ones:

1 The serviette, if folded correctly, can look well and add to the general appearance of the room whether it be a simple or difficult fold
2 Perhaps more important is the question of hygiene. The more complex fold involves greater handling to complete and its appearance, when unfolded to spread over the guest's lap, is poor as it contains creases
3 The complex fold takes much more time to complete properly than does a very simple fold

The majority of serviette folds have special names, eg:

- Cone
- Bishop's mitre
- Rose
- Prince of Wales feather
- Cockscomb
- Triple wave

The *rose* fold of serviette is one in which rolls or Melba toast may be presented at the table. The *triple wave* is an attractive fold which may be used for a special function to hold the menu and a name card.

The napkin folds shown in Figure 5.12 are, in the main, those used every day in the food and beverage service area and for special occasions. These are the simpler folds that may be completed more quickly, requiring less handling by the operator and may therefore be said to be more hygienic. The *boat* (not illustrated) is a more complex fold, requiring longer to complete, needing more handling and looking rather 'crushed' when unfolded to lay across the guest's lap.

Figure 5.12 Napkin folds
Left to right: *1 bishop's mitre 2 rose 3 cone 4 cockscomb*

Napkin folding

Shown below are four basic but decorative napkin folds. These are:

1 Bishop's mitre
2 Rose
3 Cockscomb
4 Cone

Once you become competent at these, then learn the art of folding others to extend your repertoire.

Bishop's mitre

1 Lay the napkin out flat in front of you (see Figure 5.13(a))
2 Fold it in half, straight side to straight side (see Figure 5.13(b))
3 Take the top right corner and fold it down to the centre of the bottom line (see Figure 5.13(c))
4 Take the bottom left corner and fold it up to meet the centre of the top line (see Figure 5.13(d))
5 Turn the napkin over so that the folds are now face down (see Figure 5.13(e))
6 Take the top line (edge) and fold it down to meet the base line (bottom edge), leaving the two peaks pointing away from you (see Figure 5.13(f))
7 Take the bottom right-hand side and fold it under the flap on the left side. Make sure it tucks right under the flap for a snug fit (see Figure 5.13(g))
8 Turn it completely over (see Figure 5.13(h))
9 Again take the bottom right-hand side and fold it under the flap on the left side. Now stand napkin up by pulling sides of the base out until it is circular in shape (see Figure 5.13(i))

Figure 5.13 Bishop's mitre

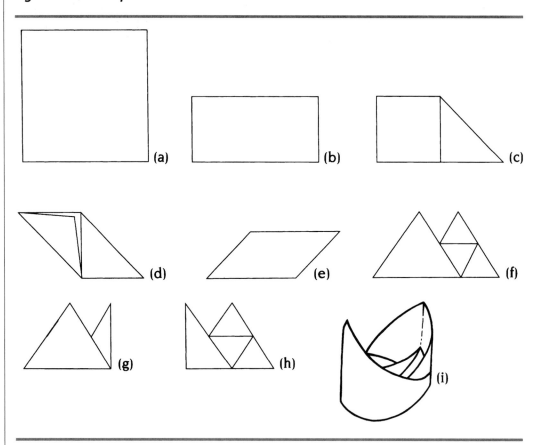

Rose

1. Unfold the napkin and lay it out in a square (see Figure 5.14(a))
2. Fold the corners into the centre of the napkin (see Figure 5.14(b))
3. Fold the corners into the centre of the napkin for a second time (see Figure 5.14(c))
4. Turn the whole napkin over so that all the corners folded into the centre are underneath (see Figure 5.14(d))
5. Fold the corners into the centre once more (see Figure 5.14(e))
6. Hold the four centre points down by means of an upturned 'Paris' goblet (see Figure 5.14(f))
7. Holding the Paris goblet steady, place your hand under each corner and pull up a folded corner of the napkin (petal) on to the bowl of the glass. You now have four petals showing. Now place your hand under the napkin, but between each of the petals, and raise a further four petals. Place on a doily on an underplate (see Figure 5.14(g))

Note: a The napkin must be clean and well starched

b Run the back of your hand over every fold to make the crease firm and sharp

Figure 5.14 Rose

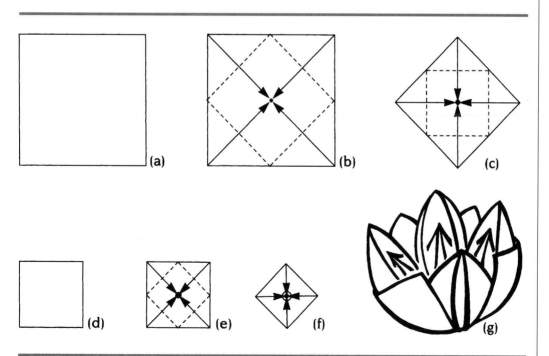

Cockscomb

1 Open the napkin into a square shape (see Figure 5.15(a))
2 Fold it in half (see Figure 5.15(b))
3 Fold it in half again to make a square (see Figure 5.15(c))
4 Rotate the square so that it now forms a diamond shape in front of you. Make sure the four single folds are at the bottom of the diamond (see Figure 5.15(d))
5 Fold the bottom corner of the diamond to the top corner. You will then have a triangular shape in front of you, with the four single folds on top (see Figure 5.15(e))
6 Take the right side of the triangle and fold it over on to the centre line (see Figure 5.15(f))
7 Do the same with the left-hand side (see Figure 5.15(g))
8 Tuck the two lower triangles (A and B) under the main triangle (see Figure 5.15(h))
9 Fold the two triangles (C and D) down from the centre line and hold it together. The four single folds should now be on top and at the peak of this fold (see Figure 5.15(i))
10 Hold this narrow fold firmly, ensuring the four single folds are away from you. In turn, pull each single fold up and towards you (see Figure 5.15(j))

Figure 5.15 Cockscomb

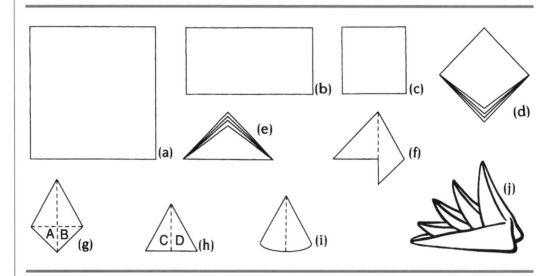

Cone

1 Open the napkin out lengthways in front of you (see Figure 5.16(a))
2 Take the top left corner and fold it diagonally on to the right end of the centre line (see Figure 5.16(b))
3 Fold the bottom square on to the top triangle (see Figure 5.16(c))
4 Take the two points at the top right corner, by placing your hand inside the napkin, and fold them back towards you as far as possible (see Figure 5.16(d))
5 Pull the base out so that it is circular and place it in the centre of the cover (see Figure 5.16(e))

Figure 5.16 Cone

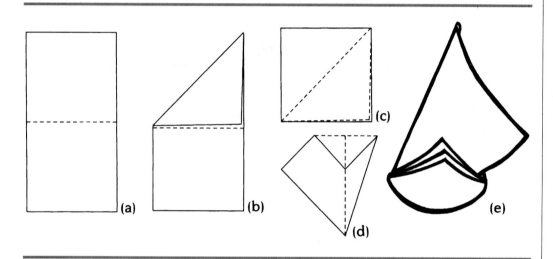

Laying covers for table service and assisted service

Cover

One of the technical terms very often used in the hospitality industry is a *cover*. What does this mean? There are two definitions according to the context.

1 When discussing how many guests a restaurant or dining room will seat, or how many guests will be attending a certain cocktail party, we refer to the *total number of guests concerned* as so many 'covers'. For example: a restaurant or dining room will seat a maximum of 85 covers (guests); there will be 250 covers (guests) at a certain cocktail party; this table will seat a party of six covers (guests).
2 When laying a table in readiness for service there are a variety of place-settings which may be laid according to the type of meal and service being offered. We refer to this *place-setting* as a certain type of 'cover' being laid. In other words a cover denotes all the

necessary cutlery, flatware, crockery, glassware and linen necessary to lay a certain type of place-setting for a specific meal.

When deciding on the laying of covers there are two basic service considerations. The first is where cutlery and flatware for the meal is to be laid before each course is served. The second is where the cutlery and flatware for the meal is to be laid prior to the start of that meal and for all the courses which are to be served. The first approach is known as the *à la carte* cover and the second is known as the *table d'hôte* cover.

À la carte cover

This cover follows the principle that the cutlery and flatware for each course will be laid just before each course is served. The traditional cover, given below, therefore represents the cover for *hors-d'oeuvre*, which is the first course in a classic menu sequence (see section 3.1, page 64). There are now a variety of differing approaches to what is laid for this form of service. This can include using large decorative cover plates and a side plate and knife only, or replacing the fish knife and fork with a joint knife and fork.

- Fish plate
- Serviette
- Fish knife
- Fish fork

Figure 5.17 A la carte cover

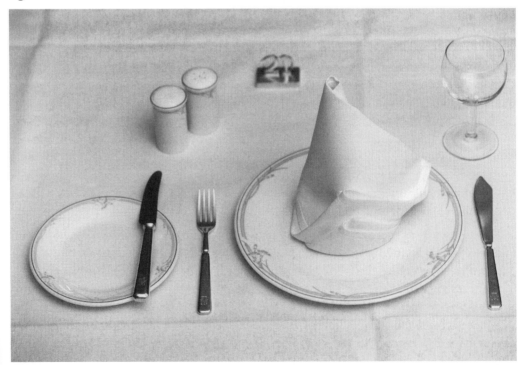

- Sideplate
- Side knife
- Wine glass

Table d'hôte cover

This cover follows the principle that the cutlery and flatware for the whole meal will be laid before the first course is served. The traditional cover is given below. Again there are some possible variations to this approach which could, for instance, omit the sweet spoon and fork.

- Serviette
- Soup spoon
- Fish knife
- Fish fork
- Joint knife
- Joint fork
- Sweet spoon
- Sweet fork
- Sideplate
- Side knife
- Wine glass

Figure 5.18 Table d'hôte cover

Laying the table

Once the table is clothed-up it should be laid in readiness for service.

- If an à la carte cover is being laid then the first item set on the table should be the fish plate in the centre of each cover

- If a table d'hôte cover is being laid then the first item to be set on the table should be the serviette or sideplate in the centre of each cover

- If the sideplate were laid in the centre of each cover it would be moved to the left-hand side of the cover once all the cutlery and flatware had been laid. The purpose of initially placing something in the centre of the cover is to ensure that the covers are exactly opposite one another and that the cutlery and flatware of each cover are the same distance apart

- Cutlery and flatware should be laid from a service salver or service plate. An alternative to this is to use a service cloth and hold the items being laid in the service cloth, giving a final polish before setting the items on the table

In some instances a cutlery trolley is used for storing the cutlery and flatware and this should be pushed around the tables and then the cutlery and flatware laid after the final polish with the waiter's cloth.

When laying a table d'hôte cover, the cutlery and flatware should be laid from inside to the outside of the cover. This ensures even spacing of the cover and normally lessens the chances of having to handle the items laid more than is necessary.

In other words the order of laying should be:

Table d'hôte	A la carte
Napkin	Fish plate (centre of cover)
Joint knife	Fish knife
Fish knife	Fish fork
Soup spoon	Sideplate
Joint fork	Side knife
Fish fork	Napkin
Sweet fork	Paris goblet
Sweet spoon	
Sideplate	
Side knife	
Paris goblet	

After the above covers have been laid, the table lay-up should be completed by the addition of the following items:

- Cruets

- Ashtrays may be laid upon request from the customer depending on the establishment policy.

- Table numbers
- Table decorations

The waiter must ensure that where applicable all cutlery and flatware is laid 1.25 cm ($\frac{1}{2}$ in) from the edge of the table and that badged crockery has the badge or crest at the head or top of the cover. The glass after polishing should be placed upside down at the top right-hand corner of the cover. Once the covers have been laid the table accompaniments should be placed on the table according to the custom of the house.

Where an à la carte cover has been laid, the cutlery and flatware required by the guest for the dishes he/she has chosen will be laid course by course. In other words there should not, at any time during the meal, be more cutlery and flatware on the table than is required by the guest at that specific time.

If decorative cover plates are used for an à la carte cover it is common for the first course plates to be placed on this plate. The first course and the cover plate are then removed when the first course is cleared.

Where a table d'hôte cover has been laid the waiter should remove, after the order has been taken, any unnecessary cutlery and flatware and relay any extra items that may be required. This means that before the customer commences the meal he/she should have all the cutlery and flatware required for the dishes chosen, set out as his/her place setting or cover.

Polishing glassware

1 The following equipment is required to carry out this technique:
   - A container of boiling water
   - A clean, dry teacloth
   - The required glassware
2 Using the base of the glass to be cleaned, hold the wine goblet over the steam from the boiling water so that the steam enters the bowl of the glass (see Figure 5.19(a))

Figure 5.19 Polishing glassware

(a) Allowing steam to enter the bowl of the glass

(b) Polishing whilst rotating the glass

3 Rotate the wine goblet to allow the steam to circulate fully within the bowl of the glass and then hold the base of the glass over the steam

4 Now hold the base of the wine goblet in the clean, dry teacloth

5 Place the other hand underneath the teacloth in readiness to polish the bowl of the glass

6 Place the thumb of the 'polishing' hand inside the bowl of the glass and the fingers on the outside holding the bowl of the wine goblet gently but firmly. Rotate the wine goblet with the hand holding the base of the glass (see Figure 5.19(b))

7 When fully polished, hold the wine goblet up to the light to check that it is clean.

8 Ensure that the base of the glass is also clean.

Table accompaniments

The table accompaniments required to complete the table lay-up are the same whether an à la carte or table d'hôte cover has been laid. These are as follows:

- Cruet: salt, pepper, mustard and mustard spoon
- Ashtray (in Smoking Sections)
- Table number
- Vase of flowers

These are the basic items required to complete the table lay-up. In some establishments certain extra items will be placed on the table prior to the service to complete its lay-up. These may include:

- Roll basket
- Melba toast
- Gristicks
- Cayenne pepper
- Peppermill
- Butter pats

If some or all of these extra items are placed on the table this would be peculiar to a particular establishment. It is worth noting, however, that in first-class service the rolls, Melba toast and gristicks are not placed on the table beforehand but offered to the assembled guests once they are seated. Butter is not placed on the table until the guests are all seated at the table – the reason for this being that if placed on the table too soon before the guests are seated it becomes warm and begins to melt, losing some of its flavour. Cayenne pepper and a peppermill are accompaniments with particular dishes and should not be placed on the table unless these particular dishes are being served.

Preparation of customer buffets and counters
Buffet service

There are various types of buffet, namely knife and fork, fork, and finger buffets. The requirements of a particular occasion and the host's wishes will determine the exact format in setting up the room. Whatever the nature of the occasion there are certain basic principles to follow. These may be listed as follows:

1 The buffet should be set up in a prominent position in the room
2 There should be ample space on the buffet for display and presentation
3 The buffet should be within easy access of the stillroom and wash-up so that replenishment of the buffet and the clearing of dirties may be carried out without disturbing the guests
4 There must be ample space for customer circulation
5 Provision should be made for sufficient occasional tables and chairs
6 The total presentation of the room should be attractive and promote the right atmosphere

Setting up the buffet

The exact equipment required when setting up the room will be determined by the occasion, eg see Section 9.4, page 346).

The buffet should be covered with suitable cloths making sure that the drop of the cloth is within 1.25 cm ($\frac{1}{2}$ in) of the ground all the way around the front and sides of the buffet. If more than one cloth is used, the creases should also be lined up and where the cloths overlap one another the overlap should be facing away from the entrance to the room. The ends of the buffet should be '*box*' pleated, thereby giving a better overall presentation of the buffet.

To achieve a neat, crisp finish the procedure needs to be carried out with as little handling as possible.

This may be achieved in the following manner:

- with assistance open the screen fold out across the table from side to side (Figure 5.20(a))

- with a person at either end unfold the cloth so that the front and sides of the table are covered and the cloth is no more than 1.25 cm from the ground

- stand in front of the table and from the edge place your thumb on the front corner and take the far side of the cloth, lift and bring it back towards you in a semi circle motion (Figure 5.20(b)) this will bring the side of the cloth horizontal with the ground

- the fold on top of the table will now resemble a triangle (Figure 5.20(c)) this should be folded back towards the side of the table ensuring that the folded edge is in line with the side of the table (Figure 5.20(d))

- use the back of your hand to flatten the fold

- repeat the procedure at the other end of the table

All creases should be in line and slip cloths may be used to finish the top of the table.

Figure 5.20 Boxing a buffet table

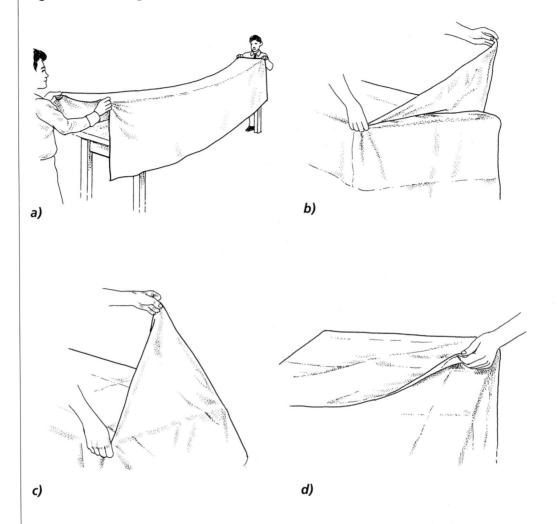

a)

b)

c)

d)

Counter service

This is a form of service whereby the customers collect a tray from the beginning of the service counter, move along the counter selecting their meal, pay cash and then collect the appropriate cutlery and flatware for their meal (see also pages 14 and 15 for different types of counter arrangements).

The menu offered would show a wide range of dishes from simple hot and cold snacks and beverages, all individually priced, to a limited table d'hôte menu with the set price of the meal being shown against the main course dishes offered.

At the entrance to the cafeteria or food service area the menus should be prominently displayed so that all customers may decide as far as possible what meal they will purchase before arriving at the service points. This saves time later and ensures that the customer turnover is as quick as possible. A tray stand should be placed at the beginning of the service counter from which each customer can collect his tray before proceeding along the counter.

The layout of the dishes on the counter is most important and it generally follows are found in the order in which they appear on the menu. This could be as follows: hors-d'oeuvre, fruit juices, fruit cocktails, cold meats and salads, bread rolls, butter, soups, hot fish dishes, hot meat dishes, hot vegetables, hot sweets, cold sweets, ice-cream, assorted sandwiches, cakes and pastries, beverages and cold drinks. Such a layout will make it more convenient for the customer as the food items are in a logical order.

An important aspect of the service counter is the presentation of the cold items to be sold. These must be well and attractively displayed, under cover for hygiene reasons and at the correct temperature.

With this form of service the meal may either be completely pre-plated or have the main meat/fish dish plated and the potatoes, vegetables, sauces and other accompaniments added according to the customer's choice. If the former is carried out it ensures a quicker turnover of customers through the various service points and requires less service top space. If the latter is the type of service offered, then the turnover of customers is much slower as the necessary potatoes, vegetables, sauces and accompaniments must be added on request. Also, more service top space is required for the vegetable and potato dishes, sauces and accompaniments to be kept hot in readiness for service. In this instance, more staff will be required for service and this in turn could increase the cost of the meal.

The length of the counter will generally be determined by the size of the menu offered, but should not be too long as it would then restrict the speed of service. At the end of the counter should be sited the cashier who charges for the meals chosen by the customers before they pass on to the seating area. Cutlery and tableware stands should be placed after the cashiers. They are placed here so that if a customer initially forgets to collect his/her cutlery or tableware, he/she may go back for it without interrupting the queue of customers.

Where this form of service is being carried out portion control equipment is used to ensure standardization of the size of portion served. Such equipment includes scoops, ladles, bowls, milk dispensers and cold beverage dispensers. At the same time great use is often made of pre-portioned foods such as butter, sugars, jams, cream, cheeses and biscuits.

Where the customer turnover rate is particularly high in a very limited period of time, a variation on the cafeteria/counter (straight line) type service operates with a number of separate/staggered service points (échelon service). Each of the service points offers a different main course dish, together with the appropriate vegetable dishes, sauces and accompaniments. Other service points offer hot and cold sweets, beverages, sandwiches, pastries, confectionery items and miscellaneous foods. In this way the customer, on entering the food service area, checks the menu to see what he/she requires and then goes immediately to the appropriate service point. Thus, someone requiring just a sandwich and a hot drink is not held up by those selecting a full meal.

This method will speed up the service as long as each of the service points is organized and staffed properly and with no delay when foods need replenishing. The seating arrangements will depend on:

- The size and shape of the food service area
- The design of tables and chairs used
- The allowance made for gangways and clearing trolleys
- The type of establishment

As a guide, an allowance of $2\frac{1}{2}$–4 sq m (10–12 sq ft) per person is sufficient. This takes account of table space, gangways and access to counters.

Checklists

Typical checklists for the preparation of a hot food counter, salad bar, dining area and take-away service in an industrial catering set-up may be as follows:

Hot food (counter preparation)

1 Turn on hot counter allowing enough time for it to heat up to the correct temperature
2 Ensure that an adequate number of plates for the day's service are available:
   - On the hot food service counter
   - In an accessible place beneath the hot food counter as back-up stock
3 Transfer regenerated hot food from oven to hot food counter
   Important: (a) Use *oven cloths* when handling hot food to avoid accidents and spillages
   (b) Always use a *tray* when transferring hot food to avoid accidents and spillages
4 Check hot food menu items for the day and ensure that before service starts there is one dish of each menu item on the hot food counter
5 Ensure that all hot food is properly covered to stop any heat loss and deterioration in quality
6 Have cleaning materials available to wipe any spills
7 Ensure that for each dish on the hot food counter there is an appropriate service implement. The implements are as follows, depending on the dish:
   - *Large spoons* for dishes such as Vegetarian Lasagne
   - *Perforated large spoons* for dishes such as boiled vegetables (to drain off any excess water)
   - *Ladles* for dishes such as Seafood Mornay and Aloo Brinjal Bhajee
   - *Food tongs* for dishes such as fried plantain and Caribbean Chicken
   - *Fish slices* for dishes such as Vegetarian Pizza
8 When service implements are not in use or have been misplaced, remember to return each one to its designated position on the hot food service counter. This prevents any confusion during a busy service period which may otherwise arise when service implements have been misplaced.

Salad bar (counter preparation)

1 Turn on the salad bar giving it enough time to chill to the correct temperature
2 Ensure an adequate number of required salad bowls and plates are available for the day's service of salads, pâtés, cold meats, cold quiches and flans, cold pies, cheeses and taramasalata/humous/tsatsiki:
   - *Bowls* are for salads only
   - *Plates* are for the other cold items detailed above
   At any one time there should be enough salad bowls and plates on the cold counter for customer service, plus a back-up stock beneath the salad bar
3 Ensure that the following service utensils are ready and placed in their designated places for service:
   - *Salad tongs* for dry salads such as freshly prepared green salad
   - *Large spoons* for wet salads such as champignons à la grecque
   - *Fish slices* for pâté, cold meats, cold quiches or flans and cold pies
   - *Large spoons* for taramasalata/humous or tsatsiki
   - *Tongs* for sliced french sticks and granary rolls
4 Have cleaning materials ready to maintain appearance and cleanliness
5 Transfer prepared salad items from the kitchen to the chilled salad bar
6 Cover all food prior to service.

Dining area (preparation)

1 Arrange tables and chairs making sure they are all clean
2 Wipe each table
3 Ensure cutlery and flatware provisions for the day's service are in place, adequate and clean
4 Ensure trays are clean and there is an adequate supply in the tray stack, ready for the customers' use
5 Ensure all salt and pepper cruets are filled and that there is one pair on each table. If using sachets of salt and pepper, ensure that there are two bowls, containing salt and pepper respectively, at the counter by the cash till
6 Fill drinking water jugs and place them in their designated place *or* make sure the water dispenser is in working order
7 Ensure the serviette dispenser is filled up
8 Ensure the clearing up trolley and lined bin are in position
9 Have cleaning materials ready, to wipe clean tables and used trays during service

Take-away service (preparation)

A variety of considerations need to be given with regard to the preparation in a take-away service. The following is a check-list for the setting up prior to service:

1 Ensure all equipment is functioning correctly and switched on
2 Check all temperature-controlled equipment is correct
3 Make sure adequate supplies of packaging, napkins and plates are available
4 See that the take-away menu and prices are clearly displayed

5 See that sufficient supplies of ready prepared food items and beverages are to hand to ensure minimum delay on receipt of orders

6 Prepare foods on a 'batch cooking' basis to ensure the quality of the product at all times

7 See that the necessary uniforms are worn in all preparation areas, ie hats, overalls and aprons

8 For safety reasons, have available such items as oven cloths, tea towels and trays

9 Have available and on show sales literature to assist in projecting your image

10 Have cleaning materials available for the purposes of wiping down and in case of spillages

11 Are all serving utensils available and to hand?

12 See that everything is in its place and therefore easily found as required. This will assist in good work method

13 Check that waste bins are available with clean plastic sacks in them

14 Ensure that all working/serving surfaces are clean and have been wiped down prior to service with relevant cleaning materials

Note: As this is a take-away service, extreme care at all times is necessary with regard to the quality of the product, hygiene, packaging, labelling and temperature control.

5.5 The order of service (table service)

Procedure for service of a meal

The procedure for service to a guest from the moment he/she enters the establishment until he/she leaves is listed in point form to make it easier to follow. This is a suggested order and it should be noted that this order may change and vary according to the establishment, the type of menu and service offered and the time available. It is generally accepted that as far as possible food is served from the left, alcoholic and non-alcoholic beverages are served from the right and dirty items are cleared from the right. There are one or two exceptions to this general rule. For example, it may depend on the position of a table and the guests seated at that table. Also sideplates, being on the left-hand side of the place setting or cover, are more easily cleared from the left thus avoiding stretching in front of the guest.

Food and beverage service staff should be on duty allowing enough time before the service is due to commence in order:

● To check the sideboards have all equipment necessary for service

● To check that tables are laid correctly

● To check the menu and have a full understanding of the dishes, methods of cooking, garnishes, the correct covers, accompaniments and mode of service

- For the allocation of stations and other duties to be made if these are not already known
- For the head waiter to check that all the staff are dressed correctly in a clean and well presented uniform of the establishment

On the guests' arrival, the following procedures should take place:

1. The guests enter and are greeted by the reception head waiter. Check to see if they have a reservation. If not, allocate a table if one is available
2. The reception head waiter asks if the guests would like an aperitif in the lounge or reception area or prefer to have one at the table
3. The guests are taken to their table. The reception head waiter indicates who is the host to the station waiter and then hands over to him/her. The station waiter passes the time of day with the guests and helps to seat them
4. The station waiter unfolds each guest's serviette and places it over his/her lap
5. The sommelier comes to the table to offer the wine list for the choice of aperitif. He/she takes the order
6. Rolls and Melba toast are offered, butter is placed on the table and water is poured
7. Menus are presented to the host and his/her guests. Allow time for the party to make their choice
8. Recognition of the host is most important
9. The station head waiter takes the order of the party through the host. He/she stands to the left of the host and should be ready to offer suggestions and advice on the menu or translate any items if necessary
10. The sommelier comes to the table to see if any wine is required with the meal, taking the order through the host. He/she should be able to advise suitable wines to accompany certain dishes
11. The waiters change the covers where necessary for the service of the first course
12. Lay the plates , serve the first course and offer any accompaniments
13. Clear the first course in the approved fashion
14. Lay the covers for the fish course
15. If wine is to be served with the fish course, the correct glasses should be placed on the table
16. The wine is presented to the host and opened. The host tastes the wine. The guests are served, ladies first, the host last. (The host may designate another guest to taste the wine, in which case they will be served last.) Remember that approximately three glasses of wine can be obtained from a half bottle and six glasses from a bottle. White wine should be served chilled and red wine at room temperature
17. Lay the fish plates and serve the fish course
18. Clear the fish course
19. Lay the covers for the main course
20. If a wine is to accompany the main course, the correct glasses should be placed on the table. Clear dirty wine glasses
21. The wine is presented to the host, opened and then tasted by the host. Serve the guests, ladies first, host last.

22 Lay the joint plates and serve the main course. The station head waiter must ensure everything required is on the sideboard before commencing service of this course. Otherwise this can disrupt the service and may mean the food is getting cold. All cold dishes should be served before hot dishes

23 Underflats should be used under vegetable dishes and sauce boats. All hot food being served should be piping hot and served on to hot joint plates. The meat should be served first and placed on that part of the plate nearest the guest or at the bottom of the cover, ie 6 o'clock. This should be followed by the potatoes, vegetables and any hot sauces and accompaniments that have to be offered

24 The sommelier should top up the wine glasses when necessary. The station head waiter should offer more rolls, Melba toast and butter as required and check that everything is satisfactory

25 Clear the main course to include sideplates and side knives, cruets, butter dishes, gristicks and accompaniments. Everything should be cleared in the approved manner

26 Crumb down

27 Change the ashtray if appropriate

28 Offer the menu for guests to choose a sweet dish. Take the order

29 Lay the sweet covers and accompaniments

30 The sommelier clears the wine glasses and wine bottle

31 Serve the sweet course. Cold dishes are served before hot dishes

32 Clear the sweet course

33 Take the coffee order

34 The sommelier presents the liqueur trolley. Serve liqueurs as required

35 The coffee service is placed on the table. Serve the coffee. Offer more coffee at the appropriate time

36 Presentation of the bill. Payment to the waiter, who has the bill receipted by the cashier. It is then returned with any change to the host

37 The station head waiter sees the guests out of the restaurant

38 Clear down the table. Re-lay it if necessary

Reception of guests

The personal skills shown by the food and beverage staff go a long way towards selling an establishment and making a guest feel at home in a friendly and relaxed atmosphere. This aspect of service is very often neglected and all employers should impress upon their staff at regular intervals the great importance attached to customer contact. A pleasant welcome to a guest can gain a sale, a poor welcome will lose a sale. *First impressions count.*

Removal of spare covers

In many instances tables are reserved for parties of guests. Where this happens the party sometimes turns up with one guest less in the party than quoted when the original booking was made. The waiter must then remove the spare cover laid on the table. Judgement must be used as to which cover he/she removes, a lot depending on the actual position of the table. It should be noted here, however, that all guests, where possible, should look into the room. The cover should be removed in the correct manner using a service plate or a service salver. When this has been done the position of the other covers should be adjusted if necessary and the table accompaniments re-positioned. The spare chair should also have been removed.

Re-laying of tables

It is very often the case in a busy restaurant or dining room that a number of the tables have to be re-laid in order to cope with the inflow of customers. Where this is the case the table should firstly be completely cleared of all items of equipment and then crumbed down. At this stage if the tablecloth is a little soiled or grubby a slip cloth should be placed over it. It can then be re-laid in the approved manner.

It is essential that this procedure is carried out as quickly as possible to ensure the maximum turnover of guests in the limited amount of time available for service. This will then allow for maximum sales which, in a well-run establishment, will mean more profit.

5.6 Taking customer food and beverage orders

Methods of order taking

Essentially there are four methods of taking food and beverage orders from customers. These are summarized in Figure 5.21.

All order taking methods are based upon these four concepts. Even the most sophisticated electronic system is based upon either the duplicate or triplicate methods even

Figure 5.21 Main methods of taking food and beverage orders

METHOD	DESCRIPTION
TRIPLICATE	Order is taken; top copy goes to the supply point; second copy is sent to the cashier for billing; third copy is retained by the waiter as a means of reference during service
DUPLICATE	Order is taken; top copy goes to the supply point; second copy is retained for service and billing purposes
SERVICE WITH ORDER	Order is taken; customer is served and payment received according to that order, eg bar service or take-away methods
PRE-ORDERED	(1) Individually, eg room service breakfast (see Section 7.2 page 252) (2) Hospital tray system (see Section 7.4, page 260) (3) Functions (see Chapter 9, page 321)

though the actual checks may not be written but communicated electronically to VDUs or print-out machines.

Triplicate checking method

This is a control system used in the majority of medium and large first-class establishments. As the name implies the food check consists of three copies.

To ensure efficient control the waiter or waitress must fill in the information required in the four corners of the check, this being:

- Table number
- Number of covers
- Date
- Signature of waiter/waitress taking the order

On taking the food order it is written from top to bottom of the food check. Where only a table d'hôte menu is in operation the guests would initially only order their first and main courses. The set price charged for this menu would be entered on the food check and circled.

A second new food check is written out for the sweet course, this being taken after the main course is finished. A third new check will be completed if any beverage such as coffee is required.

The operation for an à la carte menu is similar, although the guests may order course by course according to their requirements. It must always be remembered that all checks should be legible and that, where an à la carte menu is in operation, the price of the dishes must be put on the check.

Abbreviations may be used when taking the order as long as they are understood by everyone and not misinterpreted by the kitchen causing the wrong order to be put up, and therefore a delay in the service to the guest.

The food check

1 The top copy of the food order goes to the kitchen and is handed to the aboyeur at the hotplate
2 The duplicate goes to the cashier who makes out the guest's bill
3 The flimsy, or third copy, is retained by the waiter at his/her sideboard as a means of reference

Any checks or bills which have to be cancelled should have the head waiter's or supervisor's signature on them; so also should checks and bills which have alterations made on them.

In certain instances it is necessary to write out special checks. These would be as follows:

- Where it is necessary to write out more than one food check for a meal, eg where a sweet check is written out after the first and main course has been served. At the head of this check should be written the word *Suivant* which

Figure 5.22 Food check: before and after order is taken

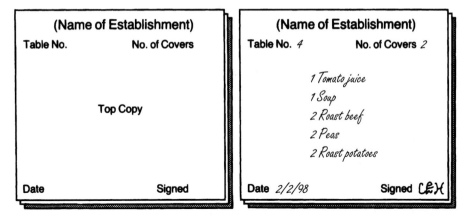

means the 'following' check, and shows that one check has already been written out for that particular table

Figure 5.23 Food check: suivant

- When an extra portion of food is required because sufficient has not been sent from the kitchen, a special check must be written out headed *Supplement* (see Figure 5.24). This means to 'supplement' what has already been previously sent. It should be signed by the head waiter or supervisor and normally there is no charge (n/c), but this depends on the policy of the establishment concerned

- Where a wrong dish has been ordered and has to be sent back to the kitchen and replaced, a special check must again be made out (see Figure 5.25). If the service being carried out is from an à la carte menu then the prices of the two dishes concerned must be shown. Two main headings are used on this special check, *Retour*, or 'return' and the name of the dish going back to the kitchen, and *En place* or 'in its place', and the name of the new dish to be served

Figure 5.24 Food check: supplement

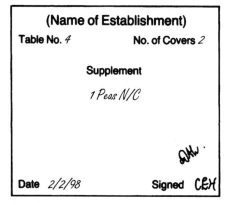

(Name of Establishment)
Table No. *4*   No. of Covers *2*

Supplement

1 Peas N/C

Date *2/2/98*   Signed *CBH*

Figure 5.25 Food check: retour/en place

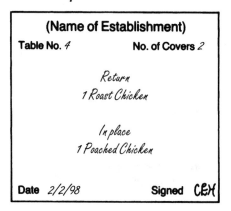

(Name of Establishment)
Table No. *4*   No. of Covers *2*

Return
1 Roast Chicken

In place
1 Poached Chicken

Date *2/2/98*   Signed *CBH*

● It occasionally happens that the waiter or waitress may have an accident in the room and perhaps some vegetables are dropped. These must be replaced without any extra charge to the guest. Here a check must be completed headed *Accident*. It will show the number of portions of vegetables required and should be signed by the head waiter or supervisor in charge. No charge (n/c) is made

Figure 5.26 Food check: accident

(Name of Establishment)
Table No. *4*   No. of Covers *2*

Accident

Potatoes N/C

Date *2/2/98*   Signed *CBH*

With modern day trends towards 'covered' dishes being presented to customers at the table it is increasingly important to identify specific orders before placing them on the table in front of the appropriate person.

A system for ensuring that the right customer receives the correct food without the constant lifting of dish covers is to identify on the order which customer is having which dish. A check pad design which might be used for this is shown in Figure 5.27. The covered dishes are then lettered at the hotplate prior to leaving the kitchen.

Figure 5.27 Check pad design enabling the waiter to identify specific orders

A		Blue Suit	G		
B		White dress	H		
C	H	Grey Suit	I		
D		Blue dress	J		
E			K		
F			L		

TABLE No. 12	COVERS 4	DATE 3/9/98	ROOM No. —

2 Smoked Salmon   AC
1 Pate   B
1 Soup   D

1 Fillet Steak medium   A
1 Dover Sole   D
2 Roast   BC

3 Vegetables   ACD
1 Salad   B

THIS IS NOT A VAT RECEIPT

WAITER _ _ _SAC_ _ _ _ _ _ _ _ _ _ _ _

T1005/1287C

T1005/1287C

T1005/1287C

Duplicate checking method

This is a control system which is more likely to be found in the smaller hotel, popular price restaurant and cafés and department store catering. It is generally used where a table d'hôte menu is in operation and sometimes a very limited à la carte menu.

As the name implies, there are two copies of each of these food checks, each set being

Figure 5.28 Example of a duplicated order pad with perforated sections

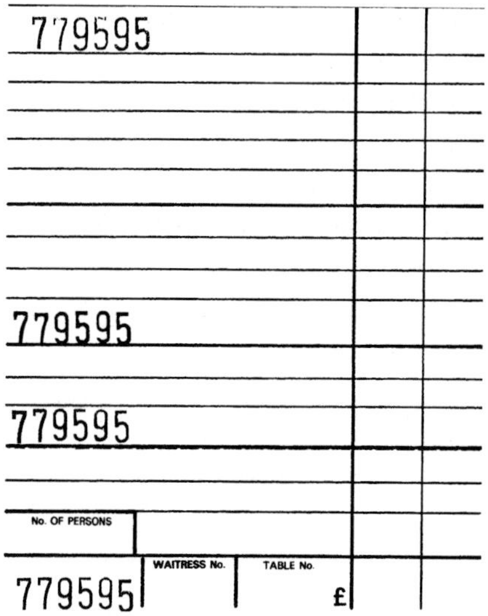

serial numbered. A check pad, or bill pad as it is sometimes termed, usually contains a set of 50 or 100 food checks. The top copy of the food check is usually carbon-backed but, if not, a sheet of carbon must be placed between the top and duplicate copy every time a fresh order is taken.

For control purposes the top copy may have printed on it a waiter's number or letter. This should be the number or letter given to a waiter on joining the staff. The control and accounts department should be informed of the person to whom the number applies, and he/she retains it throughout employment. Also on each set of food checks should be printed a serial number.

Sometimes the top copy of the set of food and drink checks is made up of a number of perforated slips usually 4–5 in number. There is a section at the bottom of the food and drink check for the table number to be entered. The top copy sometimes has a cash column for entering the price of a meal or the dishes ordered but, if this is not the case, the waiter must enter them independently on to the duplicate copy against the particular dish concerned.

When writing out a guest's order a different perforated slip should be used for each course. The waiter must remember to write out the number of covers and the price of the meal or dish concerned on each slip. Before sending each slip to the hotplate see that the details are entered correctly on the duplicate copy together with the price. Since the duplicate copy acts as the guest's bill, the waiter must ensure that everything served is charged and paid for.

As the service of a meal commences, the waiter tears off from the top copy of the food and drink check the perforated slip showing the first course ordered. This is taken to the hotplate and the required dish is put up. As soon as this happens the aboyeur will tear off the waiter's number on the end of the slip and place it with the dish concerned. This then shows which waiter the dish is for. If there is no waiter number at the end of the perforated slip, then the perforated slip itself is left with the order until collected by the appropriate waiter. The aboyeur will then retain the slip showing the course just served. As soon as the first course is served and allowing time for this course to be consumed the second perforated slip is taken to the hotplate by the waiter. This dish will then be collected as required. This same procedure is carried on throughout the meal.

It may happen that there are insufficient perforated slips on the top copy of the food and drink check for a particular guest's requirements. Very often the waiter does his/her own drink service and thus takes the drink order and enters it on a separate perforated slip. When there are not sufficient perforated slips, a supplementary check pad is brought into use.

Other checking methods

As has already been mentioned, there are many variations to the basic duplicate checking control system. These are too numerous to mention individually but three are described below very simply in order to give some idea of the possible variations available.

Menu and customer bill

This shows the menu order and customer's bill combined on one sheet and would be allocated to each party of guests. When the order is taken each of the guest's requirements would be written down in the column next to the price column. Thus if a party of two guests requested 2 cream soups, 1 mushroom omelette and chips and 1 fried cod and chips, it would be noted down as shown in Figure 5.29.

Electronic hand held check pad

The water is supplied with an electronic check pad which has itemized keys that represent each dish on the menu.

As the guest orders the waiter keys in their requirements, when the order is complete a 'send' button is pressed and the order is printed out in the kitchen.

Figure 5.29 Quick service menu and customer bill

Soup		
Cream soup	2.60	2
Hot Dishes		
Omelette served with chips		
or Bowl of salad		
Plain		

Cheese
    Ham
    Mushroom
    Tomato
	4.50	1

Fried Cod and Chips	4.75	1

Single order sheet

A further simple form of checking is shown in Figure 5.30. This may be used in cafés, quick turnover restaurants and department stores. A simple form of control such as this may also be used, or adapted for use, in various forms of take-away establishments.

The menu is normally very limited with little or no choice. The waiter takes the order and marks down the guest's requirements, calls for the order verbally over the hotplate and, when the guest requests the bill, prices the order sheet and hands it to him/her. The guest then hands it to the cashier on leaving and pays the required amount. There is only one copy of this order and bill combined and this is retained by the cashier, for control purposes, once the guest has made the necessary payment.

Figure 5.30 Example of a single order sheet used in popular catering

WAITER		Table No.	NUMBER OF CUSTOMERS		£	
WIMPY	CHEESE BURGER	EGG BURGER	BENDER ROLL	CHICKEN IN A BUN		
KING SIZE	QUARTER POUNDER	CHEESE QUARTER POUNDER	HALF POUNDER	KETCHUP SACHET		
WIMPY GRILL	WIMPY SPECIAL GRILL	QUARTER POUNDER SPECIAL GRILL	FISH GRILL	INTER-NATIONAL		
SPICY BEAN BURGER	BACON IN BUN	BACON & EGG IN A BUN	BACON, EGG, TOM. & CHIPS	EGG & CHIPS		
				2 EGG & CHIPS		
ROLL & BUTTER	SIDE SALAD	MISCELLANEOUS WHIPPED CREAM	BREAKFAST 1/2/3	CHIPS PORTION		
EGG ROLL		SOUP				
FLAPJACKS	CHILDS MEAL 1/2/3	DOUGHNUT RING	ORANGE JUICE	SPARKLING DRINKS		
HOT APPLE PIE		TEA CAKES				
BEVERAGES TEA	CHOCOLATE	ICE CREAM	ICE CREAM BROWN DERBY	CHOC NUT SUNDAE		
COFFEE	PERC COFFEE	THICK SHAKE	KNICKER BOCKER GLORY.	FRUIT SUNDAE		
MILK		SODAS or FLOATS	BANANA BOAT	STRAW-BERRY SUNDAE		

V.A.T. No. 346 5158 46

WIMPY   £

№ 33883   123 WEMBLEY PARK DRIVE, WEMBLEY

Taking orders for dispense bar beverage service

An efficient system must operate here to ensure that:

- The correct drinks are served at the right table
- The service rendered is charged to the correct bill
- A record is kept of all drinks issued from the dispense bar
- Management is able to assess sales over a financial period and make comparisons

The usual system of control is a duplicate check pad. The colour of the check pad may be pink or white, but is generally pink. This acts as an aid to the cashier and the control and accounts department in differentiating quickly between food (white) and drink (pink) checks (Figure 5.31).

When the wine order is taken it is written in duplicate. The wine service staff must remember to fill in the four items of information required, one in each corner of the check. These are as follows:

- Table number or room number
- Number of covers
- Date
- Signature

Abbreviations are allowed when writing the order as long as they are understood by

Figure 5.31 Wine check

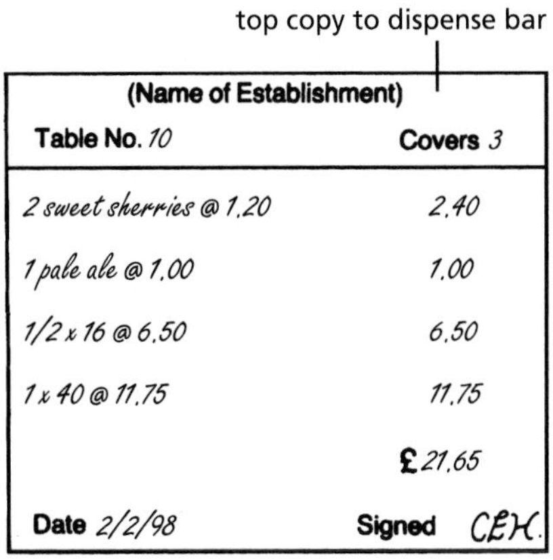

top copy to dispense bar

(Name of Establishment)	
Table No. *10*	Covers *3*
2 sweet sherries @ 1.20	*2.40*
1 pale ale @ 1.00	*1.00*
1/2 x 16 @ 6.50	*6.50*
1 x 40 @ 11.75	*11.75*
	£ *21.65*
Date *2/2/98*	**Signed** *CEK*

the dispense bar staff and the cashier. When wines are ordered only the Bin number, together with the number of bottles required, should be written down.

The Bin number is an aid to the dispense bar staff and cellar staff in finding, without delay, the wine required by a customer. Each wine in the wine list will have a Bin number printed against it. All drinks ordered should also have the price written against them, and then, at the base of the check, the total amount of cash owing for the order given should be written and circled. This is an aid to the cashier who must check all prices before entering them on the bill.

On taking the order the wine staff should hand both copies to the dispense bar staff, who retain the top copy, put up the order and leave the duplicate copy with the order. This enables the wine staff to see which is their order when they come to collect their drinks, and after serving them the duplicate copy is handed to the cashier.

Taking children's orders

Special attention should be paid by staff when taking orders for children. They need to be aware of

- The availability of children's meals and choice
- What the children's meals consist of
- Portion size, eg the number of sausages
- The cost per head
- To make a special note of any specific requests, eg *no* baked beans
- Serve young/small children first as they often become agitated when everyone else has been served and their meal is still to come
- Do not overfill cups, bowls or glasses
- Provide the children with the establishment 'give aways' in order to keep them occupied, eg a place mat to be coloured in. This can in fact encourage sales
- Always ensure children's plates are warm rather than hot to avoid mishaps

Special needs

Those customers with special needs may require your particular attention, eg customers who are hard of hearing, blind or only partially sighted (see page 165). In these instances you should consider the following:

- Where applicable, when taking the order, face the customer so he/she sees you full face
- Speak normally but distinctly
- Keep descriptions to a minimum

- Indicate precisely 'modifiers' with a specific dish, eg 'dips' available with a starter or the degree of cooking required for a grilled steak
- Read back the order given for confirmation

Other special needs may relate to either vegetarians or those with particular religious or cultural restrictions and others with special dietary needs (see page 70).

5.7 Service of food

In table and assisted service the general convention is to serve all food items from the left and to clear from the right. All beverages (both alcoholic and non-alcoholic) are served from the right. With the increase in plated service, it has become common to serve plated foods from the right. This is done for the same reason that 'dirties' are cleared from the right: the left hand (normally) is used to stack dirties whilst the right clears the plates. This ensures that the stack of dirties is behind the customer. If it falls, it will fall on the floor and not on them. With plated service, the additional plates of food are similarly held behind the seated customer.

It is also conventional always to serve cold food before hot (irrespective of the host). This ensures that, once the hot food is served, the customer may eat immediately without having to wait whilst the cold food is collected and served. This allows all customers to receive their food at the correct serving/eating temperature. Remember, courtesy demands that no customer commences eating until all have been served.

Service of soup

Soup may be served pre-plated, from a tureen at the sideboard, or on a guéridon or from an individual tureen as shown in Figure 5.32. The waiter ensures that the soup is poured away from the guest. The underflat acts as a drip plate to prevent any spillage from going on the tablecloth.

Consommé is normally served in a consommé cup on a consommé saucer with a fish plate underneath. It is traditional for this type of soup to be eaten with a sweet spoon because consommé was originally taken before going home, after a function, as a warming beverage. It was originally drunk from this large cup with a sweet spoon merely to remove any garnish. The tradition of the sweet spoon has continued, but a soup spoon would also be acceptable.

Service from flats (meat/fish)

1 The correct cover is laid prior to the food item ordered being served.
2 The service cloth is folded neatly as a protection against heat from the serving dish
3 The fold of the cloth should be on the tips of the fingers
4 The dish is presented to the guest so he/she may see the complete dish as it has come from the kitchen. This is to show off the chef's artistry in presentation

Figure 5.32 Silver service of soup from an individual soup tureen

(a)

(b)

5 The serving dish should be held a little above the hot joint plate with the front edge slightly overlapping the rim of the hot joint plate

6 The portion of food is placed in the '6 o'clock' position (ie nearest to the guest) on the hot joint plate

7 When moving to serve the second portion, the flat should be rotated on the service cloth so the next meat portion to be served will be nearest the plate

8 Note that the portion of food served, on the plate nearest to the guest, allows ample room on the plate to serve and present the potatoes and other vegetables attractively

9 If vegetables are being served on to separate plates, then the food (meat) is placed in the middle of the plate

Service of potatoes and vegetables

1 The general rule is for potatoes to be served before vegetables

2 Always when serving either potatoes or vegetables, the vegetable dish itself should be placed on an underflat with a napkin on it. This is for presentation purposes

3 The purpose of the napkin is to prevent the vegetable dish slipping about on the under-flat while the service is being carried out

Figure 5.33 Silver service of vegetables

4 A separate service spoon and fork should be used for each different type of potato and vegetable dish to be served

5 Note again the use of the service cloth as protection against heat and to allow the rotation of the vegetable dish on its underflat more easily

6 With the serving dish in its correct position the potato dish nearest the hot joint plate should be served

7 The first potato dish served is placed on the hot joint plate on the far side, allowing the server to work towards him/herself as he/she serves the remaining food items ordered and making it easier to present the food attractively

8 Creamed potato is served by placing the fork into the spoon and then taking a scoop of potato from the dish. This is then carried to the plate and the fork moved slightly. The potato should then fall off on to the plate

Note (in Figure 5.33):
1 The use of an underflat under the vegetable dishes
2 How a variety of vegetables can be served at one time by using a larger underflat
3 The use of a service cloth for protection and to prevent the underflat from slipping
4 The correct handling of the service spoon and fork
5 The separate service spoon and fork for each variety of vegetable served
6 Service from the left

Service of accompanying sauces

1 The sauce should be presented in a sauceboat on an underplate, with a sauce ladle
2 A ladleful of sauce should be lifted clear of the sauceboat
3 The underside of the sauce ladle should then be run over the edge of the sauceboat to avoid any drips falling on the tablecloth or over the edge of the hot joint plate
4 The sauce should be napped over the portion of meat already served or at the side of the meat depending on the customer's preference

Service of an omelette

1 The correct cover should be laid prior to the food item ordered being served
2 The cover here is a joint fork laid on the right of the place setting and a hot fish plate (starter course)
3 The omelette should first be presented to the guest so that it is seen as it has come from the kitchen
4 This is one occasion when two service forks may be used to serve the food item rather than a service spoon and fork. The two service forks should be placed neatly on the underflat holding the omelette until required for serving
5 Keep the holding hand, with the omelette on the hot underflat, held a little above the hot fish plate with the rim of the underflat just overlapping the edge of the fish plate
6 The end of the omelette, nearest the hot fish plate, should be trimmed off using the back of one of the serving forks

7 The underflat should then be turned on the service cloth and the second end trimmed. (The purpose of trimming the ends of an omelette prior to service is because this is the section of an omelette that dries out very quickly even if it sits on the hotplate for only a very short period of time)

8 One of the service forks should be run under the omelette to ensure it is not slightly stuck to the underflat

9 Then, spreading the two service forks apart, the omelette should be lifted carefully from the serving flat

Note: As an alternative to the two service forks and to ensure good presentation on the plate, a slice may be used for the service.

Service away from the table

Service of food away from the table includes service from trolleys at buffets and counters. Tray service is considered in Section 7.4, page 260. Guéridon service is in Section 8.2, page 272.

The main standard to be achieved in these forms of food service is that no food should be touched by hands. The food trolley should be between the staff and customer as if it were in a shop. Another point is that food is not normally served by the spoon and fork technique. Service is with one implement in one hand and another in the other hand with the service either on to plates on the buffet, for instance, or on to a plate that the customer is holding.

Figure 5.34 Sweet/cheese trolley

Sweet and cheese trolleys

These should be attractively laid from the customer's point of view and well laid out from behind for the server. Plates for dirty service equipment should therefore be to the back of the trolley. Staff should explain food items to customers either from behind the trolley, to the side of the trolley or standing by the table but not in front of the trolley.

When the customer makes a selection, a plate should be positioned near the item to be served. Then, with a service spoon in one hand and a service fork in the other (or gâteau slices, etc), food should be portioned and transferred neatly to the plate. This should then be placed in front of the customer from the right. For larger parties two people will be required: one to take the orders and place the plate with food in front of the customer, the other to stand at the trolley and portion and plate the foods.

For temperature control purposes many sweet trolleys now come with ice pack compartments which should be replenished before each service.

Buffet and counters

Food, if it has not already been pre-plated, should be served similarly to the procedure above. Food should not be sloshed on to plates but served with a spoon (or some other service implement, eg chip shovel) in one hand and a fork in the other and should be placed neatly on to the customer's plate. Additional items should be suitably arranged on to the plate and not piled on to other items already on the plate.

Counters

Checklists

Typical checklists for staff to adhere to in performance of 'standards' at service time and related to hot counter, salad bar and dining areas are given below.

Hot food (counter service)

1 Do not leave the hot food service counter unattended once service starts as this will cause a congestion in the flow of service.
   Important: arrange for someone to take your place if you have to leave the service area for any reason
2 Wipe up any spillages immediately. Spillages if left on a hot counter for too long will harden and create problems later with cleaning
3 When serving, it is important to adhere to portion control specifications
4 When a dish of hot food is only one-third full (if busy) inform kitchen that more will be needed. Do not allow food items to run out during service. If near the end of service time, check with the supervisor
5 Ensure plates are kept well stocked. If running low on plates on the service counter, replenish immediately from back-up stock underneath the hot counter

Salad bar (counter service)

1 Keep a constant eye on food levels in the salad bar

2 Never re-fill bowls or replenish plates at the counter. Take a bowl or plate to the kitchen and fill or replenish it there

3 Replace service spoons, slices, etc, in their respective bowls, dishes and plates, if misplaced by customers

4 Wipe up any spillages immediately

5 Keep the salad bar tidy, well-arranged and well-presented at all times

6 Keep a constant eye on the supply of bowls and plates for the salad counter service

7 *Remember*: do not wait for a supply of salad bowls and plates to run out before replenishing from the back-up supply (beneath the cold counter). During a busy service period this will inevitably hinder the flow of service

Dining areas (counter service)

1 Ensure the clearing station is ready in place. Checklist for the clearing station:
   - Lined bin
   - Bin liners
   - Recommended cleaning materials
   - Wiping cloth
   - Trolley with table top surface

2 Keep a constant eye on tables; make sure they are clean and tidy at all times. Change table covers regularly, as and when required. An untidy and messy table is not pleasant for the customer

3 The dining area service should be self-clearing, ie customers are requested to return their trays containing used plates and cutlery to the clearing station. Failing this, promptly clear tables of any trays

4 At the clearing station:
   - Empty contents of a tray into a lined standing bin
   - Wipe the tray clean with recommended cleaning materials

5 Return the stack of ready-cleaned trays to the tray stack, lining each tray with a paper liner before putting into place

6 Ensure there is always enough water in the drinking water jugs

7 Ensure there are enough serviettes in the serviette dispenser

8 Ensure cutlery and flatware containers are adequately stocked

Note: during service always ensure that at any one time there is an adequate supply of trays in the tray rack, ready for the customer's use.

Recommended cleaning materials may include spray sanitizers, cloths and hot water.

5.8 Service of alcoholic bar beverages and cigars

The cocktail/dispense bar may be said to be the shop window of an establishment as it is often the meeting point of customers prior to business and social events and the first impressions given here are of prime importance in gaining further sales. Therefore the presentation of the cocktail bar personnel, together with a well-stocked, organized and efficiently run bar, are essential in order to give a good service to the customer. The cocktail bar personnel must have good technical skills, knowledge and social skills in order to meet the needs of the client.

Service of apéritifs

The term *apéritif* covers a wide range of drinks which may be served before a meal. A large number of aperitifs must be stocked within the dispense bar in order to cater for the majority of tastes.

The wine butler or sommelier should present the wine list to the host for an aperitif order immediately before the butter is placed on the table and the rolls and Melba toast are offered to all the guests. This then gives the wine butler time to serve the aperitif order and the guests time to consume them, before the first course is served. An alternative to this, of course, is for aperitifs to be served in the lounge/reception area. The station waiter should take the food order here and, once the table is ready for the service of the first course, should take the customers to their table.

Service of cocktails

Cocktails should always be served well chilled in an appropriately sized glass with the correct garnish, straw, umbrella according to the policy of the establishment. Many cocktails are served in the traditional V-shaped cocktail glass but, if to be consumed as a long drink, then a larger glass such as a Slim Jim may be better suited. The key consideration here should be the total presentation of the cocktail as seen visually by the customer.

For further information on Cocktails see Section 4.6 on page 118.

Service of wines

Immediately the food order has been taken the wine list should again be presented to the host so that he/she may order wine for the party to accompany the meal they have ordered. The sommelier or wine butler should be able to advise and suggest wines from the wine list to the host if the occasion arises. This means that the wine butler must have a good knowledge of the wines contained within the wine list in order that they may be 'sold' on behalf of the management.

When the wine butler writes out the order it must be clear and legible. The top copy goes to the bar and the duplicate to the cashier. It should be remembered that all red wines are served at room temperature, white and rosé wines chilled and sparkling wines well chilled. The following basic procedure takes place when a bottle of wine has to be served.

White wines

1 Obtain the wine from the dispense bar
2 Take to the table in an ice-bucket
3 Present the bottle to the host showing the label (Figure 5.35(a))
4 Ensure the correct glasses are placed on the table for the wine to be served
5 See that a clean serviette is tied to the handle of the ice-bucket
6 Cut the foil, remove and wipe the top of the cork with the serviette (Figure 5.35(b))
7 Remove the cork in the accepted fashion. Smell the cork in case the wine is 'corked'. This happens when the wine has been affected through a faulty cork and it cannot then be served. Place the cork in the ice-bucket (Figure 5.35(c))
8 If the wine concerned is a château-bottled wine, then the cork would generally be placed on a sideplate at the head of the host's cover. This cork should have the name of the château concerned and the year of the wine printed on it
9 Wipe the inside of the neck of the bottle with the serviette
10 Wipe the bottle dry
11 Hold the bottle for pouring in such a fashion that the label may be seen. Use the waiter's cloth, folded, to catch any drips (Figure 5.35(d))
12 Give a taste to the host, pouring from the right. He or she should acknowledge that the wine is suitable – correct taste, bouquet and temperature
13 Serve ladies first, then gentlemen and the host last, always commencing from the host's right
14 Fill each glass two-thirds full. This leaves room for an appreciation of the bouquet
15 Replace the remaining wine in the wine-bucket and refill the glasses when necessary
16 If a fresh bottle is required, then fresh glasses should be placed upon the table
17 On finishing pouring a glass of wine, twist the neck of the bottle and raise it at the same time. This prevents any drips from falling on the tablecloth

Red wine

The cork should be removed from the bottle of red wine as early as possible so that the wine may attain room temperature naturally. Under no circumstances should the wine be placed on the hotplate or in the bain-marie to get it to the required temperature quickly. If the red wine to be opened is young the bottle may stand on an underplate or coaster on the table and be opened from this position, the basic procedure being similar to opening a bottle of white wine. If the wine is of age and/or is likely to have a heavy sediment, then the wine should be decanted. It should be placed in a wine basket and first presented to the customer. Placing the bottle in a wine basket keeps the bottle relatively flat and ensures that the sediment is not shaken up. It should then be opened in the basket and poured in one operation into a clean decanter. A single point light, eg a candle, should be used to view the wine as it is pouring out of the bottle. When sediment is seen reaching the neck of the bottle, the pouring should stop. There is no technical reason why red wine should

Figure 5.35 Service of wine

a) presenting the bottle

b) removing the foil

c) removing the cork

d) pouring the wine

be served with the bottle in a wine basket or wine cradle. However these are used in a number of establishments for display/presentation purposes.

Apart from the points mentioned, the basic procedure for opening and serving red wine is as for white wine above.

Sparkling wine

When we think of sparkling wines our thoughts immediately turn to champagne, but the same method is used for opening all sparkling wines. The wine should be served well chilled in order to obtain the full effect of the secondary fermentation in the bottle, namely, effervescence and bouquet. The pressure in a champagne bottle due to its maturing and secondary fermentation should be about 4.928 kg per sq cm (70 lb per sq in). Great care must therefore be taken not to shake the bottle otherwise the pressure will build up. There have been many accidents in the past and great care is demanded here.

After presenting the bottle to the host it should be replaced in the wine cooler. The neck of the bottle should be kept pointed to the ceiling during the opening process to avoid any accidents to guests should the cork be released suddenly. The thumb should be held over the cork with the remainder of the hand holding the neck of the bottle. Unwind the wire cage carefully. Holding the cork and the cage in a service cloth the bottle should be twisted slowly to release the cork.

Sparkling wine should be served in tulip-shaped glasses, from the right-hand side of each guest. It is also worth considering lifting the glass from the table so as to pour the wine more easily and to reduce the 'frothing' of the wine.

Sediment in wine

There are two sources of sediment in a bottle, which are the same for both red and white wines. These are tartrates of calcium and sodium formed by a combination of tartaric acid, which is natural in wine, and calcium or sodium. It is only the colours of red and white wine that make them appear different colours. Sugar, as it is a natural ingredient of wine, will not form crystals within the wine. Sediment is therefore not sugar even though in white wine the crystals might resemble brown sugar crystals.

On serving wine it is possible that bits of cork will be found floating in the glass. This is a result of the opening process where a piece or pieces of the cork have been broken off. This is not 'corked' wine, as it is often mistakenly termed. For an explanation of corked wine, see Section 4.8 on page 124. The bits of cork should be removed with a teaspoon and the wine enjoyed. (If the cork breaks into fine pieces, the wine may require filtering through fine muslin.)

Serving temperatures

- For red wines: 15.5–18°C (60–65°F)
- Some young red wines also may be drunk cool at about 12.5–15.5°C (55–60°F)
- White wines 10–12.5°C (50–55°F)
- Dessert wines, champagne and other sparkling white wines: 4.5–10°C (40–50°F)

Glasses

The following wines may be served in the types of glasses indicated below:

- Champagne and other sparkling wines: flute
- German and Alsace wines: German wine glass
- White wines: medium-size wine glass
- Rosé wines: flute
- Red wines: large wine glass

Figure 5.36 Wines and their appropriate glasses

Service of beer

Beer should be served at a temperature of 12.5–15.5°C (55–60°F), with lagers generally cooler than other beers at 8.0–10.5°C (48–51°F). Many different varieties of bottled beers are also served chilled. Also draught beer on its route from the keg/cask to the pump often passes through a chilling unit. Draught beers should have a small head on them, and the bar person should ensure that he/she serves the correct quantity of beer with a small head, and not a large head to make up the quantity required. One may note the good condition of beer if the head or froth clings to the inside of the glass.

When pouring bottled beer, it should be poured down the inside of the glass which is held at a slight angle. It should be poured slowly. This is especially important where a beer works a lot and may produce a large head quickly if it is not poured slowly and carefully. Such beers are Guinness and stouts.

All glasses used should be spotlessly clean with no finger marks, grease or lipstick on them. Pouring beer into a dirty glass will cause it to go flat very quickly. Extra care must be taken when pouring beer in hot weather as this causes the beer to work much more. The neck of the bottle should not be placed in the beer when pouring, especially where two bottles are being held and poured from the same hand. Where bottled beers have a sediment, when pouring a little beer must be left in the base of the bottle holding the sediment back.

Types of beer glasses

- Half pint/pint tankards for draught beer
- Pint tumblers for draught beer
- Tumblers for any bottled beer
- 34.08 cl (12 fl oz) short stemmed beer glass for Bass/Worthington/Guinness
- Lager glass for lager
- 22.72, 28.40, 34.08 cl (8, 10, 12 fl oz) Paris goblets for brown/pale/strong ales

Service of liqueurs

Liqueurs (sweetened and flavoured spirits) are generally offered from a liqueur trolley at the table. The wine butler should present the trolley immediately the sweet course is finished to ensure that any liqueurs required will be on the table by the time the coffee is served. Again the wine butler must have a good knowledge of liqueurs, their bases and flavours, and their correct mode of service. Traditionally all liqueurs were served in an Elgin-shaped liqueur glass but many alternatives are now used.

If a person asks for a liqueur to be served *frappé*, then it is served on crushed ice. A larger glass will then have to be used. The glass should be two-thirds filled with crushed ice and then the measure of liqueur poured over. Two short drinking straws should be placed into the glass and then served, eg Crème de Menthe frappé.

If a liqueur is requested with cream, then the cream is slowly poured over the back of a teaspoon to settle on the top of the selected liqueur, without mixing with it. Under no circumstances should the liqueur and cream be mixed together, eg Tia Maria with cream.

The basic equipment required on the liqueur trolley is as follows:

- Assorted liqueurs
- Assorted glasses
  – liqueur/brandy/port
- Draining stand
  25 and 50 ml measures
- Service salver
- Jug of double cream
- Teaspoon
- Drinking straws
- Cigars
- Matches
- Cigar cutter
- Wine list and check pad

Figure 5.37 Bar trolley for the service of liqueurs

Other items served from the liqueur trolley may be brandy (a grape spirit distilled from wine) and port (a fortified liqueur wine). For service, brandy requires a 25 ml measure and port a 50 ml measure.

Service of cigars

It may be as well to mention cigars here as it is the sommelier's responsibility to sell these to the guest, however some restaurants now discourage the sale of such items.

The Havana is regarded as the best of all hand-made cigars, to be savoured like a rare wine. The Jamaican cigars come a close second but are milder than Havana and much less expensive. Dutch and British cigars and Whiffs are even cheaper, with a much drier smoke. These are machine-made.

A fine cigar should be kept at between 15°C and 18°C (60°F and 65°F) and between 55% and 60% relative humidity, with as little variation as possible. A cigar will pick up any smell or moisture in the air, or dry up and smoke like tinder.

The safest way to keep cigars in condition is to buy, and offer them for sale, in tubes. These tubes are hermetically sealed and cigars stored thus will retain their good condition for a long time.

Cigars come in various sizes, three of the most important and popular being:

- *Corona* (14.5 cm) ($5\frac{1}{2}$ in)
- *Petite Corona* (13 cm) (5 in)
- *Très Petite Corona* (11.5 cm) ($4\frac{1}{4}$ in)

Some of the main importers have produced special boxes containing up to ten each of the three sizes mentioned above.

When a restaurant has a regular turnover, the best presentation and method of keeping cigars is in a humidor. This is a polished box with half a dozen sections each holding a different size and type of cigar. On the inside of the lid is a pad which is kept damp, but not wet, to maintain the humidity.

Whether a cigar is stored in a tube, humidor or specially made box, they are all either made with, or lined with cedar wood. This is done because the aroma of cedar blends well with cigar and, as cedar wood is porous, it allows the cigar to breathe. A free circulation of air around these boxes is essential.

Appearance

A cigar should be smooth, firm and even to the touch. It should always be the same size and colour as its partners in the box. The wrapper should have a healthy glow to it and the open or cut end should be smooth and even.

Smoking

- The band of the cigar should be removed before lighting

- If the cigar is not pre-cut, then a clean V-shaped cut with a cigar cutter is recommended. This allows the cigar to draw easily

- Cigars should not be pierced as this allows an inadequate draught and leaves a bitter taste in the mouth

- Cigars must be lit with safety matches or a gas lighter and not a petrol lighter whose fumes would affect the taste of the cigar

Figure 5.38 Examples of cigar presentation

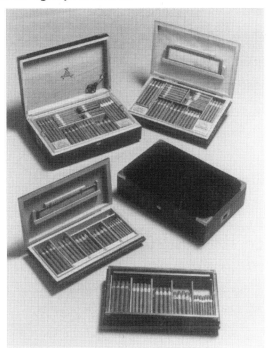

5.9 Service of non-alcoholic beverages

Tea and coffee

The following equipment is required for the service of tea and coffee:

Tea tray

- Tray or salver
- Tray cloth
- Teapot
- Hot water jug

- Jug of cold milk
- Slop basin
- Tea strainer
- Stands for teapot and hot water jug
- Sugar basin and tongs
- Teacup and saucer
- Teaspoon

Coffee tray

- Tray or salver
- Tray cloth/napkin
- Tea cup and saucer
- Teaspoon
- Sugar basin and tongs or a teaspoon according to the type of sugar offered
- Coffee pot
- Jug of hot milk or cream
- Stands for the coffee pot and hot milk jug

Variations of the above basic equipment will depend on the type of tea or coffee offered. Points to note in laying up a tea or coffee tray:

- Positioning of the items to ensure an evenly balanced tray for carrying
- Positioning of the items for convenience of the guest: beverage on the right with handles facing the guest for ease of pouring
- Ensure the beverage is placed on the tray at the last moment so that it is served piping hot

Note

1 When serving coffee the waiter must remember to ask the guest if he/she would prefer coffee with or without milk or cream
2 Remember certain coffees have flavourings added either in the blend or during the process of making:
    - Turkish coffee – vanilla
    - French coffee – chicory
    - Viennese coffee – fig

Practical techniques: service of coffee for table and assisted service

Placement of the coffee services

1 Figure 5.39(a) shows the equipment required, positioned on the service salver, assuming a table of four guests is to be served

Figure 5.39(a) Service of coffee: service salver before service

2 When the coffee is served after either lunch or dinner, then the demi-tasse, capacity 9.5 cl ($\frac{1}{6}$ pt) is used. It should be noted that there is a modern trend away from the use of demi-tasse, except at functions

3 Using this method the waiter only has to make one journey from sideboard to the table

4 Note the coffee service for each guest is made up of a demi-tasse on its saucer, placed on a sideplate, with its coffee spoon resting in the saucer and at right angles under the handle of the cup

5 The coffee service is placed on the table from the guest's right-hand side, as eventually the coffee will be served from the right

6 The coffee service is positioned on the right-hand side of the guest with the handle to the right and the coffee spoon set at right angles to the handle

7 This procedure is then repeated until all the coffee services have been placed on the table for those guests requiring coffee (see Figure 5.39(b))

(b) Service salver by the time the second customer is reached

Service of the coffee

1 Coffee is always served from the right-hand side of the guest
2 The service salver rests on a neatly folded service cloth on the palm of the hand. This allows the server to rotate the service salver so that whatever is to be served is nearest the coffee service
3 The server asks the guest if he/she requires sugar, which is always offered first
4 The required amount of sugar is placed in the demi-tasse
5 The service salver is now rotated on the service cloth so that the hot coffee pot and cream jug are in their correct positions for serving
6 The guest is then asked if he/she requires coffee with or without milk or cream
7 Keeping the service salver level, the hot coffee pot is tilted using the service salver as a base, and the coffee served
8 The service salver is again rotated a little so that the cream jug is in its best position for serving
9 Again keeping the service salver level, the cream jug is tilted using the service salver as a base, and the cream served
10 Having completed the service of the guest's coffee, the coffee service is eased into the centre of the place setting for the convenience of the guest
11 The server should always return to the table at the appropriate time, to see if the guests require their coffee to be topped up

Other methods of serving coffee are:

- Service from a pot of hot coffee held on the sideboard on a hotplate. Milk or cream and sugar are placed on the table

- Service of both hot milk (or cream) and coffee from pots, one held in each of the waiter's hands. Sugar is placed on the table for the customers to help themselves

- In function catering where larger numbers often have to be served, the hot milk/cream and sugar are placed on the table. Coffee is then served from a *one litre plus* capacity vacuum flask which may then also be held on the waiters' sideboard in readiness for replenishment should the guests require it. This means of holding and serving the coffee ensures that it is kept piping hot at all times

Dispense bar beverages

Non-alcoholic dispense bar beverages are categorized into five main groups, namely:

- Aerated water
- Natural spring water or mineral water
- Squashes
- Juices
- Syrups

Their correct service is essential in order that the customer may enjoy the beverage ordered to the full. This is where experienced bar personnel come into their own, ensuring that the drink ordered has the correct garnish, and is served at the correct temperature and in the correct glass.

Service

Aerated waters

Service: all aerated waters may be served on their own, chilled, and in either Slim Jim tumblers, Paris goblets, Highball glasses or 34.08 cl (12 fl oz) short-stemmed beer glasses, depending on the requirements of the guest and the policy of the establishment. They may also accompany other drinks as mixers, for example:

● Whisky and dry ginger

● Gin and tonic

● Vodka and bitter lemon

● Rum and Coca-cola

Natural spring waters/mineral waters

Service: natural spring or mineral waters are normally drunk on their own for medicinal purposes. However, as has been previously mentioned, some mineral waters may be mixed with alcoholic beverages to form an appetizing drink. In all cases, they should be drunk well chilled, at approximately 7–10°C (42–48°F). If drunk on their own they should be served in an 18.93 cl (6⅔ fl oz) Paris goblet or a Slim Jim tumbler.

Some examples are: Apollinaris, Buxton, Malvern, Perrier, Saint Galmier, Aix-la-Chapelle.

Squashes

Service from the bar: a measure of squash should be poured into a tumbler or 34.08 cl (12 fl oz) short-stemmed beer glass containing ice. This is topped up with iced water or the soda syphon. The edge of the glass should be decorated with a slice of fruit where applicable and drinking straws added.

Service from the lounge: all the items required to give efficient service must be taken by the wine butler or lounge waiter on a service salver. These would include:

● Tumbler or 34.08 cl (12 fl oz) short-stemmed beer glass containing a measure of squash

● Straws

● Jug of iced water ⎱ on an underplate because of the

● Small ice-bucket and tongs ⎰ condensation

● Soda syphon

● Coaster: to place the glass on in the lounge

At the side table in the lounge the coaster should be placed down and the glass containing the squash placed on the coaster. The waiter should then add the ice and enquire whether the guest wishes iced water or soda to be added. The drinking straws should be placed in the glass at the last moment if required. It may be necessary to leave the iced water and ice-bucket on the side table for the guest. If this is the case they should be left on underplates.

Juices
Service: all juices should be served chilled in a 14.20 cl (5 fl oz) goblet.

Tomato juice
Should be served chilled in a 14.20 cl (5 fl oz) goblet on a doily on an underplate with a teaspoon. The Worcester sauce should be shaken, the top removed, placed on an underplate and offered as an accompaniment. The goblet may have a slice of lemon placed over the edge as additional presentation.

Fresh fruit juice
If fresh fruit juice is to be served in the lounge, then the service should be similar to the service of squash in the lounge, with one exception. In addition to the items mentioned previously, a small bowl of castor sugar on an underplate with a teaspoon should be taken to the table.

Syrups
Syrups are never served as drinks in their own right but generally as flavourings in such items as cocktails, fruit cups, long drinks and milk shakes.

Further information on non-alcoholic bar beverages may be found in Section 4.4, page 110.

5.10 Clearing

Clearing methods

Figure 5.40 shows the various methods of clearing found in the food service industry.

Clearing tables in restaurants

Between courses and with customers in the room the procedures below should be followed:

Clearing plates

The ability to clear correctly ensures speed and efficiency around the table, avoids the possibility of accidents and creates minimum inconvenience to guests. In turn, it also allows dirties to be stacked neatly and correctly on the sideboard with the minimum delay. The correct clearing techniques allow more to be cleared, in less time and in fewer journeys between sideboard and table. In the long term, this speeds up the eating process and allows for greater seat turnover.

Figure 5.40 Clearing methods

SYSTEM	DESCRIPTION
MANUAL (1)	The collection of soiled ware by waiting staff and transportation to the dishwash area
MANUAL (2)	The collection and sorting to trolleys by operators for transportation to the dishwash area
SEMI-SELF-CLEAR	The placing of soiled ware by customers on strategically placed trolleys within the dining area for removal by operators
SELF-CLEAR	The placing of soiled ware by customers on a conveyor or conveyorized tray collecting system for mechanical transportation to the dishwash area
SELF-CLEAR AND STRIP	The placing of soiled ware into conveyorized dishwash baskets by customers for direct entry of the baskets through the dishwash

(Courtesy of Croner's Catering)

All clearing techniques stem from two main hand positions, shown on pages 225–226, and then, depending on what is being cleared, the technique is built up from that base. Remember expertise comes with practice – so practice regularly.

Clearing joint plates

- Dirties should always be cleared from the right-hand side of the guest

- The waiter should position him/herself, taking up a sideways stance at the table

- Figure 5.41(a) shows one of the two main hand positions previously mentioned, and the first dirty joint plate cleared

Figure 5.41 Clearing joint plates
(a) First joint plate cleared

- The dirty joint plate should be held firmly pushed up to the joint between the thumb and the first and second finger
- Note the position of the cutlery and flatware: the fork held firmly with the thumb over the end of its handle and the blade of the joint knife placed under the arch in the handle of the fork
- Any debris or crumbs would be pushed into that triangle formed by the handles of the joint knife and joint fork and the rim of the plate, that is nearest the holding hand
- Figure 5.41(b) shows the second dirty joint plate cleared and positioned on the holding hand

(b) Second joint plate cleared

- Figure 5.41(c) shows the second dirty joint knife positioned correctly and debris being cleared from the upper joint plate on to the lower joint plate using the second dirty joint fork cleared. This procedure is carried out as the waiter moves on to his/her next position in readiness to clear the third dirty joint plate
- Figure 5.41(d) shows the holding hand with the already cleared items held correctly and ready to receive the next dirty joint plate to be cleared
- Figure 5.42 shows the joint plates correctly stacked, with the sideplates being cleared in one journey to the table. This is an alternative to clearing the joint plates and then the sideplates in two phases

Clearing soup plates

1 Dirties should always be cleared from the right-hand side of the guest
2 The waiter should be positioned in a sideways stance at the table
3 Then, having picked up the first dirty soup plate on its underplate, this stance

(c) Clearing debris from the upper plate

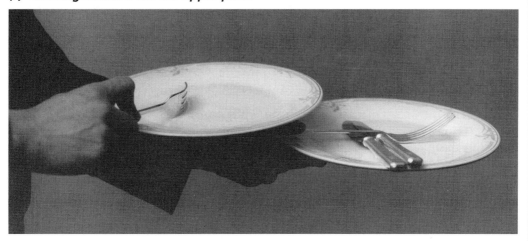

(d) Prepared to clear the next dirty plate

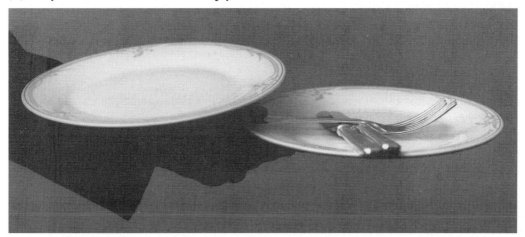

Figure 5.42 Clearing joint and sideplates in one journey

allows the waiter to pass the dirty plate from the clearing hand to the holding hand

4 Using this procedure ensures the dirty plates are held away from the table and the guests, reducing the likelihood of accidents to a minimum

● Figure 5.43(a) shows one of the two main hand positions previously mentioned, and the first dirty soup plate cleared

● This dirty soup plate should be held firmly on its underplate with the latter pushed up firmly between the thumb and the first and second fingers

● It is important that this first dirty soup plate is held firmly as succeeding dirties are built up on this one, meaning there is a considerable weight to hold

Figure 5.43 Clearing soup plates
(a) First soup plate cleared

● Figure 5.43(b) shows the second dirty soup plate on its underplate cleared and about to be positioned on the holding hand

● Figure 5.43(c) shows the position of the second dirty soup plate on the holding hand. The soup spoon is taken from the lower soup plate to be placed in the upper soup plate

● Figure 5.43(d) shows the upper soup plate with its two soup spoons now placed in the lower soup plate, leaving the underplate behind

● The third dirty soup plate with its underplate is now cleared from the right and placed on the upper underplate on the holding hand. The above procedure is then repeated each time a dirty soup plate on its underplate is cleared

(b) First stage of clearing the second soup plate

(c) Second stage of clearing the second soup plate

(d) Second soup plate cleared in preparation for the next

Clearing sideplates

Sideplates are cleared using a service salver or plate. The purpose is to allow a larger working surface on which to clear the dirty side knives and any debris remaining.

- Figure 5.44(a) illustrates the method of clearing debris from the upper dirty sideplate and on to the service salver/plate
- Figure 5.44(b) shows the holding hand having cleared four place settings with the dirty items and debris stacked correctly and safely

This method generally allows the waiter to clear more dirties in one journey between sideboard and table and is especially useful when working in a banqueting situation.

Figure 5.44 Clearing sideplates
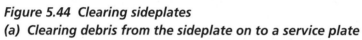
(a) Clearing debris from the sideplate on to a service plate

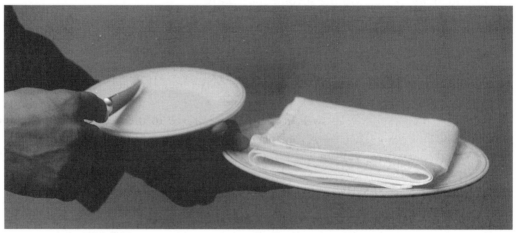

(b) Hand position having cleared four sideplates

Crumbing down

The process of *crumbing down* usually takes place after the main course has been cleared and before the sweet order is taken and served. The purpose is to remove any crumbs or debris left on the tablecloth at this stage of the meal (see Figure 5.3, page 154).

The items of equipment used to crumb down are:

- A service plate (a joint plate with a napkin on it)
- The waiter's cloth or service cloth

On the assumption that a table d'hôte cover has previously been laid, the sweet spoon and fork, prior to crumbing down, should normally be positioned at the head of the cover. However, had an à la carte cover been laid initially then, after the main course had been cleared, there should be no tableware on the table prior to crumbing down.

1 Crumbing down commences from the left-hand side of the first guest. The service plate is placed just beneath the lip of the table. Crumbs are brushed towards the plate using a folded napkin
2 This having been completed, the sweet fork is moved from the head of the place setting to the left-hand side of the cover
3 The waiter now moves to the right-hand side of the same guest and completes the crumbing down of this place setting
4 The sweet spoon is then moved from the head of the place setting to the right-hand side of the cover
5 While the sweet spoon and sweet fork are being moved to their correct positions, the service cloth is held under the service plate by the fingers of the holding hand
6 Having completed the crumbing down procedure for one place setting the waiter is now correctly positioned to commence again the crumbing down of the next place setting, ie to the left of the next guest

This method of crumbing down ensures that the waiter should never, at any time, stretch across the front of a guest to complete any one place setting in readiness for the sweet course.

Changing a dirty ashtray

This procedure may be carried out at any stage of the meal should the waiter feel it is justified.

- Figure 5.45(a) shows a dirty ashtray on the table
- Figure 5.45(b): a clean ashtray is held over the dirty ashtray
- Figure 5.45(c): the clean ashtray is placed upside down directly on top of the dirty ashtray
- The dirty ashtray covered by the clean ashtray is lifted away from the guest's table. This cover is necessary to ensure no fine cigar or cigarette ash is blown on to the tablecloth

- The dirty ashtray with its cover is transferred to the holding hand away from the table
- The clean ashtray is then placed on the table (Figure 5.45(d)).

Figure 5.45 Clearing a dirty ashtray

(a) Dirty ashtray

(b) Stage one

(c) Stage two

(d) Stage three

5.11 Billing methods

Seven basic billing methods are identified in Figure 5.46.

Bill as check

Duplicate checking system or check bill book system

When a guest requires the bill, the waiter checks everything is entered on the duplicate copy of the food and drink check and then totals the bill. It is presented to the guest as

Figure 5.46 Billing methods

METHOD	DESCRIPTION
BILL AS CHECK	Second copy of order used as bill
SEPARATE BILL	Bill made up from duplicate check and presented to customer
BILL WITH ORDER	Service to order and billing at same time, eg bar or take-away methods
PRE-PAID	Customer purchases ticket or card in advance, either for specific meal or specific value
VOUCHER	Customer has credit issued by third party for either specific meal or specific value, eg luncheon voucher or tourist agency voucher
NO CHARGE	Customer not paying – credit transaction
DEFERRED	Refers to, for example, function-type catering where bill paid by organizer

previously mentioned. One of two methods of payment may now occur. The guest may pay at the cash desk on the way out or may pay the cash direct to the waiter who will give any change that is necessary. The cashier usually keeps the bill on payment but if a guest wishes to have a receipt, then a special bill is written out and receipted.

Depending on the system used, a waiter may enter the details of his/her bills from the stubs on his/her check pads into an account slip. This account slip plus the stubs and cash received are then passed on to the control and accounts department who marry them all up.

If the waiter makes out and presents the bill to the guest and it is then paid by the guest to the cashier on leaving the establishment, then the cashier will draw up a daily summary sheet or analysis sheet to show the daily takings and also an analysis sheet showing each individual waiter's takings.

Control is effected by the control and accounts department marrying up the checks used to order food and drink from the bars, stillroom and kitchen against the bills issued by each waiter.

Separate bill

This billing method is usually found running in conjunction with the triplicate checking system. The basic differences between the duplicate and triplicate billing methods are set out in Figure 5.47.

On receiving the duplicate copy of the food check from the waiter the cashier opens a bill in duplicate according to the table number on the food check. All the sets of bills are serial numbered for control purposes. As checks are received by the cashier from the food or wine waiter, he/she enters the items ordered on to the bill together with the correct

Figure 5.47 Basic differences between duplicate and triplicate billing methods

DIFFERENCES	DUPLICATE	TRIPLICATE
TYPE OF ESTABLISHMENT	Popular price restaurants, cafes, department stores where a table d'hôte menu is in operation with possibly a limited à la carte	First-class establishments usually operating an extensive à la carte menu
NUMBER OF COPIES OF FOOD CHECK	Two	Three
THE BILL	The bill is the duplicate copy of the food and drink check and is made out by the waiter/waitress	The cashier makes out the bill, which is in duplicate
PAYMENT OF THE BILL	The guest may pay the cashier direct or pay the waiter/waitress according to the policy of the establishment	The guest pays the cashier via the waiter/waitress who returns the receipted bill and any change to the guest
AT THE END OF SERVICE	The account slip and stubs from the waiter's check pad must be handed in, together with the cash received. The cashier completes his/her summary sheet and hands it in with any cash and duplicate bills and checks to the control and accounts department	The cashier completes his/her summary sheet and hands it in with any cash and the duplicate bills and checks to the control and accounts department

prices. When this is done the bill and duplicate checks are pinned together and may be placed into a special book or file which has its pages numbered according to the number of tables in the room. The bill and duplicate checks are placed in the page corresponding to the table number. As further checks are received the items are entered on to the bill and the checks then pinned with the others to the bill.

When the guest requests the bill, the waiter must collect it from the cashier who must first check that all items are entered and priced correctly and then total it up. It is advisable for the waiter to double check the addition. The top copy of the bill is presented to the guest on a sideplate and folded in half with one corner turned up. On receiving the necessary payment from the guest, the waiter returns the bill and cash to the cashier who will receipt both copies of the bill and return the receipted top copy plus any change to the waiter. The waiter then returns this to the guest. The receipted duplicate copy with the duplicate checks pinned to it is then removed from the special book or file and put on one side until service is completed.

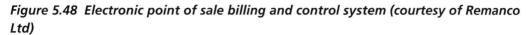

Figure 5.48 Electronic point of sale billing and control system (courtesy of Remanco Ltd)

Bill with order

This billing method may take a variety of forms depending upon the requirements of the establishment and the depth of management control information to be realized.

For example see Section 5.6:

- Menu order and customer bill, page 201
- The single order sheet, page 202

This principle of billing may also be used in bars where the customer's order is rung up as requested on a pre-set (electronic) keyboard. Here each key relates to a specified drink and its cost and a monitor is on view to the customer showing the order as it is rung up and the prices charged. When the order has been completed, the total sum owing is displayed on the monitor. On the receipt of cash for the order dispensed, the 'system' allows you to display via the monitor the change to be returned to the customer. Should it be required, a receipt or itemized bill can be obtained for the customer.

This system speeds up the process of billing to the customer and allows specific control over cash received and change given as well as controlling all stock items held.

Pre-paid

This billing method happens when pre-payment is perhaps required for a specific occasion or event and allows the organizer to determine exact numbers prior to the day. In this instance, upon arrival at the event, admission or receipt of food is obtained by handing in one's ticket or card.

Voucher

Here a customer has perhaps been issued credit by a third party, his/her employer, in the form of a luncheon voucher. This voucher can be exchanged for like goods, food and non-alcoholic beverages to the maximum value indicated by the voucher. Should the goods requested come to less than the sum shown on the voucher, no 'cash' may exchange hands to make up the difference to the purchaser. However, should the cost of the goods requested exceed the sum shown on the voucher, then the customer must pay the difference to the supplier of the goods.

In the same way vouchers may be issued to a specific value, to be given in exchange or part exchange for goods or services received. These 'credit' vouchers are then used by the supplier of the goods or services to claim *cash owing* from the employer, firm, or agency who issued them in the first instance.

No charge

This is where *no charge* is made to the customer receiving the goods or services. He/she should be asked only to sign for the goods and services received and the bill should then be sent to the firm or company supplying the hospitality.

In some instances the customer will be required to show some type of official form or letter authorizing that the 'hospitality' may take place.

Deferred/Account

In deferred or account billing a service has been requested by an individual, firm or company, which has been confirmed and taken place. The bill for the total services received is then sent after the event and will be paid by the organizing person or body. Payment in this manner will normally relate to function catering events.

5.12 Clearing following service
Clearing checklists
Table and assisted service

The supervisor should ensure that all the clearing up is completed and that it is done properly. Duties might include:

1 Clearing the cold buffet to the larder; collecting and washing all carving knives; assisting generally in clearing the restaurant
2 Collecting all linen, both clean and dirty; checking that the correct quantities of each item of linen are returned. The serviettes should be tied in bundles of ten. All linen should be placed in the linen basket and returned with the linen list to the linen room
3 Switching off the hotplate; clearing away any service silver remaining; restocking with clean china
4 Returning all the silver, together with the tableware trolleys, to the silver store. Silver should be arranged and put away neatly as shown by the shelf labels

5   Collecting all cruets and accompaniments; returning them to their correct storage place; where appropriate, returning sauces, etc, to their original containers

6   Checking all the sideboards are completely empty. Hotplates should be switched off and the dirty linen compartment empty

7   Clearing down the bar top; putting all the equipment away; washing and polishing used glasses. These should be put away in their correct storage place; removing all empty bottles, etc; completing consumption and stock sheets; locking up

8   Putting away all equipment that has been used; emptying all coffee pots and milk jugs; washing and putting away. All perishable materials should be put away in their correct storage places. The still set and milk urns should be emptied, washed out and then left standing with cold water in them

9   Emptying and cleaning all trolleys and returning them to their appropriate places. Any unused food items from the trolleys should be returned to the necessary department. Any silver used on the trolleys should be cleaned and returned to the silver room

10 Emptying the liqueur trolley; returning stock to the bar cupboard; restocking bar from the cellar. Bar shutters and doors should be properly locked

Clearing down counters

1   Turn off the electricity supply to the hot-food counter

2   Clear the hot-food counter and return all leftover food to the kitchen

3   Turn off the power supply to oven at the wall

4   Clear the oven of any remaining food

5   *Important*: write down on the day sheet the number of portions of each type of regenerated meal that is left over as waste. This exercise is essential for portion control monitoring and should give a helpful indication of the popularity or otherwise of any one particular dish. Hand in the day sheet to the supervisor who will then prepare a reconciliation of what was taken out and what is now left. This will then be entered into the analysis book

6   Clean all kitchen utensils such as serving spoons, ladles, fish slices, knives and trays that have been used during the course of the day in hot food preparation and service. Wipe them dry

7   Return all cleaned and dried kitchen utensils to the appropriate storage places ready for the next day's use

8   Check the stock of plates needed for the next day's service of hot food. *Remember*: as stocks are used up they have to be replenished if stocks are low

After service duties

At the completion of service, there are certain after service duties to be carried out by all the food and beverage service personnel. This is to ensure that all areas are left safe, clean and replenished in readiness for the next service.

Examples of what might be involved are shown in the following checklists.

Head waiter/supervisor

1   Ensure gas and electrical appliances are switched off and plugs removed from sockets

2   Return any special equipment to the appropriate work area

3 Secure all windows and check fire exits

4 Check that all tasks are completed in a satisfactory manner prior to staff completing their shift.

Station waiter/server

1 Replace all equipment in the sideboard according to the sideboard checklist

2 Wipe down the sideboard and trolleys, clearing all dirty equipment to the wash-up area

3 Clear down tables and crumb down. Relay tablecloths and slip cloths as appropriate

4 Switch off and clean sideboard hotplates

5 Return special equipment to appropriate work areas

6 Return to store cupboards any surplus china and silver

7 Remove plugs having switched off all electrical sockets

8 Return food/drink check pads and menus to the drawer in the head waiter's desk

9 Check your area of responsibility with your head waiter/supervisor

Barperson

1 All working surfaces to be wiped down

2 Ensure that all equipment is washed, dried and put away in its correct place for future use

3 See that all glassware is washed, rinsed, and dried and then stored correctly

4 Empty the bottle trolley and waste bin. Replace the bin liner in waste bin

5 Place surplus orange/lemon slices on to plates and cling film. Store in the chilling unit or fridge

6 Sweep and mop the floor

7 Return the liqueur trolley to the bar

8 Drain the glass-washing machine

9 Turn off the chiller lights

10 Complete the control system

11 Replenish bar stock

12 Make the bar secure

13 Check your area of responsibility with your head waiter/supervisor

Stillroom

1 Ensure the correct storage of such food items as bread, butter, milk, teabags and ground coffee

2 Wipe down all working surfaces

3 Clean and tidy the stillroom fridge and check its working temperature

4 Check that all equipment is left clean and stored in its correct place

5 Left over foods to be placed into clean containers and stored correctly

6 All surplus accompaniments to be stored correctly with proprietary jars and their lids to be wiped down

7 Switch off applicable electrical appliances

8 See all carrying trays are wiped down and stacked correctly

9 All surplus teapots/coffee pots and the like to be stored in the appropriate storage area

10 Check your area of responsibility with the head waiter/supervisor, or the person you are handing over to prior to leaving

CHAPTER 6

THE SERVICE OF BREAKFAST AND AFTERNOON TEA

6.1 **Breakfast service** 240

6.2 **Afternoon tea service** 246

6.1 Breakfast service

Breakfast is traditionally a British rather than a Continental meal, originating from the days of the private house and family service. At this time it was a very substantial meal, consisting of some six or seven courses, including such items as chops, liver, game and even steak (or kippers and porridge in Scotland) as the main part of the meal. For the European, a continental breakfast is of a much lighter nature and takes the form of a light snack, as their midday meal is generally taken earlier and is much more substantial than in Britain.

During the past decade, however, people in Britain have been eating far less breakfast foods, such as egg and bacon, and have turned to lighter alternatives. The current trend is for hotels to serve a continental breakfast inclusive in the room rate, and to serve the full English breakfast at an extra charge.

Breakfast may be served in the hotel restaurant or dining room, in a breakfast room set aside for this meal, or in the guest's bedroom or suite. The service of breakfast in rooms or suites is dealt with in Section 7.2, page 252.

The double checking system is normally used for breakfasts, both on the floors and in the restaurant.

Café complet

The term *café complet* is widely used on the Continent and means a continental breakfast with coffee as the beverage. *Thé complet* is also used, in this sense, with tea as the beverage.

Café simple or thé simple

Café simple or *thé simple*, is the beverage (coffee or tea) with nothing to eat.

Full breakfast menu

A full or English (or Scottish, Irish, Welsh or British) breakfast menu may consist of from two to eight courses, a specimen of which is shown overleaf. The extent and variety of the menu will depend on the type of establishment in which it is being served.

To meet the needs of the modern day customer, the 'menu content' of the full breakfast has moved towards a much more varied choice to suit all tastes. Today we expect to see on the full menu such items as fresh orange juice, fresh fruit, yoghurts, muesli, continental pastries, homemade preserves, margarines, decaffeinated coffee and mineral waters.

Continental breakfast menu

The traditional Continental breakfast consisted simply of hot croissant, brioche or toast, butter and preserves and coffee as the beverage.

The current trend in the continental breakfast menu is towards offering a wider variety of choice, including cereals, fruits, juices, ham, cheese and a wider selection of beverages.

Breakfast Menu

Chilled Fruit Juices
Orange, Pineapple, Grapefruit, Tomato

Stewed Fruits
Prunes, Pears, Apples, Figs

Cereals
All Proprietary Brands of Breakfast Cereals

Fish
Finnan Haddock, Grilled Herring, Bloaters
Fried or Grilled Kippers, Fried Smelt
Fried or Grilled Plaice or Sole
Kedgeree

Eggs
Fried, Poached, Scrambled, Boiled
Plain or Savoury Omelette

Meat
Fried or Grilled Bacon
Fried or Grilled Pork Sausages
Kidneys, Tomatoes, Sauté Potatoes

Cold Buffet
York Ham, Calf's Tongue, Breakfast Sausage

Breads
Toast, Rolls, Croissants, Brioches, Ryvita
Hovis and Procea

Preserves
Marmalade, Honey, Plum, Cherry

Beverages
Tea, Coffee, Chocolate, Tisanes

Breakfast covers

The *breakfast cover* may be divided into two types. These are:

- Full breakfast cover
- Continental breakfast cover

Cover for a full breakfast

The full breakfast consists of a number of courses, usually three or four, with a choice of dishes from within each course, as shown on the specimen full breakfast menu above. The cover will therefore include some or all of the following:

Figure 6.1 Full breakfast menu – courtesy of Forte Posthouse, Aylesbury

Full House Breakfast

Please help yourself from the Posthouse buffet table and then your order will be taken from the following range of hot dishes:

Grilled back bacon

Egg ~ fried, poached, scrambled

Sausage

Tomato

Sauté potatoes

Black pudding

Baked beans

Mushrooms

Grilled kippers

Poached haddock with poached egg

£9.95

Children's Breakfast

£3.50

Under 13's can choose our Fresh-Start Breakfast Buffet Table and Full House menu

Under 5's can eat breakfast TOTALLY FREE!

Figure 6.2 Full breakfast cover
- *The cover laid is a table d'hôte cover without the soup spoon*
- *The positioning of the items – to the right of the cover for the convenience of the guest*

- Joint knife and fork
- Fish knife and fork
- Sweet spoon and fork
- Side knife
- Sideplate
- Breakfast cup, saucer and teaspoon
- Slop basin
- Tea strainer
- Jug of cold milk
- Sugar basin and tongs
- Stands or underplates for teapot/coffee pot and hot water jug/hot milk jug
- Butter dish on an underplate with a butter knife
- Preserve dish on a doily on an underplate with a preserve spoon
- Salt, pepper

- Castor sugar
- Ashtray (depending on smoking policy)
- Napkin
- Toast rack on an underplate
- Table number
- Bread boat containing the croissant or brioche in a serviette to keep them warm

Cover for a continental breakfast

This meal consists of hot croissant/brioches or hot toast, butter, preserves and coffee or tea. The cover would be as follows:

- Sideplate
- Side knife
- Napkin
- Bread boat containing the croissant or brioche in a serviette to keep them hot, or a toast rack on an underplate
- Butter dish on a doily on a sideplate with a butter knife
- Preserve dish on a doily on a sideplate with a preserve spoon
- Breakfast cup and saucer and a teaspoon
- Stands or underplates for coffee/tea pot and hot milk/hot water jug
- Ashtray (depending on smoking policy)
- Table number
- Sugar basin and tongs

If tea is to be the beverage then the following additional items will be needed:

- Slop basin
- Tea strainer
- Jug of cold milk

The majority of the items listed for the two types of breakfast should be placed on the table as part of the *mise-en-place*, before the guest is seated. A number of items, however, are not placed on the table until the guest is seated, and these include:

- Butter dish and butter and alternatives
- Preserve dish with preserve
- Jug of cold milk
- Toast rack with toast and/or bread basket with hot rolls

Order of service for breakfasts

1 Correct cover as per the customer order
2 Serve first course
3 After first course is cleared:
  - Beverage
  - Croissant, brioche, rolls, toast
  - Butter
  - Preserves
4 Main course (plated) plus accompaniments
5 Check any other requirements

Breakfast served in the restaurant

The basic *mise-en-place* for the service of breakfast is normally carried out the evening before, after the service of dinners has finished. To ensure protection against dust until the breakfast brigade comes on duty, the corners of the cloths may be lifted up and over the basic *mise-en-place*. It will be completed the following morning before the actual service of breakfast commences. This will include turning breakfast cups the right way up, and laying the breakfast buffet with items usually served for the first course, such as chilled fruit juices, cereals and fruit compote, together with all the necessary glasses, plates and tableware required for the correct service. Also found on the breakfast buffet should be preserves and butter and alternatives. Jugs of iced water and glasses should be ready on the buffet throughout the meal, especially if the establishment is catering for American visitors. Preserves are usually now served in individual pots.

The guest should be escorted to a particular table and seated. The breakfast menu should then be presented, giving a few minutes for the guest to make his/her choice.

The food order is written on one check and sent to the kitchen; the beverage on another check which is sent to the stillroom. While the orders are being attended to in the various departments, the waiter must remember to remove any unwanted cutlery and flatware from the cover and, where appropriate, to lay fresh cutlery and flatware together with any accompaniments that may be required, eg Worcestershire sauce if the first course is to be tomato juice. The first course should then be laid on the table.

When the first course has been consumed and cleared, the beverage should be served. The teapot and hot water jug or the coffee pot and hot milk jug should be placed on the stands or underplates to the right of the lady (or the elder if more than one) in the party or, in the case of an all-male party, by the senior gentleman present. The handles of the pots should be placed in the most convenient position for pouring. Hot fresh toast and/or hot rolls should then be placed on the table together with preserves and butter before serving the main course.

The main course at breakfast is usually plated and all necessary accompaniments should be on the table before it is served. On clearing the main course the waiter should move the sideplate and knife in front of the guest and then enquire if more toast, butter, preserve or beverage is required.

The following special points should also be noted when serving breakfasts:

- Hot or cold milk, or cream should be offered when serving porridge
- Cream is not normally served with stewed fruit unless asked for

Buffet breakfast

Of all hotel meals, it is very often the service of breakfasts which seems to give management the most headaches. This is perhaps because it seems that the majority of guests arrive for breakfast within a very few minutes of one another, all requiring fast service. However well planned the service may be, this sudden influx of customers can cause havoc. To add to this, the situation may be aggravated by staff shortages. To overcome these problems and to meet the needs of their guests, some hotels have in recent years introduced a self-service breakfast buffet which has successfully provided a fast breakfast service.

For the service of this style of breakfast meal guests are presented with the breakfast menu when they sit down and from that they make their choice of either the buffet or other types of breakfast. With the buffet breakfast all items should be self-served from the buffet with perhaps the exception of any egg dishes or other cooked items and the beverage required.

6.2 Afternoon tea service

The old English tradition of taking afternoon tea at 4 o'clock is slowly dying out and in its place the trend is towards tea and pastries only, the venue changing from the hotel lounge to the coffee bars or shops and tea gardens found in shopping precincts.

However, afternoon tea is still served in many establishments and in a variety of forms which may be classified into three main types:

- Full afternoon tea as served in a first-class hotel
- High tea as served in a popular price restaurant or café
- Reception or buffet tea

Menu for full afternoon tea

The menu ususally consists of some or all of the following items, which are generally served in the order in which they are listed. Note that beverages are served first.

Menu
Hot Buttered Toast or Toasted Teacake or Crumpets
Assorted Afternoon Tea Sandwiches:
Smoked Salmon, Cucumber, Tomato, Sardine, Egg, Gentleman's Relish
Brown and White Bread and Butter
Fruit Bread and Butter
Buttered Scones
Raspberry or Strawberry Jams
Gâteaux and Pastries

Menu for high tea

A high tea may be available in addition to the full afternoon tea. It is usually in a modified à la carte form and the menu will offer, in addition to the normal full afternoon tea menu, such items as grills, toasted snacks, fish and meat dishes, salads, cold sweets and ices. The meat dishes normally consist in the main of pies and pastries, whereas the fish dishes are usually fried or grilled.

The following accompaniments (proprietary sauces) may often be offered with high tea:

- Tomato ketchup
- Worcestershire sauce
- Brown sauce (eg 'HP')
- Vinegar
- Mustard

Afternoon tea covers

The *afternoon tea cover* may be divided into two types:

- Full afternoon tea cover
- High tea cover

Cover for full afternoon tea

Figure 6.3 Cover for full afternoon tea

The following cover should normally be laid for a full afternoon tea:

- Sideplate
- Napkin
- Side or tea knife
- Pastry fork
- Teacup and saucer and a teaspoon
- Slop basin and tea strainer
- Sugar basin and tongs
- Teapot and hot water jug stands or underplates
- Jug of cold milk
- Preserve dish on an underplate with a preserve spoon
- Ashtray (depending on smoking policy)

Note: The jug of cold milk and preserve dish should only be brought to the table when the guests are seated, and are not part of the *mise-en-place*.

Cover for high tea

The cover for high tea may include:

- Napkin
- Joint knife and fork
- Sideplate
- Side knife
- Cruet: salt, pepper, mustard and mustard spoon
- Teacup, saucer and teaspoon
- Sugar basin and tongs
- Slop basin and tea strainer
- Teapot and hot water jug stands or underplates
- Jug of cold milk
- Preserve dish on an underplate with a preserve spoon
- Ashtray (depending on smoking policy)

Note: as for the full afternoon tea cover, the jug of cold milk and the preserve dish should only be brought to the table when the guests are seated and are not part of the *mise-en-place*. Any other items of tableware that may be required are brought to the table as for à la carte service.

Figure 6.4 Cover for high tea

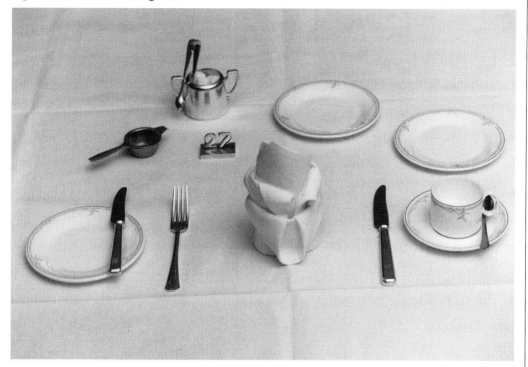

Order of service for afternoon teas

1 Beverages
2 *Hot snacks – bread and butter (sometimes salads)
3 Hot toasted items
4 Sandwiches
5 Buttered scones
6 Bread and butter
7 Preserves
8 Cakes and pastries

Note:

1 *High tea only: for the service of a high tea, the beverage should again be served first, followed by the hot snack ordered with its accompaniment of bread and butter. When this has been consumed and cleared, the service then follows that of a full afternoon tea
2 Ice-creams are becoming more popular now and are usually served last
3 Checking is usually the duplicate method

    ● **Toast, tea cakes** and **crumpets** are served in a soup plate or welled dish with a silver cover on an underplate. An alternative to this is the use of a muffin dish which is a covered silver dish with an inner lining and hot water in the lower part of the container. When serving hot buttered toast for afternoon tea, the crusts from three sides only are removed, and the toast is then cut into 'fingers' with part of the crust remaining attached to each 'finger'

- The **sandwiches** are dressed on silver flats, and are set out on the buffet prior to service
- The **scones** and **assorted buttered breads** are dressed on doilies on silver flats and are also set out on the buffet
- Preserves are served either in individual pots or in preserve dishes, both of which are served on a doily on an underplate with a preserve spoon
- **Gâteaux** and **pastries** are dressed up on doilies on silver flats or salvers. An alternative to this is the use of a pastry trolley.

Note: tea may also be served in the lounge (see Section 7.3, page 258).

Reception tea

These are offered at special functions and private parties only and, as the name implies, the food and beverage are served from a buffet table and not at individual tables. The buffet should be set up in a prominent position in the room making sure that there is ample space for display and presentation and for the guests to make their choice. As well as being in a prominent position, the buffet should have easy access to the stillroom and wash-up so that replenishment of the buffet and the clearing of dirties may be carried out without disturbing the guests.

When setting up the buffet it is necessary to ensure there is ample space for customer circulation and that a number of occasional tables and chairs are placed round the room. These occasional tables may be covered with clean, well-starched linen cloths and have a small vase of flowers and an ashtray on them (depending on the smoking policy).

Setting up the buffet

The normal afternoon tea tableware, china and serviettes should be laid along the front of the buffet in groups with the teacups, saucers and teaspoons concentrated in one or more tea service points as required. Sugar basins and tongs may be placed on the buffet or on the occasional tables that are spread round the room. The tea should be served at the separate tea service points along the buffet from silver urns which should be kept hot. Milk should be served separately from silver milk jugs. Milky non-dairy creamers and a range of sugars sometimes in packets may also be offered.

A raised floral centrepiece can be the focal point around which the dishes of food would be placed. Cake stands may also be used for presentation and display purposes.

Service

During the reception some of the staff must be positioned behind the buffet for service and replenishment of the dishes of food and the beverage. Others should circulate the room with the food and also clear away the dirties as they accumulate. As the dishes on the buffet become depleted, they should be quickly replenished or cleared away so that the buffet looks neat and tidy at all times.

CHAPTER 7

SPECIALIZED FORMS OF SERVICE

7.1	**Introduction**	252
7.2	**Floor/room service**	252
7.3	**Lounge service**	258
7.4	**Hospital tray service**	260
7.5	**Home delivery**	262
7.6	**Airline tray service**	263
7.7	**Rail service**	263

7.1 Introduction

In Chapter 1 (see pages 14–15) five groups of service methods were identified. In the first four (A: Table Service, B: Assisted Service, C: Self-Service, D: Single Point Service) the customer comes to where the food and beverage service is provided. In the last group (E: Specialized) the food and drink is taken to the customer, ie service *in situ*. The service also takes place in areas not conventionally designed for service.

This group of service methods includes *tray methods* found in hospitals and aircraft and sometimes in ODC, as well as *lounge service, room service* and *home delivery*. In this chapter information is given on this method of service and additional tasks and duties associated with specialized service are identified.

7.2 Floor/room service

Floor or room service varies from basic 'in room' tea and coffee making facilities, as well as possibly mini-bars, to vending machines on floors, or to the service of a variety of meals in rooms. Depending on the nature of establishment, the extent of service in guest rooms will vary. In five-star hotels 24-hour room service is expected, whereas two- and three-star hotels service may be limited to 'in room' tea and coffee making facilities with only continental breakfast available to be served in the room.

Full and partial room service

An example of a room service menu is shown in Figure 7.1. In this establishment full room service is offered and the room service staff are employed to provide service at the times indicated on the menus.

Service may be operated from a floor pantry: there may be one on each floor of an establishment or one sited to service two or three floors. An alternative system is where all food and beverages come from a central kitchen and are sent to the appropriate floor by lift and then taken to the rooms, possibly in a hot trolley.

Floor service staff must have considerable experience as they have to deal with the service of all types of meals. They also have to deal with the service of all alcoholic beverages and so must have a good knowledge of the licensing laws. The floor service staff work on a shift system as the service has to be provided 24 hours a day.

The guest may call for service by pressing a button which lights up a series of coloured lights in the corridor, or alternatively lights up a panel in the floor pantry which is divided into numbered sections denoting the rooms. The customers may telephone direct to the floor pantry, or telephone their request to reception or the restaurant or dining room.

A food or wine check is made out for all requests from the guests or, in the event of special luncheon or dinner parties, a bill made out and presented to the host who will sign it to show that the services listed have been received. It is most important that a signature

Figure 7.1 Example of a room service menu – courtesy of the Carlton Hotel, Bournemouth

Sandwiches

Prawns bound with Marie Rose sauce	£7.60
Smoked Salmon spiked with Black Pepper	£7.95
Roast Ham enhanced with English Mustard	£4.35
Roast Beef with creamed Horseradish	£4.35
Roast Chicken with Lettuce and Mayonnaise	£4.35
Mature Cheddar Cheese with Chutney	£4.35
Traditional Club Sandwich, toasted bread, layered with Bacon, Tomato, Lettuce, Chicken and Mayonnaise served with French Fries	£10.75
Minute Steak Sandwich layered with Tomato and Grain Mustard	£12.35

The above are served on White or Wholemeal Bread and presented with Seasonal Leaves and Crisps

Light Meals

Soup of the Day with Brown or White Roll	£4.00
Refreshing Melon of the Season	£5.95
Parfait of Chicken Livers presented on Brioche and Cumberland Sauce	£7.95
Traditional Smoked Salmon with Capers and a Lemon Pigtail	£12.00
Carlton Seasonal Salad of Bacon, Roast Chicken, Seasonal Leaves, Herbs and Spring Onion dressed with a Dijon Mustard Vinaigrette	£10.75
Tagliatelle with a Mushroom, Herb and Garlic Cream Sauce	£8.50
Char grilled Burger served in a Wholemeal Bun with Bacon and Cheddar served with French Fries and Coleslaw	£10.45
Brocolli and Cream Cheese Bake served with a Mixed Salad	£11.50
Classic Spaghetti Bolognaise with Salad	£12.75

Main Course

Medallions of Beef Fillet, Pan Roasted and coated with a Mushroom and Grain Mustard Sauce	£19.80
Char grilled Supreme of Chicken served on Tomatoes with Mozzarella and a Herb Oil	£17.00
Fillet of Salmon oven baked with a Horseradish and Breadcrumb Crust served with an Orange Butter Sauce	£19.25
A selection of Cooked Meats and Cold Salads with a Lemon Vinaigrette	£14.50

The above dishes are served with Seasonal Vegetables or Salad

Puddings

Hot Chocolate Pudding served with Vanilla and Chocolate Sauce	£5.00
A selection of Icecream or Sorbet with a Brandy Snap Basket	£4.95
Platter of British Farmhouse Cheeses served with Apple, Celery and Grapes	£7.15
Basket of Fresh Seasonal Fruits	£7.15
A choice of freshly made Gateaux or Cheesecake	£4.95

Beverages

A full selection of Wines, Alcoholic and Non-alcoholic drinks are available from 11a.m. throughout to 11p.m.

A limited choice of Alcoholic drinks are available throughout the night hours

Traditional Tea or speciality Tea with Biscuits	£2.50
Ground Fresh Coffee with Biscuits	£2.50
Milky Hot Chocolate with Cookies	£2.50

Denotes items available 24 hours a day, all other items are available from 10am until 10pm.

Vegetarian Dishes are denoted by this symbol.

We are more than happy to arrange suitable meals for our younger guests, please let us know what you would like to have!

is obtained in case of any query or complaint when the bill is presented to a guest on leaving an establishment. All checks once signed by the guest should be passed immediately to reception or control so that the services rendered may be charged to his/her account. All orders are usually taken in triplicate, the top copy going to the department supplying the food or beverage required, a duplicate going to control or reception (after being signed by the guest) and the third copy kept by the floor service staff as a means of reference.

The pantry from which the floor service staff operate may be likened to a mini still-room and holds the equipment required for the preparation and service of any meal. This equipment can include:

- Sink unit
- Hotplate

- Refrigerator
- Lift to central kitchen
- Salamander
- Open gas rings
- Small still set or other coffee making machine
- Cutting boards
- Knives
- Storage space shelves and cupboards
- China
- Cutlery, flatware and hollow-ware
- Glassware
- Cruets, Worcestershire sauce, sugars, etc
- Linen
- Guéridon trolley
- Chafing lamps and Suzette pans
- Wine service equipment, wine buckets, stands baskets, etc
- Trays

Sufficient equipment must be available to enable efficient service to be given at all times and a high standard maintained.

The service staff carry out all their own pre-service preparation (*mise-en-place*) before the service of a meal. This includes the checking and refilling of cruets and other accompaniments, laying up of breakfast trays, changing of linen, laying up of tables, washing and polishing of glasses, cleaning of trays and so on. Some establishments provide a different style and design of china, etc, for the service of meals on the floors.

Floor service staff must also co-operate with other staff within the establishment. The floor service staff should ensure that all rooms are cleared as soon as meals are finished so as not to be in the way when rooms are being cleaned.

Breakfast only service

In some hotels only breakfast service is available, which is often provided by the housekeeping staff. An example of a breakfast menu is shown in Figure 7.2.

This menu also acts as an order which, when completed, is hung on the outside of the guest's bedroom. The bottom portion of the card is detachable and sent to the billing office for charging to the guest's account. The remaining portion goes to the floor service pantry or to the central kitchen. Trays are then made up and delivered to the room within the appropriate time range.

Figure 7.2 Room service breakfast menu and order card – courtesy of Holiday Inn Crowne Plaza, Leeds

The laying-up of a breakfast tray involves the same procedure, with a few exceptions, as when laying up a table for a full English or continental breakfast in the restaurant, although as most orders for the service of breakfasts in the rooms are known in advance the tray may be laid according to the order. The main differences between laying a tray and a table for the service of breakfast are as follows:

- A tray cloth replaces the table-cloth
- Underplates are usually left out because of lack of space and to reduce weight
- There will be no ashtray or table number on the tray

With standing orders for breakfast in the rooms, the trays should be laid up the night before, placed in the pantry and covered with a clean cloth. The beverage, toast, rolls etc and first course, together with the preserves and other accompaniments that may be required according to the order given, will normally be prepared by the floor service staff in the service or floor pantry. The main course is sent up already plated from the kitchen, by the service lift. Before taking the tray to the apartment it is important to check that nothing is missing and that the hot food is hot. The beverage and toast should be the last items on the tray for this reason.

Figure 7.3 Breakfast tray laid for a continental breakfast

The positioning of the items on the tray is important. The items should be placed so that everything may be easily reached and to hand for the guest, ie beverage and breakfast cup, saucer and teaspoon to the top centre-right of the tray. This helps balance the tray and is in the correct position for pouring. Any bottled proprietary sauce required on the tray should be laid flat to avoid accidents when carrying the tray. On arriving at the apartment door, the member of staff should knock loudly, wait for a reply, and then enter, placing the tray on the bedside table.

If there are two or more people taking breakfast in the apartment, it may be necessary to lay up a table or trolley, and to serve the breakfast in the same way as in the restaurant. After approximately 45 minutes the floor service staff should return to the room, knock and wait for a reply, enter and ask if it is convenient to clear the breakfast tray away. It is important to note that all trays and trolleys should be cleared from the rooms and corridors as soon as possible, otherwise they may impede the housekeeping staff in their work, and may also inconvenience guests.

When breakfast service is finished all equipment must be washed up in the floor pantry and food-stuffs such as milk, cream, butter, rolls and preserves should be returned to the refrigerator or store cupboard. The pantry is then cleaned and the *mise-en-place* carried out for the day.

Figure 7.4 Room service tables

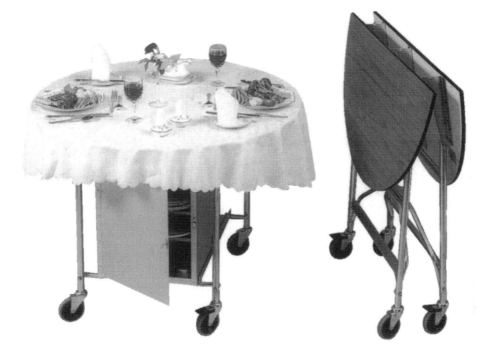

In-room facilities

Mini bar

An example of a mini bar content is shown in Figure 7.5. This card also acts as a guest self-completion bill. Mini bars are restocked each day and the consumption reconciled with the billing office.

MINI BAR			TARIFF	

Holiday Inn
CROWNE PLAZA®
LEEDS

ROOM NO _____ DEPARTURE DATE _____

PRINTED NAME _____

SIGNATURE _____

QTY IN BAR		A.B.V.	PRICE EACH	QTY TAKEN
3 CARLING PREMIER		4.70%	£1.95	
3 CAFFREYS		4.80%	£1.95	
3 BUDWEISER		5.00%	£2.50	
3 WHISKEY	50ml	40.00%	£2.95	
3 GIN	50ml	37.50%	£2.95	
3 VODKA	50ml	37.50%	£2.95	
3 BRANDY	50ml	40.00%	£2.95	
3 BACARDI	50ml	37.50%	£2.95	
3 DRY MARTINI	50 ml	14.70%	£2.95	
3 WHITE WINE	250ml	10.5/11.0%	£3.50	
3 MINERAL WATER			£0.95	
4 TONIC WATER			£0.95	
2 GINGER ALE			£0.95	
2 LEMONADE			£0.95	
2 ORANGE JUICE			£0.95	
4 PEPSI			£0.95	
4 DIET PEPSI			£0.95	
2 PEANUTS			£0.50	
4 CHOCOLATE BARS			£0.50	

TOTAL COST   £ _____

To assist with an efficient check-out, please complete daily.
Thank you for your co-operation.

Figure 7.5 Example of mini bar menu – courtesy of the Holiday Inn Crowne Plaza, Leeds

Tea and coffee making facilities

The standard stock for these facilities includes a teacup and saucer, a teaspoon (one per person), tea/coffee pot (or both), kettle (self-switching) and a selection of tea, coffee, sugar, chocolate, creamer, non-sugar sweetener and, possibly, biscuits. The stock should be a standard stock, replaced each day by the room attendants.

7.3 Lounge service

Lounge service ranges from the service of continental breakfast, morning coffee, luncheon snacks, afternoon tea, dinner or late evening snacks as well as alcoholic beverages. Although mainly associated with hotels, it is also found in public houses, wine bars and on ships. Examples of lounge service menus are given in Figure 7.6.

Organization of lounge service

In a first-class establishment lounge service staff may possibly operate from their own service pantry. However, in most instances the lounge staff work and liaise with the stillroom, or one of the dispense bars, for the service of all types of beverages required, alcoholic or non-alcoholic. The lounge staff may have a small service cupboard, of which only they have the key, and which holds a basic stock of items that they may need in case of emergency. These items may be as follows:

- Small linen stock
- Ashtrays
- Salvers
- Glasses: assorted
- Cups, saucers for the service of hot beverages
- Dry goods: coffee, tea and sugar
- Check pads, bill pads, stock sheets for alcoholic drink
- Basic alcoholic drink stock for use when guests must be served in the lounge because bars are closed to include:

– spirits	– brandies	– minerals
– apéritifs	– liqueurs	

- Cocktail snacks:

– cocktail onions	– salted peanuts	– gherkins
– cocktail cherries	– olives	– cheese sticks, etc

- Other beverages:

– Horlicks	– Bovril	– cocoa
– Ovaltine	– tisanes	– chocolate

Figure 7.6 Example of lounge service menu – courtesy of the Carlton Hotel, Bournemouth

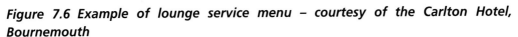

Sandwiches

Club Sandwich
- layered with Bacon, Tomato, Lettuce, Roasted Chicken, Mayonnaise, Lightly Toasted and served with French Fries £9.75

Steak Sandwich
- layered with Plum Tomatoes and Grain Mustard, served with French Fries £11.25

Smoked Salmon Sandwich
- spiced with Black Pepper £7.20

York Ham Sandwich
- with English Mustard £3.95

Roast Chicken Sandwich
- with Lettuce and Mayonnaise £3.95

Mature Cheddar
- with Chutney £3.95

Prawn Sandwich
- bound in Marie Rose Sauce £6.90

All Sandwiches are served in White or Wholemeal Bread with Seasonal Leaves and Crisps.

Beverages

Orange Juice £2.75

Your Choice of Tea:-
Traditional English, Darjeeling, Assam, Ceylon, Earl Grey, Camomile, Lemon or Mint £2.00

Your Choice of Coffee:-
A Cafetiere of Freshly Brewed Coffee, Regular or Decaffeinated £2.00

Cappuccino - by the Cup £1.50

Expresso - by the Cup £1.50

Hot Chocolate £2.00

Chilled Milk £1.50

A full range of Alcoholic Beverages and Wines are available during usual licensing hours.

Light Meals & Snacks

Soup of the Day served with Baked Rolls £3.25

Refreshing Melon on the Season £4.95

Parfait of Chicken Livers served with Brioche and Cumberland Sauce £6.75

Traditional Smoked Salmon dressed with Capers and Lemon £10.95

Carlton Seasonal Salad of Bacon, Roast Chicken, Seasonal Leaves, Herbs and Spring Onions dressed with a Dijon Mustard Vinaigrette £9.75

Tagliatelle with Wild Mushroom, Herb and Garlic Cream Sauce £6.75

Char Grilled Burger served in a Wholemeal Bun with Bacon and Cheddar, presented with French Fries and Coleslaw £9.50

Assorted Ice Creams Sorbets served in a Brandy Snap Basket £4.75

Fresh Strawberries and Cream £4.95

Side Orders

French Fries with Mayonnaise £2.00

Fried Onion Rings £2.00

Mixed Salad £2.00

Afternoon Tea

Served between 3.30pm and 5.30pm

A full Tea consists of:-
Freshly Brewed Tea or Coffee of your choice, One Round of Assorted Tea Sandwiches, A selection of Cakes and Pastries, Scones with Preserves and Clotted Cream £6.95

A Half Tea consists of:-
Freshly Brewed Tea or Coffee of your choice, Selection of Cakes and Pastries, Scones with Preserve and Clotted Cream £4.50

The lounge staff must be prepared for the service of the following in the lounge:

- Morning coffee
- Apéritifs and cocktails before luncheon
- Coffee, liqueurs and brandy after luncheon
- Afternoon tea
- Apéritifs and cocktails before dinner

- Coffee, liqueurs and brandy after dinner
- Service of late night beverages, both alcoholic and non-alcoholic
- Other snacks throughout the day depending on the type of establishment

It is normal for a chance customer to pay cash for a service rendered, but a resident may not wish to pay cash and the lounge staff must then ensure that the guest signs the check to confirm the services received. The check must have the appropriate room number against it. The amount outstanding should then be charged to the guest's account which will be paid when he/she leaves the establishment at the end of his/her visit. All checks are usually in triplicate, the top copy going to the supplying department, ie stillroom, or dispense bar. The second copy should either stay with the lounge staff if they have to make out a bill for a chance customer, or go to reception or control so the resident's account can be charged accordingly. The 'flimsy' or third copy remains with the lounge staff as a means of reference.

Stocktaking should be held at regular intervals with the occasional spot check on certain items. Stocksheets should be completed daily and are often in the form of a 'daily consumption sheet' showing the daily sales and the cash received, which may be checked against the checks showing the orders taken.

Lounge staff commence preparation in the morning ensuring all the lounge is clean. The carpets must be vacuumed, coffee tables polished, ashtrays emptied and cleaned, tables positioned correctly, brasses polished and everything ready for service. In a busy establishment once the service commences in the morning it may be almost continuous throughout the day and, therefore, it should be one of the lounge staff's duties to keep the lounge presentable at all times, the table tops clean, ashtrays emptied and all dirties removed.

Before luncheon and dinner cocktail snacks may be placed on the coffee tables and, after lunch, the tables must be prepared for the service of afternoon tea. The lounge is very often the front window of the establishment, so the standards of service should be high, reflecting the overall standards. This responsibility rests with the lounge staff and they must therefore be of smart appearance, efficient and attentive to the guests. They should have a good knowledge of food and beverage service, especially the licensing laws and their obligations to both guest and management.

Buffets

For some service in the lounge, eg afternoon tea, a buffet may be set up to display the range of foods on offer. Alternatively, a guéridon may be used to offer a selection of foods to customers seated within the lounge areas.

7.4 Hospital tray service

The development of the hospital catering service goes back to the *National Health Act 1947*. Before this time all hospitals were dependent on income from patients' fees, private donations, proceeds from garden parties and so on. Owing to this, the service of food varied considerably from one hospital to another and generally went from bad to worse. Very little consideration was being given to such things as providing an attractively served meal, correct nutritional value, supplying a wide variety of food, or serving hot and freshly cooked food.

The long-term effect of the 1947 Act was that considerable change gradually took place. Initial bad planning before 1947 and the slow growth and development of the hospital catering service meant that it took some time to achieve the major food service goals, namely, that all meals should reach the patient quickly, look attractive and have the correct nutritional value. To this end the American Ganymede Tray System was introduced in 1964.

The patient

When in hospital likes and dislikes become more important to the patient and this is an important factor that the catering officer must not overlook. Patients may be said to fall into six categories:

1 *Medical*: usually in hospital for a long time
2 *Surgical*: only stay in hospital for a short time
3 *Geriatric*: older people who require hospital treatment and may have special needs
4 *Orthopaedic*: these patients are not normally physically ill but may often be unable to move without help
5 *Maternity*
6 *Paediatric*: children

Meal times

The timing of patients' meals generally follows the same pattern:

Breakfast	7.30–8.00 am
Lunch	12 noon
Tea	3.00–3.30 pm
Supper	6.00–6.30 pm
Later hot drink	Anytime between 8.00 and 10.00 pm

Tray service

The Ganymede system, for example, is one of a number of commercially available tray service methods used in hospital catering. Basically, individual patient trays are made up on a conveyor system according to the patients' pre-ordered requirements. Differing methods are used to keep the food hot or cold, ranging from the heated or chilled pellet method to specially insulated trays. Trays once completed are transported to the wards in ambient cabinets. Beverages may be added at ward sites before presentation to the patient.

The advantages of this system are that:

- The patients receive their meal presented appetizingly on the plate and piping hot

- Labour and administration costs can be reduced
- Time originally spent in the ward 'plating up' meals may now be put to better use by completing other duties
- The patient is able to select the meal required from a given menu

The menu, on which there is a choice, is given to each patient the day before. They then mark off their requirements for lunch, dinner and breakfast for the following day by putting an 'X' in the appropriate box. These menus are then collected and sent to the catering manager. All order cards are then collated and a production schedule is drawn up.

At service time, depending on the type of dish, extra portions are available in case they are required. The patient may also mark on the card if he/she requires large or small portions. The private patient's choice of menu is larger and more varied than the main wards, and here the service is similar to hotel room service.

Microwave ovens are also used in hospitals to provide quick re-heating facilities for food at certain periods of the day and night. All forms of dishes required can be prepared the day before during 'off peak' hours in a central kitchen and blast-frozen or chilled. When required the following day the dishes can be ready for service quickly.

It can be seen that the systems are devised to boost the morale of the patient by continually presenting him/her with well-cooked food, attractively plated-up and piping hot. At the same time over the period of a week or a fortnight the patient has a wide and varied selection of dishes from which to choose.

7.5 Home delivery

Probably the first type of home delivery and the most well known is the *Meals on Wheels* service provided by local authorities as part of their welfare activities. More recently home delivery service has become a part of the profit sector. Services range from Indian and Chinese takeaway deliveries, to restaurants providing full meals (hot, or cold for customers to re-heat). One chain of establishments was specifically designed to be primarily a home delivery operation. This was a pizza operation based upon an American concept.

Methods of delivery, which endeavour to ensure preservation of the product in heat retention presentation packages, vary. The most sophisticated are the Meals on Wheels services. This is because of the nature of the customer demand being met (the elderly) where consideration for nutritional value is uppermost. The most simple, but nevertheless effective, is the pizza home delivery system which utilizes thick cardboard with internal corrigations to provide a form of insulation to keep the pizza hot. The time required for heat retention is limited by the extent of the delivery area. Indeed, the company endeavours to deliver the pizza within 30 minutes.

7.6 Airline tray service

The first catering seen on planes could best be described as a packed lunch of assorted sandwiches plus a flask of tea, and it was a case of 'take it or leave it'. Airlines now have a catering commissary. A *commissary* is a term used to cover the catering, cabin requirements, bonded stores, cleaning and other passenger requirements. It is now accepted that, where short distances and flight times are involved, only snack-type meals, or sandwiches, and beverages are offered. Where longer distances are involved, then the airline staff have time to give an extensive service of food and beverages.

For the economy and tourist flights all meals must be of the same size, with all portions identical. The meals are arranged in individual portion containers, sealed, chilled and then stored until required. For the business and first-class passenger, who often receives a food and beverage service equivalent to that of a first-class hotel or restaurant, there is little portion control. The first-class service may be such that joints may be carved from a carving trolley as it moves up the central aisle, and served with the appropriate garnish and vegetables. This, combined with the use of fine bone china, glassware, and silver plated tableware, creates an atmosphere of content and well-being whilst the meal is being served. The economy or tourist class meal is often served on a plastic or melamine tray using disposable place mats, cutlery, tableware and serviettes and disposable glasses for any drinks required. Great use is made here of pre-portioned foods such as salt, peppers, mustards, sugars, cream, cheeses, dry biscuits and preserves.

When all the food has been prepared, the required quantities of each dish are placed on trays which are either put into hot cupboards and kept hot until being transported into the plane, or alternatively are chilled and stored in the catering unit until required and, when necessary, re-heated on board the aircraft. Each airline will supply its own equipment such as tableware, china and glassware.

High-speed ovens can heat meals in 20 minutes. The tray with the meal on it is then given to the passengers on a pull-down table. In between meals tea, coffee, biscuits and cakes are served, together with cold drinks. If special dishes are required for vegetarians, children or invalids these are available. The menus and wine lists are presented in a colourful and decorative fashion. Examples are given in Figure 7.7.

All alcoholic beverages and cigarettes are drawn from the bonded stores on the catering premises under the watchful eye of a representative of Customs and Excise.

When the aircraft is in the air it is the well-trained cabin crew who provide the service to the passengers. Their job at times is very difficult especially when the time for a trip is very short, ie 45–60 minutes, in which a meal has to be served. No cooking is done on a flight.

7.7 Rail serivce

Food and beverage operations on trains are, in the main, conventional restaurant, kiosk and trolley operations. On sleepers a limited type of room service is provided. However,

Figure 7.7 Example of flight menus and bar list – courtesy of Virgin Atlantic Airways Plc

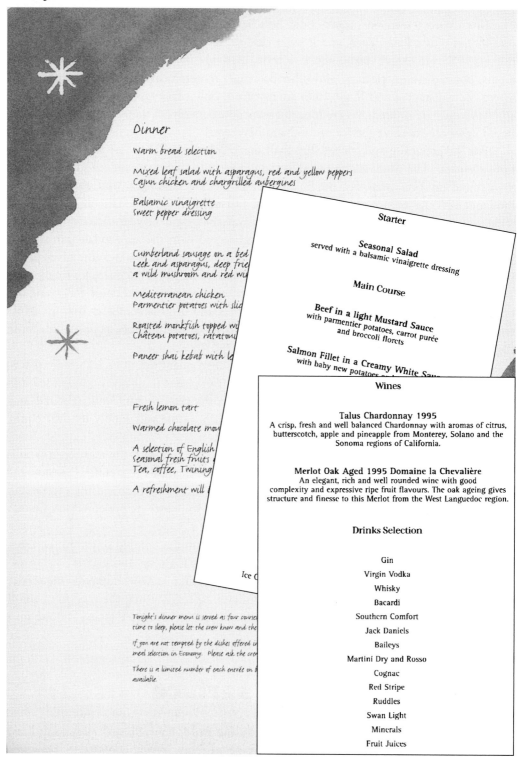

Dinner

Warm bread selection

Mixed leaf salad with asparagus, red and yellow peppers
Cajun chicken and chargrilled aubergines

Balsamic vinaigrette
Sweet pepper dressing

Cumberland sausage on a bed
Leek and asparagus, deep frie
a wild mushroom and red wi

Mediterranean chicken
Parmentier potatoes with slid

Roasted monkfish topped wi
Château potatoes, ratatoui

Paneer shai kebab with le

Fresh lemon tart

Warmed chocolate mou

A selection of English
seasonal fresh fruits
Tea, coffee, Twining

A refreshment will

Ice C

Tonight's dinner menu is served as four courses
time to sleep, please let the crew know and the

If you are not tempted by the dishes offered in
meal selection in Economy. Please ask the cre

There is a limited number of each entrée on
available.

Starter

Seasonal Salad
served with a balsamic vinaigrette dressing

Main Course

Beef in a light Mustard Sauce
with parmentier potatoes, carrot purée
and broccoli florets

Salmon Fillet in a Creamy White Sau
with baby new potatoes

Wines

Talus Chardonnay 1995
A crisp, fresh and well balanced Chardonnay with aromas of citrus,
butterscotch, apple and pineapple from Monterey, Solano and the
Sonoma regions of California.

Merlot Oak Aged 1995 Domaine la Chevalière
An elegant, rich and well rounded wine with good
complexity and expressive ripe fruit flavours. The oak ageing gives
structure and finesse to this Merlot from the West Languedoc region.

Drinks Selection

Gin

Virgin Vodka

Whisky

Bacardi

Southern Comfort

Jack Daniels

Baileys

Martini Dry and Rosso

Cognac

Red Stripe

Ruddles

Swan Light

Minerals

Fruit Juices

Figure 7.8 Example of rail catering menus – courtesy of Virgin Trains

The restaurant
Experience the pleasure of dining in the comfort of our restaurant car as we speed you through the countryside of Britain.

seasonal menu

Stilton and Bacon Salad
Pieces of ripe stilton cheese and orange segments with crisp, fried bacon and croutons on a bed of mixed leaf salad with a balsamic dressing £4.95

Soup of the Day £3.95

Moules Marinière
A large bowl of mussels cooked with white wine and herbs and served with crusty bread £6.95

Salsicotto and Pesto Mash
Grilled Italian style pork sausages served on a bed of pesto flavoured mashed potato topped with a rich tomato sauce £10.50

Confit of Duck with Frisé and Sauté Potatoes
A traditionally preserved leg of duck served on a bed of thyme flavoured sauté potatoes and frisé salad with a sharp blackcurrant vinaigrette £12.50

Roast Fillet of Cod with Braised Fennel, Leek, Bacon and Sauté Potatoes
An oven roasted fillet of cod on a bed of braised fennel with leek, bacon and lobster stock served with sauté potatoes £11.95

Fillet Steak with Mustard Butter, Frites and Salad
A prime Scottish fillet steak grilled to your liking and served with frites and a dressed salad £13.95

Fresh Pasta Bowl
Your choice of fresh penne or fusilli topped with one of the following sauces:
Creamy tomato and basil
Sun dried tomato and basil
Pepper, caper and sun dried tomato, finished with vegetarian parmesan cheese and parsley £7.95

Cheese Platter
A selection of regional cheeses offered with celery, grapes and biscuits £4.95

Tarte Tatin
An upside down puff pastry tart topped with caramelised apples and served with crème anglaise £3.75

Side Order
Mixed leaf salad £2.00
Seasonal vegetables £2.00
Sauté potatoes £1.75
Frites £1.75

Freshly brewed coffee or tea £1.50

The restaurant
Experience the pleasure of dining in the comfort of our restaurant car as we speed you through the countryside of Britain.

drinks menu

Soft Drinks

Soft Drinks
Virgin Ginger Beer
Virgin Lips Orange 65p
Virgin Lips Lemon Lime 65p
Virgin Cola 65p
Virgin Diet Cola 65p
65p

Fruit Juices and Mineral Waters
Orange Juice
Apple Juice 85p
Tomato Juice 85p
Sparkling Malvern Water 85p
Volvic Water (still) 85p
65p

Beers & Spirits

Beers, Lagers & Cider
Stella Artois
Guinness Original £1.95
Bass Draught Ale £1.90
Carlsberg Lager £1.85
McEwans Export £1.75
Strongbow Cider £1.75
£1.75

Spirits
Martell Medaillon VSOP Cognac
Johnnie Walker Black Label Whisky
Bacardi Rum £2.90
Bell's Extra Special Scotch Whisky £2.85
Gordon's Gin £2.80
Virgin Vodka £2.70
Mixers £2.70
£2.70
70p

include 17.5% VAT
rs are reminded it is an offence for any person under of 18 to be served with intoxicating liquor.

these services are provided on the move away from the home base and suppliers. The problems of rail catering are therefore similar in organization to off-premises catering.

Rail catering has also seem some operation of a tray system similar to airlines. The food and drink is served on trays to passengers at any seat, ie not within a restaurant car where tables are laid as in a restaurant.

CHAPTER 8

GUÉRIDON SERVICE

8.1	**Introduction**	268
8.2	**Guéridon service**	272
8.3	**Introduction to carving and jointing**	275
8.4	**Dishes involving work on the guéridon**	280

8.1 Introduction

The definition of the term *guéridon* is a movable service table or trolley from which food may be carved, filleted, flambéd, or prepared, and served. It is, in other words, a movable sideboard carrying sufficient equipment for the immediate operation in hand, whatever it may be, together with a surplus of certain equipment in case of emergency. It should also carry any special equipment that may be necessary. The guéridon itself may come in various forms, eg a Calor gas trolley specially made for the purpose, a plain trolley or even a small table.

The origin of guéridon service itself is hard to trace. It includes carving, salad preparation, filleting, preparation of fresh fruit and so on. This form of service is normally found in higher class establishments with an à la carte menu and service, the cost of the dishes being priced individually and the average cost of the meal being therefore higher than a table d'hôte meal. Another reason for the higher cost with an à la carte type of meal is that it demands a skilled service, and this form of labour cost in itself is much higher, and is included within the cost that the guest must pay. Also a more expensive and elaborate form of equipment must be used for the service to be carried out efficiently, which necessitates more room area for the movement of trolleys.

Flambé dishes first became popular in the Edwardian era. The first claimed flambé dish was *Crêpes Suzette* which was supposedly invented by Henri Charpentier when working as a commis at the Café de Paris in Monte Carlo (1894).

Special equipment

Flare lamps

These are an essential item of equipment for guéridon service, and are used in cooking and flambéing dishes. The maintenance of the flare lamp is very important and should be carried out very carefully, ensuring each part is fitted together correctly to maximize the life of the lamp and to minimize the possibility of accidents.

The main types of lamp being used today are fuelled in one of three ways:

Methylated spirits
These have a good flame but care must be taken to trim the wick which will help to avoid fumes. All components must fit together well as a meth's leak can cause a serious fire hazard.

Flammable gel
This is very clean and safe to refill as the gel either comes in individual lamp size containers which fit directly into the lamp or in a larger container with a dispenser However the flame can be fairly weak.

Calor gas
These lamps are very popular with replacement canisters that fit directly into the lamp. The gas is odourless and excellent control of the flame can be achieved. These lamps are often used in purpose built trolleys where the lamp is incorporated

into the structure thus giving the same working height all along the trolley top. This is much safer and there is less chance of accidents.

Chafing dish or Suzette pans

The true *chafing dish* is rarely seen nowadays. This was deeper, had a lid and was made to fit into its own individual heating unit. The shallower pans which are used today are called *Suzette pans*. They resemble frying pans in shape and size and have a diameter of 23–30 cm (9–12 in) with or without a lip. The lip is usually found on the left-hand side. The pans are generally made of silver-plated copper as this gives an even distribution of heat.

Hotplates

The hotplate's main function is to keep food hot before it is served to the guest. They are always positioned on the sideboard, but may often be found on both the sideboard and the guéridon. They come in a vast range of sizes and may be heated by gas, electricity or methylated spirits, and there are even infra-red ones available. The majority of hotplates in present-day use are heated by methylated spirits and therefore, as with the flare lamps, care should be taken in cleaning, filling and trimming the wicks. The wicks in both hotplates and flare lamps should be long enough and adequate for the service.

Guéridon (calor gas)

A guéridon may use a gas lamp connected to a Calor gas cylinder. The service top is flat as

Figure 8.1 Flambé trolley

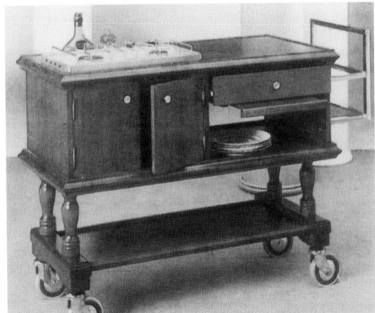

the gas lamp has been lowered into the upper casing. This makes it much safer when cooking dishes or carrying out any form of flambé work at the table. The top of the trolley is stainless steel which allows for easy cleaning. The guéridon will normally also have a control switch for the gas lamp; a drawer for surplus service equipment; a cutting board for use when cooking dishes at the table; a bracket on the lower tray used for holding bottles of spirit and liqueurs; and the indentation on top of the trolley for holding accompaniments.

Care and maintenance of equipment

There are various factors which make hygiene and safety so important in guéridon service. From a legal perspective various acts and regulations apply which hold you personally responsible for hygiene and safety incidents which arise, and these include the Food Safety Act 1990, Food Safety (general food hygiene) Regulations 1995 and the Health and Safety at Work Act 1974.

You should remember that when preparing food at the table it is a visual display that will attract many observers so all your actions should be of the highest hygiene and safety standards. This can be achieved by good planning and organization.

The following points should be observed when carrying out work at the guéridon:

- hygiene and appearance should be of the highest standard (see section 1.8)
- all equipment should be spotlessly clean and polished daily
- do not handle food with bare hands
- ensure trolleys are wiped down between each use
- never place hotplate or lamp outside the trolley legs
- the trolley should not be positioned for use close to curtains or soft furnishings
- do not leave spirits near heated trolleys or naked flames
- handle spirits carefully when flaming dishes
- do not move the trolley around the restaurant with food or equipment on it
- check that lamps are in good working order on a daily basis

A 'daily safety inspection and cleaning programme' should be enforced through the use of a cleaning rota or schedule. This work should then be carried out by the food service personnel during the normal *mise-en-place* period and under the supervision of a senior member of the team or brigade.

All items of small equipment should be checked on a daily basis using the appropriate method of cleaning such as:

- Burnishing machine
- Plate powder
- Silver dip

All large equipment such as flambé lamps, Suzette pans, hotplates, and trolleys should be hand-cleaned with the appropriate cleaners, again on a daily basis. Remember always to use the least abrasive cleaner, otherwise the surface of your equipment becomes scratched. For copper-based items a mixture of salt, lemon and a little vinegar is generally sufficient.

One should not forget that the specific maintenance of certain parts of the equipment is essential. This might include the lubrication of castors on trolleys and also any moving parts of equipment that you use, eg hinges and runners of drawers. To this end, three in one oil or *WD40* may be used.

To ensure efficiency and safety in this work a checklist should be drawn up for all staff to follow and use at the appropriate time.

Checklist

1 Gas lamps:

- Check that all moving parts move freely
- Ensure both the jet and burner are free from soot and dirt
- Clean by appropriate method – Silvo or Goddards plate powder – but remember: do not ever immerse in water

2 Gas bottles:

When changing a gas bottle consider the following factors:

- Ensure at all times there is no heated equipment or naked flames near the lamp
- Follow the manufacturer's instructions and directions, and use the correct spanner
- Check all taps are in the *off* position
- During storage all gas bottles should be kept cool

3 Spirit lamps:

- Check the amount of methylated spirit
- See that the air hole is free
- Trim the wick and check it for length
- Clean off any excessive dirt and spent matches
- Ensure all moving parts move freely
- Clean by the appropriate method – but remember: do not immerse in water
- Any decoration on equipment should be checked carefully and, if necessary, cleaned with a toothbrush

8.2 Guéridon service

Mise-en-place for guéridon service

Where necessary the top and undershelf of the guéridon should be covered with a folded tablecloth. This of course depends on the nature of the guéridon itself and its general appearance. For convenience of working, the cutlery and flatware lay-out should be similar to that of the sideboard. This saves time and speeds up the service. From right to left:

- Service spoons and forks (joint)
- Sweet spoons and forks
- Soup, tea and coffee spoons
- Fish knives and forks. Special equipment including a soup and sauce ladle
- Joint and side knives

The hotplates or table heaters are generally placed on the left-hand side on the top of the guéridon. These heaters may be gas, electric or methylated spirit. If the latter, then coffee saucers should be placed under the burners. Also on the top will be found a carving board, knives for carving and filleting and a selection of basic accompaniments such as oil and vinegar, Worcester sauce, English and French mustard and castor sugar.

Underneath will be found a service plate and service salver, sideplates, and some joint plates for dirty tableware when an operation is being carried out. There should also be some silver underflats of assorted sizes for the service of vegetables and sauces. A selection of doilies is useful for the presentation of sauces and other accompaniments. Any other *mise-en-place* required, such as coffee saucers, accompaniments and check pads, will be on the waiter's sideboard, together with a surplus of all the guéridon equipment in case of emergency.

Taking the order

Remember first and foremost that you are a salesperson. You must sell the dishes, which will involve you in work at the table. Suggest to the customer items on the menu, thus focusing attention on dishes you may wish to sell. Use the carving trolley and sweet trolley as visual selling aids.

You must always have a good knowledge of the menu so as to give good descriptions to the guests of the dishes available. Recognition of the host is an important factor.

1 Stand to left of the host. Each guest should have a menu, including the host. Have one yourself for reference purposes
2 Do not position yourself too close to guests as this may cause embarrassment
3 Size up your host and guests according to age, dress and nature of the party (business lunch/eating out/celebration and so on). This should then give you some indication as to the type of dishes one may suggest

4 Take all orders through the host. Try to ascertain the length of time available for the meal as this could determine the type of dishes sold (ie à la carte). Warn customers of waiting times
5 Take note as to whether the party is all male, female or male/female
6 Always take the order as soon as possible (ie if acceptable, in the bar)

Method of serving a dish at the table

First present the dish to the customer and state the name of the dish eg 'your Dover sole, madam', then return to the guéridon. Place the hot plates on the side of the trolley, with the food for service standing on the hotplate. The food for service is then carved or filleted if necessary, and is placed on to the plate of the guest. Unlike silver service, when the spoon and fork are used together in one hand, guéridon service requires that the spoon and fork are used one in each hand.

The vegetables and potatoes are then placed on to the plate by the waiter while the plates are still on the guéridon. The sauces are also placed on to the plates by the waiter and the plates are then placed in front of the guests.

It should be noted that, when there are more than two people at one table, the main dish is served as described but the vegetable and potato dishes are served as for normal silver service, and will be kept hot in readiness for service on the hotplate on the waiter's sideboard. During this operation it will be the commis or debarrasseur's function to keep the guéridon clear of dirty dishes and equipment

The guéridon

In many establishments where guéridon service is carried out it is policy to standardize the basic *layout* of the guéridon. This is to ensure that the required standards of service are met and that *safety* is a prime consideration of all the service staff.

There are many designs of guéridon available on the market today, but the basic format for the guéridon lay-up is shown in Figure 8.2.

Figure 8.2 Example of a basic guéridon lay-up

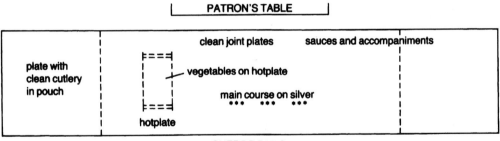

General points

1 Guéridon service is essentially a chef and commis service. Therefore there must be complete liaison and teamwork between them and every member of the brigade

2 Always push the guéridon and never pull it. This helps to avoid accidents, as one is able to see more easily where one is going

3 When the service is finished at one table wipe down the guéridon and move on to the next table immediately. It will then be ready for the commis coming from the kitchen with a loaded tray

4 The guéridon should be kept in one position for the service of a complete course and not moved from guest to guest

5 Where more than two covers are being served from the guéridon, only the main dish of each course should be served from the guéridon, potatoes and vegetables, sauces and accompaniments being passed in the normal manner. This speeds up the service as generally there is not sufficient room on the guéridon for the service of the complete meal

6 The service spoon and fork are not used as in silver service, but held with the spoon in one hand and the fork in the other. This gives more control when handling the food for service

7 When transferring foods and liquids from the silver to the plate, always run the fork along the underside of the spoon to avoid drips marking the plate

8 Never fillet or carve on a silver dish. Use either a carving board or a hot joint plate. When using a fork in carving, always work with the curved side downwards, otherwise the prongs will puncture the meat

9 The commis must always keep the guéridon clear of dirties

Sequence of service

Presentation of all dishes for all courses is very important both before the actual service commences and in placing the meal upon the plate, especially when filleting and carving.

1 *Hors-d'oeuvre or other appetisers*: these are served in the normal way except for speciality dishes such as *pâté de foie gras*, which may have to be cut into slices. Accompaniments passed in the normal manner

2 *Soup*: always served from the guéridon, whether in individual soup tureens or in larger soup tureens requiring a ladle. All accompaniments passed

3 *Fish*: filleted where necessary and served from the guéridon

4 *Meat*: carved where necessary and served from the guéridon

5 *Potatoes and vegetables*: served as previously mentioned together with sauces and accompaniments

6 *Sweet*: served from the guéridon if a flambé type dish or from the cold sweet trolley. All accompaniments passed

7 *Savoury*: served from the guéridon

8 *Coffee*: normal silver service unless speciality coffees are required

There are many different types of liquors used for various purposes in lamp cookery and flambé work. For example:

Types	Purpose
Spirits	To flambé
Fortified wines	To sweeten
Sparkling wines	To colour
Still wines	To balance flavours
Beer	To determine correct consistency
Cider	To remove excessive fat/grease
Syrups	

8.3 Introduction to carving and jointing

The following extracts have been taken from an article published in the *Caterer and Hotelkeeper* (8 October, 1987, pp 32–4). They indicate the dedication required and the practical and social skills and knowledge necessary to project a successful image as a trancheur.

'A good carver in the restaurant can ensure that the customer is served well-presented, tender meat which is a joy to the palate. Carving is a skill of real value to the restaurant trade . . .'

'How much nicer it is when a saddle of lamb is brought to you and you see it being carved. This gives the customer so much more than simply presenting a piece of meat on a plate. We are in show business. People also have their likes and dislikes, rare or medium, thick or thin slices. With a carver it is easier for guests to ask for what they want. It is there in front of them . . .' (Willy Bauer)

'Presentation and tenderness are determined by how well the meat is cut. If you carve in the wrong way the meat can be tough or, at least, not as tender as it might be . . .' (Anton Edelmann)

'If the meat is cut with the grain, you have to chew. Cutting across the grain means the fibres are shorter so the meat is easier to eat . . .' (Francis Edward)

'To leave a professional impression requires more than carving skills. You also need social skills . . .' (Anton Edelmann)

'You carve as you pull the knife back towards you and not by pushing the knife forwards as some people believe. That imbalances both you and the joint.' (Francis Edward)

Carving

The carving of a joint is a skilled art only perfected by continual practice. The following points should be noted:

- Always use a very sharp knife, making sure it is sharpened beforehand and not in front of the customer. Remember you are going to carve a joint and not cut it to pieces
- You must cut economically and correctly, at the same time being quick
- Meat is carved across the grain, with the exception of saddle of mutton or lamb which are sometimes cut at right angles to the ribs
- The carving fork must hold the joint firmly. This is the only time the fork pierces the meat
- Practise as much as possible to become perfect

Selection of tools

- For *most joints* a knife with a blade 25–30 cm (10–12 in) long and about 2.5 cm (1 in) wide is required
- For *poultry* or *game* a knife with a blade 20 cm (8 in) long is more suitable
- For *ham* a long, thick, flexible carving knife is preferred
- A carving fork is needed to hold the joint

Carving hygiene

The standard of cleanliness of the trancheur, the equipment and during the practical application of the craft are of the utmost importance. To this end the following should be noted:

- Always wear spotlessly clean protective clothing. Remember you are on show as well as demonstrating your craft
- Ensure that your personal cleanliness is given priority as you are working in the vicinity of your clients as well as handling food
- No excessive deodorants or after-shave should be used
- Always pre-check your work area and equipment to ensure good and adequate hygiene practices
- Never handle the meat, poultry or game excessively
- Carve as required and do not pre-carve too much or too early
- Keep all meat, poultry or game under cover, be it hot or cold, and at the correct serving temperature
- Be constantly vigilant by using your senses of sight and smell for any sign of deterioration in the product being sold.
- At the conclusion of each service your equipment should be scrubbed thoroughly in hot soda water and then well rinsed

Preparation of joints

The correct preparation of joints before cooking is very important, and any bones which make carving difficult should be removed prior to cooking. You should ensure that the larder chef has a knowledge of your requirements to ensure maximum economy and a saving in food cost and waste. At the same time, the person carving must have a knowledge of the bone structure of a joint in order to carve correctly and thus acquire the maximum number of portions.

Therefore the *carver* must be able to:

- *Recognize* the joint, poultry or game to be carved
- *Be aware* of the bone structure and muscle fibre of the product being carved
- *Recognize* the correct carving implements for the task in hand
- *Handle* the carving implements correctly and safely
- *Steel* a knife correctly

Methods of carving

The carving of all hot food must be performed quickly so that no heat is allowed to escape.

- *Beef and ham*: always cut very thinly
- *Lamb, mutton, pork, tongue and veal*: carved at double the thickness of beef and ham
- *Boiled beef and pressed meats*: cut a shade thicker than roasts and each portion of the former will include some fat
- *Saddle of lamb*: carved along the loin in long, thickish slices
- *Shoulder of lamb*: this has an awkward bone formation. Starting from the top, cut down to the bone, then work from top to bottom, then turn the piece over and work gradually round
- *Cold ham*: carved on to the bone from top to bottom in very thin slices
- *Whole chicken*: medium-sized bird is dissected into six portions
- *Broilers*: generally dissected into four portions
- *Poussin*: may be either offered whole or split into two portions
- *Duckling*: may be carved into four/six portions, two legs, two wings and the breasts cut into long strips
- *Turkey*: slice the breast into nice even portions and give each guest a slice of brown meat off the leg as well as a share of the stuffing
- *Salmon*: is first skinned whether it be hot or cold. It is then served in fillets,

one from each side of the bone. Cut slices up to 10 cm (4 in) long and 2.5 cm (1 in) thick

- *Lobster and crayfish*: hold firmly. Pierce vertically with a strong knife and cut with a levering motion towards tail and head. Hold shell down with a spoon on a dish, slowly lifting out the meat with a fork. Slice the meat diagonally

- *Sole*: first the bones along either edge are removed. Then the fillets are drawn apart with the aid of two large forks. Serve a top and bottom fillet per portion

Carving trolley

The carving trolley is a very expensive item of equipment. Because of this, great care must always be taken with the maintenance and use of the carving trolley to ensure that it functions correctly.

Maintenance

The carving trolley should be cleaned at regular intervals with the aid of plate powder, ensuring that all the powder is finally polished off so that none comes into contact with any food stuffs. A toothbrush may be used for cleaning any intricate design work.

Function

The function of the carving trolley is to act as an aid to selling. At all times the waiting brigade must be salespeople and sell the dishes on the menu by brief and accurate description. The carving trolley supplements this by being a visual aid to selling and should be at the table as orders are taken by the waiter so that he/she may suggest and show off particular items to the guest. Always remember to push the trolley and not pull it.

The carving trolley is heated by two methylated spirit or flammable gel lamps. The container on which the carving board rests contains hot water. This container has a steam outlet which, for safety reasons, should not be covered at any time.

Note the plate rest for hot joint plates and the two containers for gravy and sauces. When making up the carving trolley ready for service these two containers should always be placed at the end nearest the plate rest. This is for ease of service.

Nothing should be placed on the upper shelf of the trolley. The reason for this is that when the cover of the carving trolley is in the lowered position it would come into contact with anything placed on the upper shelf, knocking them over and thus causing delays and maybe accidents during the service. The lower shelf should be used for carrying the service plate, spare service cutlery and flatware and a clean joint plate.

Safety factors

There are certain safety factors to observe in the handling of the carving trolley and these must be carefully adhered to:

Figure 8.3 Carving trolley

- Ensure the lamps are functioning properly, with trimmed wicks and holders filled with methylated spirits. There must be sufficient to last over the service period

- Ensure the base is filled with hot water before the lamps are lit

- Ensure the safety valve is set on correctly and screwed down tight. There is a small hole set in the safety valve which allows the surplus steam to escape. This must never be covered over. If it is, the pressure builds up within the base which can buckle the trolley and may cause an accident

Presentation of trolley

When in use the carving trolley must be presented at the table in the correct manner. It should be placed next to the table, in between the customer and yourself. This ensures that the customer can see every operation performed by the trancheur and appreciate the skills involved. It should be positioned in such a way that the lid is drawn back from the trolley towards the trancheur and the safety valve is positioned on the side away from him/her. The latter ensures that the trancheur will not be scalded in performing his/her duties.

Mise-en-place

For its satisfactory operation in the restaurant, the correct *mise-en-place* must be placed on the carving trolley:

- Carving board
- Carving knives/fork
- Sauce ladles
- Service spoons and forks
- Joint plates for dirty cutlery and flatware
- Spare serviette and service cloth

The trancheur must always ensure that the carving trolley is correctly laid up before it is taken to the table.

8.4 Dishes involving work on the guéridon

Hors-d'oeuvre or other appetisers
Smoked eel (anguille fumée)

Cover
fish knife and fork and cold fish plate

Accompaniments
horseradish sauce – cayenne pepper – peppermill – segment of lemon – brown bread and butter

Equipment for guéridon
smoked eel on a board – small sharp knife and a joint fork – spare plate for skin and bone – spare plate for dirty cutlery and flatware – service spoon and fork

Service
1 Commence at the tail end
2 Cut a section about 10 cm (4 in) long
3 Insert the knife between skin and flesh on one side and loosen the skin
4 Insert the skin between the prongs of the fork and roll up on the fork towards the backbone
5 Cut round the backbone
6 Roll the skin off the other side and cut free with the knife

7 Fillet each side removing the backbone

8 Place on to a cold fish plate and serve

Note: this is a dish which is very often carved on the buffet rather than on the guéridon because of the length of the whole eel and the room needed in order to have it on a flat surface for carving.

Smoked trout (truite fumée)

Cover

fish knife and fork and cold fish plate

Accompaniments

horseradish sauce – cayenne pepper – peppermill – segment of lemon – brown bread and butter

Equipment for guéridon

smoked trout dressed on a silver flat – service spoon and fork – spare plate for dirty cutlery and flatware – service spoon and fork

Service

1 Present dish to customer – return to guéridon

2 Place little crisp lettuce leaves and tomato on the fish plate

3 Place the smoked trout on to a cold joint plate before removing the head and tail

4 With the aid of the service spoon and fork, remove both the head and tail

5 Set the smoked trout neatly on to the cold fish plate and serve

Smoked salmon (saumon fumé)

Cover

fish knife and fork and cold fish plate

Accompaniments

cayenne pepper – peppermill – segment of lemon – brown bread and butter

Equipment for guéridon

smoked salmon on a board – carving knife and a joint fork – service spoon and fork – spare plate for dirty cutlery and flatware

Service

1 Remove the black line in the middle of each slice by making a small 'V' shaped incision in the side of smoked salmon before carving

2 Carve each slice wafer thin, giving 2–3 slices per portion

3 Insert the edge of the slice of smoked salmon between the prongs of the joint fork and roll up

4 Lift over to the cold fish plate and unroll neatly. Serve

Note: for the same reasons as with smoked eel, the smoked salmon is more often than not carved on the buffet.

Caviare (roe of the sturgeon)

Cover

caviare knife on the right-hand side of the cover – cold fish plate

Accompaniments

hot breakfast toast – butter – segments of lemon – sieved hard-boiled white and yolk of egg/chopped shallots

Equipment for guéridon

caviare pot in a dish of crushed ice on an underflat – sweet spoon or two teaspoons for service – spare plate for dirty cutlery and flatware

Note: if a caviare knife is not available then a side knife is an adequate substitute.

Service

1 If a sweetspoon is used then generally one spoonful, which will weigh approximately 30 grams, is recognized as being a portion
2 If two teaspoons are used, the caviare is moulded in the two spoons, 3–4 teaspoonfuls per portion
3 When served direct from the pot in this fashion the caviare is usually weighed before and after service and charged according to the amount served

Note: Caviare may also be served already pre-plated by the larder or already pre-portioned by the larder and silver served on to the cold fish plate using a spoon.

Whole melon (melon frappé)

The main varieties are: Cantaloupe, Honeydew, Charentais

Cover

sweet spoon and fork or sweet spoon and fork plus a small (side) knife (this is in case the melon is a little unripe) – cold hors-d'oeuvre or fish plate

Accompaniments

ground ginger – castor sugar

Equipment for guéridon

melon in small container of crushed ice – cutting board – sharp knife – clean serviette – spare plate for debris of melon – spare plate for dirty cutlery and flatware – soup plate for pips from melon – service spoons and fork – cocktail cherries in small silver or glass dish – cocktail sticks in a holder

Service

1 The melon should be in a small container of crushed ice. Ensure all *mise-en-place* required is to hand before commencing the service
2 Lift the melon with the aid of a clean serviette on to a board. Trim both ends
3 Stand the melon on end and cut out the required portion or portions. Use your judgement as to the size of a portion but, as a guide, there should be approximately six portions to one whole melon

4 Place the cut portion on your clean serviette and hold it firmly in your left hand. Scoop out any pips with the aid of a service spoon into remainder of the whole melon. If there is less than half the melon left then scoop the pips straight into a soup plate

5 Trim the base of each portion so it stands squarely on the cold fish plate and will not roll or slide about

6 If required the waiter may cut the flesh of the melon from the rind and slice

7 Decorate with a cocktail cherry on a stick. Serve

Note: Charentais melon, which is usually served half to a portion, requires a teaspoon which is placed on the plate or on the right-hand side of the cover.

Globe artichoke (artichaut)

A globe artichoke can be served either hot or cold, and either as an hors-d'oeuvre substitute or as a separate vegetable course

Cover
hot or cold fish plate as appropriate – large (joint) fork on the right-hand side of the cover (used to consume the heart) – fingerbowl containing lukewarm water and a slice of lemon placed on a doily on an underplate, and positioned at the top left-hand corner of the cover – spare serviette placed at the head of the cover

Accompaniments
if served hot: sauce hollandaise or beurre fondue – if served cold: sauce vinaigrette (see page 297)

Equipment for guéridon
lamp if served hot – globe arthichoke on a silver flat – service spoons and forks – spare plate for dirty cutlery and flatware – sauceboat of sauce on an underflat, with a sauce ladle

Service
1 Present the dish to the customer – return to the guéridon
2 With the service spoon and fork transfer the globe artichoke from the silver flat to the hot or cold fish plate
3 Lift out the centre leaves and arrange neatly on the edge of the hot or cold fish plate
4 Pour the appropriate sauce into the resultant space
5 Serve, ensuring the correct cover and accompaniments are already on the table

Pâté de foie gras

The true pâté is made from the goose's liver, and the geese are specially bred and fattened for this purpose. However, the more commonly known is *pâté maison* – pâté of the house or establishment – where each recipe may vary slightly according to the individual who prepares this particular dish.

Cover
small side knife and a sweet fork – cold fish plate

Accompaniments

hot breakfast toast, with crusts removed, cut into triangles and served in a serviette on a sideplate

Equipment for guéridon

terrine (pot) of *foie gras* – two teaspoons – silver jug of very hot water – if *pâté maison* is being offered, then a side knife will be required – service spoons and forks – spare plate for dirty cutlery and flatware

Service

1 Present dish to guest – return to the guéridon
2 If *terrine de foie gras* is being offered, place the two teaspoons in the silver jug of very hot water
3 Using each in turn, drawing the teaspoon across surface of the *foie gras*: 'curls' of *foie gras* may be formed
4 Give four or five per portion and, as they are formed, place them on the cold fish plate
5 Decorate with little crisp lettuce leaves and some segments of tomato. Serve
6 If *pâté maison* is being offered, then the waiter must use the side knife frequently dipped in hot water to cut two or three slices per portion. Decorate as above and serve

Note: it should be noted that in some instances the 'pâté' may come already sliced from the larder and dressed on to a silver flat. In this case serve as for silver service.

Shellfish cocktail (cocktail de crevettes)

Cover

teaspoon – oyster fork – shellfish cocktail holder on a doily on a sideplate

Accompaniments

brown bread and butter

Equipment for guéridon

small glass dishes with teaspoons, to hold the ingredients, all placed on a silver salver – soup plate for mixing the sauce – service spoons and forks – spare plate for dirty cutlery and flatware

Ingredients

shellfish – shredded lettuce – tomato concassé – sieved hard-boiled white and yolk of egg – mayonnaise – tomato ketchup – Worcester sauce – lemon juice – chopped parsley – slice of lemon

Note: the oyster fork and teaspoon may be placed to the right and left of the cover, or on the doily on the sideplate on either side of the shellfish cocktail holder.

Service

1 Ensure there is some crushed ice around the base of the shellfish cocktail holder and that it is well chilled
2 Place the tomato concassé in the base of the shellfish cocktail holder

3 On top of this place some shredded (*chiffonade*) lettuce followed by the shellfish which may be prawns or shrimps. Keep one or two shellfish by for decorating the finished dish

4 Make up the sauce by mixing together the mayonnaise, tomato ketchup, Worcester sauce and a little lemon juice in the soup plate

5 Coat the shellfish with the tomato flavoured mayonnaise. Be careful not to put too much mayonnaise in as this then overpowers the rest of the ingredients

6 Now decorate the top with the sieved hard-boiled yolk and white of egg, and chopped parsley

7 Place the remaining shellfish and slice of lemon over the edge of the holder and serve

Soup

Clear soup with sherry (consommé aux xérés)

Cover

sweet spoon – hot consommé cup on consommé saucer on an underplate

Accompaniments

brown bread and butter (offered to the guests) – segments of lemon in a lemon press, placed on a sideplate at the head of the cover – cheese straws (offered to the guests) – measure of warm sherry: added by the waiter at the guéridon

Equipment for guéridon

portion of soup in a soup tureen – measure of sherry (or Madeira etc) – sauce ladle – lamp

Service

1 Served from the guéridon

2 Re-heat on the lamp and then pour into the consommé cups which will be sitting on the consommé saucer on an underplate

3 The measure of sherry may be warmed and added to the soup at the last moment in the kitchen, or it may be heated in a sauce ladle over the lamp, flambéd and then poured over the soup

4 Serve immediately

Fish

Grilled sole or sole meunière (sole grillée ou meunière)

Cover

fish knife and fork – hot joint plate

Equipment for guéridon

silver flat with the sole – service spoons and forks – hot joint plate for filleting – lamp – spare plate for dirty cutlery and flatware – spare plate for debris

Service

Method A

1 Present the dish to the customer – return to the hot plate or lamp

2 Remove the fish from the silver flat on to the hot joint plate
3 With the aid of a service spoon and fork remove the side bones (Figure 8.4(a))
4 Run the tip of the spoon down the backbone
5 Place two large forks back to back at the head of the fish and on the backbone. Press the forks down, so that the tips of the forks pierce the flesh on either side of the backbone (Figure 8.4(b)). Now ease the fillets slowly away from the backbone
6 Continue to do this working the forks gradually down the backbone towards the tail
7 Lift out the bone (Figure 8.4(c))
8 Place the fillets back together in their original shape on the silver flat. Re-heat as necessary
9 Coat with beurre fondue or replace garnish and serve

Figure 8.4 Preparation of a Dover sole

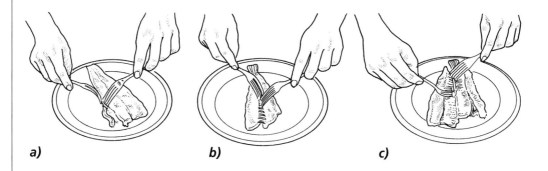

a)   b)   c)

Method B
1 1–4 as in **A** above
2 Start at head of fish and, with the aid of a service spoon and fork, loosen the two top fillets
3 Hold the fish firmly with the spoon and run the fork down from head to tail between the two top fillets and the backbone
4 Repeat this with the other two fillets, placing fork between the bottom fillets and the backbone
5 Lift out the backbone
6 8/9 as in **A**, above

Poached sole (sole pochée)

Cover
fish knife and fork – hot fish plate or hot joint plate if to be served as a main course

Accompaniments
according to garnish

Equipment for guéridon
sole on silver flat – hot joint plate for filleting – service spoon and fork – two joint forks – lamp – spare plate for dirty cutlery and flatware

Service

1 Present the dish to the guest – return to the guéridon
2 Remove the sole from the silver flat on to hot joint plate
3 Remove the side bones with the aid of the joint fork
4 Run the tip of the service spoon down backbone of the sole
5 With the aid of two joint forks, fillet sole as in *sole grillée ou meunière*, disturbing the glazed sauce, coating the fillets as little as possible
6 Replace the fillets together in the shape of the fish on the silver flat
7 Recoat with sauce and serve

Deep fried sole (sole frite)

Cover
fish knife and fork – hot joint plate

Accompaniments
sauce tartare – segments of lemon

Equipment for guéridon
service spoon and fork – hot joint plate for filleting – spare plate for debris – spare plate for dirty cutlery and flatware – lamp

Service

1 Ensure the guéridon is laid up fully with all required *mise-en-place*
2 Present the dish to the guest
3 Lift the sole on to the hot joint plate
4 Remove the side bones as for *sole grillée*
5 Run the point of the spoon down the centre of the sole, from head to tail, making a slight incision
6 Cut off the tail approximately 2.5 cm (1 in) from the end
7 Hold the spoon curved side upwards and insert the point between the fillet and the bone at the tail end of the fish
8 Hold the sole firmly with the fork and push the spoon up towards the head, lifting off one top fillet
9 Repeat for other top fillet, and then lift the two loosened top fillets off the backbone
10 Lift out the backbone
11 Replace the top fillets on the bottom ones on the silver flat and re-heat and then place on to a hot joint plate for service
12 Add a garnish of lemon and serve

Poached or grilled salmon (saumon poché ou grillé)

This type of dish is generally served in an earthenware dish, and therefore it is not necessary to remove it to a hot joint plate for skinning and filleting the *darne* (thick slice across the bone).

Cover
fish knife and fork – hot fish plate or hot joint plate if to be served as a main course

Accompaniments
according to the garnish, eg Hollandaise, Doria

Equipment for guéridon
service spoon and fork – lamp – spare plate for debris – spare plate for dirty cutlery and flatware

Service
1 Present to the customer. Return to the lamp on the guéridon
2 Hold the salmon firmly in place with the fork
3 With the point of the spoon curved side outwards, run round the edge of the *darne* removing the skin
4 As an alternative to this method of removing the outer black skin you may use a joint fork, inserting the skin between the prongs of the fork. Now twist the fork around the outer edge of the *darne*, rolling the skin up on the fork as you proceed
5 Insert the point of the spoon between the flesh and the centre bone and push the fillets away from the bone
6 Remove the bone
7 Lift the two fillets on to the hot fish plate or joint plate, being careful not to break the flesh, and add the garnish. Serve

Blue trout (truite au bleu)

Cover
fish knife and fork – hot fish plate or hot joint plate if to be served as a main course

Accompaniments
hollandaise sauce or beurre fondue

Equipment for guéridon
fish knife and fork – service spoon and fork – lamp – spare plate for dirty cutlery and flatware – spare plate for debris

Service
1 Ensure the guéridon is correctly laid up
2 Present the dish to the customer and return to the guéridon. This dish should come from the kitchen in an individual copper fish kettle
3 Lift out on a draining tray
4 Remove the garnish of sliced carrots and onions
5 With the point of the fish knife make an incision from the head to tail on the thin line showing on the side of the trout. Cut only the skin, not the flesh

6 Lift off the skin below that line with the knife and also above the line to the backbone

7 Turn the fish over and repeat the process of removing the skin on the second side, remembering to remove the fins

8 Lift trout carefully on to a hot fish plate or joint plate and decorate with a few slices of carrot and onion. Moisten with a little stock

9 Serve and then offer the appropriate accompaniment

Flambéd scampi with a cream sauce (scampi à la crème flambée)

Cover
fish knife and fork – hot fish plate or joint plate if to be served as a main course

Accompaniment
peppermill

Equipment for guéridon
lamp – pan on an underplate – service plate with service spoons and forks – spare plate for dirty cutlery and flatware

Ingredients
dishes of sliced mushrooms, onions and portion of floured scampi – glass of sherry, white wine, vermouth and spirit – eg brandy, pernod or whisky depending on the specific dish – butter, oil, seasonings: salt, peppermill, cayenne and tabasco on a service plate – sauce boat of single cream

Method
1 Place the pan on a slow heat to melt the butter; add a little oil

2 Sauté off the onions lightly and add mushrooms

3 Place in scampi and seal. Add flavouring liquor

4 Season with salt, peppermill, tabasco and cayenne

5 When the scampi are cooked, quickly flambé and douce with acidulated cream

6 Reduce the cream and thicken the sauce

7 Serve on to a hot fish plate or joint plate and offer to the guest

8 It is a good idea to serve scampi into a nest of riz pilaff

Note:
1 This dish has many adaptations by using different flavouring liquor and flambé spirits

2 It can be combined with fresh fruit to offer a subtle blend of foods – fresh black grapes, pineapple chunks, peaches, etc

3 Variations include *Scampi Boulvarde*, *au Pastis* or *Crêpes*

Steaks
Double entrecôte steak (entrecôte double)

(coming from the boned sirloin)

Cover

steak knife and joint fork – hot joint plate

Accompaniments

English and French mustard

Equipment for guéridon

silver flat with the double entrecôte steak on it – board for portioning the entrecôte steak – sharp knife for carving – service spoons and forks – two sideplates, for pressing the trimmed ends to extract all the juices – spare plate for dirty cutlery and flatware – lamp – pan

Service

1 Present the dish to the customer – return to the guéridon
2 Lift the double entrecôte steak from the silver flat on to the board
3 Trim the ends
4 Cut on the slant into two portions. Place back on the silver flat on the lamp
5 Press the trimmed ends between two hot sideplates, allowing juices extracted to fall over the two portions of steak
6 Place the portions of steak on to the hot joint plates and add the garnish. Set it out attractively. Serve

Note: it must always be remembered that this is a dish that must be ordered by a party of two guests. When taking the order the waiter should ask how the guests wish the steak to be cooked. If one guest wants their steak to be *rare* and the other guest *medium*, then the steak will come in from the kitchen rare and, once carved, one portion may be cooked a little longer in a pan on the lamp at the table

Double fillet steak (Châteaubriand)

Although the Châteaubriand is commonly termed a *double fillet steak* it may be large enough to serve a party of two, three, four or five guests as required.

The *cover*, *accompaniments*, *equipment* required for guéridon and *service* are as for *Entrecôte double*; with the following exception:

Figure 8.5 Carving of Châteaubriand

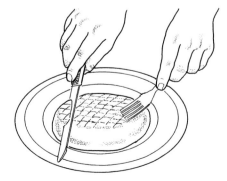
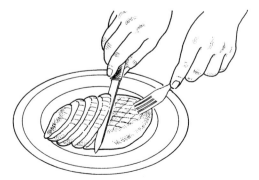

- When the *Châteaubriand* is being carved each portion will be carved into approximately two or three slices, each 13 mm ($\frac{1}{2}$ in) thick, rather than being left in one whole piece as is the case with an *Entrecôte double*.

'T' bone steak/Porterhouse steak

This is a steak made up of part sirloin and part fillet, the whole being held together by the backbone, with a rib separating the sirloin from the fillet.

Cover
steak knife and joint fork – hot joint plate

Accompaniments
English and French mustard

Equipment for guéridon
silver flat containing the Porterhouse steak – board for carving – sharp knife – spare plate for debris – spare plate for dirty cutlery and flatware – service spoons and forks – lamp

Service
1 Present the dish to the customer – return to the guéridon
2 Remove from the silver flat on to the carving board
3 Cut out the 'T' bone to give two separate pieces of meat: one of sirloin and one of fillet
4 Return the two pieces of meat to the silver flat: re-heat quickly
5 Dress attractively on to the hot joint plate with the garnish
6 If the Porterhouse steak is for more than one person then carve the fillets as for a *Châteaubriand*

Steak tartare

Cover
joint knife and fork – cold joint plate

Accompaniments
cayenne pepper – peppermill

Equipment for guéridon
soup plate – service spoons and forks – spare plate for debris – spare plate for dirty cutlery and flatware – containers for the various ingredients

Ingredients
portion of chopped raw fillet steak, moulded into a cake shape and presented on a round silver flat – one egg – chopped gherkins, capers, parsley and shallots – oil and vinegar – peppermill – salt – French mustard – Worcester sauce

Note: the portion of raw fillet steak must be welled in the centre to hold a whole egg. Only the yolk of the egg will be used.

Service

1 Ensure your guéridon has all the necessary *mise-en-place* before proceeding to make the sauce

2 Put the seasoning of salt, pepper and French mustard in the soup plate. Mix well

3 Separate the yolk from the white of egg, placing the yolk into the soup plate and the white into a spare container

4 Beat the yolk and seasoning together using a service (joint) fork

5 Add vinegar and mix in and then add a little oil according to the amount of sauce you wish to make and mix in

6 Be careful of the quantity of sauce you make as the finished product should be moist but not runny or too liquid

7 Add the chopped gherkins, capers, parsley and shallots and bind the whole together well

8 Now place in the raw chopped fillet steak together with a dash of Worcester sauce, incorporating the sauce and fillet steak together well

9 Shape into a round flat cake and place on the cold joint plate. Serve

Steak Diane

Cover

steak knife and joint fork – hot joint plate

Accompaniments

English and French mustard

Equipment for guéridon

lamp – pan on an underplate – service spoons and forks – teaspoons – plate for dirty cutlery and flatware

Ingredients

minute steak on a plate – chopped shallots – chopped parsley – fines herbes – cayenne pepper and peppermill – cruet – oil and butter – Worcestershire sauce – measure of brandy – jug of double cream

Service

1 Ensure the guéridon is correctly laid up with all the *mise-en-place*

2 Enquire of the customer how he/she would like the steak cooked.

3 Place some butter and a little oil in the pan and allow to melt. The oil will prevent the butter from burning

4 Season the steak with cruet, cayenne pepper and peppermill

5 Place the chopped shallots in the pan and sweat without colouring until cooked

6 Place the steak in the pan and cook as required

7 Add a dash of Worcestershire sauce, and then sprinkle with some chopped parsley and *fines herbes*

8 Add a measure of brandy and flambé

9 Serve immediately from the pan on to a hot joint plate at the table

10 Before serving, if requested, a thickened sauce may be made by the addition of a little double cream. Bring up to simmering point but do not boil

11 If a sauce is made, the steak must be kept on a hot joint plate on the hotplate, and covered whilst the sauce is being prepared

12 Coat the steak with the sauce and serve, ensuring it is piping hot

Note: there are many variations in the making of Steak Diane, each done to an establishment's traditional recipe or being a speciality of the waiter carrying out the operation according to his/her own particular techniques.

Figure 8.6 Equipment lay-up for Steak Diane

Monkey gland steak

Cover
hot joint plate – joint knife and fork

Accompaniments
mustards – tossed salad

Equipment for guéridon
flare lamp – pan on an underplate – service spoon/fork on a service plate – plate for dirty cutlery and flatware – teaspoons/timbales for ingredients all on a large salver

Ingredients
flattened fillet steak on a plate – chopped shallots – chopped parsley – jug of double

cream – garlic (optional) – set of cruets/peppermill/cayenne pepper – oil and butter – Worcestershire sauce – mustards (French and English) – measure of whisky

Method
1 Ensure *mise-en-place* is correct
2 Social skills – explain seasonings to clients
3 Melt butter in pan and add a little oil
4 Season steak and spread the steak with mustard on both sides
5 Sauté shallots to 'pearl' stage; add garlic if required
6 Sauté the steak as required
7 Season with Worcestershire sauce
8 Flambé with whisky
9 Finish with cream and chopped parsley
10 Serve on to a hot joint plate and place in front of the customer
11 Offer mustards

Beef stroganoff (filet de boeuf stroganoff)

Cover
hot joint plate – joint knife and fork

Accompaniments
none

Equipment for guéridon
lamp – pan on a service plate – service spoons and forks on a service plate – plate for dirty cutlery and flatware – teaspoons/timbales for ingredients (on a large silver flat)

Ingredients
fillet steak cut in 'batons' – chopped shallots – chopped parsley – sliced button mushrooms – chopped chutney (mango) – jug of double cream – cayenne pepper/peppermill – set of cruets – oil and butter – Worcestershire sauce – measure of brandy – garlic (optional) – fried rice

Method
1 Ensure *mise-en-place* is correct
2 Social skills – explain the seasonings to the client
3 Melt the butter in a pan and a little oil
4 Season the steak
5 Sauté the shallots to the 'pearl' stage; add garlic if required and mushrooms
6 Sauté the steak; season with Worcestershire sauce
7 Add mango chutney to the desired taste
8 Flambé with brandy
9 Finish with double cream and chopped parsley
10 Serve on to a hot joint plate and place in front of the customer
11 If fried or savoury rice is to be served then make a nest of rice and place the Stroganoff in the centre

Veal escalope suédoise (escalope de veau suédoise)

Cover
joint knife and fork – hot joint plate

Accompaniments
None

Equipment for guéridon
flambé lamp – pan on an underplate – service spoons and forks on a service plate – plate for dirty cutlery and flatware

Ingredients
escalopes on a plate – chopped shallots – chopped parsley – French mustard – orange curaçao – Worcestershire sauce – butter and oil – cruet set/peppermill/cayenne pepper – sliced mushrooms – brandy – double cream

Method
1 Ensure *mise-en-place* is complete
2 Melt the butter and add a little oil
3 Season the escalopes
4 Sauté off the onions without colouring, then add mushrooms
5 Add the escalopes and cook
6 Season with salt, pepper, cayenne pepper and Worcester sauce
7 Add curaçao without flambéing
8 Ensure the escalopes are cooked and flame with spirit (brandy)
9 Add double cream and correct the consistency
10 Serve on to a hot plate and finish with a little chopped parsley

Salads

Varieties of salad

Basically there are two main types of salad. Firstly, a *plain salad* which consists entirely of vegetables and secondly a *compound salad* which is a plain salad plus other ingredients, such as meat, fish and mushroom. A green or fruit (orange) salad is generally offered as an accompaniment with a main course dish such as chicken, duck, or grilled steak.

All salads should be served chilled, crisp, and attractive. Remember a salad is not complete without a well-made salad dressing or sauce, such as vinaigrette or mayonnaise.

The cover for a salad when offered with a main course dish should be a salad crescent-shaped dish, or a small round wooden bowl with a sweet fork, or a small wooden spoon and fork. The prongs of the small or sweet fork should be pointing downwards when placed over the rim of the salad crescent as part of the cover. This is to avoid tarnishing the silver with the acid in the dressing.

Examples of salads are:

- *Française*: lettuce hearts, sections of skinned tomato, hard boiled egg, vinaigrette separate
- *verte*: lettuce hearts, vinaigrette separate
- *Saison*: lettuce hearts, plus salad vegetables in season, vinaigrette separate
- *d'orange*: lettuce hearts, in sections, filleted orange, fresh cream separate
- *Mimosa*: lettuce hearts, filleted orange, grapes skinned and stoned, sliced banana, sprinkle with egg yolk, acidulated cream, dressing separate
- *Japonaise*: lettuce, bananas, apple, tomatoes all in dice, shelled walnuts, fresh cream separate
- *Lorette*: corn salad, julienne of beetroot, raw celery heart, vinaigrette separate
- *Russian*: vegetable salad decorated with tomatoes, eggs, anchovies, lobster, ham, tongue, mayonnaise sauce
- *Niçoise*: French beans, tomato quarters, sliced potatoes, anchovies, capers, olives, *sauce vinaigrette*
- *Endive*: hearts of lettuce, endive, *sauce vinaigrette*

Dressings

Equipment required on the guéridon when preparing a salad dressing

the ingredients, depending on the type of dressing required – soup plate – service cloth – service spoon and fork – salad crescent or wooden salad bowl – sweet or small fork or a small wooden spoon and fork – glass bowl for tossing the salad – teaspoon: for tasting the dressing – spare plate for dirty cutlery and flatware

Service

1 The dressing required should be prepared by the waiter on the guéridon at the table
2 The dressing and salad are tossed together in the glass bowl
3 The salad or fruit should then be dressed on to the salad crescent which is then placed at the top left-hand corner of the cover before serving the dish which it accompanies.

The seven main types of dressing are as follows:

1 French dressing

Ingredients

French mustard – seasonings of salt, pepper, cayenne pepper – three parts oil to one part vinegar

Equipment for guéridon

soup plate – service cloth – service spoons and forks on a service plate – salad crescent – sweet fork – wooden bowl for tossing the salad with the made up dressing – teaspoons in a jug of cold water for tasting

Method

1 Place the French mustard and seasonings in a soup plate which is resting on the folded service cloth at an angle, thus retaining the mixture in one part of the soup plate to make mixing easier
2 Blend the seasonings together with a service fork
3 Add the measure of vinegar to the seasonings and mix well into a smooth mixture
4 Now add the oil and blend all together with the service fork
5 Taste – adjust seasonings if required
6 Place a portion of green salad in a wooden bowl, add French dressing and toss together
7 Dress on to a salad crescent. Garnish with cucumber, watercress

2 English dressing

As for French dressing with the exception that English mustard replaces the French mustard, the proportions of oil to vinegar are one to two, and one teaspoon of castor sugar is added to the seasonings.

3 Sauce vinaigrette

This should be mixed by the waiter in a soup plate at the guéridon.

Ingredients

one teaspoonful French or English mustard – seasoning (salt, peppermill) – one tablespoon vinegar – two tablespoons oil

Method

1 Place the mustard, seasoning and vinegar in a soup plate and mix together using a fork
2 Add the oil, mixing slowly
3 The proportions of vinegar and oil used are according to individual taste
4 Once the vinaigrette is made to the guest's liking, the salad should be tossed with the dressing in a salad bowl

4 Roquefort dressing

This form of dressing is again made according to taste and in a soup plate.

Ingredients

Roquefort cheese – vinegar (see Method A) – olive oil (see Method A) – sauce mayonnaise (see Method B) – seasoning (salt)

Method A

1 Break down the Roquefort cheese into small lumps or cream it right down by mixing in a soup plate with a little wine vinegar or lemon juice
2 Add the olive oil and season with salt. This will help to bring out the full flavour of the cheese. A little single cream may be added
3 Toss the salad with the dressing in a salad bowl

Method B
1 Break down the Roquefort cheese into small pieces in a soup plate
2 With the aid of a large fork, fold the pieces of Roquefort cheese into some sauce mayonnaise
3 Season with salt to help bring out the flavour
4 Toss the salad with the dressing in a salad bowl

5 Acidulated cream dressing

This form of dressing is mainly offered with salads containing fruit, such as orange salad.

Ingredients
lemon juice – seasoning (salt) – single cream – paprika

Method
1 Mix the lemon juice with seasoning
2 Add the single cream
3 Toss the fruit from the salad with the dressing
4 Place on a bed of lettuce leaves on the salad crescent and sprinkle with paprika pepper

Other forms of dressings are:

6 Mustard cream:
$\frac{1}{3}$ litre ($\frac{1}{2}$ pt) cream
Tablespoon of mustard
Juice of a lemon
Seasoning

7 Lemon dressing:
Oil
Lemon juice
Seasoning

Poultry
Roast chicken (poulet rôti)

Cover
joint knife and fork – hot joint plate

Accompaniments
bread sauce – roast gravy – parsley and thyme stuffing – bacon rolls – game chips – watercress

Equipment for guéridon
carving board – sharp carving knife – service spoons and forks – spare plate for dirty cutlery and flatware – spare plate for debris – lamp – chicken on a silver flat

Service
1 Present the whole chicken to the host at the table – return to the lamp on guéridon
2 With the service spoon and fork lift the chicken from the silver flat on to the carving board, draining off any liquid that may be inside
3 Lay the chicken on its side on the board from right to left in front of you, with a leg uppermost
4 Holding the bird firmly on the board with the flat of the knife, insert the service fork beneath the leg joint and raise the leg until the skin surrounding it is taut
5 Cut round the taut skin surrounding the leg with the tip of the knife, at the same time pulling the leg away from the joint and cutting the flesh where necessary
6 Cut the leg into two pieces through the joint, also removing the claw end
7 Place the two pieces of leg on to the silver flat
8 Proceed in the same manner with the other leg
9 Turn the chicken on to its back. Insert the joint fork into the base of the carcass to hold it firmly
10 Carve part of the breast and down through the wing joint, giving one piece made up of the wing and a little breast
11 If necessary turn the chicken on its side and, with the aid of the service fork, lever the wing away from the carcass, at the same time holding the chicken firmly with the flat of the knife
12 Proceed in the same manner with the other wing

Figure 8.7 Carving a roast chicken

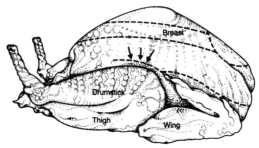

13 Position the bird on its back. Cut down one side of the breastbone and lever off half the breast
14 Proceed in the same manner with the other side of the breast
15 An alternative method of removing the breast is by turning the chicken on its side and cutting through the wishbone joints
16 Turn the chicken on to its breast, holding it firmly in place with the service fork
17 Insert the knife between the flesh and the wishbone. Holding the whole breast on the board with the knife lever the carcass away with the aid of the service fork
18 Cut the whole breast into two portions lengthways
19 Replace the carved chicken on the lamp. If necessary whilst the carving operation is being carried out add a little liquid (gravy) to the silver flat to prevent the carved portions of chicken from burning
20 Serve the chicken giving some brown and some white meat per portion. Remember to add some game chips, bacon rolls and watercress if these make up the garnish

Note: having completed the carving of the chicken, the carcass should be turned over. The 'oyster' piece is found on the underside of the carcass and is a small brown portion of meat found on either side of the back.

Poussin (young chicken 6 weeks old)

Cover
joint knife and fork – hot joint plate

Accompaniments
as per menu garnish

Equipment for guéridon
poussin on silver flat – lamp – board – knife – service spoons and forks on a service plate – plate for dirty cutlery and flatware – plate for debris

Service
1 Present to the customer – return to the guéridon
2 Lift the poussin from the silver flat on to the carving board with the aid of the service spoon and fork
3 Insert the service fork into the base of the carcass and hold firmly on the board with the breast uppermost
4 With the tip of the knife cut the poussin in half down through the breast
5 Take the half poussin attached to the backbone and remove the backbone
6 Place the two portions of poussin on the silver flat and re-heat if necessary
7 Present attractively on to the hot joint plate. Add garnish and/or sauce. Serve

Roast duck (canard rôti)

Cover
joint knife and fork – hot joint plate

Accompaniments
apple sauce – sage and onion stuffing – roast gravy

Equipment for guéridon
duck on a silver flat – lamp – carving board – sharp carving knife – service spoons and forks on a service plate – spare plate for dirty cutlery and flatware – spare plate for debris

Service

Note: before commencing to carve a duck the waiter should remember that the joints are much tighter and more compact than those of a chicken and are therefore more difficult to find and cut through when carving. Also the wing joints lie a little further under the base of the carcass than those on a chicken.

Figure 8.8 *Carving a duck*

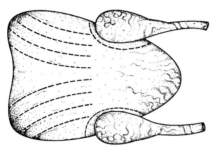

The initial stages in carving a duck are the same as for a chicken until the legs and wings have been removed:
1 Hold the duck firmly on the carving board with the aid of a joint fork in the base of the carcass
2 The breastbone on a duck is wide and flat in comparison with that of the chicken. It is therefore easier to remove the complete half breast from the breastbone
3 Now cut into long thin slices (*aiguillettes*) on the carving board
4 Repeat with the other half breast
5 Dress back onto the silver flat. Reheat if necessary. Serve with the appropriate accompaniments

Note:
1 In the case of a duckling, very often the wing and breast are carved all in one portion.
2 When carving the breast, a cut on an angle should be made with the carving knife along the length of the breast. The reason for this is that, as the meat is shallow, to carve straight down on to the flat breast bone would take the edge off the carving knife. This method allows you to carve *aiguillettes* with the breast still on the carcass.

Pressed wild duck (canard sauvage à la presse)

The following method is based on a further extract published in the *Caterer and Hotelkeeper* (8 October 1987, pp. 32–4) indicating the techniques and experience of one of the Savoy's long-serving carvers, Francis Edward ('Eddie' as he is known to colleagues and customers):

Method
1 Commence the sauce by reducing two parts red wine to one part port. Add one teaspoonful of brandy, together with two to three strips of orange and lemon peel for a tangy, citrus flavour
2 Next carve the duck, which must be undercooked. The legs are removed first and returned to the kitchen to be finished *diable* (devilled) with Dijon mustard and breadcrumbs
3 All traces of skin and fat must be removed from the duck as this can be detrimental to the sauce
4 Now carve slices from both sides along the length of the breast
5 The backbone is now broken, folded in half and placed in the duck press. The wheel is then tightened until the first pressure is felt
6 A pre-prepared mixture of two-thirds duck liver and one-third turkey liver paste, mixed with one ounce of butter and well-seasoned with salt, pepper and red pepper is now added to the wine reduction. The mixture and the reduction are well blended together and allowed to cool to avoid curdling when the duck's blood is added
7 Now tighten the wheel of the duck press to extract all the blood from the carcass. This blood is run off into the pan containing the sauce
8 The ingredients of the sauce, reduction, mixture and blood are liaised together over a low heat on the lamp. Do not boil. Finish with a few spots of fresh lemon juice
9 Place the slices of duck carved from the breast in the sauce and coat. The finished sauce should shine
10 Present to the guest on a hot joint plate and serve with the devilled legs from the kitchen

Roast turkey (dindonneau rôti)

Cover
joint knife and fork – hot joint plate

Accompaniments
cranberry sauce – bread sauce – chestnut stuffing – chipolatas – gravy – game chips – watercress

Equipment for guéridon/buffet
turkey on a silver flat – lamp – carving board – sharp carving knife – service spoons and forks on a service plate – spare plate for dirty equipment – spare plate for debris

Service
1 The legs and wings should be separated, but not entirely removed from the carcass (ie

Figure 8.9 Carving a turkey

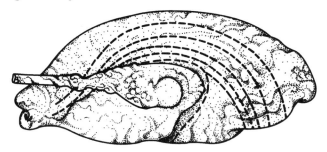

pulled to one side) This is to allow the trancheur to carve thin slices the full length of the body on either side

2 If possible, carve and serve the stuffing with the slices

3 As with roast chicken, the dark meat from the legs should be carved and a portion made up of both white and dark meat. Serve with accompaniments

Flambéd chicken breast (suprême de volaille flambée)

Cover
joint knife and fork – hot joint plate

Accompaniments
none or possibly salad

Equipment for guéridon
flare lamp – pan on an underplate – service spoons and forks on a service plate – spare plate for dirty equipment – butter knife – sauce ladle

Ingredients
prepared suprêmes on a silver flat (if required the suprêmes may be marinaded in wine or liqueur beforehand) – glass of red or white wine – Drambuie – butter – oil – tomato concassé (in a small glass bowl) – sliced mushrooms (in a small glass bowl) – onions finely chopped (in a small glass bowl) – seasonings of salt, pepper, cayenne pepper – double cream in a sauceboat

Method
1 Place pan on a low heat to melt the butter, add a little oil

2 Season the sûpremes

3 Sauté off the onions to pearl stage without colouring and add the mushrooms

4 Add the supremes and cook as quickly as possible without browning too much

5 Add the wine and reduce the liquor

6 Flambé with Drambuie and add the double cream

7 Reduce the cream as quickly as possible and finish by combining tomato concassé into the cream sauce

8 Serve on to the hot joint plate and offer to the guest

Note:

1 During cooking time a salad dressing could be prepared, adding to the salad once the main course is served.
2 There are many variations: by adding ingredients such as curry powder and other seasonings, and by altering the wines and flambé spirit.

Game
Grouse (grouse)

Season 12 August to 12 December. Grouse is regarded as a particularly choice dish. If small it is generally served whole. Otherwise it should be split into two portions by carving down through the middle of the breastbone.

Note:

1 A larger bird may be carved into three portions as indicated – from either side of the bird remove a leg and wing in one piece. This gives two portions. The third portion is made up of the remainder of the breast separated from the carcass.
2 Partridge may be carved in exactly the same fashion (see below).

Figure 8.10 Carving a partridge or grouse

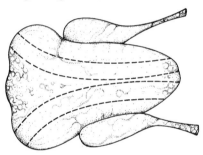

Partridge (perdeau)

Season 1 September to 1 February. Depending on its size the partridge may be carved into two or three portions. If large, the three portions would consist of:
1 One leg and one wing with a little of the breast attached
2 As for 1
3 The breast left on the bone.

If small it would be split into two portions by carving down through the breastbone.

Woodcock (bécasse)

Season 1 August to 1 March. Split into two portions as for grouse or partridge. Generally served on a *croûte* spread with a pâté made from the giblets of the woodcock.

Snipe (bécassine)

Season 1 August to 1 March. Served whole as snipe are too small for carving into portions.

Pheasant (faisan)

Season 1 October to 1 February. The flesh of the pheasant is very dry and the waiter should use a very sharp knife. Remove the legs as for chicken or duck. These are normally not served. Carve in thin slices on either side of the breast down to the wing joint. One does not normally remove the wing as a separate portion.

Wood pigeon (pigeon)

Season 1 August to 15 March. Carved in half through the breast to give two portions

Saddle of hare (selle de lièvre)

Season 1 August to 28 February. Carved in slices lengthwise as in a saddle of lamb. The flesh is dark in colour.

Joints

These would be carved on the carving trolley at the table. *Mise-en-place* as previously mentioned on page 278.

Boned sirloin of beef (contre-filet de boeuf)

Accompaniments
roast gravy (from the trolley) – Yorkshire pudding (from the trolley) – English and French mustard (placed on the table by the waiter) – horseradish sauce (placed on the table by the waiter)

Note:
1 Carved in thin slices giving mainly lean meat and a little fat per portion.
2 The beef itself should be a little underdone.

Sirloin of beef on the bone (aloyau de boeuf)

The *accompaniments* offered would be as for a *contre-filet*.
It may be said that a sirloin is comprised of two parts:

- The undercut
- The uppercut

1 The *undercut* can be removed from the sirloin and may be served separately, either as fillets or tournedos, or larded and roasted. If it is to be carved, then this should be done across the joint and not parallel to the side with the grain. A piece of fat should be served with each portion.
2 With the uppercut the portions should be carved in thin slices down towards the ribs. On reaching a rib-bone the waiter must release the meat attached to the bone by running the knife along and between the bone and the sirloin. This then allows the slices of meat carved to fall free

Figure 8.11 Carving a sirloin of beef

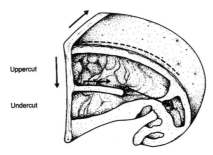

Note:

1 Boiled beef will be carved with the grain as this prevents shredding. A little cooking liquor should accompany each portion.
2 Ribs of beef are carved in a similar fashion to the uppercut of the sirloin.

Best end of lamb (carré d'agneau)

Accompaniments
roast gravy – mint sauce – redcurrant jelly

Carve two cutlets per portion.

Method A

1 Hold the *carré* firmly on the board by inserting a service fork into the base at one end
2 Turn the *carré* upright
3 Carve into cutlets using the exposed end of the ribs as a guide to the correct amount per portion

Method B

1 Lay the *carré* flat on the board with the exposed end of the ribs pointing downwards
2 Holding the *carré* firmly with a service fork and using the exposed ends of the ribs as a guide, carve into cutlets

Saddle of lamb (selle d'agneau)

Note:

1 The loin may be roasted, boned, stuffed, rolled and roasted, or may be cut into chops.
2 The two loins undivided make up a *saddle*.

Accompaniments
roast gravy – mint sauce – redcurrant jelly

There are two alternative methods of carving the saddle:

Method A

1 Remove the whole side loin from the saddle
2 Carve into slices parallel with the ribs and approximately 6 mm thick ($\frac{1}{2}$ in)
3 Serve some lean meat and some fat per portion

Figure 8.12 Carving a saddle of lamb (method A)

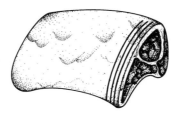

Method B

1 Cut down one side of the backbone reaching approximately halfway along the length of the saddle
2 Cut right down the side of the backbone to the short ribs
3 Where you finished cutting halfway along the backbone, turn the knife at right angles and cut down through the meat and fat
4 Cut out lengths of meat from the saddle, commencing at the backbone, parallel to the backbone where the initial incision was made
5 Work outwards to the edge of the saddle
6 Each wedge of meat should then be carved into thin slices lengthwise

Note:

1 With Method A each customer is given a portion of some lean meat and a little fat.
2 With Method B if the waiter is not careful it is possible for one customer to have a portion of all lean meat and another to receive nearly all fat and very little lean meat.

Figure 8.13 Carving a saddle of lamb (method B)

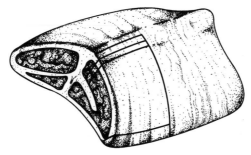

Leg of lamb (gigot d'agneau)

Accompaniments
roast gravy – mint sauce – redcurrant jelly

Service
1 The waiter should remember that initially he/she should carve on to the bone
2 Take out a small V-shaped portion of meat just above the knuckle

3 Proceed to carve the portions of meat by carving on to the bone from the V-shaped cut. This part of the joint is known as the *nut* and is the most choice part

4 After the initial portions have been carved from the nut of meat, the succeeding portions should be carved: a slice from the nut and a slice from the underside

Note:

1 When carving a leg of lamb, to keep it steady on the board, the waiter should hold the knuckle in a clean serviette.

2 The flesh of lamb should be cooked evenly and be rosé (pink) in colour.

3 Always cut generously.

Figure 8.14 Carving a leg of lamb

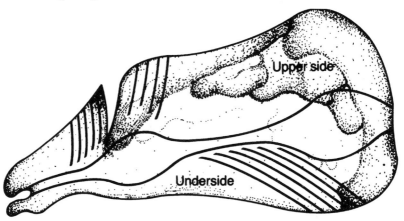

Leg of pork (cuissot de porc)

Accompaniments

roast gravy – apple sauce – sage and onion stuffing

Service

Carved in a similar fashion to a leg of lamb, but the slices carved here should be thin.

Ham (jambon)

There are two methods of carving hams, namely:

1 *French*: the ham is cut into very thin slices down the length of the ham.

2 *English*: the ham is carved at the thick end where the meat is at its most tender.

Note: if the ham is boned and rolled it will then be carved in slices across the fibre of the meat.

Flambé sweet dishes

The flambé trolley

As with the guéridon, the flambé trolley may be set up following a certain basic format, for the reasons already given. The lay-up can be seen in Figure 8.15.

Figure 8.15 Basic lay-up for flambé sweets

Safety points

- Always know where the flame damper is for the flare lamp
- Have an empty joint plate beside the lamp for the hot pan
- Place the flammable spirit away from the lamp
- Never move the trolley near to curtains or hangings

Peach flambé (pêche flambée)

Cover
sweet spoon and fork – hot sweet plate

Accompaniment
castor sugar

Equipment for flambé trolley
lamp – pan on an underplate – matches – spare plate for dirty cutlery and flatware – service spoons and forks on a service plate

Ingredients
measure of brandy – castor sugar – portions of warmed peaches in peach syrup in a timbale

Service
1 Place peach syrup in the pan and heat
2 Add the portion of peaches

3 Pierce the peaches with a fork to allow the heat to penetrate more quickly

4 Baste the peaches occasionally, allowing the peach syrup to reduce right down until it is almost caramelized

5 At this stage sprinkle with castor sugar. This speeds up the caramelizing effect and aids flambéing

6 Ensure the hot sweet plate is now placed in front of the guest

7 Pour over brandy and flambé

8 Serve from the pan on to hot sweet plates at the table, or serve on to hot sweet plates at the flambé trolley

Pear flambé (poire flambée)

As above using pears and pear syrup instead of peaches and peach syrup

Banana flambé (banane flambée)

method 1

Cover

sweet spoon and fork – hot sweet plate

Accompaniment

castor sugar

Equipment for guéridon

lamp – pan on an underplate – service plate with service spoons and forks – spare plate for dirty cutlery and flatware – carving board and small carving knife (12.5 cm – 5 in)

Ingredients

banana – measure of rum (or Pernod depending on the specific dish) – butter – castor sugar

The initial layout of the flambé trolley can be seen in Figure 8.14.

Service

1 Prepare the banana as explained on page 320

2 Place the butter in the pan and melt

3 Pierce both halves of the banana with a fork, to allow the heat to penetrate more quickly

4 Place the banana round side down in the pan and heat. Baste with the butter occasionally and then turn the banana over

5 When golden brown add a little fresh orange juice and blend well. This produces the sauce and removes the surplus fat from within the sauce

6 At this stage place the hot sweet plate on the table in front of the guest

7 When heated sufficiently, flambé with the rum

8 Serve at the table from the pan on to the hot sweet plates, or serve on to hot sweet plates on the flambé trolley

Note: be careful not to overheat the banana at any stage.

Figure 8.16 Equipment lay-up for banana flambé

method 2

Cover
sweet spoon and fork – hot sweet plate

Accompaniment
castor sugar

Equipment for flambé trolley
lamp – pan on an underplate – matches – service spoons and forks on a service plate – spare napkins – sauce ladle – spare plate for dirty equipment – small carving board – small sharp knife – hot sweet plate

Ingredients
1 portion of banana – 3 sauce ladles full of fresh orange juice in a sauceboat – creamed mixture: 40 g demerara sugar; 40 g butter – 1 measure rum

Service
 1 Check you have all necessary equipment and ingredients
 2 Place the pan on a low heat, add the creamed mixture and allow to melt and colour slightly
 3 Place the banana on a carving board and remove the skin as described on page 320
 4 Split the banana in two lengthways
 5 Pierce the banana, to allow heat to penetrate
 6 Add orange juice to the pan, blend together well to produce a clear smooth sauce
 7 Place the banana in a pan – rounded side down
 8 Heat quickly, baste, turn over
 9 Sprinkle with castor sugar – heat well
10 Place the hot sweet plate in front of the guest

11 Flambé with rum

12 Serve from the pan on to hot sweet plate at the table

Cherries flambé with kirsch (cerises flambées au kirsch)

Cover

sweet spoon and fork – hot sweet plate

Accompaniment

castor sugar

Equipment for guéridon

lamp – pan on an underplate – service plate with service spoons and forks – spare plate for dirty cutlery and flatware

Ingredients

portion of cherries in syrup in a timbale – measure of Kirsch – castor sugar

Service

1 Place the cherries and cherry syrup into the pan and heat

2 Reduce the cherry syrup to a minimum

3 Sprinkle with castor sugar to help caramelize the remaining syrup and as an aid to flambéing

4 Place the hot sweet plate on the table in front of the guest

5 Add the Kirsch and flambé

6 Serve at the table from the pan on to a hot sweet plate, or serve on to a hot sweet plate on the flambé trolley

Cerises flambées au glace vanille

As above with the vanilla ice-cream being served immediately before the *Cerises flambées*

Cherries jubilées (cerises jubilées)

Cover

sweet spoon and fork – cold sweet plate

Accompaniment

castor sugar

Equipment for guéridon

lamp – pan on an underplate – service plate with service spoons and forks – spare plate for dirty cutlery and flatware

Ingredients

portion of cherries in syrup in a timbale – measure of brandy – castor sugar

Service

1 As exact timing is required to serve this dish correctly, ensure that your flambé trolley is correctly laid up with all your *mise-en-place* before commencing

2 Light the lamp. Place the portion of cherries in the syrup in the pan and heat up to simmering point

3 Allow the syrup to reduce quickly until almost caramelized

4 When the syrup is reduced to a minimum, sprinkle with castor sugar. This is an aid to flambéing and speeds up caramelization

5 The measure of brandy is now added to the cherries and they are flambéd

6 Serve immediately from the pan

Rum omelette (omelette au rhum)

Cover
sweet spoon and fork – hot sweet plate

Accompaniment
castor sugar

Equipment for flambé trolley
lamp – pan on an underplate – matches – spare plate for dirty equipment – service spoons and forks on a service plate – measure of rum – castor sugar – omelette received from the kitchen on a silver flat at the last moment. It should be cooked *baveuse*

Service
1 Present the omelette – return to the lamp

2 Trim the ends of the omelette with the aid of a service spoon and fork

3 Sprinkle with castor sugar

4 Pour a measure of rum round the edge of the flat

5 Heat quickly, light with a match

6 Serve immediately on to a hot sweet plate at the table or on to a hot sweet plate on the flambé trolley

Strawberries Romanoff (fraises romanoff)

Cover
sweet spoon and fork – cold sweet plate

Accompaniment
castor sugar

Equipment for guéridon
glass bowl – service plate with service spoons and forks – spare plate for dirty cutlery and flatware (see Figure 8.17)

Ingredients
portion of strawberries – portion of double cream in a bowl – measure of Orange Curaçao or Grand Marnier – castor sugar

Service Method A
1 Pour the liqueur to be used over the strawberries and allow to macerate for a few minutes

2 Stir the double cream until it thickens

3 Remove two-thirds of the strawberries plus the liquid into a glass bowl and cream together with the aid of a service fork

4 Add the thickened double cream a little at a time until the mixture is firm

5 Set on to a cold sweet plate and decorate the top with the remaining strawberries. Sprinkle with a little castor sugar and serve

Service Method B

1 Stir the double cream until it starts to thicken

2 Place two-thirds of the strawberries in the glass bowl with the portion of thickened cream

3 Cream together with the aid of a service fork, blending the strawberries and double cream together well

4 Allow to macerate for a few minutes: this mixture should now be firm

5 Add the measure of liqueur (orange curaçao or Grand Marnier)

6 Blend together well

7 Set neatly on to the cold sweet plate

8 Decorate the top with the remaining strawberries

9 Sprinkle with a little castor sugar and serve

Note alternatives are:

1 *Eton Mess* – flavoured with curaçao and lemon juice

2 *Fraises royale* – flavoured with Van der Hum, Kirsch and orange juice

3 *Pêches à la royale* – strawberries and peaches combined with brandy and cream

Pineapple flambé (ananas rafraîchi au kirsch flambé)

Cover

hot fruit plate or sweet plate – fruit knife and fork or a sweetspoon and fork

Accompaniment

castor sugar

Equipment for guéridon

lamp – pan on an underplate – service plate with service spoons and forks – spare plate for dirty cutlery and flatware – carving board and carving knife (at least 20 cm – 8 in)

Ingredients

fresh whole pineapple with small jug of syrup or tinned pineapple slices with jug of syrup from the tin – cherries for garnish – measure of Kirsch – butter – castor sugar

Service

1 If the pineapple is fresh prepare as explained on page 319

2 Place the sugar syrup in the pan and heat

3 Pierce with a fork to allow the heat to penetrate more quickly

4 Place the portion of prepared pineapple into the heated sugar syrup

5 Allow to heat quickly, reducing the liquid to the stage where it is almost caramelized

6 At this point sprinkle well with castor sugar. This helps caramelize the sugar syrup and aids flambéing

7 Place the hot fruit or sweet plate in front of the guest on the table

8 Pour Kirsch over the pineapple, allow to heat, then flambé

9 Serve on to the hot fruit or sweet plate from the pan, at the table

Crêpes Suzette

Cover
sweet spoon and fork – hot sweet plate

Accompaniment
none

Ingredients (two portions)
85 g (3 oz) castor sugar –half lemon – zest 2 oranges – 85 g (3 oz) butter – 1 measure orange curaçao – 1 measure brandy – 4 pancakes

Equipment for flambé trolley
lamp – pan on an underplate – service spoons and forks on a service plate – 2 teaspoons on a sideplate – 2 sweet forks on a sideplate – oval flat with a doily for a portion of pancakes – oval flat with 3 small sauceboats for the creamed mixture, orange juice and lemon juice – brandy and liqueur glass on an underplate – 1 bottle of Orange Curaçao and 1 of brandy – 2 hot sweet plates

Figure 8.17 Equipment lay-up for Strawberries Romanoff

Service

1 Pour out the required measure of liqueur
2 Place the creamed mixture of castor sugar, butter and zest into the pan and melt. Allow to colour slightly to a light golden shade
3 Add three sauce ladles of orange juice and blend well
4 Add the juice of half a lemon if required – according to taste
5 Add one measure of Orange Curaçao
6 Mix well, stirring with a large fork – taste
7 Place in the pancakes, one at a time, heat well, turn over and then fold
8 During this process the sauce should be reducing all the time and thickening
9 When the sauce is reduced sufficiently, add the measure of brandy and flambé
10 Serve on to the hot sweet plates from the pan, at the table

Dessert

Fresh fruit and nuts (dessert)

Cover

fruit knife and fork – fruit plate – one finger bowl on a doily on an underplate with cold water, or a small glass bowl if more than two portions of grapes are to be served – second finger bowl on a doily on an underplate containing warm water and a slice of lemon – spare sideplates for shells and skins – spare serviette – nutcrackers – grape scissors

Accompaniments

castor sugar – salt

Service

1 Present the fruit basket to the guest, allowing him/her to make his/her choice
2 If the guest chooses grapes, the required portion must be cut from the main bunch, held in the grape scissors, and rinsed in the finger bowl or glass bowl containing the cold water before being placed on to the fruit plate
3 If the pineapple, oranges, pears or bananas are chosen then these must be prepared on the guéridon by the waiter

Orange salad (salade d'orange)

Accompaniment

castor sugar

Equipment for guéridon

small very sharp knife – sweet fork – two oranges on plate – fruit plate – spare plate for dirty cutlery and flatware – small glass dish – board

Service

1 Cut a slice from one end of the orange with the aid of the sharp knife
2 Pierce the cut slice with the fork to act as a guard when sectioning the whole orange

Figure 8.18 Preparation of an orange

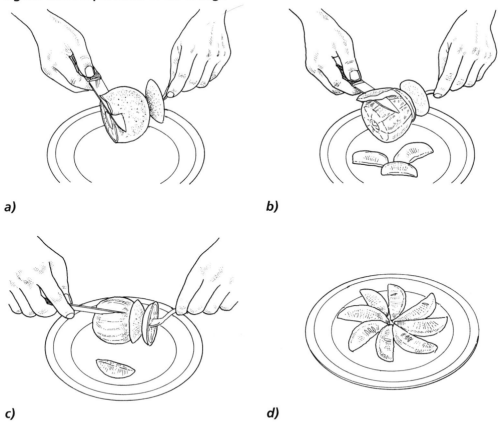

a)

b)

c)

d)

3 Now pierce the whole orange with the fork from the uncut end, so that it is firmly held on the fork

4 Make an incision around the uncut end of the whole orange through the skin to the flesh (through the rind and pith)

5 Remove the peel and pith by cutting strips from the cut end to the incision made around the orange

6 At this stage you should now have a whole orange on your fork with the peel and pith removed

7 Holding the orange over the glass bowl cut out each section of the orange leaving the pith on the fork. Let the sections of orange fall into the glass bowl

8 With the aid of a second fork squeeze the pith over the glass bowl to remove all the juice

9 Sprinkle with castor sugar

10 Dress on to the fruit plate and serve

Apple or pear (pomme au poire)

1 cut a cone from the top of the apple or pear around the stalk approximately 2.5cm in diameter and put aside for later use

2 cut the base of the apple or pear

Figure 8.19 Preparation of an apple

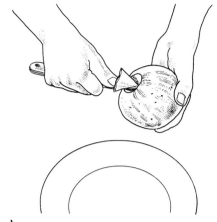

a)

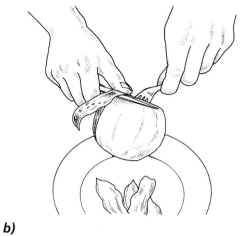

b)

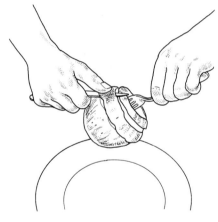

c)

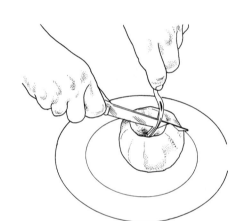

d)

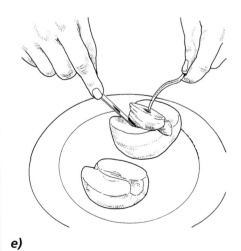

e)

f)

3 place a fork into the top of the apple or pear where the stalk cone was removed from
4 peel the apple in strips from top to bottom or in a spiral from top to bottom
5 cut the apple into two then into quarters
6 remove the core from each quarter
7 decorate on the plate using the stalk cone to garnish

Pineapple (ananas)

1 holding the pineapple by the stem with a clean napkin remove the base of the pine-apple

Figure 8.20 Preparation of a pineapple

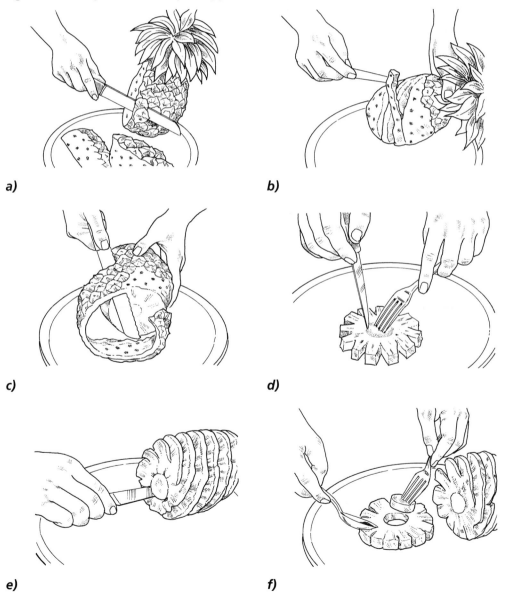

a)

b)

c)

d)

e)

f)

2 peel the pineapple in strips from top to bottom or cut the pineapple in a spiral from bottom to top

3 remove the eyes by cutting a V shaped channel. Note that each channel should go from left to right this will give a less complex spiral that does not all run into one

4 slice the pineapple

5 remove the core using the point of a paring knife or a apple corer

Banana (banane)

1 remove the end of the banana

2 slice through the banana and through the stalk lengthways to give two even slices. Your knuckles may rest against the board to keep the knife straight

3 insert a fruit fork into the end of the stalk and peel the skin back using your knife on the outside of the skin to fold it away from the flesh

Figure 8.21 Preparation of a banana

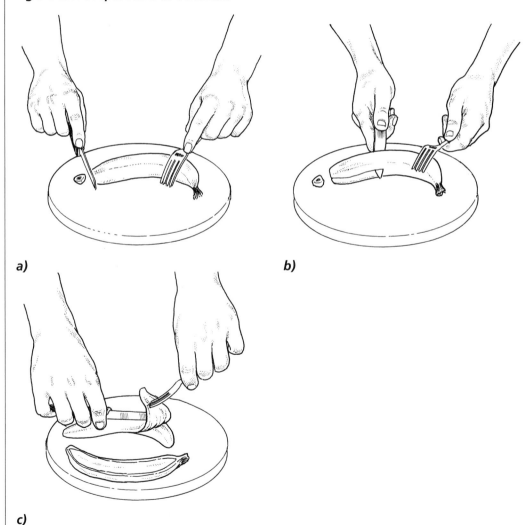

a)

b)

c)

CHAPTER 9

FUNCTION CATERING

9.1	**Introduction**	322
9.2	**Function administration**	330
9.3	**Function organization**	337
9.4	**Weddings**	345
9.5	**Outdoor catering (off premises catering)**	350

9.1 Introduction

Function catering is the term used to cover the service of special functions for specific groups of people at specific times, the food and beverages provided being pre-determined. It includes occasions such as luncheon parties, conferences, cocktail parties, weddings and dinner-dances. In the large first-class establishments all functions take place within the banqueting suites and are under the administrative control of the banqueting manager. In the smaller hotel these functions normally take place in a room set aside for the purpose and come under the jurisdiction of the hotel manager or assistant manager. There are also specialist, banqueting conference centres. Most of the staff available for functions are employed on a casual basis. At busy periods there may be a number of functions running at the same time.

Figure 9.1 Function room ready for service

Functions are as popular as ever but it may be said that their purpose and style are changing. Theme evenings, for example, appear to be becoming increasingly popular. The trend is also for less formality, going for the more informal style table plans and away from the top table and sprigs. At the same time guests are expecting a better overall standard of décor, lighting effects and in the glass and china used. We are perhaps becoming more sophisticated in our tastes and want higher standards of food and comfort.

Types of function

There are two main types of function:

- *Formal meals* (sometimes called banquets)
  Luncheons
  Dinners
  Wedding breakfasts

- *Buffet receptions*
  Wedding receptions
  Cocktail parties
  Buffet teas

  Dances
  Anniversary parties
  Conferences

A further breakdown of the types of function may be as follows:

- *Social*
  Dinners (Old Boys)
  Luncheons (Rotarians)
  Receptions

  Cocktail parties
  Charity performance

- *Conferences*
  Political conferences
  Trade Union

  National and international
  sales conferences

- *Public Relations*
  Press party to launch a new product
  Fashion parade

  Dealer's meetings
  Seminars
  Exhibitions

Function service staff and responsibilities

In large first-class establishments there is generally a small nucleus of permanent staff dealing with functions alone. This includes the banqueting/conference manager, one or two assistant banqueting managers, one or two banqueting head waiters, a dispense barman and a secretary to the banqueting manager. In smaller establishments where there are fewer functions the necessary administrative and organizational work is undertaken by the manager, assistant manager and head waiter.

Sales administrative manager

The main purpose of the sales administration manager is to sell the function catering facilities of an establishment to a client and, where necessary, to make the initial approach and contact. After this the client is referred to the banqueting manager concerned.

Owing to the varied make-up of each function suite in the various establishments, the sales administration manager must have an extensive knowledge of room specifications, size, light switches, electric points, heights of doorways, maximum floor loads and so on. This enables him/her to give positive and negative answers to any requests at the initial meeting with a client without causing any delay to either party.

A certain approach is required when meeting a client, who must be made to feel at ease immediately. The first thing to determine is how much the client has available to spend per head, and to decide whether requests come within that particular price range. If not, this must be made clear right from the start. The client is usually given a booklet of menus to study by the sales administration manager. These must be well presented and therefore act as a good selling point for the establishment concerned. The menus and price ranges should be varied with a choice for each season of the year to include such seasonable foods as game.

The sales administration manager must also be a person of ideas. For very special occasions he/she should be able to make suggestions for that function. For instance a theme might be introduced to be carried throughout the meal.

Banqueting/conference manager

The banqueting/conference manager is responsible for all the administration: the meeting of prospective clients, discussing of arrangements with them concerning menus, table plans, costs, wines, bands, toastmaster and so on.

He/she must communicate to all the departments concerned the date of a function, numbers, and any other details that might be applicable to a certain department.

Secretary

The secretary works with the banqueting manager and is responsible for handling all incoming and outgoing mail, for seeing any memos dictated are sent to the appropriate departments and for the correct filing of any correspondence. The secretary should handle all telephone calls and, in the absence of the banqueting manager, may take provisional bookings for functions ensuring the details are entered on the correct form (banqueting memorandum, see page 331). Bookings are generally made in one of three ways: by telephone, by letter, or by interview. All enquiries, however made, should be confirmed by letter.

Banqueting head waiter

The banqueting head waiter is in charge of the banqueting suites plus the organization required to prepare them for various forms of functions. He/she may also be responsible for the engaging of staff, on a casual basis, to cover the various duties at a function. The banqueting head waiter would normally have a list of names and addresses and telephone

Figure 9.2 Example of a banqueting sales package – courtesy of The Café Royal, London

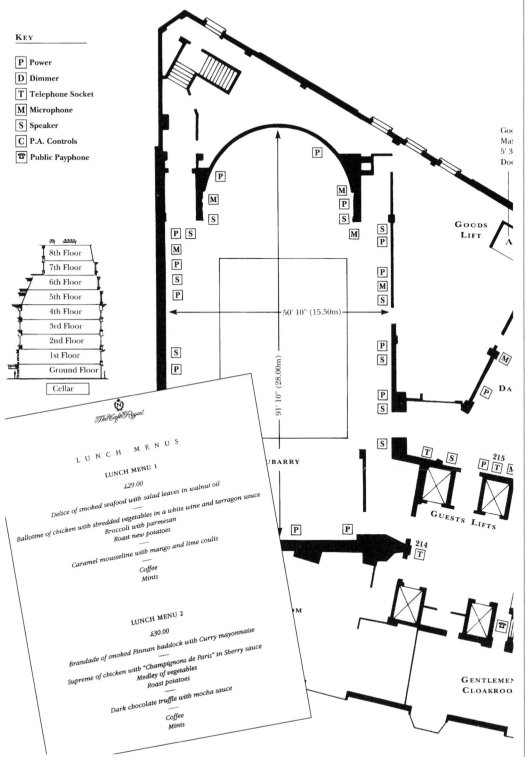

numbers of the best casual staff, and will ensure that they are well employed. This shows results in that the staff work well together as a team, producing a good all-round result which benefits both the client and management.

Dispense bar staff

If they are members of the permanent banqueting staff, the dispense bar staff are responsible for the allocation of bar stock for various functions, the setting up of bars, the organization of the bar staff, control of stock and cash during service and for stocktaking when a function is completed. They are also responsible for the restocking of the banqueting dispense bar.

Banqueting head wine waiter

The banqueting head wine waiter may work in conjunction with the dispense bar staff or, if there are no permanent dispense bar staff, may take over the latter's duties together with those of organizing the banqueting wine waiters and allotting them stations, giving them floats if there are cash wines and discussing the service with them.

Permanent waiting staff

The permanent waiting staff are usually experienced chefs de rang who can turn their hand to any job concerning banqueting and who generally do most of the *mise-en-place* before the function (the laying of tables, etc). Their job during service is mainly wine waiting, but they may also help to clear after service is completed.

Casual staff

Care is taken as to the type of casual staff employed. They normally report approximately one hour before a function commences and are then allocated stations and given a brief talk with regard to the procedure for the service of a particular function. They are normally paid by the hour. After service they are paid and then dismissed.

Porters

There are generally two or three porters on the permanent banqueting staff. They are essential members of staff as there is a great deal of heavy work to be carried out.

Points to note concerning the work of function waiters and wine waiters

A *waiter* at a banquet is generally expected to serve between 10 and 12 covers on a station

- Establishments vary on the service of guests at banquets: generally the waiter commences at one end of a station and works along to the other end. He/she may, however, commence at the left of his/her station for one course and from the right for the next course, or for smaller parties he/she may serve from the right of the host and then right round the table

- Apart from the top table no precedence is given to rank or sex at banquets

Figure 9.3 Example of part of a conference and meetings sales package – courtesy of the Holiday Inn Crowne Plaza, Leeds

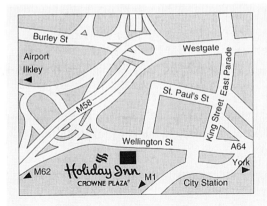

HOLIDAY INN CROWNE PLAZA

LEEDS

Wellington Street, Leeds LS1 4DL
Tel: (0113) 2442200
Fax: (0113) 2440460

LOCATION/TRANSPORTATION FACTS
- From M1 follow signs to City Centre. At City Square left into Wellington Street
- Rail station 400m.
- Leeds/Bradford Airport 13 km.
- Manchester Airport 97 km.

ACCOMMODATION
- 6 Floors with 125 guest rooms
- Three different types of suites available
- Non-smoking bedrooms
- Executive bedrooms
- Facilities for the disabled
- Air-conditioning
- 24-hour room service
- In-room computer connection facilities

DINING/ENTERTAINMENT
- "Hamiltons" Restaurant/Cocktail Bar serves a variety of menus - breakfast, lunch and dinner. Overlooks pool
- "Buongiorno's" Italian Restaurant
- "Roundhay" Bar for residents or non-residents

SERVICES/FACILITIES
- Car rental
- Indoor and on-site parking
- Limousine service available
- Bus parking available

RECREATIONAL/AMUSEMENT FACILITIES
- Health & Leisure Club with indoor swimming pool, sauna, steamroom, solarium, fitness equipment and whirlpool
- Aerobics classes. Jogging trails
- Local tours available
- Yorkshire Dales 25 km.
- Bolton Abbey, Harewood House & Pennines 20 km.
- Yorkshire's top Golf Course within 10 km.

MEETING FACILITIES
- Meeting facilities to 200 featuring a Business Centre, Training Centre and Executive Boardroom
- 3 dedicated syndicate rooms opposite the Main Training Room with cloakroom
- Roundhay Suite can separate into 3 sections
- Daylight and blackout capability in most meeting rooms
- Completely self-contained Training Centre on second floor has 2 adjoining Executive Club bedrooms, 3 dedicated syndicate rooms, the Main Training Room and Lounge with cloakroom
- Smaller rooms on first floor make excellent interview rooms

MEETING EQUIPMENT
- A/V, microphone and sound equipment
- Enhanced staging capabilities (dance floor, podiums) with 24 hours' notice
- Back projection capability
- Speaker phones and mobile/cordless phones

MEETING SUPPORT SERVICES
- Business Centre services
- Secretarial assistance. Translation service
- Flower arrangements, photographer, costume rental. Cat walk
- Extended hours concierge
- Dictaphone, stenographer
- Courier service

A MEETINGS SELECT HOTEL

- The waiters should all be numbered, once the stations are allocated, so that the waiter with a station furthest from the service entrance will be nearer the head of the queue at the hotplate
- The waiters on the top table are always at the head of the queue and enter the room first with each successive course
- No waiter commences service on his/her station until those on the top table have commenced their service

A banqueting *wine waiter* will serve approximately 25 covers, but this depends on the type of function, the amount of wines on offer, and whether any wine is inclusive in the price of the menu or if cash drinks are being served.

- The wine waiters will normally aid the food waiters with the service of vegetables and sauces for the main course
- When cash drinks are served the wine waiters are normally given a float with which they may pay the cashier or barperson as drinks are ordered and collected from the bar. The responsibility then rests with the wine waiter to collect the cash for any drinks served. This should be done immediately the liqueurs are served and before the toasts commence
- If any guests sign their bills or wish to pay by cheque, this must first of all be confirmed by someone in authority
- The wine waiters may also be required to serve aperitifs at a reception before the meal and if so they will be required to do the necessary *mise-en-place* to ensure the reception area is ready, ie ashtrays, cocktails snacks, setting-up of portable bar, polishing glasses, etc. They must also ensure there are plenty of small tables available

Service methods in function catering

Generally it is recognized that at functions the *service method* may take any of the following forms:

- Silver
- Family
- Plate
- Assisted-service
- Self-service

The type of service method chosen is usually determined by the:

- Host's wishes
- Time factor
- Skills of the service staff available

- Equipment available
- Type of function

Formal functions

For formal functions it is normal practice for the banqueting head waiter to organize his/her staff so that at a given signal the top table service staff can commence to serve/clear, immediately followed by all the service staff. It should be remembered, therefore, that the top table service staff always commence to serve/clear first. Correctly the banqueting head waiter will not give any signal to clear a course until all guests have finished eating.

All staff should leave and enter the room led by the top table staff and followed by the other service staff in a pre-determined order. This pre-determined order generally means that those staff with stations furthest from the service doors should be nearer the top table service staff in the line-up. Theoretically this means that, when entering the room, all service staff reach their stations at more or less the same time. Each member of staff then serves his/her own table using the appropriate service method – either full silver service or a combination of plate and silver service and so on. However, when deciding on the pre-determined order, another factor that should influence the final decision is that of safety. In other words, as far as is possible, any cross-flow of staff and bottlenecks in their movement to and from the room should be avoided.

Less formal functions

An alternative to the above method is that used at less formal functions in which the staff double up with regard to the service of the main course. This means that two members of staff act as a team, with one serving the main meat dish, and the other the potato and vegetable dishes, followed by the sauce if served apart. This method can also be used at formal functions to speed up the service to each table and ensure that the food reaches the plate at the correct temperature for the guest.

It should be noted here that the current trend seems to be for the starter and sweet course to be plate served, whilst the fish and main course are silver served. Coffee may be offered by the full silver service method, by serving black coffee and placing the sugar and cream on the tables for guests to help themselves, or by two members of staff working together as a team, in which case the sugar would be placed on the table, black coffee served to each guest by the first waiter, followed by a second waiter offering cream.

Buffet-style functions

At buffet style functions, guests approach the buffet at its various service points to select their requirements course by course. Most ancillary items may also be collected, if needed, at the buffet. These might include rolls, butter, sauces, napkins, tableware and the like. The guests then return to their tables to consume the meal. Any dirties are then removed by clearing staff at the appropriate time.

9.2 Function administration

Booking and organization of functions

At the initial meeting of the banqueting manager and the client, a file must be opened recording all points mentioned concerning the particular function and to hold all correspondence received. If the enquiry is not immediately a firm booking, then the provisional details should be only pencilled in until the booking is confirmed. It should then be written in ink. The banqueting manager should have available specimen luncheon and dinner menus with the costs per head and photographs of the various table layouts for different numbers. This gives the client a clear picture of the facilities available in the price range he/she can afford.

After the initial meeting, the booking having been confirmed, the following basic points should have been noted:

- Type of function
- Date
- Time
- Number of covers (final numbers 24–72 hours beforehand)
- Price per head
- Menu and method of service
- Wines – inclusive or cash
- Type of organization
- Table plan

Depending upon the nature of a particular function, its requirements may vary and it is useful for the banqueting manager to have a checklist of these possible requirements. Other than those points listed above, the following should also be considered:

- List of toasts
- Floral décor for the tables, rooms, reception area, and possibly button holes
- Audio-visual equipment required
- Special licence
- Car-parking
- Cloakrooms
- Artists
- Accommodation
- Telephones
- Lectern
- Secretarial facilities
- Syndicate rooms
- Photographer
- Sign-posting
- Private bar facilities
- Function cancellation fee
- Date for final inspection by clients
- Security
- Marketing
- Toastmaster
- Band, cabaret, dancing
- Place cards
- Seating plan
- Type of menu for printing

Figure 9.4 Example of a function confirmation form – courtesy of Forte Posthouse, Aylesbury

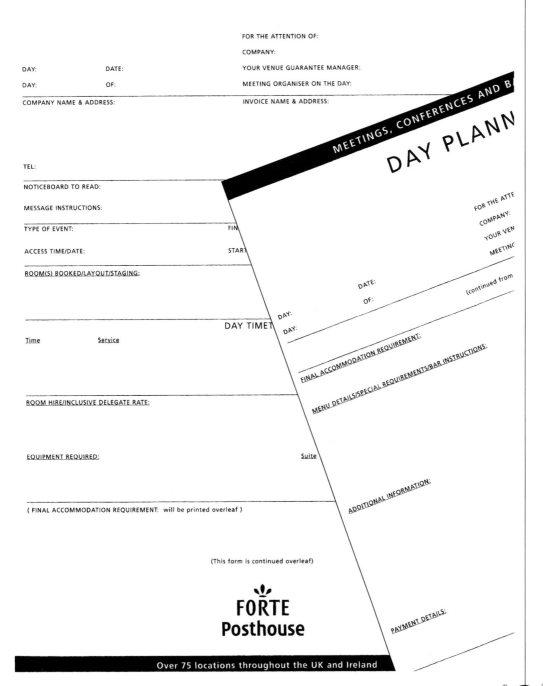

MEETINGS, CONFERENCES AND BANQUETING

DAY PLANNER

FOR THE ATTENTION OF:

COMPANY:

DAY: DATE: YOUR VENUE GUARANTEE MANAGER:

DAY: OF: MEETING ORGANISER ON THE DAY:

COMPANY NAME & ADDRESS: INVOICE NAME & ADDRESS:

TEL:

NOTICEBOARD TO READ:

MESSAGE INSTRUCTIONS:

TYPE OF EVENT: FIN

ACCESS TIME/DATE: START

ROOM(S) BOOKED/LAYOUT/STAGING:

DAY TIMET

Time   Service

ROOM HIRE/INCLUSIVE DELEGATE RATE:

EQUIPMENT REQUIRED: Suite

(FINAL ACCOMMODATION REQUIREMENT: will be printed overleaf)

(This form is continued overleaf)

FORTE
Posthouse

Over 75 locations throughout the UK and Ireland

MEETINGS, CONFERENCES AND B

DAY PLANN

FOR THE ATTE

COMPANY:

YOUR VEN

MEETING

DATE:

OF: (continued from

DAY:

DAY:

FINAL ACCOMMODATION REQUIREMENT:

MENU DETAILS/SPECIAL REQUIREMENTS/BAR INSTRUCTIONS:

ADDITIONAL INFORMATION:

PAYMENT DETAILS:

Figure 9.5 Summary of administrative procedures

If you receive an enquiry

Per telephone

Write down all details on enquiry form

Check diary

If fully booked,
offer alternate dates

If available

Per letter

Check diary

If available

If fully booked,
offer alternate dates

If not acceptable, regret

Send letter of regret
and file under "regret"

If acceptable

If acceptable

If not acceptable, regret

Send letter of regret
and file under "regret"

Pencil in date in diary

Send letter "reply to enquiry"

Send letter "please confirm"

After one week, file in "awaiting confirmation" unless an old file already exists

If response is negative, cancel in diary

Send letter "sorry you cancelled" and file
under "cancellation" (Cancellation file
to be classed into types of function and
used by sales dept. for follow up when needed)

If confirmation is received, ink
booking into diary and open file

Write out function sheet and book all extra requirements

Update as more details become available

Include party in forward banqueting list.
(If list is already issued send out "additional booking form")

Distribute function sheet two weeks in advance

Confirm final numbers three days in advance and inform head chef, porters and head waiter

On the day before: meeting of banqueting managers and heads of departments

One day in advance: issue table plan

On the day: Check last minute changes. Headwaiter to advise
office in writing of covers booked and actual numbers

On the day after: invoice to be handed to the banqueting co-ordinator plus function
checks from: manager, headwaiter, bar man; checks from flowershop; charges for audio / visual;
charges for security and other charges. Used to compile and complete function account

(bottom copy filed on function file)

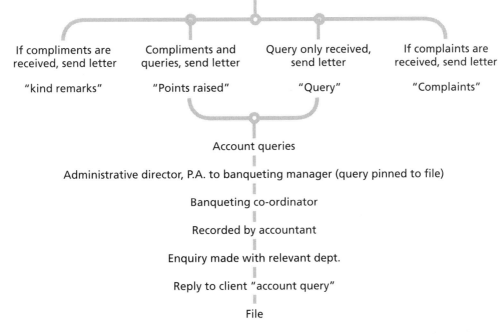

Top copy and file passed to control for checking

Bill to go out same day with accompanying letter

Office to send out letter "see you again"

"provisionally booked" (pencil date in diary)

If compliments are received, send letter	Compliments and queries, send letter	Query only received, send letter	If complaints are received, send letter
"kind remarks"	"Points raised"	"Query"	"Complaints"

Account queries

Administrative director, P.A. to banqueting manager (query pinned to file)

Banqueting co-ordinator

Recorded by accountant

Enquiry made with relevant dept.

Reply to client "account query"

File

Function menus

There should be a varied choice of menu within a wide price range, with special menus available for occasions such as weddings, twenty-first birthday parties and New Year's Eve. As functions are booked up months in advance, special care is called for with regard to foods in season. The minimum number of courses is often four, plus beverages. They are made up of, for example:

- Hors-d'oeuvre or other appetizers
- Soup or fish
- Meat – with a selection of seasonal vegetables
- Sweet
- Coffee – with a selection of petits fours

The above is generally popular today, but extra or alternative courses such as entrées, cheese or and savouries may be added.

Figure 9.6 Examples of function menus. These examples of function menus are a small sample from those available at, and are reproduced courtesy of, The Café Royal, London

Luncheon

Paupiettes of smoked salmon, prawns and
Japanese seaweed with a cucumber and
pickled ginger salad

–

Thick cut roast beef with a trio of
peppercorns and Cognac sauce
Potato galette
Tomato with spinach

–

Tiramasu with mocha sauce

–

Coffee with petits fours

Tartar of gravadlax with dill cucumber
and Vodka cream

–

Breast of corn-fed chicken with a
Provençale herb and tepenade crust and
roast pepper coulis
Baked sweet potato cake
Green and yellow courgettes in garlic oil

–

Caramel mousseline with mango and
lime sauce

–

Coffee with Mints

Dinner

Salad of Mediterranean seafood with
artichokes and saffron vinaigrette

–

Essence of beef with old Sherry

–

Supreme of guinea fowl with foie gras and
truffle 'en croûte'
Dariole of spinach
Glazed carrots and celeriac

–

Prune and Armagnac parfait with
chocolate sauce

–

Coffee and Petits fours

Salad of artichokes, wild mushrooms and
green beans with balsamic vinegar and
pumpkin seed oil

–

Pithivier of prawns and mushrooms with
tomato beurre blanc

–

Tournedos of beef with celeriac gratin and
truffle sauce
Buttered French beans
Noisette potatoes

–

Lemon and raspberry meringue with
pistachio sauce

–

Coffee and Petits fours

Buffet

Cold items
Seasonal melon   Seafood roulade   Pâté with Cumberland sauce
Honey roast ham with asparagus   Display of charcuterie and pickles
Mediterranean seafood and vegetable salad
Assortment of smoked seafood with horseradish
Herring and apple salad with sour cream   Selection of salads, vinaigrettes and sauces

Hot items
Fricassée of chicken with oriental spices   Salmon 'en croûte' with shredded vegetables
Spinach ravioli with mushrooms and parmesan
Minted new potatoes   Stir-fried vegetables

–

Farmhouse cheeseboard   Chef's selection of sweets

–

Coffee , Tea

Wines

The banqueting wine list is generally small, but contains good wines from the main wine list. Wines may be inclusive with the meal or on a cash basis, the money being payable to the sommeliers who may work on a float system. Very often the aperitif served before a function is also inclusive with the meal but, if not, there may be a 'cash bar' set up in the reception area.

Tabling

The type of table plan put into operation for a particular function depends upon a number of major factors, these being:

- Organizer's wishes
- Nature of the function
- Size and shape of room where the function is to be held
- Number of covers

For the smaller type of function a *U-* or *T-shaped* table may be used, or where the luncheon or dinner party is more formal there may be a top table and separate tables, round or rectangular for the various parties of guests. Where the function to be held has a very large number of covers, then the generally accepted form of table plan is a top table and sprigs.

However, before these various table plans can be shown to the organizer when a function is being booked, a great amount of consideration must be given to spacing, ie widths of covers, gangways, size of chairs and so on. This is to allow a reasonably comfortable seating space for each guest and, at the same time, to give the waiter sufficient room for the service of the meal. Also the gangway space must be such that two waiters may pass one another during the service without fear of any accident occurring. Remember that these factors must always be borne in mind to ensure that the maximum number of covers are seated in a limited area, thus gaining maximum income from the particular room being used.

Spacing

- It is generally recognized that the minimum space between sprigs should be 2 m (6 ft). This is made up of two chair widths: from the edge of the table to the back of the chair (46 cm or 18 in) plus a gangway of 1 m (3 ft), allowing each waiter passing space: total of 2 m (6 ft)

- Table widths are approximately 75 cm (2 ft 6 in)

- The length along the table per cover should be 50–60 cm (20–24 in)

- The space from the wall to the edge of the table should be a minimum of 1.4 m (4 ft 6 in). This is made up of a 1 m (3 ft) gangway, plus one chair of width 46 cm (18 in)

- The height of the chair from the ground will vary according to the style and design, but is approximately 46–50 cm (18–20 in)

- The length of the table used is generally 2 m (6 ft) but 1.2 and 1.5 m lengths (4 and 5 ft) may be used to make up a sprig

- Round tables would be 1.0, 1.5 or 2 m (3, 5 or 6 ft) in diameter with the appropriate extensions

- Suggested area allowance for sit-down functions per person is approximately 1.0–1.4 sq m (12–15 sq ft); for buffets the allowance is 0.9–1.0 sq m (10–12 sq ft)

Laying of cloths

The minimum size of banqueting cloths is 2 m (6 ft) in width by 4 m (12 ft) in length. However, they are available in longer lengths (eg 5½ m or 18 ft etc). These cloths are used on top tables and sprigs, thus often avoiding the necessity of overlapping that occurs when smaller-sized tablecloths are used.

When laid, the centre crease should run straight down the centre of the table, with the overlap the same all round the table. All cloths should be in the same fold and have the same pattern. Any overlap of cloths should face away from the main entrance so that the join is not visible to the guests as they look down the room on arrival. When laying the cloth it may require three or four waiters to manipulate it (depending on size) thus ensuring that it is laid correctly without creasing or becoming dirty.

9.3 Function organization
Seating arrangements

Of the total number of people attending a function it must be determined how many will be seated on the *top table*, and how many on the *sprigs*, round or oblong tables, making up the full table plan. It must be known whether the number on the top table includes the ends, and care should be taken to avoid seating 13 on this table.

All tables, with the exception of the top, should be numbered, again avoiding using the number 13. In its place it is permissible to use *12A*. The table numbers themselves should be on stands of such a height that they may all be seen from the entrance of the banqueting room, the approximate height of the stands being 75 cm (30 in). After the guests are seated and before the service commences these stands are sometimes removed. If left they are an aid to the sommelier when checking for cash wines.

As far as possible when formulating the table plan, one should try to avoid seating guests with their backs to the top table. Normally there are three copies of the seating plan. These go to:

- The *organizer*: so that he/she may check all necessary arrangements
- The *guests*: this seating plan should be placed in a prominent position in the entrance of the banqueting suite so that all guests may see where they have been seated, who else is sitting at their table, and the position of their table in the room
- The *banqueting manager*: for reference purposes

Examples of banquet layouts
The use of a top table and sprigs

Dinner of 110 guests: 15 guests on top table; 3 sprigs required

METHOD OF WORK (PLAN 1)
1 *Length of table required for top*
   15 guests × 60 cm (2 ft) = 9 m (30 ft) or 5 × 2 m (6 ft) tables
2 *Number of covers on each sprig*
   110 − 15 = 95
   95 ÷ 3 = 32, 32, 31
   Therefore each side of a sprig will have 16 covers, except one which will have 15 covers
3 *Length of sprig*
   16 covers × 60 cm (2 ft) = 9.7 m (32 ft) or 5 × 2 m (6 ft) tables

4 *To check if three sprigs may be fitted on top table*

3 sprigs × 75 cm (2 ft 6 in) (width)	= 2.25 m (7 ft 6 in)
2 gangways × 1 m (3 ft) (width)	= 2 m (6 ft)
4 chair width × 46 cm (18 in)	= 2 m (6 ft)
Total	= 6.25 m (19 ft 6 in)

Thus there is plenty of room (see Figure 9.7)

Figure 9.7 Top table and sprigs

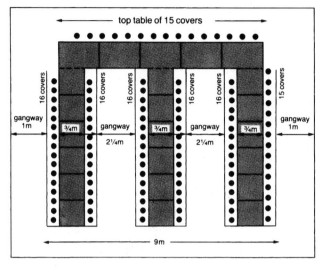

TABLE AND SEATING PLAN (GENERAL)

● *Plan 1* allows for five extra covers in case of emergency

1 either end of the top table	= 2
1 either end of the sprigs	= 3
Total	= 5

If the host had so wished, could a similar plan have been evolved making the layout more compact, for use in a slightly smaller room? ie: *can we get four sprigs on a 9 m (30 ft) long top table?*

4 sprigs × 75 cm (2 ft 6 in)	= 3 m (10 ft)
3 gangways × 1 m (3 ft)	= 3 m (9 ft)
6 chair widths × 46 cm (1 ft 6 in)	= 3 m (9 ft)
Total	= 9 m (28 ft)

Therefore four sprigs will give a more compact layout and bring everyone closer to the speakers on the top table. This alternative plan allows for 12 covers on each side of the sprigs and additional seating at the sprig ends if required.

The use of a top table and round tables

Total covers is 110: 15 on top table, 95 covers on round tables
Dimension of room = 18 m (60 ft) long by 11 m (36 ft) wide

1 *To find the circumference of a round table*

   diameter $\times \pi$ (where $\pi = 22/7$)

Therefore, circumference is 'diameter' $\times$ 22/7

2 *Circumference of a round table 1 m (3 ft) in diameter*
   - 1 m $\times$ 22/7   = 3 1/7 ie 3 m
   - 3 ft $\times$ 22/7   = 9 3/7 ie 9 ft

3 *Number of covers available per round table*
   (allowing 60 cm (2 ft) per person)
   - 3 m $\div$ 0.6 m = 5.0
   - 9 ft $\div$ 2 ft   = 4.5

   ie number of covers is 4–5 per round table

4 *Round table of diameter 1.5 m (5 ft)*
   Number of covers available:
   - (1.5 m $\times$ 22/7) $\div$ 0.6 m   = 4.7 m $\div$ 0.6 m   = 8
   - (5 ft $\times$ 22/7) $\div$ 2 ft   = 15 5/7 ft $\div$ 2 ft = 8

   ie number of covers is 8 per round table

5 *Round table of diameter 2 m (7 ft)*
   Number of covers available:
   - (2 m $\times$ 22/7) $\div$ 0.6 m   = 6.3 m $\div$ 0.6 m = 11
   - (7 ft $\times$ 22/7) $\div$ 2 ft   = 154/7 ft $\div$ 2 ft = 11

   ie number of covers is 11 per round table

METHOD OF WORK

1 *Length of table required for top*
   15 guests $\times$ 60 cm (2 ft) = 9 m (30 ft) or 5 $\times$ 2 m (6 ft) tables

2 *Number of round tables required*
   110 − 15 = 95 covers to be laid on round tables
   Assuming using tables all same diameter (1.5 m, 5 ft), ie 8 covers per table
   Number of tables required is 95 $\div$ 8 = 11.875
   ie 12 tables (11 $\times$ 8 covers and 1 $\times$ 7 covers)

3 *To check if tables as per the table plan will fit in length of the room (ie 18 m, 60 ft)*
From wall behind the top table:

Gangway	= 1 m	(3 ft)
Top table chair	= 0.46 m	(1 ft 6 in)
Top table	= 0.75 m	(2 ft 6 in)
Gangway	= 1 m	(3 ft)
Total	= 3 m approx	(10 ft approx)
Round table	= 1.5 m	(5 ft)
Chairs	= 1 m	(3 ft)
Gangway	= 1 m	(3 ft)
Total	= 3.5 m	(11 ft)
Total $\times$ 4	= 14 m	(44 ft)

Total length = 3 m (10 ft) + 14 m (44 ft) = 17 m (54 ft)
The length of the room is 18 m (60 ft) so the proposed table plan fits

4 *To check if the tables as per the table plan will fit in the width of the room (ie 11 m, 36 ft)*

3 round tables each 1.5 m (5 ft) diameter	= 4.5 m (15 ft)
6 chair widths each 0.46 m (1 ft 6 in)	= 3 m (9 ft)
4 gangways each at 1 m (3 ft)	= 3.5 m (12 ft) (by reducing the size slightly
Total	= 11 m (36 ft)

The proposed table plan fits (see Figure 9.8)

Figure 9.8 Top table and round tables

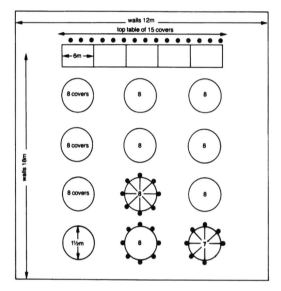

Instructions to staff

The purpose of the staff instruction sheet is to ensure that all duties are covered, that a particular function is laid up and everything is in order in the shortest possible time and to give working methods to casual staff.

Allotting stations

When all the necessary *mise-en-place* has been completed and all the staff are assembled together, the stations are allotted to the waiters and wine waiters. Care must be taken in the allocation of the top table and usually one of the more experienced and proficient members of the brigade will be given this job. One must bear in mind the age and agility of the staff when allotting stations, giving the older members of the brigade the stations nearest the service doors.

When the waiters queue up at the hotplate for each course this should be done in an orderly fashion with the waiter for the top table at the head of the queue and then the various waiters in order according to the distance of their station from the service hotplate. This order must be maintained throughout the service.

After the service of each course the brigade should remain outside the banqueting room and in readiness to clear and serve the next course.

EXAMPLES OF ALLOTTING STATIONS, STAFF REQUIRED, AND THE ORDER AT THE HOTPLATE

Dinner of 84 covers
12 on the top table
and
24 on each sprig (12 on each side)

Table requirements (plan: Figure 9.9)
Top: 4 × 2 m (6 ft) tables = 8 m = 60 cm (24 in) allowance per person
Sprigs: 4 × 2 m (6 ft) tables = 8 m = 60 cm (24 in) allowance per person.
A total of 3 sprigs in all: 12 covers on each side

Stations: Top: 12 covers   12
           Sprig: 6 × 12 covers   72

Order at hotplate
1
2
3
4
5
6
7
Stations 7 × 12 = 84 covers

Figure 9.9 Example of allotting stations and the order at the hotplate

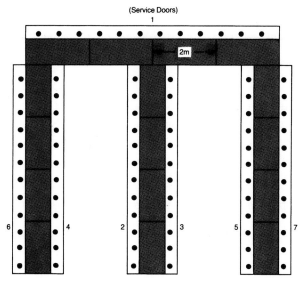

TITLE	INTRODUCTION	VERBAL ADDRESS	PLACE CARDS
THE ROYAL FAMILY			
The Queen	'Her Majesty the Queen'	'Your Majesty' and subsequently 'Ma'am'	
The Duke of Edinburgh	'His Royal Highness, Prince Philip, The Duke of Edinburgh'	'Your Royal Highness' and subsequently 'Sir'	
The Queen Mother	'Her Majesty, Queen Elizabeth, The Queen Mother'	'Your Majesty' and subsequently 'Ma'am'	
A Royal Prince	'His Royal Highness, Prince Charles, The Prince of Wales'	'Your Royal Highness' and subsequently 'Sir'	His Royal Highness, The Prince of Wales
	'His Royal Highness, Prince Andrew, The Duke of York'	'Your Royal Highness' and subsequently 'Sir'	His Royal Highness, The Duke of York
	'His Royal Highness, The Prince Edward'	'Your Royal Highness' and subsequently 'Sir'	His Royal Highness, The Prince Edward
A Royal Princess	'Her Royal Highness, The Princess Margaret	'Your Royal Highness' and subsequently 'Ma'am'	Her Royal Highness, The Princess Margaret
A Royal Duke	'His Royal Highness, The Duke of Gloucester'	'Your Royal Highness' and subsequently 'Sir'	His Royal Highness, The Duke of Gloucester
A Royal Duchess	'Her Royal Highness, The Duchess of Gloucester'	'Your Royal Highness' and subsequently 'Ma'am'	Her Royal Highness, The Duchess of Gloucester
PEERS, BARONETS AND KNIGHTS			
Duke	'The Duke of Somerset'	'Duke'	The Duke of Somerset
Duchess	'The Duchess of Somerset'	'Duchess'	The Duchess of Somerset
Earl	'Lord Salisbury'	'Lord Salisbury'	Lord Salisbury
Countess	'Lady Salisbury'	'Lady Salisbury'	Lady Salisbury
Viscount	'Lord Wilton'	'Lord Wilton'	Lord Wilton
Viscountess	'Lady Wilton'	'Lady Wilton'	Lady Wilton
GOVERNMENT			
The Prime Minister	By appointment or by name	By appointment or by name	The Prime Minister
Chancellor of the Exchequer	By appointment or by name	'Chancellor' or by name	Chancellor of the Exchequer
Ministers	'Mr Salmon'	'Minister' or 'Mr Salmon'	Mr Roy Salmon

TITLE	INTRODUCTION	VERBAL ADDRESS	PLACE CARDS
THE CLERGY			
Archbishops	'The Archbishop of York'	'Archbishop' (socially)	His Grace, The Archbishop of York
Bishop	'The Bishop of Downton'	'Bishop' (socially)	The Lord Bishop of Downton
LOCAL GOVERNMENT			
Lord/Lady Mayor	By appointment or appointment and name	'My Lord/Lady Mayor' or 'Lord/Lady Mayor'	The Lord/Lady Mayor
Mayor	By appointment or appointment and name	'Mr/Madam Mayor'	The Mayor of Woodfalls
Mayor's Consort	By appointment or appointment and name	'Mayoress'	The Mayoress of Woodfalls

Figure 9.10 Precedents and forms of address

Forms of address

It is not unusual at very formal functions for royalty or other dignitaries holding certain '*office*' to be entertained. As a result, etiquette demands a certain order of precedence when proposing and replying to toasts, and the correct mode of address should be adhered to.

The above list gives some examples of the correct modes of '*introduction*' and '*address*' for both formal and social occasions. For all functions, formal and informal, etiquette is very important and great care should be taken to ensure the correct forms of address are used to suit the occasion.

Note:

- It should be remembered that *formality* is always followed on occasions involving members of the Royal Family.

- The social forms of address are given for Peers, Baronets and Knights. For details related to more formal events one should consult *Debrett's Peerage and Baronetage* or *Debrett's Correct Form*

- The Members of the Royal Family listed are shown in order of precedence

Loyal toast

Correctly at any formal function no guest should smoke until after the Loyal Toast. This toast is generally announced by the toastmaster as soon as the sweet course has been cleared, but before the coffee is to be served. Staff should ensure at this time that all glasses have been *charged* in readiness for the coming toasts.

The Loyal Toast should be announced by the toastmaster and is then normally proposed by the host for the evening – Chairman or President of an Association. The Loyal

Toast is a toast to the reigning monarch: 'The Queen'. Immediately afterwards, the toast-master indicates that the company present has the 'Chair's permission to smoke'. Staff should ensure that at this time ashtrays have been placed on the tables.

Example of an order of service for a formal function

1 Dinner announced by the toastmaster
2 Grace
3 Guests seated. Chairs pulled out by waiters. Serviettes across laps
4 If first course is not already on the table, proceed to hotplate to collect first course
5 Line up as previously mentioned, top table first
6 Serve first course – top table waiter to commence service first
7 All waiters (food) to leave room after each course is served
8 Take in fish course plates
9 Clear first course and lay fish plates
10 Take out dirties and collect fish course
11 Serve fish course. Leave room taking dirty silver
12 Take in meat plates
13 Clear fish course and lay meat plates
14 Take out dirties and collect potato and other vegetable dishes
15 Deposit on sideboard or sidetable on a hotplate
16 Return to hotplate and collect main meat dish
17 Present on each table and serve
18 Serve accompanying potatoes and vegetables
19 Leave room taking dirty silver
20 Continue until end of the meal

Note: the head waiter will control all the food waiters at the hotplate, and variations on this service may be adopted according to the situation. The head waiter also controls the exit from hotplate into the banqueting room.

The order of service on the top table at functions, especially very formal occasions, is the one time when the host is always served first, or at exactly the same time as the Guest of Honour should they be seated on different stations.

Reception and ordering of wines

If required, a bar must be set up in the reception area away from the main entrance, so as to avoid overcrowding in one area as the guests are arriving and being announced by the toastmaster. The bar should be clothed up as a buffet, with the cloth within 1.3 cm ($\frac{1}{2}$ in) of the ground in front with both ends boxed in. Keep the rear of the bar open so it may be used for storing extra supplies of drink, glasses and any necessary equipment such as glass jugs, soda syphons, extra ice, and so on. Always allow ample working space behind the bar. The latter is generally higher from the ground than the average table and, if no shelves are available for storage purposes, then sometimes smaller tables may be incorporated under the bar to fulfil that particular function.

There should always be a good stock of drink, which is generally brought from the cellar approximately 45 minutes before the reception is due to commence. Once the drink is at the bar there should always be one barman on duty at all times. Depending on the function, drinks may be served either *cash* or *inclusive*. Whichever may be the case, a stock-take should be made when service is completed. Where necessary do not forget to have on hand price lists, till, floats, notices regarding size of measures, occasional licence (if required).

When the drinks are to be served on a cash basis, this can very often be a lengthy process. To speed this up there should be a wine waiter on duty near the table plan in the reception area together with a commis. They should have a:

● Wine list

● Menu

● Check pads

● Wine waiters' names

● Stations

● Table plan

Note: the object here is to get as many orders as possible for wine to accompany the meal prior to the meal service commencing.

The order should be written in duplicate with the guests name at the top of the check to assist in identifying customers orders at the tables. One copy should go to the cellar or dispense bar and the duplicate to the correct wine waiter. The order should be prepared by the dispense barman or cellarman and when the wine waiter shows the duplicate he should be given the required order. Do not open until the guests arrive at the table – red wine at room temperature and white wine chilled. At a cash reception the wine waiters very often act as lounge waiters and therefore are always to hand to receive any orders in readiness for the service.

As for food service, the top table must always be served first with drink. The toasts very often commence immediately the coffee is served. By this stage the wine waiters should have taken all the liqueur orders, served them and collected all the cash outstanding in the case of cash drinks. Whilst the speeches are going on all the food waiters should be out of the room. The wine waiters may circulate if necessary.

On completion of the function and when the food and wine waiters have cleared their stations and the latter returned any floats, they should be paid off after returning service cloths, jackets, and other equipment provided for the service.

9.4 Weddings

Wedding functions are usually of two main types:

- Wedding breakfast
- Wedding reception (buffet)

At the initial meeting of the client and the banqueting manager when a wedding function is being arranged similar points should be borne in mind as those for 'booking a function', already mentioned. The requirements of the client depend on the type of wedding function, the number of guests attending and the cost per head to be paid.

Some main points to bear in mind which require discussion with the client are requirements concerning a wedding cake stand and knife and whether a room should be available for the bride and bridegroom to change prior to leaving the function to go on their honeymoon. Also it should be noted whether the wedding presents will be displayed and, if so, how much space will be needed, and whether the services of a photographer will be required.

Wedding organization

The type of menu offered will depend on the cost per head to be paid. For a wedding the menu is often printed in *silver*, together with the names of the couple and the date as they are usually kept as souvenirs. If the wedding is a *sit-down* affair then the same points should be noted as previously mentioned with reference to spacing of tables, covers, gangways, and service. In this instance the cake will be cut at the end of the meal, after the coffee, and will be followed by any necessary toasts.

A seating plan should be available for a wedding breakfast and the table plan may be either U-shaped, top table and sprigs or top and rounds. Room allowance for a sit-down function is usually 1–1.4 sq m (12–15 sq ft) per person, and 0.9–1 m (10–12 sq ft) per person for buffets.

Wedding reception (buffet)

The buffet itself should be placed in such a position that it is on view to all guests as they enter the room, but within easy access of the service doors for ease of clearing and re-stocking. The buffet should be clothed up correctly in that the buffet cloth should reach within 1.27 cm ($\frac{1}{2}$ in) of the floor and both ends should be boxed neatly. The creases along the top and front of the buffet should all be lined up. Adequate room should be left between the buffet and wall to allow two people to pass and for any extra supplies and equipment required. If the function is being carried out in a marquee in private grounds then the ground should be covered with canvas or a form of corded matting. Behind the buffet and in the service areas duck-boards may be used on canvas to avoid walking on wet ground or in mud and carrying it into the main part of the marquee.

The buffet itself may be split into three sections for ease of service of *food, tea and coffee*, and *wines and spirits*.

- The *food* should be presented appetizingly and attractively on the buffet and the cutlery, flatware and china required placed conveniently near the service points and in a decorative manner. Food for replenishing the buffet should be close to hand. The centre of the buffet may be raised in order to show off the dishes to greater effect.

- The section set up for the service of beverages, *tea and coffee*, should have all the relevant equipment close to hand. This will include teacups and saucers, teaspoons, sugar basins, cold milk jugs, tea and coffee urns, and hotplates for the pots of hot milk. The service of beverages does not normally take place until after all the toasts have been completed. It is advisable to allow a little more in quantity than is actually required.

- The section of the buffet required for *alcoholic and non-alcoholic drinks* should have all the correct size glasses for the drinks to be served (spirits, soft drinks and mineral waters, cocktails, wines and champagne), plus ice-buckets for the white, sparkling and rosé wines to be chilled, service salvers, waiters' cloths, and all the ancillary equipment required for mixing drinks and cocktails to give the correct form of service. Any champagne or other sparkling wine used for the toasts must be well chilled to approximately 7°C (45°F). A surplus of glasses should be kept under the buffet in their appropriate boxes. Diet, low calorie and low alcohol drinks should be on hand if required.

Note: should it be appropriate this 'drink section' may be set up as a separate service point, away from the main buffet, to improve the efficiency of the service to the guests.

The floral arrangements are an important aspect of the decoration and help show off the room to best effect. A large vase of flowers should normally be placed near the entrance to be noted on arrival by all the guests. A further large centrepiece of flowers may be placed in the centre of the buffet and other smaller arrangements of flowers placed at intervals around the room on the occasional tables. The final floral arrangements will depend on the cost involved. The front of the buffet cloth may be decorated with some greenery (smilac) of some sort, or some coloured velvet may be draped along in order to take away the plainness of the white buffet cloth. One may also use purpose-made pleating to enhance the front and overall appearance of the buffet. This pleating may be purchased in a variety of colours.

The wedding cake may be used as a separate focal point away from the buffet and should be placed upon its stand with a knife on a special table clothed-up for the purpose. This is a very important aspect of the dressing of the room, as the main formalities of the function take place, at a certain stage of the proceedings, around the wedding cake. It must, therefore, be in full view to everyone in the room. The bride's and bridesmaid's bouquets are often placed on the table around the base of the wedding cake, together with any telegrams of congratulations that are to be read out by the best man or toastmaster.

Occasional tables should be placed at regular intervals around the room and clothed up in a suitable manner. Groups of chairs should be placed around each table ensuring there is still space left for people to walk around and meet.

All the ancillary items required for the efficient service of the meal should be placed upon the occasional tables. Items might include butter, rolls/French bread, sideplates, side knives, serviettes, sugar basins and tongs, accompaniments for cold meats and salads, and ashtrays. Where possible some large free-standing ashtrays should be used as well. Thus the majority of the brigade on duty can be either serving drinks or clearing away items, and not be involved in the service of food which will be done from the buffet by other members of the brigade or one or two chefs if there is any carving involved.

It should be noted that the buffet itself may be used entirely for displaying the food, and separate service points may be set up for the service of beverages, both alcoholic and non-alcoholic. This depends upon the exact nature of the function, the room available, number of guests, requirements of the client and the type and amount of drinks to be served. Cigars and cigarettes should be supplied at additional cost and placed on the occasional tables.

The client may also request that you arrange for a photographer to be present and this then is a further charge that has to be made. The photographer will probably take photographs of the bride and bridegroom on arrival at the reception, together with a group photo of those in the *receiving line*, one of the bride and bridegroom cutting the cake and maybe one or two of the buffet while it is complete. The photographer will develop all the photographs and return the proofs for everyone to see before the function is over.

Fully attended cloakrooms must be available for all guests on arrival.

Staff

The number of staff required will depend on the nature and requirements of a particular function. As a guide, at a buffet type reception, which is the more popular type of wedding function, one would need:

Brigade: 1 head waiter/banqueting head waiter
            1 waiter to every 25–30 covers
            1 wine waiter to every 40 covers
            1 barman to every 3 wine waiters
            1–2 commis for fetching and carrying and clearing
            1 chef to every 35–40 guests for service

Procedure at a wedding buffet reception

1 Any casual staff required should report approximately one hour beforehand to complete the necessary *mise-en-place*, to be allocated duties and to be briefed on the procedure to be carried out

2 If a toastmaster is to be on duty, he should arrive approximately 30 minutes before the arrival of the bride and bridegroom to acquaint himself with the room where the function is being held and to enquire what his duties will be with regard to the announcing of guests on arrival. He must liaise with the best man to discuss the timing of cutting the cake, the toasts, and who is to give them. If there is to be a social evening afterwards then the toastmaster may act as MC for the duration of the function

3 The bride and bridegroom should arrive first from the church. Some photographs may be taken at this stage and an aperitif offered or a glass of champagne

4 Immediately following the bride and bridegroom should be the parents of the bride and bridegroom and bridesmaids and/or pages. These people will generally make up the 'receiving line' to greet the guests as they are announced by the toastmaster

5 All the guests should generally arrive together. Cloakrooms at this stage must be fully staffed. Guests announced by toastmaster then pass down the receiving line and enter the room

6 The toastmaster should 'count' guests entering the room. This is a help to management for costing purposes

7 The wine waiters should be placed at strategic points in the reception area for the service of aperitifs or champagne to the guests as they move on from the 'receiving line'. These trays should be replenished with full, fresh glasses. No bottles handled. The wine waiters at the initial briefing should be allocated different sections of the room for service after the reception so as to ensure efficient service for all guests in the room

8 After the reception the buffet should be open for service. The turnover on the buffet should be quick and efficient so as to avoid any major delays which may cause congestion. The wine waiter at this stage should be going round serving drinks and topping up glasses. An important factor to note during the service of the food and drink is to ensure that there are always some members of staff circulating, keeping the tables clear of any dirty equipment. Ashtrays should be changed as and when necessary

9 At the agreed time the toastmaster should announce the cutting of the cake by the bride and bridegroom. Portions of the cake should then be passed around to all guests and champagne taken round by the wine waiters. When this has been done the toasts should commence, being announced by the toastmaster, who should have all the principal people concerned in a group by the wedding cake, or in a central position so they can be seen and heard by everyone present

10 After the toasts any remaining cake and tiers must be packed ready to be taken away by the host. The top tier is sometimes kept for a christening

11 The bride and bridegroom should then change. If required, food and champagne should be placed in the changing rooms. Here liaison is demanded between floor service housekeeping and banqueting staff to ensure that timing is correct as far as the movements of the bride and bridegroom are concerned

12 When the bride and bridegroom have left the reception the flowers should be packed up for the host to take away

Family line-up to greet guests at reception

I Toastmaster
   Entrance
   1 Bride's father
   2 Bride's mother
   3 Bridegroom's father

II Toastmaster
    Entrance
    1 Bride's father
    2 Bride's mother
    3 Bride

4	Bridegroom's mother		4	Bridegroom
5	Bride		5	Bridegroom's father
6	Bridegroom		6	Bridegroom's mother
7	Best man		7	Best man
8	Bridesmaid/Matron of honour		8	Bridesmaid/Matron of honour

Note: the best man sees that everyone gets away from the church and that no one is left. He therefore does not always arrive in time for the beginning of the reception

Procedure for toasts

Method A

1 Cutting of cake
2 Whilst it is being cut telegrams may be read out by best man
3 Pass cake and champagne for toasts
4 Toastmaster announces toast to bride and bridegroom, proposed by bride's father or near relation
5 Response of bridegroom. Proposes health to bridesmaids
6 Best man replies on behalf of bridesmaids
7 Any other toasts: close relative of bride or bridegroom

Method B

1 Pass champagne for toasts
2 Toastmaster announces toast to bride and bridegroom, proposed by bride's father or near relation
3 Response by bridegroom. Proposes health of bridesmaids
4 Best man replies on behalf of bridesmaids
5 Any other toasts: close relative of bride or bridegroom
6 Cutting of cake: reading of telegrams of congratulations by best man. Pass cake and more champagne

9.5 Outdoor catering (off premises catering)

The business of an outdoor catering firm should, as far as possible, continue throughout the year to ensure the plant (equipment provided for a particular function) and staff are used to the full. At each function carried out the organizer should aim to give a fully comprehensive sales service, covering not only meals and drinks but such things as confectionery, cigarettes and hot-dog kiosks. As in function catering the organization must be planned to the last detail and an initial survey should be exact and thorough. The following points should be included in the initial survey:

- Type of function

- Date

- Site and distance from depot

- Local transport

- Local commodity purchase

- Staff recruitment

- Layout of site

- Number of people expected to attend

- Availability of water, gas, electricity, drainage, refrigeration

- Spending power of people attending

- Kiosk and stand details

- Time allowance for setting up catering units and dismantling

- Type of licence: if required

- Mobile units adaptable to hot and cold food

- Lines of communication to ensure control of staff and continuous supplies

- Photographers

- Press

- Changing room and toilets

- Insurance against weather/fire

- First aid

- Cost of overheads on a particular site

- Type of service: find the one most suited to each particular catering operation
  - buffet style service may be preferred to restaurant service
  - provision of the take-away meal service in disposable containers
  - supply of some simple hot dishes: soup, fish and chips and so on
  - flexibility of drink service: hot or cold – according to weather

- Washing-up facilities

- Containers supplied for litter and disposable items

Each outdoor catering operation is different and varies to some extent in the main points that have to be noted during the initial survey. From the basic list shown above one appreciates the organization needed beforehand and some of the problems that may arise at the outset or during an operation. The person in charge needs to be decisive, quick-thinking, able to command, adaptable to varying situations and circumstances and, above all, needs to have the respect of the staff working under him/her.

The majority of staff employed at outdoor catering functions are either taken on as casual staff which may involve a lot of administration for the organisers and the scrutiny of staff must be very thorough to ensure the quality of the personnel.

The organization of outdoor catering functions must be very thorough as, once on site, it is often virtually impossible to rectify errors. Any items forgotten, or not packed on the transport, have to be gone without. This is to the detriment of the function, and could well result in the loss of 'repeat' business at a later date.

CHAPTER 10

SUPERVISORY ASPECTS OF FOOD AND BEVERAGE SERVICE

10.1	**Legal considerations**	354
10.2	**Food and beverage revenue control**	370
10.3	**Beverage control**	379
10.4	**Performance measures**	386
10.5	**Customer relations**	390
10.6	**Staff organization and training**	393
10.7	**Sales promotion**	403

10.1 Legal considerations

There are a wide variety of legal requirements for food and beverage operations. These range from company law to the licensing regulations or employment law. In a book of this kind which aims to provide a foundation in food and beverage service it is not possible to cover all legal aspects which affect food and beverage operations. We have, however, attempted to provide a summary of the principal legal requirements as they affect the relationship between the food and beverage operator and the customer.

Licensing

Licensed premises must, in order to sell alcoholic liquor, obtain what is called a *Justices Licence*. Licences are granted from 5 April each year. The Annual Licensing Meeting is held in the first fortnight of February, called the *Brewster Session*. In addition there must be held at least four, but no more than eight, licensing sessions at regular intervals throughout the year. These are called *Transfer Sessions*.

Licences are granted for the premises in whole or in part. Any alteration proposed must be agreed by the justices. The premises must be 'fit', ie meet the requirements of the local authority, police and fire authority.

Furthermore, *good order* must be maintained, ie:

- No drunkenness
- No violence
- No riotous conduct
- No prostitutes
- No gaming (justices may authorise certain games)

Licences are held for particular premises by a licensee, but may also be held jointly by two people.

The magistrates can revoke or refuse to grant licences for the following reasons:

- If the licensee or the applicant is not considered a fit and proper person
- If they feel that the premises are not used or intended to be used for the purpose stipulated in the licence
- If the premises are unsuitable due to the risk of fire
- If the customary main meals are not being habitually served (in the case of a Restaurant Licence)
- If the premises are being used mainly by unaccompanied persons who are under 18 years of age

Licensed premises generally may be classified according to the way in which they are controlled. There are two types:

1 *Free house*: a licensed premises that is privately owned and which has no attachment to any particular supply source
2 *Tied house*: tenanted or managed:
   (a) Tenanted: the tenant leases the property from the brewery and is tied to that brewery for the purpose of beer and perhaps other drinks. This is similar to a franchise operation. The tenancy agreement lays down the conditions of operation
   (b) Managed: the brewery owns the property and a manager is paid a salary to run the premises for the brewery

Full on-licence

The full on-licence allows the licensee to sell all types of alcoholic liquor for consumption on and off the premises. An '*on*' licence may be limited by the licensing justices as to the type of alcohol that may be sold, eg beer only.

Restricted on-licences

RESTAURANT LICENCE

This can be granted for premises which are structurally built or adapted and are used in a *bona fide* way or intended to be used for the habitual provisions of the main midday and/or the main evening meal.

The licence will authorize the sale or supply of intoxicants on the premises to people who take table meals there, but such liquor must be as an ancillary to the meal. In other words, customers must not frequent these establishments merely to drink.

For this purpose, the meal must be a *table meal*. This means it must be eaten by a person seated at a table, or a counter, or at some other structure which serves the purpose of a table. Another aspect is that drinks other than intoxicants must be available to the diners, should they require them.

There is no provision that the drinks must be taken at the table. A diner can buy a drink before or after a meal, even in another room, but it must be ancillary to that meal.

RESIDENTIAL LICENCE

This may be granted for premises used, or intended to be used, for the purpose of habitually providing (for reward) board and lodging, including breakfast and at least one of the other customary main meals. This could apply to a boarding house if it provided bed, breakfast and either lunch or an evening meal. Many private hotels easily fulfil this qualification.

A residential licence will authorize the sale or supply of alcoholic beverages on the premises to people residing there, or to their private friends, who are genuinely entertained by such guests at their own expense.

Under this licence the drinks can be sold or supplied at any time, because there are no licensing hours. Any abuse of such a licence could lead to its removal. It is normal for magistrates when granting this type of licence to make it a condition that there is at least one other room in which drinking is not allowed, and which can be used by children and those persons not wishing to drink alcohol.

COMBINED LICENCE

This is granted for premises which fulfil the conditions required both for a restaurant licence and a residential licence, eg a private hotel with a public dining room attached. Residents can enjoy the provision of intoxicants in their own bar, whilst the public can visit the premises for a meal in the dining room, at which intoxicants can be served. When granting a combined licence, the magistrates may impose a condition that the drinks are not supplied to the public in the dining room outside the normal permitted hours for the locality. This restriction would not of course apply to the residents.

The other conditions applying to the restaurant and residential licences also apply to the combined licence, ie other beverages must be available, there must be a sitting room for non-drinkers, and the meals must be table meals.

Licensed and registered clubs

LICENSED CLUB

Normally a licence to run a club which is operated by individuals or a limited company as a commercial enterprise and alcoholic drink is sold only to members.

REGISTERED CLUB

A licence to run a club, normally by committee members, and the members own the stock of liquor; a non-profit making organization.

Off-licences

A licence authorizing the sale of alcoholic liquor for consumption '*off*' the premises. Off-licences include specialist outlets, corner-shop grocers, supermarkets and 'cash and carries'.

Occasional licence

This licence is granted by magistrates to holders of 'on', restaurant or combined licences. It enables these licence holders to sell alcoholic beverages at another place for specified times, eg for outdoor catering work.

Occasional permission

This is a licence available from licensing justices for '*eligible organizations*' to sell intoxicating liquor. It is similar to an occasional licence but may be applied for by non-licence holders, eg a football club or for a specific fund raising activity.

Note: the definitions for all licences quoted above apply to England and Wales. In Scotland, the licensing pattern is similar although there are differences in the definitions and in restrictions in permitted hours. Licensing definitions in Northern Ireland are similar to those in England and Wales.

Permitted hours

Permitted hours are currently *:

Weekdays	11.00 to 23.00 hours (off-licences 08.00 to 22.30 or 23.00 including Good Friday)
Sundays and Good Friday	12.00 to 22.30 hours (off-licences may open from 10.00 on Sundays)
Christmas Day	12.00 to 15.00 hours and 19.00 to 22.30 hours (off-licences are the same)

The local magistrates may allow opening on weekdays from 10.00

* (as at August, 1997)

Within these hours, licensees can chose when and for how long they open their premises.

EXCEPTIONS TO PERMITTED HOURS

- The first 20 minutes after the end of permitted hours for consumption only

- The first 30 minutes after the end of permitted hours for those taking table meals. Again this is for consumption only

- Residents and their guests (as long as only the resident purchases the alcoholic beverages)

Note: permitted hours in Scotland are broadly similar to those above.

EXTENSIONS TO PERMITTED HOURS

Special order of exemption

This is an extension of the normal permitted hours of on-licensed premises for any special occasion, eg wedding, buffet dance, dinners and carnivals. Normally 'special occasions' do not continue for more than a few days, and the term does not cover such occasions as market days held on one day every week of the year. The duration of the extension is determined by the licensing authority and can only be determined by references to the order itself.

General order of exemption

This allows a licence to be exempted from the normal permitted hours during a certain day, or for a certain time. Such a notice must be displayed outside the premises for all to see. The effect of a general order of exemption is to extend the licensing hours to whatever time the licensing authority sees fit, either on one particular day, or several days, or generally throughout the week. The general order of exemption therefore is for the benefit of people who, for example, might attend a local market at times during which licensed premises would normally be closed, or for those following a particular trade which results in their working, and hence requiring refreshments, during hours when licensed premises would normally be closed. The licensing authority is not bound to grant a general order of exemption and need only do so at its discretion, and may at any time revoke or vary any order.

Supper hour certificate

This is a grant by the licensing justices, once they are satisfied that the premises are suitable, of an additional hour to the permitted hours in a licensed restaurant for the sale and consumption of alcoholic liquor with a table meal. This certificate also allows any other bars and dispensing bars to remain open for the additional hour after the end of the permitted hours. The half an hour drinking-up time in the licensed restaurant would still be allowed after the additional hour.

The effect, therefore, of a supper hour certificate is to extend the normal permitted hours in the evening. Such extensions only apply to those parts of the premises set aside for the service of table meals. A supper hour certificate may be withdrawn if the premises at any time cease to qualify within the laid down conditions, but otherwise it continues in force without need for renewal.

Special hours certificate

Where this certificate is in force the permitted hours in such licensed premises will be extended until:

West End of London	3.00 am with consumption until 3.30 am
Elsewhere	2.00 am with consumption until 2.30 am.

This certificate will only apply if the following conditions are fulfilled:

- The establishment itself is licensed

- A music and dancing licence has been obtained

- All, or any part, of the premises are structurally adapted and intended to be used for the purpose of providing 'live' music and dancing and substantial refreshment, to both of which the sale of liquor is ancillary

This certificate, if granted, will only apply to that part of the premises which qualifies as above. The premises must be such that they always provide, on a regular basis, the facilities indicated above. Therefore a special hours certificate will not be granted for one isolated special occasion, or for any area in which a music and dancing licence is not required. In the latter case the licensee must make do with an extended hour certificate.

A special hours certificate may be removed at any time if it appears that:

- The premises no longer possess a music and dancing licence

- The certificate has not been used

- The certificate is being used for the wrong purposes

- The premises have been conducted in a disorderly or unlawful manner

It is perhaps as well to note here that it is possible for different parts of the same licensed premises to be licensed in different ways. It is therefore possible to have a normal public bar closing at 11.00 pm, a licensed restaurant remaining open for the sale of liquor with meals until 12.00 midnight and a separate ballroom operation under a special hours certificate until 2.00 am.

Extended hours certificate

This extension is for the benefit of premises which qualify for a supper hour certificate and which also provide regular musical or other entertainment (live), together with the table meal. Here the sale of liquor is ancillary to both the table meal and the entertainment. The refreshment and entertainment must be provided in a part of the premises normally set aside for the purpose.

This certificate extends the permitted hours up to 1 am. The service of drink must cease when either the entertainment or service of table meals cease. The service of drink must finish in any case at 1 am. There is a *drinking up time* of 30 minutes allowed after the service of drink has ceased.

If granted the extended hours certificate may be limited to certain evenings in the week. The licensing justices have complete discretion as to whether or not they grant this certificate, and it may be revoked at any time if it appears that the premises no longer qualify or that the use of such a certificate has led to noisy and disorderly conduct.

It should be noted that the usual half-hour *drinking up time* allowed at the end of each period of permitted hours, during which drinks were purchased with table meals, is allowed at the end of any of the following if they are in force:

- General order of exemption
- Special order of exemption
- Supper hour certificate
- Special hours certificate
- Extended hours certificate

Late night refreshment houses

This licence is allowed for certain premises, which are open for public refreshment, resort and entertainment at any time between 22.00 and 05.00 hours the following morning.

Entertainment licences

These are not liquor licences. Generally licences are required for public music and dancing, although the law varies according to the particular place. These licences are granted by local councils but are not required for:

- Radio
- Television
- Recorded music
- Not more than two live performances

If dancing takes place, however, a licence is required. Music and dancing licences are not available for Sundays, if payment is to be required.

However care needs to be taken not to infringe copyright and permission by way of licences are usually required. Further information may be obtained from either the Performing Right Society or Phonographic Performance. Ltd.

Weights and measures

BEER OR CIDER

Unless sold in a prepacked container (quantity must be stated), beer and cider may only be sold in quantities of $\frac{1}{3}$ pint, $\frac{1}{2}$ pint or multiples of $\frac{1}{2}$ pint. It must be provided in a capacity measure (eg a lined glass) unless sold through a dispensing meter. The $\frac{1}{3}$ and $\frac{1}{2}$ pint measures do not apply to mixtures of two or more liquids, eg shandy or lager and lime.

SPIRITS

Since 1st January 1995 whisky, gin, vodka and rum must be sold in 25 mls *or* 35 mls or multiples thereof (measures of other spirits are usually based on these also). A notice must be displayed indicating the measure being used in the establishment. The restriction does not apply to the mixtures of three or more liquids, eg cocktails.

Figure 10.1 gives a guide to the number of measures that may be obtained from the various bottles.

Figure 10.1 *Examples of measure per bottle*

	BOTTLE SIZE	**METRIC MEASURE**
Spirits	75 cl	30 × 25 ml or 21 × 35 ml
Spirits	70 cl	28 × 25 ml or 20 × 35 ml
Spirits	65 cl	26 × 25 ml or 18 × 35 ml
Vermouths	75 cl	15 × 50 ml
Fortified wines	75 cl	15 × 50 ml
Liqueurs	varies according to bottle size but likely to be in measures of 25 ml or 35 ml	

WINES

There is no specific quantity if the wine is sold in sealed containers.

Open carafes, however, must be 25, 50 or 75 centilitres or 1 litre.

Wine by the glass must be sold in quantities of 125 millilitres and/or 175 millilitres or multiples of either quantity.

Young persons

It is an offence to knowingly, or now unknowingly, serve a person under 18 in a licensed bar. It is also an offence to allow persons under 18 to consume alcoholic beverages in a bar. Similarly, it is an offence for the person under 18 to attempt to purchase, or to purchase, or consume alcoholic beverages in a bar. The position regarding young persons is summarized in Figure 10.2.

Figure 10.2 Young persons and the law

AGE	PURCHASE IN A BAR	DRINK IN A BAR	ENTER A BAR	WORK IN A BAR	BUY IN A RESTAURANT	CONSUME IN A RESTAURANT
UNDER 14	No	No	No[1]	No	No	Yes[2]
UNDER 16	No	No	Yes	No	No	Yes[2]
UNDER 18	No	No	Yes	No	Yes[3]	Yes

[1] See note on childrens' certificate below
[2] As long as the alcholic beverage is bought by a person over 18
[3] Only beer, cider or perry
Note: tobacco should not be sold to persons under 16

CHILDRENS' CERTIFICATE

This Certificate allows, if the environment is suitable, for persons under 14 year of age to enter a bar as long as they are accompanied by an adult. The Certificate usually covers the period up to 21.00 hours but may be later. Meals and non-alcoholic drinks must be available during the hours when the Certificate is in force.

Contract

A contract is made when one party agrees to the terms of an offer made by another party. In food and beverage service there are essentially two types of customer: those who *pre-book* and those who do not (often called *chance* or *casual* customers).

For those who pre-book the offer is made by them, eg a requirement for a table of four at 1 pm. If the restaurant suggests an alternative, eg 'We do not have a table at 1 pm, but we have one at 1.30 pm', then the offer is made by the restaurant.

There is a requirement for a price list to be shown (see page 363). In operations where the customer may not have or is not required to pre-book (eg fast food operations) it is likely to be considered, in law, that the price lists constitutes an offer.

If customers fail to turn up on time, then the table need not be held. Similarly if the party is only two and not the four previously booked, then restaurants may seek compensation. Alternatively, if the food and drink is not as expected then the customer can refuse to pay but must provide proof of identity and their home address. Only if fraud is suspected may the police be involved, as fraud is a criminal offence.

However, contracts may be broken if one party is induced to enter into a contract by false statement, eg if promised a certain menu which is not available. In this case there is no obligation for the customer to continue with the contract. Also, if either party is unable to meet the terms of the original contract due to unforeseen circumstances, eg illness of customer, or the restaurant burning down, then the contract becomes *frustrated* as it cannot be fulfilled.

Care should be taken with *minors*: contracts cannot be made with persons under 18 unless it is for 'goods and services suitable to the minor needs and his station in life'.

Sale of goods and trades descriptions

The *Sale of Goods Act 1979* (as amended by the Sale and Supply of Goods Act 1994) applies to the sale of goods by description. It clarifies that there is an implicit contract when the caterer accepts the order of a customer.

According to the Act, the customer can refuse to pay or can demand replacement:

- If the goods supplied do not correspond with the description, eg roast chicken which is in fact poached and then quick grilled
- If a displayed item is not what it seems, eg a sweet trolley where the cream, which reasonably one would expect to be fresh, is in fact artificial. (It makes no difference if the customer has partly or entirely consumed the purchase)
- If it is inedible

The *Trades Description Acts 1968/1972* make it a criminal offence to misdescribe goods or services. Care must therefore be taken when:

- Wording menus and wine lists
- Describing menu and beverage items to customers
- Describing conditions, eg cover and service charges or extras
- Describing the service provision

A person charged under the Act will have to prove that reasonable precautions were taken to ensure that descriptions would not be misleading. However, the Act also provides that defence of a charge would be if the description was:

- The result of pure mistake
- The result of information from another person
- The fault of someone else
- The result of accident or other cause beyond the control of person concerned
- The person charged could not reasonably know the description was misleading

Discrimination

The *Sex Discrimination Act 1975* and the *Race Relations Act 1976* seek amongst other things to legislate against discrimination on grounds of colour, race, creed or sex. The Acts also define what *to discriminate* might mean. There must not be:

- *Direct discrimination*: eg refusing service to customers of particular colour, race, creed or sex
- *Indirect discrimination*: eg denying consumer services by the imposition of

unjustifiable conditions or requirements which have colour, race, creed or sex implications

- *Discrimination through victimization*: (a) eg refusal of provision: refusal of admission on basis of ethnic origins or sex; (b) eg omission of provision: providing services to ethnic customers that are markedly inferior to those available to the public in general or which may only be available at a price premium

Providing services

The food and beverage operator is under no specific requirement to serve anyone unless the food and beverage operation is within an establishment covered by the *Hotel Proprietors Act (HPA) 1956* and the customers seeking food and beverage service provision are resident in the hotel. Reasons for refusal to provide provision might be as follows:

- There is no space left on the premises
- The person is intoxicated
- The person is under the influence of drugs
- The person does not comply with the dress requirements of the operation
- The person is unable to pay admission charge
- The person is a known trouble-maker
- The person is an associate of a known trouble-maker
- The person is under legal minimim age for licensed premises or does not comply with an age policy set by local management

Under the *Licensed Premises (Exclusion of Certain Persons) Act 1980* an exclusion order can be made against a particular person. Under the *Licensing Act 1964*, the licensee has the right to refuse any person who is drunk, violent, quarrelsome or disorderly and the police may be brought in to assist. Under *HPA 1956*, innkeepers are relieved of the obligation to serve if the customer is not in a fit state or appears unable to pay. Additionally the *Licensing Act 1964* makes it an offence to sell intoxicating liquor to a drunken person or those under 18 years of age.

Price lists

Under the *Price Marking (Food and Drink on Premises) Order 1979*, prices of food and drink must be displayed in a clear and legible way by persons selling food by retail for consumption on the premises. However this does not apply:

- Where the supply is only to members of a bona fide club or their guests
- At staff restaurants or works canteens
- At guest houses where the supply is only to people staying there

Also excluded from the requirements are specially agreed menus at prices agreed in advance, eg in function catering.

The main provisions of the order are that:

- Prices must be displayed so as to be seen by customers before reaching the eating area. If access is from the street then the list must be at the entrance or be able to be read from the street. If this area is part of a complex then the list must be at the entrance to the eating area

- For self-service premises the list must be at the place where the customer chooses food and at the entrance unless it can otherwise be seen from there

- Both food and drink must be included

- Table d'hôte menu prices must be given

- VAT must be included and service and/or cover charge must be prominently shown as an amount or a percentage

There is no longer a requirement for alcoholic strength to be displayed on price lists, wine lists and menus.

Service, cover and minimum charges

Part III of the *Consumer Protection Act 1987* came into force on 1 March 1989. This part of the Act deals with misleading prices and amongst its provisions it states that it is an offence to give misleading price information and authorizes the issue of a Code of Practice. The 'Code of Practice for Traders on Price Indications' recommendations on service, cover and minimum charges in hotels, restaurants and similar establishments are that:

If your customer in hotels, restaurants or similar places must pay a non-optional extra charge, eg a 'service charge':

(i) incorporate the charge within fully inclusive prices wherever practicable, and

(ii) display the fact clearly on any price list or priced menu, whether displayed inside or outside (eg by using statements like 'all prices include service').

Do not suggest optional sums, whether for service or any other item, in the bill presented to the customer.

Cover charges and minimum charges should be 'shown as prominently as other prices on any list or menu, whether displayed inside or outside'.

While compliance with the Code is not obligatory, failure to do so can be relied on by a prosecutor as evidence that an offence has been committed. Copies of the Code are available from the Department of Trade and Industry.

Customer property and customer debt

There is liability for guests' property under the *Hotel Proprietors Act 1956* for those who have booked overnight accommodation. Other than this, establishments have no automatic liability for guests' property unless negligence can be proved by the customer. However, care should be taken by staff so as to minimize potential loss or damage. Notices warning guests of 'no responsibility' may help in defence but do not guarantee exemption from liability for the food and beverage operator.

If customers are unable to pay, no *right of lien* exists except in inns (the right to hold property against non-payment of an account, the *Hotel Proprietors Act 1956*). The only action for the food and beverages operator is civil proceedings unless the proprietor believes that fraud has been attempted in which case the police should be called in.

Health, safety and security

There is a common law duty to care for all lawful visitors. The Acts of which affect health and safety issues include the *Occupiers Liability Act 1957, the Health and Safety at Work Act 1974* and the *Fire Precaution Act 1971*, as well as the *Food Hygiene (General) Regulations 1970*, the *Food Act 1984* and the *Food Safety Act 1990* and the *Food Safety Regulation* 1995.

Essentially safety is a civil duty and negligence is a criminal offence. The implications for staff under the above legislation are that they should:

- Understand the food hygiene regulations and that it is their responsibility to act within the bounds of these regulations
- Notify management of any major illnesses
- Perform duties in any area concerned with the handling of food in a hygienic manner and keep within food and hygiene regulations
- Make themselves familiar with all escape routes and fire exits in the building
- Ensure that fire exits remain clear and unblocked in any way
- Participate in fire evacuation drills and practices
- Take reasonable care for the health and safety of themselves and of others, and ensure that health and safety regulations are followed
- Report to heads of department or duty managers any hazards which may cause injury or ill-health to customers and/or staff
- Not interfere with or misuse anything provided in the interests of health, safety and welfare
- Co-operate with employers in order to carry out duties within the context of the Acts

Maintaining a safe environment

One of your responsibilities to yourself, your work colleagues and the customer is to be aware of 'hazards' that may arise due to either you or others not taking enough care when carrying out your various tasks as required in the work environment.

Should an accident occur you should immediately call a qualified first aider and until this assistance reaches you remain calm giving any help that you can, eg keeping the patient warm.

A detailed record should be kept of all accidents, however minor they may initially appear. Those involved, including witnesses, should sign the 'accident book' to show they agree with the report made out.

Many accidents occur through carelessness or through lack of thought, eg:

- Not having the correct protective clothing such as an apron
- Not wearing sensible shoes
- Delay in clearing spillages or picking up items of equipment that have fallen on the floor
- Not being aware of customer's bags placed on the floor
- Items of equipment not stored correctly
- Broken glass or china not wrapped up sufficiently before being placed in the bin
- Forgetting to unplug electrical appliances prior to cleaning
- Putting ashtray debris into rubbish bins containing paper (a fire hazard)
- Forgetting to switch off and unplug an appliance after use, or at the end of the 'service'
- Not being observant with tablelamps or lit candles on a buffet
- Overfilling coffee pots, soup tureens, glasses and the like
- Using cups, glasses, soup bowls, etc, for storing cleaning agents
- Stacking trays incorrectly
- Trays carrying a mix of equipment, such as tableware, china and glass
- Carpet edges turned up
- Faulty wheels on trolleys or castors on sideboards
- Being unaware of customers' walking sticks and crutches
- Lack of adequate space for the 'safe' service of food and drink due to bad planning
- Lack of knowledge in carrying out certain tasks, ie opening a bottle of sparkling wine

You *must* consider your work method and sequence of events in everything that you do – for the safety of all.

Procedure in the event of an accident

All employers should have provision to provide first aid should such a need arise, so in the event of an accident your first course of action should be to acquire the service of trained first aid staff.

If you are treating the casualty yourself do not move them unless absolutely necessary and if the accident has been caused by electric shock switch the mains supply off before touching them

Under the *Health and Safety at Work Act* employers must keep a record of all accidents that occur in the work place.

If you are involved in or witness an accident you will be required to give information or complete an accident form.

For this reason it is wise to make notes on the event at your earliest convenience. The information should include

- time of accident
- location of accident
- witnesses
- a statement of the event
- treatment administered

Procedure in case of fire

As an employee you should be given 'fire drill' training within your induction programme. This should be followed up by regular training sessions related to procedure to be taken in the event of fire. This training should include:

- Fire procedures in your own specific area of work
- An awareness of 'fire drill' instructions as applicable to both customers and staff
- A knowledge of where the nearest 'fire points' are to your particular area of work
- An indication of where the fire exits are located
- A knowledge of the appropriate assembly point to your area of work
- A knowledge of the correct type of fire extinguisher to be used in relation to the type of fire. See chart in Figure 10.3 on page 368
- An indication of your own specific responsibilities in the event of fire.

Note: in the event of the fire alarm ringing you should:

1 Follow the fire instructions as laid down for your establishment
2 Usher all customers and staff out of your work area promptly and quickly
3 Pay special attention to those customers with special needs such as mobility problems
4 Walk quickly but do not run. Display a sense of urgency
5 Remain calm and do not panic as your composure and lead will be followed by others
6 Proceed as promptly as possible to the nearest assembly point
7 Ensure that someone watches to see that there are no stragglers
8 Follow the exit route as laid down in your fire instructions. Never use a lift
9 Never re-enter the building until told it is safe to do so
10 Do not waste time to collect personal items

As an employee it is your responsibility to assist in fire prevention, control and safety. You must therefore be aware of the following:

- To ensure that fire exits are not obstructed

- That fire-fighting equipment is not damaged or mis-used

- That 'no smoking' rules are observed at all times

- As far as is possible to switch off all electrical and gas equipment

- To close all doors and windows not being used for evacuation purposes

- Never wedge open or keep locked your fire doors

- Ensure that sufficient ashtrays/stands are available for the disposal of cigarette ends and used matches

- To know the procedure for making an emergency fire call

Figure 10.3 Fire extinguishers and their uses

Contents	WATER	FOAM	CO$_2$	DRY POWDER	HALON
Colour	Red	Cream (yellow)	Black	Blue	Green
Electrical suitability	Danger electrically conductive		Safe non-electrical conductive		
Suitable for	Solids	some liquids	electrical	liquid	liquid
Unsuitable for	oil	electrical	solids	very little	solids

Maintaining a secure environment

Depending upon the nature of the establishment in which you work the security measures laid down may vary considerably. As an employee you should be aware of all such measures as they relate to you in your own work environment. You should therefore give consideration to the following aspects of security:

- The need to wear some form of recognized identity badge

- To be observant and report 'suspicious' persons and/or packages

- Not to discuss your duties to your customers outside of the workplace
- To allow all bags and packages to be searched upon request when either entering or leaving the workplace
- To be aware of the security procedures to be searched upon request when either entering or leaving the workplace
- To be aware of the security procedures for your establishment should sudden and urgent action have to be taken
- Ensure external fire doors are kept shut and not left ajar in error
- Should you be responsible for 'locking up' duties then ensure all areas have been vacated. Check all toilets/cloakrooms very carefully
- At the same time check all windows and doors as appropriate have been locked
- Keys should only be handled by someone in authority. A signing out book should be available when staff request keys
- At no time should keys be left unattended
- When handling cash, check all large denomination notes most carefully as well as all cheque and credit card payments. The purpose being to prevent fraud, the passing of illegal notes and acceptance of altered credit cards
- Be alert and observant at all times and do not hesitate to report anything suspicious to your immediate superior

Dealing with a suspicious item or package

All employees should be constantly alert for suspicious items or packages, otherwise lives may be put at risk:

- Should you find such an object then you must immediately alert your security officer, manager or supervisor
- Do not touch or attempt to move the object
- If there are customers in the immediate vicinity, you may discreetly attempt to establish ownership of the object
- Should you be successful, ask the customer to keep the 'object' with them, or to hand it in for safe keeping
- If no immediate ownership is established, then the area should be cleared, and
- The appropriate authorities notified without delay

Dealing with a bomb threat

Immediate action needs to be taken as a bomb could go off at any moment. As a result staff should:

- Be aware of and follow establishment policy with regard to bomb threats and evacuation procedures
- Evacuate your immediate work area
- Search your work area should this be your responsibility
- Evacuate the premises and usher all guests/staff through appropriate exits to specified assembly areas. A count should be taken of all persons to determine their safety and minimize the risk of fatal accidents.

10.2 Food and beverage revenue control

A control system covering the sale of all food and beverages in a catering establishment is essential to achieve maximum returns. The type of control system used varies from one operation to another. How this is carried out depends on management and the degree of training and instruction that is given to staff on the job. In a large establishment a control and accounts department would be in overall charge of the efficient running and working of the control systems used. In a smaller establishment this may be taken over by an assistant manager, who would personally carry out the daily and weekly checks that were necessary. All control systems should be as simple as possible, making it easier for the food and beverage service staff to operate and for the control and accounts department staff to check for any errors and omissions and to have them rectified.

Function of a revenue control system

A control system essentially monitors areas where selling takes place:

- There must be efficient control of all items issued from the various departments
- The system should reduce any pilfering and wastage to a minimum
- Management should be provided with any information they require for costing purposes, so that they may estimate accurately for the coming financial period
- The cashier should be able to make out the customer's bill correctly so that the customer is neither overcharged nor undercharged
- The system should show a breakdown of sales and income received in order that adjustments and improvements may be made

The main control methods in use in catering establishments are:

- Triplicate and duplicate checking methods (see Section 5.6, page 195)

- Sales analysis sheets

- Operational statistics (see Section 10.4, page 386)

The process of food and beverage revenue control through checking methods is summarized in the chart given in Figure 10.4. This chart is based upon the triplicate method for food and the duplicate method for the dispense bar. The chart indicates that all top copies go to the dispense points (bar, kitchen) and follows the flow of information through until top and second copies are matched up by control.

The cashier

Before the start of service the cashier should have made all relevant checks and have the required materials to hand.

Each establishment will have its own procedure but the following checks will generally apply:

- check float: if it is incorrect follow the company procedure

- is the cash drawer properly organised with notes and coins in the relevant compartments?

- do you have enough credit card vouchers, till rolls, promotional items, bill folds stapler or paper clips and pens?

On receiving the duplicate copy of the food check from the waiter/waitress, the cashier opens a bill in duplicate according to the table number on the food check. All the sets of bills are serial numbered for control purposes. As checks are received by the cashier from the food or wine waiter, he/she enters the items ordered on to the bill together with the correct prices. When this is done the bill and duplicate checks are pinned together and may be placed into a special book or file which has its pages numbered according to the number of tables in the room. The bill and duplicate checks are placed in the page corresponding to the table number. As further checks are received the items are entered on to the bill and the checks then pinned with the others to the bill.

Figure 10.4 Flow chart of food and beverage checks

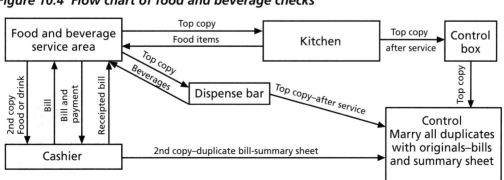

When the guest requests the bill the waiter must collect it from the cashier who must first check that all items are entered and priced correctly and then total it up. It is advisable for the waiter to double check the addition. The top copy of the bill is presented to the guest on a sideplate and folded in half with one corner turned up. On receiving the necessary payment from the guest the waiter returns the bill and payment to the cashier who will receipt both copies of the bill and return the receipted top copy plus any change to the waiter. The latter then returns this to the guest. The receipted duplicate copy with the duplicate checks pinned to it is then removed from the special book or file and put on one side until service is completed.

At the conclusion of service all the items from all the bills are entered on to a cashier's summary sheet. This shows an analysis of all cash taken and must be balanced by the cashier before going off duty. Once it is balanced it should be handed to the control and accounts department, together with all the duplicate bills and their checks, and the money received through the service plus the float. A receipt must be obtained for the monies handed in.

Where services are provided to residents in the lounges and on the floors, cash does not always change hands for the service rendered and therefore all checks written out must be signed by the resident concerned to show he/she has received a particular service. These checks should then be immediately passed on to the control and accounts department. It is their job to co-ordinate and marry up all checks, bills and money coming in via the various service departments. In this way all residents' bills are up to date and all services provided are charged for. When a resident signs a check for a service rendered the waiter must ensure the correct room number is placed on the check so that the charge can be made on the right bill.

Figure 10.5 Example of a bill

(Name of Establishment)		
Serial No.057531		
Table No. 4	Date 2.2.98	
2 Couvert @ £12·00		24·00
2 Café @ 90		1·80
Wines – 1 × 16 @ 11·00		11·00
Spirits –		
Liquers – 2 Tia Marias @ 1·80		3·60
Beers and Minerals –		
057531		
	Total	40·40

The cashier's duties for table and assisted service may be summarized as follows:

- Issuing and recording of check books
- Counter-signing spoilt checks
- Receiving all unused checks
- Maintaining of cash floats
- Preparation of bills
- Receiving of cash (which may include credit card and cheque payments as well as luncheon vouchers or other forms of prepaid voucher)
- Making up sales summaries
- Banking of cash

Note: 1 Alternatively, payment may be taken by individual servers.

2 Cashiers on cafeteria check-outs may have similar duties but excluding tasks regarding checks.

Methods of payment

There are various means of making payment for goods or services received, some of which have already been indicated under Billing Methods (see page 232). The following are the main methods of payment:

Cash

The amount of cash received by the operator should always be checked in front of the customer and when change is given it should be counted back to the client. The change should always be accompanied by an itemized and receipted bill.

Any 'notes' received by the operator should always be checked to ensure they are not forgeries.

Cheque

Payment by cheque should always be accompanied by a cheque card. The operator receiving the cheque should check the following points – that the cheque is:

- Dated correctly
- Made payable to the correct firm or company
- Filled in with the correct amount
- Signed by the person indicated on the cheque
- The signature is the same as that on the cheque card
- The bank code is the same as on the cheque card

The operator should also check that the cheque card is valid – it has not expired in relation to the dates indicated.

Cheque guarantee card

This indicates that the bank concerned will meet the cheque payment. This will be the case even if the person writing the cheque has insufficient monies in his/her account.

It should be noted that some credit and debit cards also pass as cheque guarantee cards. An example of this would be Barclaycard.

Credit cards

On receipt of a credit card the operator should check that it is still valid. A voucher is then made out and the appropriate details filled in. The customer is then requested to sign the voucher after which the operator should check the signature with that on the credit card. The customer receives a copy of the voucher as a receipt.

In certain instances the validity of the credit card is checked by passing it through an electronic machine, after which the details of the transaction are printed in the form of an itemized bill which the customer then signs. A copy of this itemized bill is then given as a receipt.

Debit cards

This is used in a similar way to a credit card which results in the amount due being immediately deducted from the customer's bank account. Examples here are the Switch and Connect cards.

Charge cards

Here the customer is normally invoiced once a month for all services rendered during that month. The account must then be paid up in total and no credit is allowed. Examples here are the American Express and Diners Club cards. Payment by either debit or charge cards is similar to that by credit card.

Traveller's cheques

These may be issued by either your travel agent or bank in the traveller's own country. They may be issued in sterling, US dollars and many other currencies, this being determined by the rate of exchange.

The traveller's cheque must be signed once when issued and again when used to pay for something or when exchanging for cash. Your rate of exchange will be that at the time of the transaction.

All traveller's cheques come in different values and this value is guaranteed as long as the two signatures match.

When a payment is made by traveller's cheque the customer must:

● Be asked to date the cheque or cheques required

- Make them payable to the establishment concerned
- Sign the cheque or cheques for a second time in the appropriate place

The cashier will then:

- Match the two signatures
- Ask for other identification to check the two signatures against. Such identification might be the customer's passport
- Give change where needed in the currency of the traveller's cheque

Eurocheques

These are cheques issued by banks for use in other countries. When used for payment they should be accompanied by a cheque guarantee card. The method of payment is then as for a normal cheque.

Vouchers and tokens

Vouchers, such as Luncheon Vouchers, may be offered in exchange for food in those establishments accepting such vouchers. These vouchers have an expiry date. Should food be purchased over the value of the voucher, the difference would be paid for in cash.

Tokens might be exchanged for specific meals or for certain values. If food purchased is more than the value of the token then the difference is again paid in cash. No change can be given for purchases valued at less than the token being exchanged.

Dealing with discrepancies

Prevention is better than cure! So when dealing with cash do not allow anyone to interrupt you while dealing with a transaction or to get involved with the counting of money. This will only serve to confuse things.

- Always double check cash received before placing it in the till and change before giving it out.
- If you make a mistake always apologise and remain polite. If you feel you cannot deal with a situation gain the assistance of your supervisor or manager.
- Notes should be checked for forgeries and if they are found to be fake they must not be accepted. You should explain why you cannot accept them, advising the guest to take the note to the police station.
- If credit card fraud is suspected the card should be retained at the request of the card company and suggest to the guest that they contact the company to discuss the matter. You may wish to offer the use of a telephone with some privacy.

Sales summaries

Sales summaries are sometimes also called *restaurant analysis sheets*, *bill summaries*, or *records of restaurant sales*. They provide for:

- The reconcilation of items with different gross profits
- Sales mix information
- Records of popular/unpopular items
- Records for stock control

The basic information required includes:

- Date
- Food and beverage outlet (if more than one)
- Period of service
- Bill number
- Table number
- Number of cover per table
- Bill total
- Analysis of eg food, beverages, tobacco or more detailed, eg per menu and wine and drink list items
- Cashier's name

It could also include individual staff or till breakdown. An example of a sales summary is given in Figure 10.6.

Figure 10.6 Example of a cashier's summary sheet

BILL No	TABLE No	No. OF COVERS	ROOM No	AMOUNT PAID	CREDIT	KITCHEN	BEVERAGE COFFEE	WINES	LIQUEURS	BEERS AND MINERALS	CIGARS AND CIGARETTES	FLOWERS	EXTRAS	SUNDRIES	TOTAL
0631	6	3	64		48·25	22·00	1·20	21·20	1·35		2·50				48·25
0632	10	2		38·16		22·40	1·30	11·00	2·10		1·36				38·16
Total				38·16	48·25	44·40	2·50	32·20	3·45		3·86				86·41

£ 86·41

LUNCHEON SERVICE   DATE 21/1/98

All bills to be entered in numerical order according to the serial numbers.

Consumption control

In food and beverage service areas there may be displayed:

- Cold tables
- Carving trolleys
- Sweet trolleys
- Liqueur trolleys
- Buffets
- Food and beverage counters

For these services a consumption control method is used which identifies the number of portions/measures, etc, issued to the area. Following service, returns are deducted. This equals the consumption. The consumption is then checked with actual sales to identify shortages/surpluses.

This method of control is also found in room and lounge service.

Figure 10.7 Example of a consumption sheet

Date:			Consumption Control Service: Luncheon			
Item	Portions issued	Portions returned	Portions consumed	Billed portions	Discrepancy +	−
Fruit Salad	24	6	18	15		3
Gateau	20	5	15	14		1
Flan	30	10	20	16		4
Etc						

Electronic point of sale control (EPOS)

The inducement on today's caterers is to purchase an electronic cash register (ECR) system which can provide a more efficient service at the point of sale itself, as well as improving the flow and quality of information to management for control purposes. Broadly speaking the advantages will vary from one system to another, but may be as follows:

- There are *fewer errors* in entering sales information. In all but the simplest of ECRs, mistakes in the sequence of entries required for a particular transaction are not permitted, and where an automatic 'price look-up' or pre-set key is used this avoids the possibility of error by the assistant in keying in the price and other details

- Transactions may be *processed faster*. This may be achieved by:
  a) The automatic reading of price-tags using a hand-held wand
  b) Single key entry of prices
  c) Eliminating any manual calculation or hand-writing by the assistant

  Therefore the ECR can handle more transactions than the equivalent older electro-mechanical equipment and also raises the productivity of the staff

- *Training time* may be reduced from days on the conventional register to hours on the ECR. This is because many ECRs have a sequencing feature which takes the user through each transaction step by step. This is often achieved by lighting up the instruction for the next entry on a panel display

- *Instant credit checking*: a customer's rating can be obtained by having the ECR compare the account number with a central computer file

- *More detailed information* may be provided for management. ECRs provide more information in a computer-readable form directly. This should improve both the detail and quality of computerized stock control and accounting systems, and make them more economic for relatively small establishments

- Most ECR systems have *additional security features*. These include such things as:
  - Locks which permit the ECR to be operated only by authorized personnel, and totals etc to be altered and reset only by supervisors and managers
  - Not disclosing at the end of the day the sum of money that should be in the cash drawer until the assistant has entered the amount actually in it

- *Advanced calculating facilities*: most ECRs can be programmed to calculate the total price when a number of items of the same price are purchased, there are a number of items at various prices, or if VAT has to be added. If required the ECR can be switched to a so-called calculator mode and used by management as an electronic calculator to assist with accounts

- The ECR gives *improved print out* compared with the electro-mechanical equipment:
  - The quality and the amount of information contained on the customer's receipt may be improved quite considerably
  - Receipts may be overprinted with sales and VAT
  - Both alphabetic and numeric information can be presented in one or two colours
  - The receipt can contain an alphabetic record of the goods purchased as well as, or instead of, a simple reference number

- ECR's have a much *improved appearance* and styling to fit into present day modern catering environment

The ECR equipment available falls roughly into six categories:

- Cash tills, eg for bars
- ECRs similar to older electro-mechanical machines with a few additional features such as a calculator option and more totals but no data-capture facilities

- ECRs which, in addition to the above, have storage facilities that record information on all items purchased, cash taken in different categories and so on, all for subsequent processing

- For larger establishments there are units available which work on their own in separate food and beverage outlets but which transmit all the information entered over a link to a central billing area

- More sophisticated systems are those in which all the cash registers within the establishment work with, and are controlled by, a central computer

- Finally, there are those systems suitable for a large chain in which the cash registers in the individual outlets either are under the continuous control of the group's central computer at its head office, or, at regular intervals, transmit the information they have collected to the central computer and receive back instructions from head office such as changes in price levels

From this brief insight into ECR systems one is able to appreciate their value in all facets of control over both cash and materials and can see how they allow for accurate planning and forecasting for the future. Individual caterers will need to determine which system of control best suits their needs and gives them the information they require.

10.3 Beverage control

The system of beverage control is basically the same as for food. The sales mix is easier to determine than with a regular menu, as the number of bottles of spirit consumed compared with gallons of beer is readily available without a special effort being made to record items sold.

Administration
Stocktaking

It is essential that a physical alcoholic beverage stock be taken at least on a monthly basis, and more if it is felt necessary. To enable a result to be achieved records need to be kept.

GOODS RECEIVED BOOK
All deliveries should be recorded in full detail in the *goods received book*. Each delivery entry should show basically, the following:

- Name and address of supplier
- Delivery note/invoice number
- Order number
- List of items delivered
- Item price

- Quantity
- Unit
- Total price
- Date of delivery
- Discounts if applicable

You may also record here or in a separate *returnable containers book* the amount and deposit cost of all containers such as kegs, casks and the number of CO2 cylinders delivered.

ULLAGE, ALLOWANCE, OFF-SALES BOOK

One must ensure that each sales point has a suitable book for recording the amount of beer wasted in cleaning the pipes, broken bottles, measures spilt, or anything that needs a credit.

Either in the same book or in a separate one, the *off-sales book*, must be recorded the number of bottles, whether beer or spirits, sold at off-sales prices and the difference in price. This difference will be allowed against the gross profit.

A pre-determined amount should be allocated per member of staff, per day, times the number of working days in the week to give a *weekly beverage allowance cost* figure for staff.

GROSS PROFIT

Gross profit is determined by deducting the *beverage cost* from the *sales*. The proportion of beer to spirits consumed will sometimes help explain why a certain month's gross profit is low (a lot of beer sold) or high (more spirits have been sold).

The mark-up on spirits should give at least 60 per cent gross profit, whereas on beer it is difficult to realize 50 per cent gross profit. There are, however, other reasons for a high or low gross profit. This is an area where the Food and Beverage Manager needs to be forever vigilant as it is here that most can be done to upset one's forecasting, planning and profit margins.

A number of points to look out for may be as follows:

- *Underringing* and keeping the difference, eg by ringing perhaps 0.50 instead of 1.50, whereby the bar loses a £1. The cash register should be sited so that both the customer and the management are able to check visually the amount rung up

- *Too many 'No sales'* on the till roll may give a clue to shortages. It is not always possible to prohibit the use of the 'No sale' key altogether. Therefore the till roll should be examined each time it is removed. Then excessive use of the 'No sale' key may be queried at the time.

  The *till roll* itself can be very revealing. It is sometimes found that there are a lot of very small sales recorded, or that the average sale is lower than usual, or lower with one operator than with another. Such indications should put you on your guard.

  The *efficient manager* will count the money first and then read the till rather than read the till first and then ask for the money, which is often done by the inexperienced manager. In busy bars it is good practice to collect most of the cash before the end of a session, leaving a temporary receipt in the drawer

- Working with the *drawer open*, if the till is not set on 'closed drawer' giving change without ringing the amount up

- Never let *bar staff cash up* as this may throw suspicion on everyone if there is cause for concern

- All *off-sales* should be kept apart from the bar where measures are sold, and a separate stock used. All off-sales should be entered into a separate book. The difference between tot prices and off-sales prices will be needed by the stocktaker

- *Lounge sales* or sales at a table away from the bar may also be vulnerable. The till ticket provides one simple method of control. If each waiter or waitress is provided with a float and has to pay for drinks at the time of collecting, then he/she can have a ticket to present to the customer. The customer then knows that the money has gone into the till, and this gives the customer confidence in the establishment.

  The other advantage is that, unless there is collusion, the barstaff will not overcharge the waiter or underring the transaction. Even though this is a simple method of control it is still open to abuse. Staff have been known to use the same chit twice, but only if they are able to get drinks without paying for them

- The introduction of more recently developed *electronic equipment* may help to reveal that losses have taken place, but it will not in itself prevent them. Most of this electronic equipment is designed primarily to facilitate the analysis and recording of sales. Such equipment may, for example, provide automatic pricing for up to 1,000 items, such as a half-pint and pint of beer, whisky, gin, gin and tonic, and thereby greatly reduce the likelihood of miscalculation and make underringing easier to detect

TRANSFER BOOK

With multi-bar units one must minimize the movement of stock between bars otherwise you will end up short. If this does happen then you must make sure a record is kept in a *transfer book.*

CELLAR STOCK LEDGER

The *cellar stock ledger* is an essential part of beverage control and may be used as either an extension of, or in place of the goods received book. It therefore shows movement of all stock into the establishment and issues out to the bars or dispensing points. All movements of stock *in and out* of the cellar is often shown at cost and selling price.

BIN CARDS

If *bin cards* are to be used they must show the physical stock of each item held in the cellar. Therefore the movement of all stock 'in and out' of the cellar should be recorded on each appropriate bin card. The bin cards are often used to show what is termed the *maximum stock* and *minimum stock.*

The minimum stock determines the reordering level, leaving sufficient stock in hand to carry over until the new delivery arrives. The maximum stock indicates how much to reorder and is determined by such considerations as storage space available, turnover of a particular item, and to some extent by the amount of cash available within one's budget.

REQUISITION

Each unit dispensing alcoholic beverages should use some form of *requisition* to draw items from the cellar. These requisitions may be controlled either by colour or serial number, and are normally in duplicate or triplicate. The copies are sent as follows.

- Top copy to the cellar
- Duplicate to the beverage control department
- Triplicate would be used by each unit to check its goods received from the cellar

Information listed on the requisition would be:

- Name of the dispensing unit
- Date
- List of items required
- Quantity and unit of each item required
- Signature of the authorized person to both order and receive the goods

The purpose of the requisition is to control the movement of items from the cellar into the dispensing unit and to avoid too much stock being taken at one time, thus overstocking the bar. The level of stock held in the bar is known as *par* stock. The amount ordered on the requisition, each day, should bring your stock back up to par. The amount to reorder is determined simply by taking account of the following equation: *opening stock plus additions* (requisition) *less closing stock equals consumption* (the amount to reorder, each item to the nearest whole unit).

OVERAGE – SHORTAGE

An analysis of alcoholic beverage sales and stock held allows one to gain two important pieces of information. Firstly, the *gross profit* and, secondly, the *overage* or *shortage* of the estimated monetary revenue and stock in hand. The gross profit is determined by finding the difference between revenue and the cost of the alcoholic beverage consumed.

To determine the overage or shortage it is necessary to estimate how much money one should have taken during a given period of time, based on the consumption at selling price. The consumption must be priced out bottle by bottle, keg by keg.

For example, a bar has sold 12 bottles of whisky (which sells at £2.20 per 25 ml tot), 6 bottles of sherry (at £1.70 per 50 ml tot) and 5 kegs (9 gallons each) (selling at £2.00 per pint):

Whisky: $12 \times 30 \times £2.20 = £792.00$
Sherry: $6 \times 15 \times £1.70 = £153.00$
Kegs: $5 \times 72 \times £2.00 = \underline{£720.00}$

Note: 9 gallons $\times$ 8 pints = 72 pints

Estimated takings   = £1665.00
Actual cash takings   = £1683.26
Surplus   £   18.26

£18.26 is 1.69% of estimated takings

Goods ordered, received and issued from the cellar

When any alcoholic or non-alcoholic drinks need to be purchased for an establishment to keep up the level of stock, this is done by the cellarperson. The cellarperson's order should be written in duplicate on an official order form. The top copy is then sent to the supplier and the duplicate remains in the order book for control purposes when the goods are delivered. In some instances there may be three copies of the order sheet. If so they are distributed as follows:

- Top copy: supplier
- Duplicate copy: control and accounts department
- Third copy: remains in the order book

When the goods are delivered to an establishment they should be accompanied by either a delivery note or an invoice. Whichever document it may be, the information contained thereon should be exactly the same, with one exception: *invoices* show the price of all goods delivered whereas *delivery notes* do not. The goods delivered must first of all be counted and checked against the delivery note to ensure that all the goods listed have been delivered. An extra check may be carried out by the cellarperson by checking the delivery note against the copy of the order remaining in the order book. This is to ensure that the items ordered have been sent and in the correct quantities and that extra items have not been sent which were not listed on the order sheet, thereby incurring extra cost without immediately realizing it. At this stage all information concerning the goods delivered must be entered in the necessary books for control purposes.

No drinks should be issued by the cellarperson unless he/she receives an official requisition form, correctly filled in, dated and signed by a responsible person from the department concerned. The cellarperson should have a list of such signatures and ought not to issue anything unless the requisition sheet is signed by the appropriate person on the list. In order to aid the cellarperson, all requisitions should be handed into him/her at a set time each day, when all issues will be made. In certain instances, however, depending on the organization of an establishment, it may be necessary to issue twice per day, once before opening time in the morning and again before opening time in the evening. All requisition sheets are written in duplicate. The top copy going to the cellar for the items required to be issued, and the duplicate to remain in the requisition book for the barstaff to check their drink on receipt from the cellar.

Figure 10.8 Summary of basic steps in bar and cellar control

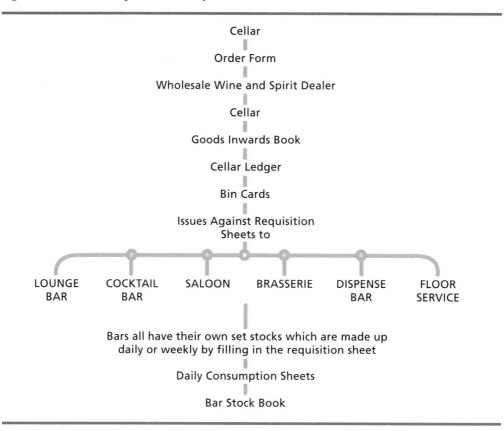

Cellar

Order Form

Wholesale Wine and Spirit Dealer

Cellar

Goods Inwards Book

Cellar Ledger

Bin Cards

Issues Against Requisition
Sheets to

| LOUNGE BAR | COCKTAIL BAR | SALOON | BRASSERIE | DISPENSE BAR | FLOOR SERVICE |

Bars all have their own set stocks which are made up
daily or weekly by filling in the requisition sheet

Daily Consumption Sheets

Bar Stock Book

Cellar control

In any catering establishment where a large percentage of the income received is through the sale of drink, a system of cellar control and costing must be put into operation. The system used depends entirely on the policy of each establishment. Some or all of the books listed below may be necessary depending upon the requirements of management:

- Order book
- Goods inward book
- Cellar ledger
- Bin cards
- Goods returned book
- Stock book
- Departmental requisition book
- Daily consumption sheets

The cellar is the focal point for the storage of alcoholic and non-alcoholic liquor in an establishment. All the service points for such liquor, such as the lounge, lounge bar, cocktail bar, saloon bar, brasserie, dispense bars and floor service should draw their stock on a daily or weekly basis from the cellar, this being determined largely by the amount of storage space available and the turnover of sales. All the bars within an establishment hold a set stock of liquor which is sufficient for a period of one day or one week. At the end of this period they requisition for the amount of drink consumed in that one day or week, thus bringing their total stock up to the set stock required. This is known as a *par* stock, ie bringing one's stock up to a particular set level, which is determined by turnover.

In the cellar where bin cards are used, every time a wine is received or issued it must be entered on the appropriate bin card and the remaining total balance shown. Thus the bin cards should show at any given time the total amount of each particular wine held in stock. They also show where applicable a maximum and minimum stock – this being a guide to the cellarperson when ordering and dependent on the storage space available.

Figure 10.9 Bin card

Name of Wine		BIN No.	
Date	Received	Balance	Issued

Figure 10.10 Daily consumption sheet

Name of drink	BIN no.	Mon.	Tues.	Wed.	Thurs.	Frid.	Sat.	Sun.	Total

Figure 10.11 Stock book

Name of drink	BIN no.	Opening stock	Received	Total	Closing stock	Consumption	Price per unit	£

In the dispense bar, as all drink is checked for before issue, a daily consumption sheet is completed each day after the service by copying down the sales shown on the top copy of the wine checks. The consumption sheet will list the complete stock held in the dispense bar.

Bin cards may also be completed for checking the wines. At the end of the week the consumption sheets may be totalled up, thereby showing the total sales for that period. These totals may then be transferred on to a bar stock book for costing purposes. Where drink consumed is not checked for in any way then either a daily or weekly stock is taken so that the amount to be requisitioned from the cellar may be noted. This then brings the bar stock back up to its required level, which is the par stock. The daily or weekly consumption (sales) would then be costed and the cash total for sales arrived at would be related to the daily or weekly income. That is cash in the till.

10.4 Performance measures

In Figure 1.5 (page 8) a variety of performance measures or operating statistics are identified. This section provides information on these various measures (also see 'Level of Demand', page 394).

Sales mix

Sales mix figures may be taken from a sales summary sheet (see Figure 10.6, page 376) and shown in a simple report, as in Figure 10.12 or 10.13.

Food and drink sales may be broken down further to provide *sales mix* data. This not only reconciles sales of items with differing gross profits but also provides information on:

- Popular/unpopular items on the menu/drinks lists
- Records for stock control, eg helping predict future demand
- Changes in customers' interests
- Where profits/losses are being made

Figure 10.12 Simple sales report

SERVICE	TOTAL £	FOOD £	LIQUOR £
LUNCHES	90	60	30
DINNERS	80	50	30
SNACKS	15	15	—
DAILY TOTAL	185	125	60

Figure 10.13 Application of percentages

SERVICE	TOTAL £	%	FOOD £	%	LIQUOR £	%
LUNCHES	90	49	60	67	30	33
DINNERS	80	43	50	62	30	38
SNACKS	15	8	15	100	—	—
DAILY TOTAL	185	100	125	68	60	32

Elements of cost

In catering there are three *elements of cost*:

- *Food or beverage costs* (often called *cost of sales*)
- *Labour* (eg wages, salaries, staff feeding, uniforms)
- *Overheads* (eg rent, rates, advertising, fuel)

Sales in catering are always equal to 100%. The relationship between costs and profits in catering operations may be seen in Figure 10.14.

Note: in kitchen operations gross profit is sometimes called kitchen percentage or kitchen profit.

Figure 10.14 Elements of cost

FOOD AND BEVERAGE COSTS	COST OF SALES
LABOUR COSTS	
OVERHEAD COSTS	GROSS PROFIT
NET PROFIT	
SALES	REVENUE 100%

Costs, eg labour, may be classified in relation to sales. Thus all costs can be attributed to a return in revenue.

Figure 10.15 Labour cost percentages

SALES		DIRECT LABOUR COSTS	% OF TOTAL LABOUR COSTS	% OF DEPARTMENT SALES
FOOD	£125	£35	78%	28%
LIQUOR	£60	£10	22%	17%
TOTAL	£185	£45	100%	24%

$$\text{Percentage of total wages cost} = \frac{\text{Department labour cost}}{\text{Total wage cost}} \times 100$$

$$\text{Percentage of sales} = \frac{\text{Labour cost}}{\text{Revenue}} \times 100$$

Seat turnover

Seat turnover is a pointer to efficiency, ie how many times a seat is being used in a service period. It is calculated by dividing the *number of covers served* by the actual *number of seats available* per service period. Thus:

- In a snack bar seat turnover might be four to five times per service period
- In an expensive restaurant seat turnover might be once per service period

In operations where customers do not occupy covers (eg in cafeterias or take-aways), customer throughput may be calculated by the number of till transactions per service period or time period (eg per hour).

Figure 10.16 Example of seat turnover calculation

SERVICE	No OF COVERS	SEATS	TURNOVER
LUNCH	60	80	0.75
DINNER	85	80	1.06

Average check

Average check is also called *spend per head*. The calculation of the average spend assists in interpretation of sales figures. For example, if revenue goes up is it due to higher selling prices or more customers being served? If, however, the revenue reduces is it due to fewer customers being served or to customers spending less? Average check is calculated by dividing the *total sales per department* by the *number of people or covers served*.

Figure 10.17 Example of average check calculation

SERVICE	TOTAL £	No OF COVERS	AV CHECK £
LUNCHES	90	12	7.50
DINNERS	80	10	8.00
SNACKS	15	7	2.14
TOTAL	185	29	6.38

Index of productivity (alternative method of showing labour costs)

The *index of productivity* is calculated as follows:

$$\frac{\text{Sales}}{\text{Labour costs (including any staff benefit costs)}}$$

The index of productivity varies depending on the type of operation, eg a fast-food operation should have a high index of productivity as the labour costs should be relatively low, whereas a restaurant with a high ratio of staff to customers should have relatively low index of productivity. As payroll costs can be controlled and should be related to the forecasted volume of business, a standard index of productivity can be established over time to measure how accurately the two elements are related.

Stock turnover

The rate of *stock turnover* gives the number of times that the average level of stock has turned over in a given period. It is calculated as follows:

$$\text{Rate of stock turnover} = \frac{\text{Cost of food or beverage consumed in specific period}}{\text{Average stock value (food or beverage) at cost}}$$

The *average stock holding* is calculated by taking the opening stock value, adding the closing stock value and dividing by two. High stock turnover should be expected in a restaurant using predominantly fresh foods. Low stock turnover indicates usage of convenience food. Too high a turnover indicates potential problems through panic buying and lack of forecasting. Too low a turnover indicates capital being tied up in unused stocks.

Sales per seat available

Sales per seat available shows the sales value that can be earned by each seat in a restaurant, coffee shop, etc and is used for comparison of different types of operation as well as a record of earnings per seat over a period of time. It is calculated by dividing the *sales figures* by the *number of seats* available in the dining area.

Sales per square metre

An alternative method of comparison is to calculate the *sales per square metre* or foot. This is particularly useful in bars or take-away operations where earnings per seat cannot be calculated. It is calculated by dividing the *sales* by the *square meterage* of the service area.

10.5 Customer relations

In Section 5.2 (page 157) interpersonal skills for staff were highlighted. Also in Chapter 5 various interpersonal skills were identified as associated with different tasks and duties in food and beverage service.

Customer relations is concerned with the conditions staff work under which may assist or prevent good standards of interpersonal skills being maintained. There are two aspects to this: firstly, the *physical staff conditions* and, secondly, the *satisfaction* or otherwise customers receive from the food and beverage service experience.

Developing and maintaining good customer relations requires two skills in the supervisor:

- The ability to *recognize* the symptoms of a deterioration in customer relations
- The ability to *minimize* the causes of customer relations problems

What are the symptoms of customer relations problems?

- Increasing complaints: about products/staff
- Increasing accidents
- Mistakes by staff in orders, etc
- Customers arriving without previous bookings being noted
- Arguments between staff
- Poor morale of staff
- Breakages or shortages of equipment
- High turnover of staff

Minimizing customer relations problems

The following is a series of questions that the supervisor should consider in order to minimize customer relation problems:

- *Why is that member of staff not smiling or being courteous to customers?*
  - a) If a waiter is not smiling his/her feet might be hurting: no amount of telling him/her to smile will change this. His/her shoes might be the problem
  - b) In the society in which we live we are trained from an early age to be polite. We all know to say *please* and *thank you*. In catering the use of *sir, madam, please, excuse me*, and *thank you* is expected. If it is not being done:
    - Are the staff in the wrong job?
    - If they are in the right job, then what is the problem?

- *What are the problems of each department in working with other departments?*
- *How does each department's problems affect the others?*
- *What are the difficulties that a guest could experience?*

  For example, lack of information or direction signs

- *Is the emphasis in the work areas put on the customer?*

  For example, a barman eating behind the bar takes the emphasis away from the customer

- *What problems can be solved by physical changes?*

  For example, staff congregating round a central sideboard will face inwards and not outwards to observe customers

- *What problems exist because information to customers is insufficient other than that which can be obtained from staff?*
- *Are staff given enough information about the establishment and locality before they meet customers?*
- *Are foreseen problems minimized?*

  For example, large parties organized in advance

- *Are staff informed of set procedures for foreseen problems?*

  For example, running out of food items

- *Are complaints used as an opportunity to show care for guests?*
- *Are there set procedures for dealing with complaints?*
- *How can staff be encouraged to identify and propose solutions for their problems?*

Handling complaints

Should a problem arise and the customer makes a complaint the following should be observed: do not interrupt the customer. Let them have their say and then, when they have made their point,

- APOLOGISE   but only for the specific problem or complaint
- RESTATE   the complaint briefly to show you understand
- AGREE   eg 'you are right to bring that up sir', this shows you are looking at the problem from their perspective
- ACT   quickly, quietly and professionally

Never

- lose your temper
- take it personally

- argue
- blame another department

Valid complaints are a restaurant's feedback and should be used to improve service.

Customer satisfaction

In Section 1.5 (page 10), the factors contributing to the meal experience were summarized. Factors which might affect the customer's enjoyment of a specific meal experience in a particular operation could be:

- The welcome, the décor, the ambience
- Efficiency, eg has the booking been taken properly, using the customer's name?
- Location of the table
- Menu and drinks list (presentation and cleanliness)
- The order being taken: recognition of the host
- Availability of dishes/items
- Speed and efficiency of service
- Quality of food and drink
- Courteousness of staff
- Obtrusiveness/attentiveness of staff
- Ability to attract the attention of staff
- Other customers' behaviour
- Method in which complaints are handled
- Method of presenting bill/recovery payment
- Departure attentiveness

The supervisor is responsible for minimizing potential customer relations problems. He/she should be as much concerned with the physical aspects of the service as with the way in which the service is operated and with the interpersonal interaction between customers and staff.

In food and beverage service operations, interaction also takes place with people outside the service areas, eg kitchen staff, bill office staff, dispense bar staff, still room staff. It is important that the provision of food and beverages within an establishment is seen as a joint effort between all departments, with each department understanding the needs of the others in order to meet the customers' demands.

10.6 Staff organization and training

Staff organization

Staff organization in food and beverage service centres on having sufficient trained and competent staff on duty to match the expected volume of customer demand.

The first step in staff organization is to determine the expected volume of customer demand. This can be done from sales records, and is often called *customer throughput*.

There is a relationship between the *volume of customers* served and the *length of time* they stay on the premises. The time customers take in different types of operation varies. An indication of these times is given in Figure 10.18.

Figure 10.18 Seating/consumption times in various types of operation

OPERATION	CONSUMPTION TIME (mins)
RESTAURANT	60–120
CARVERY	45–90
POPULAR CATERING	30–60
CAFETERIA	15–40
WINE BAR	30–60
PUB (FOOD)	30–60
TAKE-AWAY WITH SEATING	20–40
FAST-FOOD WITH SEATING	10–20

There is also a relationship between the *volume of customers* and the *opening times* of the operation. For example, in a full service restaurant the seating time of customers might average one and a half hours. If the restaurant is open for four hours, then it might be possible to fill the operation twice. If, however, the opening hours are only two and a half, then this would not be possible.

Opening times are determined by the consideration of:

- Local competition
- Local attractions, eg theatre
- Location of the premises, eg city centre/country/suburb catchment area
- Transport systems
- Staffing availability
- Volume of business
- Local tradition

Level of demand

Customer throughput in table and assisted service operations

Since all customers are usually seated in both table and assisted service methods, throughput can be estimated for new operations as it is limited by the length of seating time and the opening hours of the operation. For existing operations sales records will provide a guide to potential throughput. Staffing for each service period can then be estimated and allocated to specific jobs. Staffing will also need to be estimated for *mise-en-place* duties and for clearing following service. Thus a restaurant open for two and a half hours at lunch time may require staff for up to five hours.

To calculate the total staffing required:

1 Estimate the number of staff required per service period in one week
2 Multiply the number of staff per service period by the number of hours to be worked in each period
3 Divide total staff hours by full-time working week hours. This will give the full-time equivalent of number of staff required
4 Mix part-time and full-time staff hours to cover all service periods
5 Draw up staff rota which may need to be on two or three week cycle to allow for days off, etc

For example: A restaurant opens six days per week for luncheon and dinner; maximum of 80 covers

Volume of customers

	M	Tu	W	Th	F	S
Luncheon	65	75	85	80	85	54
Dinner	85	90	120	140	135	160

Opening times

Luncheon	12.30 pm to 2.30 pm	Last order 2.00 pm
Dinner	6.30 pm to Midnight	Last order 11.30 pm

Staff time
11.00 am to 3.00 pm (4 hours)
6.00 pm to 1.00 am (7 hours)

The number of staff to each service period can now be calculated and a rota drawn up.

Similar approaches for estimating staffing requirements exist for the other service method groups although the calculation of throughput differs as follows:

Customer throughput in cafeteria operations

There are five factors which influence potential throughput in cafeterias. These are:

- *Service time*: the time it takes each customer to pass along or by the counter and reach the till point

- *Service period*: the time the cafeteria is actually serving
- *Till speed*: the time it takes for customer to be billed and payment taken
- *Eating/seating time*
- *Seating capacity*

The main criterion is seating capacity. The speed required in the queue is determined by the seating capacity and the average seating time.

For, say, 186 seats and with a till speed of nine per minute it will take 20.66 minutes to fill the cafeteria. If the customers' seating time is 20 minutes, then the cafeteria will be filled just after the first customers are leaving. A faster till speed will mean that the last customer through the till will have nowhere to sit. Too slow a till speed will mean the cafeteria is not being fully utilized. For one till, four to six people per minute is a maximum.

Assuming the service period is to be one hour, then this cafeteria will be able to provide service to:

- *55* (60 min less 5 min service time) × *9* (people per minute till speed) = *495 people*
- The cafeteria would need to be open for *1 hour + 20 minutes* (1 hour service period and 20 minutes for the last person to finish eating)

To calculate the seating capacity of a cafeteria required to serve 200 people in one hour; service time = 5 minutes, average seating time = 20 minutes.

1a All customers will need to be served in:

	60 min	(opening time)
less	20 min	(seating time)
less	5 min	(service time)
	35 min	(service period)

b The number of seats required will be:

$$\frac{200 \text{ (people)} \times 20 \text{ (seating time)}}{35 \text{ (service period)}} = 114.25 \text{ seats}$$

There will need to be 115 seats in the cafeteria

c The till speed will need to be:

$$\frac{115 \text{ (seats)}}{20 \text{ (seating time)}} = 5.75 \text{ people per minute}$$

2a If the seating time is reduced to 15 minutes then all customers will need to be served in:

	60 min	(opening time)
less	15 min	(seating time)
less	5 min	(service time)
	40 min	(service period)

b The number of seats required would then be:

$$\frac{200 \text{ (people)} \times 15 \text{ (seating time)}}{40 \text{ (service period)}} = 75 \text{ seats}$$

This is 40 fewer seats than above, which represents a considerable saving in seating provision

c Till speed will reduce to:

$$\frac{75 \text{ (seats)}}{15} \backslash \text{(seating time)} = 5 \text{ people per minute}$$

Hence the service speed will also reduce which may mean a saving in staffing

Generally, if the seating time is greater than the service period then the actual number of seats will need to equal the total number of customers. If the eating time is less than the time it takes to serve all the customers then the number of seats may be less than the actual number of people to be served. However, the queue may need to be staggered to avoid excessive waiting before service.

Customer throughput in single point service operations

Customer throughput in single point service operations may be taken from records of till transactions. Increases and decreases in service are proved by increasing or decreasing the number of till points (or in the case of vending, additional machines). If seating areas are provided then similar calculations as for cafeterias are carried out, assuming there is a known percentage of customers using the seating facility.

Customer demand in specialized service

For hospital and airline tray methods there is a capacity limitation. For other forms of specialized service methods there are records or estimates of potential take-up of services in specific locations, eg hotel rooms, lounges or home delivery.

Duty rota

Figure 10.19 gives an example of a duty rota for pre-service duties in table service and shows how they may be allocated. The exact nature of the duty rota varies with every establishment according to the duties to be performed, the number of staff, time off, and whether a split/straight shift is worked.

The object of a duty rota is to ensure that all the necessary duties are covered in order that efficient service may be carried out. It also provides the basis for staff training. Task and duty lists for each of the tasks and duties given are drawn up. These will also identify standards to be achieved.

Cleaning programmes

All food and beverage service staff should be made aware of the importance of cleaning programmes to reduce and minimize the build up of dust, bacteria and other forms of debris.

Figure 10.19 Example of a daily duty rota

Waiter	1-6-98	2-6-98	3	4	5	6	7	8	9	10	11	12	13	14-6-98	Task No.
A	1	11	10	9	8	7		6	5	4	3	2	1		1. Menus
B	2	1	11	10	9	8		7	6	5	4	3	2		2. Restaurant cleaning
C	3	2	1	11	10	9		8	7	6	5	4	3		3. Linen
D	4	3	2	1	11	10	D	9	8	7	6	5	4	D	4. Hot plate
E	5	4	3	2	1	11	E	10	9	8	7	6	5	E	5. Silver
F	6	5	4	3	2	1	S	11	10	9	8	7	6	S	6. Accompaniments.
G	7	6	5	4	3	2	O	1	11	10	9	8	7	O	7. Sideboard.
H	8	7	6	5	4	3	L	2	1	11	10	9	8	L	8. Dispense bar
I	9	8	7	6	5	4	C	3	2	1	11	10	9	C	9. Stillroom.
J	10	9	8	7	6	5		4	3	2	1	11	10		10. Miscellaneous
K	11	10	9	8	7	6		5	4	3	2	1	11		11. Day off

For this reason, together with the considerations you need to give with regard to both safety and hygiene, full attention needs to be paid by all concerned to cleaning tasks and when they should be carried out.

Remember failing to empty ashtrays or waste bins may turn out to be a fire hazard, whilst lack of attention to personal hygiene or in daily routine cleaning tasks may result in the spread of dust and bacteria.

Whatever cleaning tasks have to be done, in any area, a cleaning programme should be set up. Some tasks are done daily, even twice daily, for instance, the steaming and polishing of china before each service period.

Other tasks might, for instance, be done weekly, monthly or every six months. Certain items of equipment would need cleaning immediately after each service period is finished.

Examples of such tasks are as follows:

- *Immediately after use*:
  - Carving trolley
  - Sweet trolley
  - Copper pans
  - Refrigerated trolleys
  - Flare lamps

- *Daily*:
  - Vacuuming
  - Damp dusting chairs
  - Polishing sideboard tops

- Cleaning brasses
- Clearing ashtrays

- *Weekly*:
  - Silver cleaning
  - Cleaning pictures
  - Defrosting fridges
  - Wipe down door frames and all high ledges
  - Washing cellar/china store
  - Floors

- *Monthly plus*:
  - Shampoo carpets
  - Dry clean curtains
  - Maintenance checks on still set, chilling units, fridges, air conditioning systems
  - All lighting

Points to note:

- Always use the correct cleaning materials for the task in hand

- Clean frequently

- Rinse all surfaces well

- Dusters should only be used for dusting and not other cleaning tasks

- Use cleaning procedures which clean adequately and efficiently

- Cloths used in cleaning toilets must not be used for any other purpose

- Clean and store your equipment safely and in its correct place

- Do not use cleaning cloths for wiping down food preparation surfaces

- Consider safety at all times and do not stretch or stand on chairs to reach high 'points'. Use a step ladder

Remember: regular maintenance, in whatever form, makes your service area look attractive and will project the right image for your establishment.

Staff training

Training is the *systematic development of people* and the general objectives are to:

- Increase the quantity and quality of output by improving employee skills

- Reduce accidents

- Increase the return to the employee in personal rewards, ie increase pay, recognition and other benefits which the employee wants from the job

- Make the operation more profitable by reducing the amount of equipment and material required to produce or sell in a given unit

- Make it possible for the supervisor to spend less time in correcting mistakes and to spend more in planning
- Minimize discharges because of inadequate skills
- Improve morale and achieve a more satisfactory working environment
- Enable new employees to meet the job requirements and enable experienced employees to accept transfers, adapt to new methods, increase efficiency and adjust to changing needs
- Encourage willingness, loyalty, interest and the desire to excel

Advantages of well-produced training programmes and the role of the supervisor

The advantages of well-produced training programmes include:

- Standards of performance required are identified
- Improved ability of staff
- Availability of a means of measuring ability
- More efficient working
- Clearer responsibilities

The role of the supervisor in training is to:

- Ensure that staff are competent to carry out the duties required of them
- Ensure that legal and company requirements are met (eg no staff under 18 on dangerous machinery)
- Develop and train staff as required
- Develop existing staff to train others
- Identify training needs of staff now and in the future
- Develop the necessary skills in order to achieve the points made on the advantages of well-produced training programmes.

What is a training need?

A *training need* is present when there is a gap between:

- The knowledge, skills and attitudes displayed by people in their jobs, and
- The knowledge, skills and attitudes needed for them to achieve the results the job requires both now and in the future

Identifying training needs

In our own establishment or departments we probably think we know what the 'gap' is – we see the evidence every day. However, it is worth trying to find the specific answers to questions like the following:

PRESENT NEEDS

Staffing
- Who have we got on our staff?
- Where do they fit in?
- How long do they stay and why?
- Where do they come from?
- How do we choose them?
- How many people do we take on and how often?

Agreed job descriptions
- What do our staff do in theory and in practice?
- Do they know clearly what they have to do?

Standards and performance
- What results and standards do we expect from our staff?
- Are they aware of these?
- How well do they meet our requirements?
- What stands in the way, if requirements are not being met?

Present training
- How do our staff learn their jobs now, and from whom?
- How well do they learn?
- How quickly do they learn?

Key problems
- Are there any special difficulties:
  - In the skills people have to learn?
  - In the circumstances under which they work?
  - In organizing training?

Resources
What training facilities exist within or outside the organization which can be used or developed?

FUTURE NEEDS

Any change brings a training need with it, so we need to ask questions which will show us what future training is needed, for instance:

Normal staff changes and development
- What is the age structure of our staff?
- What posts are we likely to have to fill due to:
  - Retirement?
  - Normal replacements?
  - Transfers?

- Is anyone 'earmarked' for promotion?

- What potential for promotion is there?

- What have we in mind for our craft or other trainees?

Other changes

- What plans, if any, are there for:
  - Expansion?
  - New equipment?
  - New methods?

- How will existing jobs have to be changed to meet this?

- What further training will existing staff need?

- Will new staff be required?

Terms used in training

Job

All the tasks carried out by a particular employee in the completion of prescribed duties, within the setting of particular working environment.

Job analysis

The process of examining a job in order to identify its component parts and the circumstances in which it is performed.

Note: this would normally require an examination of:

- The *purpose* of the job – what it exists for and what key results are expected from it

- The *setting* of the job – the physical, organizational and social conditions of the job

- The main *tasks* that have to be performed in order to achieve the results – what the employee does

- The *resources* or facilities available to the employee – what people, equipment, services, etc, he/she can call upon

Job description

A broad statement of the purpose, scope, duties and responsibilities of a particular job

Note: this would normally include:

- Job title

- Place of work

- Purpose and scope of job

- To whom responsible

- For whom responsible
- Main duties
- Main characteristics and conditions

Task

An identifiable element of a job, by means of which a specific result is achieved.

Task identification

The process of identifying, listing and grouping the tasks that go to make up a job.

Task analysis

The detailed and systematic examination of the skills used by an experienced worker in performing a task to the required standard

Job specification

A detailed statement of the tasks involved in a job, the standards required and the corresponding knowledge and skills involved.

Syllabus

A statement, usually under main headings, of what a trainee needs to learn, based on the comparison between the job specification and his/her present knowledge and competence.

Training programme

A broad outline of training, indicating the stages or sequence of the training and the time allowed for each part.

Training manual

This is a guide for the training staff and trainees specifying the points to be covered in training, standards to be achieved, methods of instruction to be used, equipment and materials, forms and records to be kept, and any tests or targets to be given to the trainee.

Induction training

Not specifically related to the job but covers such things as:

- Health and safety
- Procedures/policies
- Other departments
- Period of notice

- Sickness
- Holidays
- Where things/people are
- Duty rota

Planning of training

The contents of this book have been based upon an 'operations hierarchy' (see Figure B, page ix). This led to the identification of tasks and duties in food and beverage service operations which forms the basis of the content of this book. For individual operations a similar list of tasks and duties can also be drawn up specific to that particular operation. The set of tasks and duties, when compiled, are then analyzed to identify specific knowledge, skills and attitudes required for each task. In other words, each task and duty is defined and standards of performance identified. Existing staff are then assessed against these criteria. The 'gaps' are the training needs, and plans should then be drawn up to carry out the training required.

Training skills, however, are not innate. The Hospitality Training Foundation offers a variety of training skills courses depending on the specific training responsibilities of different personnel within the organization.

Further information may be obtained from the Hospitality Training Foundation, International House (3rd Floor), Ealing, London W5 5DB.

10.7 Sales promotion

Chapter 1 considered the range of food and beverage operations within the hotel and catering industry. Sectors were identified based on the nature of demand being met rather than the types of operation. In addition the factors which affect the customer's enjoyment of a meal were identified. This section considers various aspects of sales promotion relevant to food and beverage operations.

Sales promotion involves activities designed to promote temporary sales – mainly to increase business at slack periods such as:

- Mondays
- Early evenings (happy hours)
- January/February

Examples of such activities include: reducing prices; offering free wine (or a 'buy one get a second free' deal); offering a free soup or starter as part of the meal package.

Also included are special product sales – mainly to increase sales by promoting particular products:

- Festival promotions
- Wine and spirit promotions (possibly in association with suppliers)
- Children's menus
- Diabetic menus
- National eating out week (sometimes also includes temporary sales offers)
- Taste of England, Scotland, etc
- Products to complement calendar dates, etc

The number of innovations in sales promotions is growing all the time.

For food and beverage operations, three aspects of sales promotion are considered, these are:

- Sales promotion through advertising
- Sales promotion through merchandising
- Sales promotion through personal selling.

Advertising

There are many different definitions of advertising. Each text book tends to take the business of advertising in a slightly different context. Some to consider are:

'Advertising is *paid* communication by an identified sponsor'
Hotel and Food Service Marketing, Francis Buttle
'Advertising is any *paid* form of non-personal presentation and promotion of goods or services by an identified sponsor'
American Marketing Association in *Food Service Operations*, Peter Jones

'Advertising is that function of an organization concerned with contacting and informing the market of an operation's product and persuading it to buy'
Food and Beverage Management, Davis and Stone

The first two definitions tend towards the marketing angle. The third tends to encompass all aspects including sales promotions, direct mail, etc.

Advertising media

The following are examples of advertising and media:

BROADCAST
- Radio
- Television

PRINT

Newspapers
- National daily
- Regional daily
- National Sunday
- Regional Sunday
- Weekly regional and free distribution

Consumer publications
- Directories (eg, Yellow Pages, Thompsons)

Guides

Business publications
- Executive travel publications

- Technical and professional publications
- Journals

Other magazines
- Including local free one

OTHER MEDIA

Transport
- Bus

- Underground stations

- Escalators

- Train stations

- Posters

- Cinema

POSTAL ADVERTISING
- Direct mail

- Hand drops (not really postal as such but may be useful on very local basis)

In addition it is always worth considering the use of mailing lists to advise existing customers of special events, etc. Retaining existing customers is always less costly than finding new ones.

Merchandising

Merchandising is related mainly to point-of-sale promotion. Its main role is to improve the average spend per head of the customer. However, it is also used to promote particular services or goods.

Examples of food and beverage merchandising tend to be mainly visual, but may also be audio, such as in-store broadcasts or hotel audio systems, or audio-visual, such as hotel room videos.

Food and beverage merchandising stimuli can include:

- Aromas

- Bulletin/black boards/floor stands

- Directional signs

- Display cards/brochures

- Displays of food and drinks
  - trolleys (sweet, liqueurs etc)
  - buffets/salad bars
  - self-service counters – bar displays, flambé work, etc

- Drink/placemats
- Facia boards
- Illuminated panels
- Menus/drinks and wine lists
- Posters
- Tent cards
- Other customers' food/drink

However, most merchandising stimuli must also be supplemented by good personal selling techniques.

Personal selling

Personal selling refers specifically to the ability of the staff in a food and beverage operation to contribute to the promotion of sales. This is especially important where there are specific promotions being undertaken. The promise of a particular type of menu or drink, a special deal or the availability of a particular service can often be devalued by the inability of the staff to fulfil the requirements as promised. It is therefore important to involve service staff in the formulation of particular offers and to ensure that briefing and training are undertaken so that the customer can actually experience what has been promised.

Personal selling does not, however, relate solely to supporting special promotions. The contribution of staff to the meal experience is vital. The service staff contribute to the customers' perception of value for money, hygiene and cleanliness, the level of service and the perception of atmosphere that the customer experiences.

Within the context of selling, the service staff should be able to:

- Detail the food and drink on offer in an informative way, and also in such a way as to make the product sound interesting and worth having.

- Use the opportunity to promote specific items or deals when seeking orders from the customer.

- Seek information from the customer in a way that promotes sales. For example, rather than asking *if* drinks are required with the meal, ask *which* drinks are to be required with the meal. Or, for instance, rather than asking if a sweet is required, ask which of the sweets is required.

- Use opportunities for the sales of additional items such as extra garnishes, special sauces or accompanying drinks such as a dessert wine with a sweet course.

- Provide a competent service of the items for sale and seek customers' views on the acceptability of the food, drinks and the service.

Good food and beverage service staff must therefore have a detailed product knowledge, be technically competent, have well developed interpersonal skills and be able to work as part of a team.

ANNEX A

Foods in Season

The following information below should only be seen as a guide. The seasonality of foods, largely due to buying on a world rather than local basis, has now meant that most foods are available all year round, although there is sometimes a price premium – foods tend to be cheaper when in season and plentiful. In some cases the dates have very traditional associations and are related to calendar dates in animal breeding, for example the game seasons, and therefore changes in these dates are limited.

	NAME	SEASON	FRENCH MENU TERMINOLOGY
FISH (POISSON)	Barbel	June–March	Barbeau
	Bream (sea)	July–end of December	Brème
	Brill	August–March	Barbue
	Cod	May–February best	Cabillaud
	Dab	July–December	Limande
	Eel	All the year (poor quality summer)	Anguille
	Flounder	January–May	Flet
	Haddock	All the year	Aiglefin
	Hake	September to February	Merluche
	Halibut	All the year	Flétan
	Herring	Best September–April	Hareng
	Lemon sole	October–March	Limande
	Mackerel (red)	December–May	Rouget
	Plaice	Best May–January	Plie/carrelet
	Salmon	February–September	Saumon
	Salmon trout	March–September	Truite saumonée
	Smelt	October–May	Eperlan
	Skate	October–May	Raie
	Sole	All the year (poor quality in spring)	Sole
	Sturgeon	December–April	Esturgeon
	Trout (river)	March–October	Truite de rivière

	NAME	SEASON	FRENCH MENU TERMINOLOGY
	Turbot	February–September	Turbot
	Whitebait	February–September	Blanchaille
	Whiting	August–February best	Merlan
SHELLFISH (CRUSTACES ET MOLLUSQUES)	Crab	Preferably summer	Crabe
	Crayfish	October–March	Ecrevisse
	Crawfish	January–July	Langouste
	Lobster	Preferably summer	Homard
	Mussel	September–May	Moule
	Oyster	1 September–30 April	Huître
	Prawn	September–May	Crevette rose
	Shrimp	All the year	Crevette grise
	Scallop	September–April	Coquille St Jacques
BUTCHER'S MEAT (VIANDE)	Beef	All the year	Boeuf
	Lamb	Best spring and summer	Agneau
	Mutton	All the year	Mouton
	Pork	September– end of April	Porc
	Veal	All the year	Veau
GAME (FEATHERED)	Wood grouse	12 August–12 December	Coq de bruyère
	Partridge	1 September–1 February	Perdreau
	Pheasant	1 October–1 February	Faisan
	Ptarmigan	August–December	Ptarmigan
	Quail	All the year	Caille
	Snipe	August–1 March	Bécassine
	Woodcock	August–1 March	Bécasse
	Teal	Winter–spring	Sarcelle
	Wild duck	September–March	Canard sauvage
	Wood pigeon	1 August–15 March	Pigeon des bois
GAME (FURRED)	Hare	1 August–end of February	Lièvre
	Rabbit	Preferably Autumn–spring	Lapin
	Venison	Male best May–September Female best September–January	Venaison
POULTRY (VOLAILLE)	Chicken	All the year	Poulet
	Duck	All the year	Canard

NAME	SEASON	FRENCH MENU TERMINOLOGY
Duckling	April–May–June	Caneton
Goose	Autumn–winter	Oie
Gosling	September	Oison
Guinea fowl	All the year	Pintade
Spring chicken	Spring (cheapest)	Poussin
Turkey	All the year	Dinde

	NAME	SEASON	FRENCH MENU TERMINOLOGY
VEGETABLES (LÉGUMES)	Artichoke Globe	Best summer–autumn	Artichaut
	Artichoke Jerusalem	October–March	Topinambour
	Asparagus	May–July	Asperge
	Aubergine	Best summer–autumn	Aubergine
	Beetroot	All the year	Betterave
	Broad bean	July–August	Fève
	Broccoli	October–April	Brocolis
	Brussels sprout	October–March	Chou de Bruxelles
	Cabbage	All the year	Chou
	Capsicum (peppers):		
	Pimento (large)	September–December	Piment
	Chilli (small)	September–December	Chili
	Cardoon	November–March	Cardon
	Cauliflower	All the year	Chou-fleur
	Carrot	All the year	Carotte
	Celery	August–March	Céleri
	Celeriac	November–February	Céleri-rave
	Cep	July–October	Cepe
	Cucumber	Best summer	Concombre
	Chicory (Belgian)	Best winter	Endive belge
	Endive (frizzled)	November–March	Endive
	Flageolet	Fresh in summer, dried all year	Flageolet
	French bean	July–September	Haricot vert
	Leek	October–March	Poireau
	Lettuce	Best summer	Laitue
	Mushroom	All the year	Champignon
	Onion	All the year	Oignon
	Pea	June–September	Petit pois
	Parsnip	October–March	Panais
	Pumpkin	September–October	Citrouille
	Radish	Best summer	Radis
	Runner bean	July–October	Haricot d'espagne
	Salsify	October–February	Salsifis

	NAME	SEASON	FRENCH MENU TERMINOLOGY
	Sea kale	January–March	Chou de mer
	Shallot	September–February	Echalotte
	Spinach	All the year	Epinards
	Swede	December–March	Rutabaga
	Sweetcorn	Autumn	Maïs
	Tomato	All the year (best summer)	Tomate
	Turnip	October–March	Navet
	Vegetable marrow	July–October	Courgette
FRESH HERBS (FINES HERBES)	Bay leaf	September	Laurier
	Borage	March	Bourrache
	Chervil	Spring–summer	Cerfeuille
	Fennel	March	Fenouil
	Garlic	All the year	Ail
	Garlic (clove)	All the year	Une gousse d'ail
	Marjoram	March	Marjolaine
	Mint	Spring–summer	Menthe
	Parsley	All the year	Persil
	Rosemary	August	Romarin
	Sage	April–May	Sauge
	Thyme	September–November	Thym
	Tarragon	January–February	Estragon
FRUIT (FRUITS)	Apple	All the year	Pomme
	Apricot	May–September	Abricot
	Blackberry	Autumn	Mûre
	Cherry	May–July	Cerise
	Cranberry	November–January	Airelle rouge
	Currant (black & red)	Summer	Groseille
	Damson	September–October	Prune de Damas
	Gooseberry	Summer	Groseille à maquereau
	Greengage	August–September	Reine-Claude
	Grapes	All the year	Raisin
	Melon (Cantaloup)	May–October	Melon
	Nectarine	June–September	Brugnon
	Peach	All the year (best June–September)	Pêche

ANNEX B

Glossary of cuisine and service terms

The following is a selection of common classic and other cuisine and service terms and their definitions.

TERM	DEFINITION
Aiguillettes	Long, thin, vertically cut strips of meat from the breast of ducks and other poultry
Ail	Garlic
A la broche	Cooked on a spit
A l'anglaise	English style
Aspic	Savoury jelly
Assiette de	Plate of
Au bleu	Method of cooking trout; when applied to meat it means 'very underdone'
Au four	Baked in the oven
Au naturel	Uncooked
Baba	Yeast sponge or bun
Bain-marie	Hot water bath or well
Bard (barder)	To cover or wrap poultry, game or meat with a thin slice of fat bacon so that it does not dry out during roasting
Baron de boeuf	Double sirloin
Barquette	A boat-shaped tartlet case, filled in a variety of ways
Beard (ébarber)	To remove the beard from oysters, mussels, etc
Béchamel	Basic white sauce
Beurre manié	Butter and flour kneaded together and used to thicken soups and sauces
Beurre noisette	Golden brown butter
Bind (lier)	To thicken soups or sauces with eggs, cream, etc, to mix chopped meat, vegetables, etc, with sauce
Bisque	A fish soup, made with shellfish
Blanc	Water to which flour has been added, used to keep vegetables white, eg celery

TERM	DEFINITION
Blanch (blanchir)	To part cook a food without colouring, eg Pommes frites
Blanquette	A white stew
Bleu	Steak very underdone
Bombe	Iced sweet
Bordelaise	Rich brown sauce flavoured with red wine
Bouchée	Small puff paste patty; tiny savoury or hors d'oeuvre tit-bit; Bouchées may be filled in a variety of ways, Bouchées à la reine
Bouillon, court	Liquor for cooking fish
Braisé	Braised
Braiser	To brown meat, game and poultry thoroughly and then finish cooking in a covered vessel with a little liquid or sauce. Vegetables are usually braised without browning in broth containing very little fat
Braising pan (braisière)	A covered dish
Breadcrumb (paner)	To cover a piece of meat, fish, poultry, etc, with breadcrumbs after first dipping it in beaten egg or liquid butter. See breadcrumbs
Breadcrumbs	Remove the crusts from stale white bread and rub through a coarse wire sieve. Used for breadcrumbing for deep and shallow frying, etc
Brioche	Type of yeast roll
Brochette	On a skewer
Brunoise	A name used to describe vegetables, ham, or chicken cut in tiny dice. It is also a garnish for a clear soup
Butter (beurrer)	To coat or brush the inside of a mould or dish with butter
Carré	Best end
Caviar	Roe of female sturgeon
Célestine	Strips of savoury pancake
Champignons	Mushrooms
Châteaubriand	Double fillet steak
Chaudfroid	Sauce for cold buffet work
Concassé	Rough chopped (tomato)
Confiture	Jam
Citron	Lemon
Canapés	Small pieces of bread, plain, grilled, or fried, garnished and served mainly as hors'd'oeuvre
Caramel	Burnt sugar, commonly known as 'Black Jack'
Caramelise (caraméliser)	To line a mould thinly with caramel sugar; to coat fruit with, or dip it in, crack sugar
Casserole	A fire-proof earthenware saucepan, casserole
Chiffonnade	Leaf salads or vegetables cut in fine shreds and simmered in butter

TERM	DEFINITION
Choucroûte	See Sauerkraut – pickled cabbage
Clarify (clarifier)	To clear aspic or bouillon by mixing it with egg white beaten with a little water or mixed with chopped meat, bringing it to the boil and letting it simmer; broth is clarified by simmering gently and skimming off the impurities as they rise to the top
Coat napper	To cover a dish or a sweet entirely with a sauce, a jelly or a cream. To mask, to dip
Cocotte	Small round fire-proof dishes for cooking an egg, a ragoût, etc, also used to describe a larger oval casserole for cooking chicken, etc
Court bouillon	Fish stock with white wine or vinegar and mirepoix
Croquettes	Minced fowl, game, meat or fish, bound with sauce and shaped like a cork. They are usually egg and breadcrumbed and deep-fried
Croustades	Deep, scalloped tartlet cases which may be served with a variety of fillings
Croûtons	Fried bread, used as garnish. For soups they are cut in small cubes, for other dishes in a variety of fancy shapes
Courgettes	Baby marrows
Darne	Thick slice of a round fish, including the central bone
Du jour	Of the day
Dariole	A small beaker-shaped mould
Daube	A method of cooking food very slowly in a hermetically sealed dish in order to preserve its full flavour
Decant (décanter)	To let liquid stand and then pour it gently into another container, leaving the sediment behind
Demi-glace	A basic sauce of fairly thin consistency, frequently used to improve other sauces, soups and stews
Devilled (à la diable)	Generally applied to fried or grilled fish or meat prepared with the addition of very hot condiments and sometimes a highly seasoned spiced sauce
Dorer	To egg wash pastry with yolk or egg mixed with water Some baked goods are brushed with milk
Duxelles	A mixture of chopped onions, mushrooms and other ingredients, used for stuffing vegetables and in making sauces
Escalopes	Thin slices of flattened veal or beef
Entrée	A meat dish served with a sauce. Formerly regarded as an intermediate dish, it is nowadays frequently served as the main course

TERM	DEFINITION
Entremets	Sweet, dessert
Étuver	A method of simmering food very slowly in butter or very little liquid in a closed casserole
Farce	Stuffing
Filet mignon	Fillet from the saddle of lamb
Fines herbes	Mixed herbs
Frappé	Chilled
Flambé	Flamed with spirit or liqueur
Foie de veau	Calves' liver
Foie gras	Liver of a fattened goose
Fromage	Cheese
Flame (flamber)	To pour brandy or liqueurs over a dish and set them alight
Fleurons	Crescents and other fancy shapes of baked puff pastry. Used to garnish a variety of dishes
Fricassée	A white stew in which the poultry or meat is cooked in the sauce
Fumet	Essence of fish or herbs, game or poultry
Gâteau	Sponge cake
Glace	Ice-cream
Galantine	A fine cold dish of poultry or meat, boned, stuffed, braised in concentrated stock and coated and garnished with aspic
Garnish	An ingredient which decorates, accompanies or completes a dish. Many dishes are identified by the name of their garnish
Glaze (glacer)	To dust a cake or sweet with icing sugar and brown under a grill; to simmer vegetables cut in fancy shapes in butter until they have a shining coating; to give meat a shiny appearance by frequent basting; to give cold dishes, cakes and sweets a shiny appearance by coating with aspic or jelly that is on the point of setting
Gnocchi	Classified as a farinaceous type dish, made from semolina or other flour bases
Gratin (au)	A dish is described as 'au gratin' when the top has been sprinkled with grated cheese, possibly mixed with breadcrumbs, and a little butter and then browned under a grill or in a hot oven
Hachis	Minced meat
Haché	Minced
Hang	To keep freshly killed meat or game in a cool place for a time so that it becomes more tender

TERM	DEFINITION
Hors-d'oeuvre	Preliminary dishes intended to act as appetizers. Hors-d'oeuvre may be hot or cold and are served before the soup
Embrocher	To place on a spit for spit roasting or on skewers for grilling or frying
Jardinière	Matchstick shape cut of spring vegetables
Jus lié	Thickened gravy
Julienne	Term used to describe vegetables cut in very fine strips. Used as a garnish in soups
Knead (fraiser)	To work dough on a pastryboard or marble slab with the ball of the hand
Lard (larder, piquer)	To draw strips of larding bacon through the middle of a piece of meat by means of a larding tube (larder); to lard the surface by means of a larding needle (piquer)
Lardons	Strips of fat bacon used for larding meat or fish
Macédoine	Mixture of diced vegetables
Mise-en-place	Preparation beforehand
Macerate	To pickle briefly, to steep, to macerate or to souse. Generally applied to fruit, usually diced, sprinkled with caster sugar and liqueurs in order to improve flavour
Maître d'hôtel butter	Herb butter containing parsley and lemon, served with grilled meat
Marinade	To soak meat, game, etc, for a short while to improve flavour and make more tender
Marmite	An earthenware pot in which soups and stews are cooked and served at table. The name is also given to some dishes cooked in such a pot
Meat glaze (glace de viande)	Boiled down bone broth of marrow bones, etc, reduced to the thickness of jelly, used for glazing cooked meats, and improving their appearance
Medallion (médaillon)	A round slice of meat, lobster, etc
Mirepoix	A garnish of diced, browned onions, bacon and carrots with various herbs used to flavour soups, sauces, stews, etc
Mousse	A light and fluffy mixture, which may be sweet or savoury, hot or cold
Mousseline	Purée strained extra fine and mixed with cream
Morilles	An edible fungus with a delicate flavour
Nature	Plain boiled
Poulet	Chicken
Poussin	Spring chicken
Purée	Passing food through a sieve; term applied to soup and vegetables

TERM	DEFINITION
Panada	A dough used to bind forcemeat; made from flour, milk or water, eggs and butter
Pasta	Pastes made from wheaten semolina in a variety of shapes and dried. Among the best known are macaroni, spaghetti, vermicelli, noodles, ravioli
Paupiettes	Slices of meat rolled up with forcemeat
Paysanne	Vegetables cut in very thin slices; size of a 1p piece
Pilaff	Rice cooked with meat, poultry or fish, etc
Pipe	To force a soft mixture or dough through a forcing bag with a nozzle, plain or fancy, in order to arrange it in a desired pattern or shape
Piquer	See Lard
Poach (pocher)	To simmer dishes in a mould in a bain-marie until done. To cook food in water that is kept just on boiling point without actually letting it boil
Poêler	To casserole in butter in a covered dish with no liquid added. The lid is removed shortly before the end to allow the contents to brown. Used only for the better cuts of meat and poultry
Profiteroles	Small balls of choux paste. Garnish for soup. Sweet of same name
Quenelles	A kind of dumpling, made from various kinds of forcement and poached, made in different shapes, balls, ovals, etc
Ragoût	A rich, seasoned brown meat stew
Reduce	To add wine or other liquid to a roux or to pan residue; to boil down to a desired consistency
Ris de veau	Calf sweetbreads
Roast (rôtir)	To roast
Roux	Flour stirred into melted butter, used for thickening soups and sauces. It may be white, blonde or brown
Royale (à la)	A garnish
Salmis	Game birds and ducks, boned after roasting, placed in a rich sauce and served as a game stew
Salpicon	Consists of one or more kinds of food, diced small and bound with sauce
Sauerkraut (choucroute)	Pickled, finely shredded white cabbage, preserved in brine and fermented with salt, caraway seeds and juniper berries. A national dish of Germany and Alsace, served hot with bacon and sausages
Sauter	A quick cooking process. To brown quickly in a sauté or frying pan or toss in fat anything that requires quick cooking at considerable heat

TERM	DEFINITION
Sauteuse	A shallow pan with sloping sides and a lid in which food may first be fried and then braised
Shred (émincer)	To cut meat or vegetables into thin slices or strips
Skim (dépouiller)	To remove impurities and fat from the top of soups and broths being cooked for a long time by means of a skimming ladle
Soubise	A smooth onion pulp served with various meat entrées
Spaetzele (spaetzeli)	A Swiss and Austrian paste speciality made by pressing an egg noodle dough through a colander and boiling it in salt water
Suprêmes	The best parts, eg suprêmes de volaille – chicken breasts and wings
Tabasco	A pungent Indian pepper sauce, also used extensively in countries with a hot climate
Tartare	Cold sauce, base of mayonnaise
Timbale	A half-conical tin mould; a dish cooked in such a tin
Tournedos	Fillet steak cut in round, neatly trimmed slices; usually fried or grilled
Tronçon	Portion of flat fish cut across the body (turbot)
Truss	To bind or truss poultry or game birds for cooking to give them a better shape, using a special needle
Velouté	Velvety, smooth. A rich white sauce made from chicken stock, cream, etc. Also a name given to certain cream soups
Vol-au-vent	A round or oval case made of puff pastry

ANNEX C

Cocktail Listing and Recipes

Whisk(e)y cocktails

Whisk(e)y cocktails	Ingredients	Methods
HIGHLAND COOLER	2 measures Scotch whisky 1 teaspoon sugar 1 oz lemon juice 2 dashes Angostura bitters Ginger ale	Shake whisky, lemon juice, sugar and Angostura with ice. Serve in glass with ice and top off with ginger ale
RUSTY NAIL OR KILT LIFTER	1 measure Scotch whisky 1 measure Drambuie	Always serve on the rocks with ice partially crushed
SCOTCH MIST (Bourbon Mist, Rye Mist, etc.)	1 measure Scotch whisky Crushed ice Lemon twist Short straws	Fill an Old-Fashioned glass with crushed ice and pour whiskey over ice. Decorate with lemon and add straws
ROUND THE WORLD	1 measure banana liqueur 1 measure Scotch whisky Dash Cointreau Dash orange squash Orange slice Ice	Put banana liqueur and whiskey in mixing glass with plenty of ice. Add Cointreau and undiluted orange squash. Stir and strain into cocktail glass. Add orange and serve
THISTLE	1 measure Scotch whisky 1 measure sweet vermouth 1 dash Angostura bitters	Put ingredients in a mixing glass with ice. Stir and strain into cocktail glass
WHISKEY SOUR	1 measure American rye whiskey 2 teaspoons sugar 1 measure lemon juice	Shake ingredients with ice until sugar is dissolved. Strain into Sour glass. Garnish with slice of orange and a cherry

Variations are: GIN SOUR, BOURBON SOUR, RUM SOUR (light rum), SCOTCH SOUR, DAQUIRI

Whisk(e)y cocktails	Ingredients	Methods
WHISKEY COLLINS	1 measure American rye whiskey 2 teaspoons sugar 1 measure lemon juice	Collins is a Sour served on the rocks in a Collins glass, filled with soda. Garnish as a Sour but add straws
MANHATTAN	2 measures American rye whiskey 1 measure sweet vermouth	Pour into shaker and stir until well chilled. Strain into Cocktail glass
DRY MANHATTAN	Substitute dry vermouth for sweet	
OLD FASHIONED	2 measures rye whiskey Angostura bitters Sugar	In an Old Fashioned glass saturate either one lump of sugar, or one heaped teaspoon sugar with Angostura and add a dash of water. Muddle, add whiskey. Fill glass with ice. Stir. Garnish with slice of orange and a cherry

Gin cocktails

Gin cocktails	Ingredients	Methods
SINGAPORE SLING	1 measure gin $\frac{1}{2}$ measure cherry brandy 1 fl oz lemon juice Soda	Shake with ice. Serve in a Highball glass, garnish with orange slice and a cherry
PINK LADY	2 measures gin Dash grenadine Half white of egg	Shake and strain into a Cocktail glass
FALLEN ANGEL	1 measure gin Dash lime juice 2 dashes crème de menthe Dash Angostura bitters	Shake and serve Cocktail glass with ice
SATANS WHISKERS	1 measure gin 1 measure Grand Marnier 1 measure dry vermouth 1 measure sweet vermouth Orange juice Dash orange bitter	Shake contents and serve in Collins glass with ice

Gin cocktails	Ingredients	Methods
AFTER ONE	1 measure Gin 1 measure Galliano 1 measure sweet vermouth 1 measure Campari	Shake and serve with ice in Highball glasses, and cherry and orange slice
SNAKE IN THE GRASS	1 measure gin 1 measure Cointreau 1 measure dry vermouth 1 fl oz lemon juice	Shake with ice and pour into glass with ice
ORANGE BLOSSOM	1 measure gin 1 measure fresh orange juice	Shake and strain into a Cocktail glass
TOM COLLINS	1 measure gin 2 teaspoons castor sugar 1 measure fresh lemon juice	Shake, strain into a Cocktail glass
PINK GIN	1 measure gin 2 drops Angostura bitters Iced water	In Spirit glass swill round Angostura bitters and then tip out. Fill glass with ice and pour over gin. Serve with iced water according to taste

Brandy cocktails

Brandy cocktails	Ingredients	Methods
ALEXANDER	1 measure cognac 1 measure cream 1 measure crème de caçao	Shake well and strain into Cocktail glass
SIDECAR	2 measures cognac 1 measure Cointreau 1 measure lemon juice	Shake well and pour into Highball glass with ice
BETWEEN THE SHEETS	1 measure cognac 1 measure Cointreau 1 measure white rum 1 measure lemon juice	Shake well and pour into an Old Fashioned glass with ice
DEPTH CHARGE	1 measure cognac 1 measure Calvados 2 dashes Grenadine 4 dashes lemon juice	Shake well and strain into a Cocktail glass

Brandy cocktails	Ingredients	Methods
OLYMPIC	1 measure cognac 1 measure orange curaçao Orange juice	Shake well and serve with ice in Highball glass. Garnish with orange
B & B	$\frac{1}{2}$ measure cognac $\frac{1}{2}$ measure Benedictine	Serve straight up in a Liqueur glass
STINGER	$\frac{1}{2}$ measure white crème de menthe 2 measures cognac	Shake well, until icy cold and serve in a Cocktail glass

Rum cocktails

Rum cocktails	Ingredients	Methods
BETWEEN THE SHEETS	1 measure rum 1 measure brandy 1 measure Cointreau Dash lemon juice	Shake all together and strain into an Old Fashioned glass
JUMP UP AND KISS ME	1 measure white rum 1 measure Galliano Dash apricot brandy Dash lemon juice 1 measure pineapple juice 1 egg white	Shake well with crushed ice, serve in Highball glass
PINACOLADA	1 measure white rum 1 measure coconut cream 1 bottle pineapple juice	Shake well and strain into a Collins glass and garnish. Add straws
SHANGHAI	1 measure white rum 1 dash Pernod 1 measure lemon juice 2 dashes Grenadine	Shake together and serve in Old Fashioned glass with ice
CUBA LIBRE	1 measure white rum 1 measure lemon juice 1 bottle Pepsi Cola	Pour white rum and lemon juice into Collins glass with ice and lemon slice. Top up with Pepsi Cola

Vodka cocktails

Vodka cocktails	Ingredients	Methods
BLACK RUSSIAN	1 measure vodka 1 measure kahlua Ice	Serve on the rocks. Stir contents
BLOODY MARY	1 measure vodka 1 bottle tomato juice	Season, serve in Old Fashioned glass if 'on rocks', otherwise serve in Collins glass To make 'spicy' tomato juice add salt, pepper, Worcester Sauce. Flavour can be improved by adding any of the following: Dash Tabasco Basil Leaves Juice of one quarter lemon Pepper from pepper mill Garnish can be varied – stick of celery, carrot stick, wedge of lemon
HARVEY WALLBANGER	1 measure vodka 1 bottle orange juice $\frac{1}{2}$ measure Galliano	Stir vodka and orange juice in a Collins glass with ice. Float Galliano on top
PIANO PLAYER	1 measure vodka 1 measure crème de cacao 1 measure fresh cream	Shake and strain into Cocktail glass
BLUE LAGOON	2 measures vodka 1 measure blue curaçao Lemonade 1 measure fresh cream on top	Shake vodka and blue curaçao and pour onto ice in a Collins glass, add lemonade and float cream
QUIET SUNDAY	1 measure vodka $\frac{1}{2}$ measure Amaretto Bottle orange juice Dash of Grenadine	Amaretto and orange juice. Pour into Collins glass with ice and add a dash of grenadine

Tequila cocktails

Tequila cocktails	Ingredients	Methods
SUNRISE	1 measure tequila 2 dashes Grenadine 1 bottle orange	Serve with ice in Collins glass, with straws
MARGARITA	1 measure tequila 1 almost full measure lemon juice 1 measure Cointreau	Shake well, strain and serve in a Cocktail glass, rimmed with salt
BRAVE BULL	1 measure tequila 1 measure Kahlua	Serve in Old Fashioned glass with partly crushed ice
MOCKINGBIRD	1 measure tequila 3 fl oz grapefruit juice Dash lime juice	Mix and pour into Old Fashioned glass with ice. Garnish with a cherry

Other cocktails

Other cocktails	Ingredients	Methods
GOLDEN DREAM	1 measure Galliano 1 measure Cointreau 1 fl oz orange juice 1 fl oz cream	Shake well and strain into Cocktail glass
GRASSHOPPER	1 measure cream 1 measure crème de menthe 1 measure crème de cacao	Shake well and strain into Cocktail glass
AMERICANO	1 measure Campari $\frac{1}{2}$ measure sweet vermouth Soda	Pour into Old Fashioned glass and top up with soda. Stir well in glass generously loaded with ice. Garnish with slice of orange
NEGRONI	1 measure gin 1 measure sweet vermouth 1 measure Campari Dash soda	Use mixing glass. Serve in Collins glass with ice and soda to taste. Garnish with a slice of lemon

Other cocktails	Ingredients	Methods
DRY MARTINI (GIN AND FRENCH)	2 measures gin $\frac{1}{2}$ measure of dry vermouth	Pour gin and dry vermouth into shaker. Stir until chilled. Garnish with stoned or stuffed olive on a stick, or a twist of lemon. Serve in Cocktail glass
SWEET MARTINI (GIN AND ITALIAN)	Substitute sweet vermouth for dry	Garnish with red Maraschino cherry
VODKA MARTINI	Substitute vodka for gin	Garnish with olive or twist of lemon
KIR	1 glass white wine 1 measure cassis	Stir and serve in wine glass

Note: Kir Royale contains sparkling wine in place of white wine

FIZZES	1 measure American rye whiskey 2 teaspoons sugar 1 measure lemon juice	A Fizz is a Collins served off the rocks, topped with soda from syphon, and the only garnish is a cherry. Serve in Old Fashioned glass
GIN FIZZ	Substitute American rye whiskey with gin	
SILVER FIZZ	Same as Gin Fizz	Add white of egg before shaking
GOLDEN FIZZ	Same as Gin Fizz	Add yolk of egg before shaking
ROYAL FIZZ	Same as Gin Fizz	Add whole egg before shaking

Note: A Royal Fizz with at least one whole split of soda added is an excellent hang-over remedy

CHAMPAGNE/SPARKLING WINE COCKTAIL	$\frac{1}{2}$ sugar cube Angostura bitters Chilled champagne/sparkling wine/babycham 1 teaspoon brandy	Place sugar cubes soaked in Angostura in flute shaped Champagne glass. Pour in well chilled champagne, float brandy on top. Garnish with slice of orange, or cherry

Other cocktails	Ingredients	Methods
BUCKS FIZZ	$\frac{1}{3}$ fresh orange juice $\frac{2}{3}$ chilled champagne	Prepare in a flute shaped champagne glass by pouring in the orange juice first and top up with the champagne
BELLINI	$\frac{1}{3}$ fresh peach juice $\frac{2}{3}$ chilled champagne	Prepare in a Paris goblet by pouring in the peach juice and topping up with the champagne

Non-alcoholic cocktails

Non-alcoholic cocktails	Ingredients	Method
SHIRLEY TEMPLE/ROY ROGERS	Ginger ale Dash Grenadine	Serve 'on the rocks' with full fruit garnish and straws
VARIATIONS	Ginger ale and lime Ginger ale Lime cordial (to taste)	
TROPICANA	This is made from pineapple juice and orange juice	
PUSSYFOOT	2 measure orange juice 1 measure lemon juice 1 measure lime cordial $\frac{1}{2}$ measure Grenadine 1 egg yolk Soda water	Shake all ingredients together. Serve on ice, strained into Collins glass and top up with soda water
FRUIT CUP	$\frac{1}{2}$ baby bottle orange juice $\frac{1}{2}$ baby bottle grapefruit juice $\frac{1}{2}$ baby bottle apple juice Lemonade/soda water	Pour all ingredients onto ice in a glass jug and stir well. Add sliced fruit. Top up with lemonade or soda water. Serve well chilled in Highball glasses

INDEX

à la carte menu, 66
à la carte cover, 182
à point, 33
aboyeur, 31
accident check, 198
accident procedure, 367
accompaniments, 72
    appetizers, 79, 280
    cheese, 87
    dessert, 93, 316
    egg dishes, 83
    fish, 84
    game, 116, 378–80
    hors-d'oeuvre, 78, 280
    meat, 85
    pasta and rice dishes, 83
    poultry, 86
    salads, 295
    savouries, 92
    soups, 81, 285
    steaks, 289
    sweets, 87
    vegetables, 86
acetification, 124
acidulated cream dressing, 298
addressing customers, 159
advertising, 404
aerated waters, 111
after meal drinks lists (digestifs), 117
afternoon tea, 246
    covers, 247
    menu, 246
    order of service, 249
airline tray service, 263
alcohol over consumption, 163
alcoholic strength, 117
alcopops, 118
allergies, 71
American service, 14
apéritifs, 114, 212
apple and pears, service of, 93, 317
apprentice, 17
asparagus tongs, 57
assistant station waiter/demi-chef de rang, 17
assisted service, 12, 14
atmosphere, 10
attributes of personnel, 20
automatic conveyor dishwashing method, 31

automatic vending, 39
average check, 388
average spend per head, 388

banana flambé, 310
banquet layouts, 337
banqueting sales package, 326
banqueting/conference manager, 324
banqueting/conference/exhibitions, 5
banqueting head waiter, 324
banqueting staff, 326
banqueting wine lists, 117
bar, 15
    control, 384
    dispense, 34, 172
    equipment, 35, 37
    mise en place, 172
    planning, 38
    service, 212
bar and cocktail lists, 116
bar and lounge areas, 46
bar spoon, 35
barquettes, 92
baveuse, 33
beer, 142
    faults, 146
    measures, 114
    service of, 212
    storage and equipment, 146
beverages
    alcoholic, 118–145
    non-alcoholic, 94, 96–113
beverage control, 379
bien cuit, 33
bill as check, 232
bill with order, 235
billing methods, 322
bin cards, 381, 385
bitters, 120
blind and partially sighted customers, 166
bomb threat, 369
bone china, 52
booking a function, 330
booking sheet, 167
booth, 46
Boston shaker, 35
botrytis cincerea, 122
brandy, 139

brasserie, 69
breakfast, 240
breakfast covers, 241
breakfast menu, continental, 240
    full, 240
    traditional, 311
breakfast service, 240, 254
breakfasts, order of service, 245
buffet and counters, 173, 210
buffet assistant/buffet chef/chef de buffet, 18
buffet breakfast, 245
buffet service, 260
burnishing machine, 28
butler/French service, 14
butter knife, 57

café, 5
café complet, 240
café simple, 240
cafeteria service, 14
cafetière, 105
camomile tea, 100
Campari, 121
cappucino, 107
captive customers, 10
carrying
    clean cutlery and flatware, 152
    coffee services, 152
    glasses, 152, 154
    plates, 150
    trays, 157
carte du jour, 66
carver/trancheur, 17
carvery-type operations, 33
carving and joining, 275, 299
carving trolley, 279
cash, 373
cashier, 18, 233, 371
catering china, 52
catering cycle, viii
caviar knife, 57
cellar control, 384
cellar management, 147, 384
cellar stock ledger, 381
cerises flambées, 312
cerises jubilées, 312
chafing dish, 269
chairs, 46
champagne glass, 59, 216
changing a dirty ashtray, 231
charge cards, 374
checking methods, 195
cheese, 65, 87
cheese knife, 57
cheese, service of, 87
cheese trolley, 93, 174
chef de buffet, 18
chef de rang, 17
chef de salle, 18
chef d'étage, 17
cheque, 373
cheque guarantee card, 374

cherries flambé, 312
children, dealing with, 165, 361
children, lost, 164
children's orders, 204
china, 50
China tea, 98
cholesterol, 71
cider, 145
cigars, service of, 218
classic menu sequence, 64
cleaning programmes, 396
cleanliness and hygiene, 10
clearing, 224
    down, 237
    following service, 236
    glasses, 155
    joint plates, 224
    plates, 151
    sideplates, 154
    soup plates, 226
    tables in restaurants, 224
clearing checklists, 236
clothing-up, 175
club goblet, 59
cocktail bar equipment, 35
cocktail bar staff, 18
cocktails, 118
    brandy, 421
    gin, 420
    making, 119
    non-alcoholic, 426
    other, 424
    rum, 422
    tequila, 424
    types of, 118
    vodka, 423
    whisk(e)y, 419
coffee, 100
coffee making, 102
coffee shop menu, 70
coffee, speciality, 109
coffee tray, 220
Coffey still, 138
cognac, 139
cold buffet, 64
combined licence, 356
commis debarasseur, 17
commis de rang, 17
communication difficulties, 166
compiling of menus, 66
complaints, 22, 391
consumption control, 377
continental breakfast, cover for, 314, 244
contract, 360
cooking terms, 32, 411
copita, 59
corked wines, 124
corn on the cob holders, 57
cost provision sectors, 4, 7
counter assistants, 18
counter service, 14, 210
cover, general, 181

covers
    afternoon tea, 246
    à la carte, 182
    appetizers, 79, 280
    cheese, 87
    continental breakfast, 244
    dessert, 93
    egg dishes, 83
    fish, 84
    full breakfast, 241
    game, 86
    high tea, 248
    hors-d'oeuvres, 78
    meat, 85
    pasta and rice dishes, 83
    poultry, 86
    salads, 65, 78, 295
    savouries, 92
    soups, 81
    sweets, 87
    table d'hôte, 183
credit cards, 374
crêpes suzette, 315
crockery, 212
crumbing down, 153, 231
customer debt, 365
customer mobility, 165
customer property, 162, 365
customer relations, 390
customer satisfaction, 392
customer throughput, 394
cutlery, 55

daily consumption sheet, 385
debit cards, 374
decaffeinated coffee, 108
décor, 43
deferred payment, 236
deferred wash dishwashing method, 30
demi chef de rang, 17
department store, 19
deputy manager, 16
dessert, 65, 93, 316
diabetic, 71
diets, 70
dining arrangements, 46
dip-sticks, 146
discrimination, 362
dishwashing methods, 30
dispense bar, 34, 172
dispense bar beverages
    non-alcoholic, 222
dispense bar service, 222
display buffet, 173
disposables, 60
drive-in, 15
Dubonnet, 128
duplicate check, 179
duty, ix
duty rota, 396

echelon cafeteria, 14

egg dishes, 64, 83
Egyptian coffee, 108
electronic point of sale control, 377
elements of cost, 387
Elgin sherry glass, 58
entrée, 64
espresso coffee, 107
Eurocheques, 375
extended hours certificate, 359

family line-up, 349
family service, 14
farinaceous dishes, 64
fast food, 5
faults, beer, 146
filter coffee, 106
fire, procedure, 367
fish, 64, 84, 280, 285
flambé sweet dishes, 308
flare lamps, 268
flatware, 55
flight conveyor dishwashing method, 30
floor service staff, 17
floor/room service, 252
floor service staff/chef d'étage/floor waiter, 17
food and beverage manager, 13
food and beverage orders, 195
food and beverage service personnel, 13
food and drink, 10
food check, 195
food court, 15
food hygiene regulations, 365
foods in season, 407
formal function, 322, 345
forms of address, 343
free-flow cafeteria, 14
French dressing, 296
French menu and cooking terms, 411
French service, 14
fresh fruit and nuts, 65, 93, 316
fresh herbs, 410
front of house manager, 16
fruit, 93
fruit, service of, 93
fruit teas, 100
fruitarian, 72
full afternoon tea, 246
full on-licence, 355
function administration, 330
function catering
    buffet-style, 329
    confirmation, 331
    formal, 229
    menus, 333
    organization, 337
    service methods, 328
    service staff, 324
    types of, 323
function catering/banqueting staff, 19
furniture, 45

game, 65, 87, 304

Ganymede system, 261
gâteau slice, 57
general manager, 16
General Order of Exemption, 357
gin, 139
    cocktails, 118, 212, 419
glassware, 36, 58
    carrying, 152, 154
    clearing, 155
    for the service of wine, 216
    polishing, 185
    sizes, 59
    types, 58, 217
goods received book, 383
gourmet spoon, 57
grapefruit spoon, 57
grape scissors, 57
grapes, service of, 93
grey rot, 122
gross profit, 380, 387
guéridon, 269
guéridon, dishes served using a
    appetizers, 280
    dessert, 316
    fish, 285
    game, 304
    hors-d'oeuvre and substitutes, 280
    joints, 305
    poultry, 299
    salads, 295
    salad dressings, 296
    soups, 285
    steaks, 289
    sweets, 308
guéridon, mise-en-place, 272
guéridon service, 272

Hawthorne strainer, 35
head waiter/maître d'hôtel/supervisor, 16
health and eating, 70
health and safety, xi, 365, 366
head waiter/supervisor, 16
herbal teas, 100
high density seating, 46
high tea, 247
Hindu, 71
hock glass, 58, 216
hollow-ware, 55
home delivery, 15, 262
hors-d'oeuvre, 64, 78, 280
hospital tray service, 260
hospitality industry, 2
hotel earthenware, 62
Hotel Proprietors Act (HPA) 1956, 363, 365
hotels, 5
hotplate, 31
hotplate language, 32
housekeeping duties, 168

ice-cream spoon, 57
iced coffee, 108
iced tea, 99

illness of guest, 163
index of productivity, 389
induction training, 402
industrial catering, 6
Indian tea, 98
in-room facilities, 257
in situ, 12, 46
instant coffee, 104
interpersonal skills, xii, 115
Irish coffee, 109

Jews, 71
jug method for coffee, 105
juices, 113, 224
Justices licence, 354

kiosks, 15

labour cost, 387
lager glass, 58
laying covers, 181
laying the table, 184
laying the tablecloth, 175
legal considerations, 354
leisure attractions, 5
lemon tea, 99
level of demand, 394
level of service, 10
licensed and registered clubs, 431
licensed premises, 354
Licensed Premises (Exclusion of Certain Persons)
    Act 1980, 363
licensed trade, 6
licensing, 354
lien, right of, 365
lighting and colour, 43
linen, 49
liqueurs, 141
    service of, 217
    types of, 142
liqueur wines, 127
lobster pick, 57
loose module seating, 46
loose random seating, 46
lost property, 162
lounge service, 15, 258
lounge staff/chef de salle, 18
loyal toast, 343
Lussac, Gay, 117

machine dishwashing method, 30
Madeira, 127
maderization, 124
maître d'hôtel, 16
manual clearing, 224
manual dishwashing method, 30
Marsala, 127
meal experience, 9, 11
meat, 65, 85, 277, 289
menu, the, 64
    airline, 263
    afternoon teas, 246

à la carte, 66
banqueting, 333
breakfasts, 240
classes, 66
classic sequence, 64
coffee shop, 70
floor service, 252
influences on, 70
lounge service, 258
origin, 64
room service, 252
table d'hôte, 66
menu terms
fish, 407
fresh herbs, 410
fruit, 410
game, 409
meats, 408
poultry, 408
shellfish, 408
vegetables, 409
merchandising, 405
method, ix
mineral waters, 111
mini bar, 257
minimum charges, 364
mise en place, 168
mixing glass, 34
modes of address, 343
module seating, 46
Moselle glass, 58, 216
motorway service stations, 6
Muslims, 71

napkin folding, 177
National Vocational Qualifications, vii
natural spring waters/mineral waters, 111
nett profit, 387
noble rot, 122
non-alcoholic beverages, 110
service of, 94, 219
non-captive customers, 9
nut crackers, 57

occasional licence, 356
occasional permission, 356
off board, 32
off-licences, 356, 381
OIML scale, 117
operation, ix
operations hierarchy, ix
orange salad, 296
oranges, service of, 316
order of service, 192
order taking, methods of, 195
outdoor catering (off premises catering), 6, 350
overheads, 387
oyster fork, 57

Paris goblet, 59
pasta and rice dishes, 83
pastry fork, 57

pastry slice, 57
patent still, 138
payment methods, 372
peach flambé, 308
pears
season, 410
service of, 317
pear flambé, 310
percolated coffee, 105
performance measures, 8, 386
permitted hours, 357
perry, 146
personal selling, 406
Phylloxera vastatrix, 122
pineapple flambé, 319
pineapple, service of, 319
planning of training, 402
plate/American service, 14
plate powder, 29
plate room, 28
polishing glassware, 185
Polivit, 29
popular catering, 5
menus, 70
porcelain, 53
port, 127
port glass, 58
pot still, 138
poultry, 65, 86, 299
pourriture gris (botrytis cincerea), 122
pourriture noble, 122
preparation for service, 168
price lists, 363
Price Marking (Food and Drink on Premises)
Order 1979, 363
prix fixe, 66
procedure for taking bookings, 166
productivity index, 389
profit orientated sectors, 7
proof, 117
property, customer's, 162, 365
providing services, 360
purchasing of equipment, 24

rail service, 267
reception head water, 13
reception tea, 250
relevés, 64
religion and the menu, 70
residential licence, 355
restaurant licence, 355
restaurant manager/supervisor, 13
restaurant wine lists, 116
restaurants, 5
restricted on-licences, 355
retail stores, 5
retour, 161, 197
returned food, 161, 197
revenue control, 370
roast, 65
Roman Catholic, 71
room service drinks list, 117

room service, 15, 252
rum, 140
rum omelette, 313
Russian service, 14

saignant, 33
Sake, 18
salads, 65, 78, 295
Sale of Goods Act 1979, 362
sales mix, 386
sales per seat available, 385
sales per square metre, 385
sales promotion, 403
sales summaries, 376
saucepan method, coffee, 105
sauces, 73
savouries, 65, 91
Scotches, 205
Scottish Vocational Qualification, vii
seasons, for foods, 407
 fish, 407
 fresh herbs, 410
 fruit, 410
 game, 408
 meat, 408
 poultry, 408
 shellfish, 408
 vegetables, 409
seat turnover, 388
secondary fermentation, 124
section supervisor, 16
sector, ix, 4
secure environment, 368
sediment (in wine), 212
self-clear, 225
self-clear and strip, 225
self-service, 12, 14
semi-automatic dishwashing method, 30
semi-captive customers, 10
semi-self-clear, 225
separate bill, 233
server, 18
service of
 apéritifs, 212
 appetizers, 79, 280
 beer, 216
 beverages, alcoholic, 212
 cheeses, 210
 cigars, 212, 218
 cocktails, 212
 coffee, 94, 102, 220
 dessert, 93, 316
 fish, 84, 280, 285
 food, 205, 272
 hors-d'oeuvre, 78, 280
 liqueurs, 217
 non-alcoholic beverages, 219
 omelette, 208
 potatoes and vegetables, 207
 soup, 205, 285
 sweets, 210, 308
 tea, 94, 97, 219
 wine, 212
service areas, 24
service away from the table, 209
service, cover and minimum charges, 364
service charges, 364
service from flats (meat/fish), 205
service methods, 11
service of a meal, 192
service of accompanying sauces, 208
service personnel, 12
service plate, 153
service salver, using a, 152
service spoon and fork, 150
serviette folds, 176
sherry, 127
sideboards, 48, 171
Sikes, 117
Sikhs, 71
silver, 55
silver cleaning methods, 28
silver dip, 30
silver/English service, 14
silver or plate room, 28
silver serving vegetables, 153
single order sheet, 202
single point service, 12, 15
skills and knowledge, ix
snails, service of, 57
sodium/salt, 71
sommelier, 18
sorbets, 65
soup, 64, 81, 285
spare linen store, 34
Special Hours Certificate, 358
Special Order of Exemption, 357
special needs, 70, 165, 204
speciality coffees, 109
specialized service, 12, 15
spend per head, 388
spillages, 159
spirits, 138
 measures, 37, 360
 production of, 138
 types of, 138
sprigs, 328
squashes, 113
staff organization and training, 393, 398
stainless steel, 56
Standard Industrial Classification, 2
station head waiter/section supervisor, 16
station waiter/chef de rang, 17
station waiter/server, 16
steaks, 86, 289
still-set, 108
stillions, 147
stillroom, 25
stillroom beverages, 110
stock book, 385
stock turnover, 389
stocktaking, 379
stoneware, 52
strawberries Romanoff, 313

sundae spoon, 57
supermarket cafeteria, 14
supervisor, 16
Supper Hour Certificate, 358
suspicious item or package, 369
suzette pans, 269
sweet, 65, 87, 308
sweet and cheese trolleys, 210
syrups, 14

table clearers, 19
table d'hôte cover, 183
    menu, 66
table service, 12, 14
table waters, 113
tablecloth, 49
tables, 47
tableware, 55
take-away service, 5, 15
taking bookings, 166
tank method, washing up, 30
task, ix
tea, 96
tea, making of, 97
tea tray, 219
teas, speciality, 99
technical skills, 150
thé simple, 240
tisanes, 100
Trades Description Acts 1968/1972, 362
trainee commis debarrasseur/apprentice, 17
training needs, 399
training, terms used, 401
trancheur, 17
transfer book, 381
transport catering, 6
traveller's cheques, 374
tray service, 15
    airline, 263
    floor, 252
    hospital, 260
    rail, 263
triplicate check, 196
trolley
    carving, 174, 278
    cheese, 174
    flambé, 269
    hors-d'oeuvre, 78
    service, 209
    sweet, 174
trolley service, 15
trolleys, 174
Turkish coffee, 108

ullage, allowance, off-sales book, 380
underplates, 73
unsatisfactory appearance, 64

vacuum infusion, coffee making, 105
value for money/price, 10
vegan, 72
vegetarianism, 72
vending, 15, 39
vermouth, 128
vinaigrette, 297
vine species, 123
vinification, 123
vins doux naturels, 127
vodka, 140
voucher, 236, 375

waiter/server/commis de rang, 17
wash-up, 30
wedding, 345
weights and measures, 360
welfare catering, 6
whisk(e)y, 141, 419
wine and drinks list, 114
wine and food, 135
wine bar, 6
wine butler/wine waiter/sommelier, 18
wine, 121
    alcohol-free, de-alcoholized and low alcohol,
        127
    aromatized, 127
    check, 203
    fortified, 127
    label, 129
    observations on, 133
    organic, 127
    quality of, 122, 130
    sediment in, 124
    sparkling, 125
    still, 125
    storage, 148
    taste guide, 134
    tasting of, 132
    types, 125
wine service, 212
    red wine, 213
    sparkling wine, 215
    taking orders, 203
    temperatures, 214
    types of glassware, 216
    white wine, 213

young persons, 360